The Winter Road

A Story Of Legacy, Land And A Killing At Croppa Creek

Kate Holden

16pt

Copyright Page from the Original Book

Published by Black Inc.,
an imprint of Schwartz Books Pty Ltd
Level 1, 221 Drummond Street
Carlton VIC 3053, Australia
enquiries@blackincbooks.com
www.blackincbooks.com

Copyright © Kate Holden 2021
Kate Holden asserts her right to be known as the author of this work.

ALL RIGHTS RESERVED.
No part of this publication may be reproduced, stored in a retrieval system,
or transmitted in any form by any means electronic, mechanical, photocopying,
recording or otherwise without the prior consent of the publishers.

This work was drafted on the Dharawal land of the Wodi Wodi peoples,
which was never ceded. The author acknowledges the traditional custodians
of country throughout Australia and their connections to land, sea and community.
The author pays respect to their Elders past and present, and extends that respect
to all Aboriginal and Torres Strait Islander peoples today.

 A catalogue record for this book is available from the National Library of Australia

Cover design by Mary Callahan
Text design and typesetting by Typography Studio
Author photograph by Darren James Photography

Printed in Australia by McPherson's Printing Group.

TABLE OF CONTENTS

PROLOGUE	vii
PART ONE: TRESPASS	
1	3
2	30
3	78
4	107
5	133
6	149
7	167
PART TWO: MURDER	
8	195
9	225
10	247
11	277
12	292
13	322
14	338
15	363
16	394
PART THREE: INHERITANCE	
17	415
18	437
19	468
20	486
21	522
22	544
23	564
24	578
CODA	619
ACKNOWLEDGEMENTS	621
BIBLIOGRAPHY	628
NOTES	670

BACK COVER MATERIAL

PRAISE FOR *THE WINTER ROAD*

'Compellingly told, shattering in its reverberations, *The Winter Road* is a story for our times – a battle that is being fought the world over as we try to find a better way of managing the land and respecting the forces of nature that sustain us.'
—**Isabella Tree, author of *Wilding***

'This book is a major contribution to the canon of Australian land and social history: a bedfellow with Francis Ratcliffe, W.E.H. Stanner, Tim Flannery, Bill Gammage and Bruce Pascoe ... Its power is in exposing a hidden, suppurating sore in the psyche of our nation.'
—**Charles Massy, author of *Call of the Reed Warbler***

'Holden brilliantly telescopes centuries of history and law into fatal conversations at a farm gate. As one man stalks another on a winter road, the whole psyche of modern Australian settlement comes under trial. An

enthralling and disturbing tale told with deep insight and compassion.'
—**Tom Griffiths, author of *The Art of Time Travel***

'This is a special book, and I cannot thank Holden enough for writing it.'
—**Anna Krien, author of *Into the Woods* and *Night Games***

'Holden finds the epic thread in this crime.'
—**Chloe Hooper, author of *The Tall Man* and *The Arsonist***

'An incredible writer.'
—**Books+Publishing**

ALSO BY KATE HOLDEN

In My Skin: A Memoir (2005)
The Romantic: Italian Nights and Days (2010)

Dedicated to the dispossessed, to the dismayed and to the defenders

And to my brave and clever Tim

The first man who, having enclosed a piece of ground, bethought himself of saying 'This is mine', and found people simple enough to believe him, was the real founder of civil society. From how many crimes, wars, and murders, from how many horrors and misfortunes might not any one have saved mankind, by pulling up the stakes, or filling up the ditch, and crying to his fellows: 'Beware of listening to this imposter; you are undone if you once forget that the fruits of the earth belong to us all, and the earth itself to nobody.'
—**Jean-Jacques Rousseau,** *Discourse on Inequality,* **1754**

We could say well that the settlement of these plains saw a tragedy which arose from both sides being true to their natures.
—**R.J. Webb,** *The Rising Sun: A History of Moree and District 1862–1962,* **1962**

Why did the man cut down the tree? Because it was there.
Why didn't the man cut down the tree? Because it wasn't there.

—**Andy Griffiths and Terry Denton,**
The Treehouse Joke Book, 2019

PROLOGUE

The crunch of the ute's tyres down the road. The sound of his breathing. His heart: he thought it would kill him. And his mouth was that dry.

He had hoped the dark would hasten, for cover. He had been watching it coming: the dusk soaking down the trees, the shadows dissolving. They might make it, if only the winter dark could arrive. Robert Strange had heard the fear in Glen Turner's voice, there in the shadows, crouched behind the ute. But he had also feared the dark because as it rose to hide them, Turnbull's gun would begin to hurry.

They were on Talga Lane, a broad dirt groove in the farming country heading east–west in the flat lands between Moree and Croppa Creek, in northwest New South Wales. The road went straight to the horizon. Lined with scrub on either side, and to the left and right, occasional properties, palisades of vegetation, and enormous quilts of cleared, cropped land.

viii

It was just before six o'clock. Knock-off time, nearly tea time. The road had been empty for the last forty minutes. Just Strange and Turner and Ian Turnbull, the two white utes, the brigalow scrub, the koalas and other little animals keeping quiet, the cloudless sky slowly lifting into the night.

Then the raised gun. The quiet, urgent voices. The shots. The pleas.

Now Turnbull's rasping voice was gone and Turner's panicked breath was gone and Strange could stop talking, stop this mad monologue to Turnbull holding the .22, saying we're unarmed, we're not here to hurt you, sir, please put the gun down, and to Turner, stay down, Glen, move up a little bit, Glen, move up, move, move, he's coming; his mouth so dry he could barely get the words out and he needed to keep talking.

There had been six explosions from the mouth of the gun.

In the silence afterwards, Turnbull's red tail-lights had grown small. The dark came down like a door, only a little light in the sky to the west.

The tall scrub, the black grass, the man now lying on the earth with his head towards the trees. Such hush.

Strange got in their ute and turned on the engine, trundling off the road to shine the headlights on the fallen man. He kneeled down next to Turner, who was still breathing, faintly. He got some water out of the car, took a mouthful and poured some over Turner. He talked to him. He said they were both going to be okay.

Weak pulse. He rubbed Turner's head. He poured more water over the man's face. The water glistened in the white light.

Turner, trees above him, earth beneath, receiving his blood. Strange, holding Turner. The men were bathed in a channel of light that bled across the rough grass. Behind, the scrub. Behind the scrub, the fields and the huge sky.

Strange heard a vehicle approaching. He thought, He's coming back. I've got no service and he's coming back. Hang in there, hang in there, Glen.

He let go of Turner. He ran out onto the road. If it wasn't help, he didn't want to see what was going to happen. In the winter dark, on the winter road, he closed his eyes.

The car slowed, a solid young man behind the wheel staring at him. The man stopped, backed up. Strange said his colleague had been shot. Andrew Uebergang rang triple zero on his phone. He said to Strange, *You have to talk, I can't talk,* handed the phone over with a shaking hand. Strange got into Uebergang's white ute to explain and give directions.

Far away in Dubbo, Strange and Turner's boss at the Office of Environment and Heritage, Arthur Snook, was getting a call that Turner's Emergency Position Indicating Radio Beacon (EPIRB) had been activated. He tried Turner's phone. He tried Strange's. Tried again.

Strange's phone came to life. 'Arthur, is that you? Arthur, Glen's been shot, chase the ambulance, he's bleeding badly.'

'Where are you?' Snook shouted down the line.

'Talga Lane, Talga Lane.'

The call dropped out.

The ute driver said he'd go for help. His white lights swung away. Strange went back out to Turner. He pulled him to a sitting position, cradling his head. Blood came out of Turner's mouth, shining in the cold light of the headlights. He wasn't breathing.

Strange dropped him. Pressed his big hands against Turner's chest. Pumped. Pumped. 'Come on, Glen. Come on, Glen, you can't do this. We've got to get home.'

And he realised Glen was dead.

PART ONE
TRESPASS

1

The interior landscape responds to the character and subtlety of an exterior landscape; the shape of the individual mind is affected by land as it is by genes.
—**Barry López, *Crossing Open Ground,* 1988**

His name is Ian Robert Turnbull. A classic man of the district: iron-grey hair, barrel chest with great gripping arms, creaky legs from years on a tractor. A check shirt under a woollen jumper. Big tough hands of a farmer, the skin on the back of his neck creased by weather.

He's patriarch of the clan, with four sons and fifteen grandchildren. Been married to Robeena, Rob, for fifty-five years. He's been a big man of the little town, given money when locals needed a hand, but kept out of the papers – nothing exhibitionist, nothing showy. Mates with everyone important, and the best lawyers. Began with one farm, and now look at him. Not afraid to think big, to think of his family to come. He's travelled with the Australian Wheat Board, went to the United States twenty years back: much impressed by the large-scale farms there, the respect for the landholder, the rights of property owners, who aren't told how to run things.

His health as a child had been bad, with four bouts of rheumatic fever, inflaming the heart and its valves. But it didn't stop him. He was the cheeky jackdaw in a kindergarten play. Won 'best individual boy' at primary school, snapped in a proud soldier's uniform.

His dad farmed a bit, around Inverell and Moree, but Ian grew up to work with wood. He was a carpenter and joiner, not a farmer. Then his chance arrived: a property came up for sale. 'Yambin' was on the slope above Croppa Moree Road, the slice of bitumen that linked the hamlet of Croppa Creek to the town of Moree. Later he bought little 'North Yambin', across the road from it. He got 'Lima' from Rob's dad, along with 'Buckie'; then 'Wallam', 'Allendale', 'Erralee', 'Elgin'. And now 'Strathdoon' and 'Lochiel', next to each other on County Boundary Road. One of them is for his son Grant, and Grant's a smart cookie; he'll turn it to profit, like his other holdings. He's already renamed 'Lochiel' to 'Colorado', stamping his mark. Turnbull helped Grant get started and now it's grandson Cory's turn, got him set up now too on the other block, used his own mortgage as a guarantee. He has four sons, though Doug and Sam don't farm, and Roger – best not to talk about him. But Roger's lad Cory is sound. So those two properties, they're not really his, as such, just he has an arrangement with the boys.

Between them, the Turnbulls have nearly 9000 acres of the best agricultural land in the country – the black soil of the Golden Triangle goes for thousands of dollars the hectare now. And to think it was all under scrub once. He might be seventy-nine and getting tired, but he's going to see his family right before he goes.

It's all big wide monoculture fields around here. Mostly wheat and barley, but some chickpeas too. You can do anything in this soil; the country's biggest pecan farm isn't far, and there's cotton to the west. Though Moree runs on artesian bore water, out this way, an hour east, there's usually enough rain.

A nice little place, Croppa: pretty creeks, and hills here and there. Only a few dozen people in the town itself, but more out on the properties, and it's got the tennis and golf clubs, the little school, the general store. Australian flags on top of the cabs. Lawrence Tibbins' collection of old farm machinery lined up right around a block. Now and then he gets them going – the kids help fix them up, and they even take the creaky old harvesters out into the fields to have a go. Turnbull is known for his quiet generosity – sending a heap of seed to a new farmer, lending his best dog to a muster, paying for a neighbour's gravel and putting in to build the local nursing home; city kids screaming with delight on his tractor, clutching a special sample of sheared wool. Croppa Creek is less than a hundred years old but it's doing better than a lot of little towns, and that's thanks to the farms, the money brought in, the hard work people have done on the land for decades. The fields reach to the horizon – big, smooth blankets of gold. There's a bit of scrub left on the fencelines and boundaries, of course, it keeps the wind off these basalt plains. But look at the place. It's earning its living, and that's thanks to people like him.

The old Scott brothers owned 'Strathdoon' and 'Lochiel', just on the other side of the road from 'Buckie' and 'Lima', their whole lives. The blocks have been let go, half grown over with scrub since they were cleared a bit and grazed on back in the day. It was all grazing for a hundred years round here; then when Turnbull was young the scientists told everyone to plough and sow, and it was crops, crops, crops, while the Scotts' blocks just sat there. Good soil waiting. Now, if he can get rid of the bloody scrub and get a tractor through with the seeds, those blocks will do well.

*

'IF YOU PULL UP on County Boundary Road to the southern side of the property, you'll hear the dozer,' a man's voice told him. Glen Turner knew what this meant. By the day of that phone call in June 2012, the compliance officer already had six months' worth of files on the Turnbulls. His department, the Environmental Protection Agency, had written a letter advising the old man before he'd even bought 'Strathdoon' half a year before that he couldn't clear without permission: 'While the EPA fully expects that you will comply with legislative requirements, our aim is to ensure that you are fully aware of your responsibilities...' They'd been warned he'd try. But the block was covered in native vegetation, and everyone knew it was probably protected by law.

Turner had actually been out that way a fortnight earlier, inspecting another property near Croppa Creek. He'd seen a new crop planted on 'Strathdoon' and taken photos. After what he'd seen in February, March and April, it wasn't really a surprise. The person who called in June had been in touch before, and he seemed reliable. Turner was busy, but he rang Ian

Turnbull the next morning. If the dozers were running the previous day, they'd probably still be going.

'Have you got some pimp out here reporting on us?' asked Turnbull sharply. He had observed keenly how his neighbours had been treated by the regulators in the past. Small communities: not everyone respects the local ways.

Turner told him about the anonymous tipster. Turnbull digested this. 'You can come out,' he said, 'but I need forty-eight hours' notice.' As a compliance officer, Turner was used to this response. A lot could be cleared away in two days.

Two days later, Turner headed out on the three-hour drive, picking up the quietly spoken ecologist Chris Nadolny to take along with him. The two had been on this case together from the start. On the roadside boundary the Turnbulls had left ten or so metres of fenceline vegetation as required, but the visitors could see immediately that more clearing had been done on 'Strathdoon' – all along the boundary with 'Colorado' and further into the property.

County Boundary Road is unsealed, a pale tan ribbon grooved between wide grass verges and fences fringed with remnant scrub: brigalow, belah, box trees, smaller shrubs. The tree boughs arc towards the road, and the shaggy dark greenery is thick, but in places only a few metres deep. Native flowering shrubs wander towards the bitumen, and there are crags of prickly pear bedded in among the bush. Beyond are low fences.

The entrance to 'Strathdoon' has a short driveway, then a double metal gate. The white four-wheel drive pulled in alongside the one already waiting. A tall, grey-haired man was standing by it. Turner and Nadolny got out and, not for the first time, the three men shook hands. Turner commented drily on the new work.

'We've cleared,' said Turnbull, meeting his gaze, 'because this is prime agricultural country.'

He acted as if he didn't understand the problem. This was one of the last blocks still covered in scrub around here, he said. Though it was poor grazing country and had been eaten out by sheep, the soil was good under all that mess. It had had sixty or seventy years of brigalow on it, fixing nitrogen into the soil; in other parts of the country, you had to put the nitrogen in. It had just been let go. 'Colorado' next door had never even been rung – that is, the bark removed in a ring so that the trees died. Turner and Nadolny, gazing around, saw what they knew were remnant populations of protected species. But what Turnbull saw was, he explained with satisfaction, the last of the black soil.

***

CROPPA CREEK, LESS THAN an hour from Boggabilla on the border between New South Wales and Queensland, is a speck of human habitation in a sea of vegetation. That vegetation used to be the grassy woodlands of brigalow and box and native grasses kept open by the Murri people of the Kamilaroi. Flinders, Kangaroo and perennials, which look dead in drought but revive after rain, flourished here. Edible herbs once grew between the clumps too.

There are small hills and ranges to the east, and beyond them the mountains are visible, where Tenterfield, Glen Innes and other towns of New England brim the foothills of the Divide; further still is the coast where Glen Turner grew up, in Telegraph Point, among the warm coastal forests. Tamworth is hours to the southeast over tumbling hills; Narrabri and Gunnedah on the plains south are distant, too. There are little townships and localities sprinkled around, often based on former stations. On road maps the highways are scant red lines loosely strung across spaces, hours of driving between them.

Croppa Creek and nearby small towns Warialda and Pallamallawa form a triangle on basaltic soil between the Gwydir and Macintyre rivers, which run roughly east–west before curling around to the south; Croppa Creek itself cuts diagonally across, meeting up with sister creeks in a skein of precious wet in the mostly flat expanse west of the Divide. To the southwest of Croppa is Moree, a town of over 7000 people; Warialda, once the district centre but now much shrunken, lies to the southeast.

This is country just sufficiently close from the arid inland, just soaked enough with rain, just mineral-rich enough from millions of years of basalt ground to powder, that from the moment an escaped convict reported its riches, men were drawn here to make wealth.

It is good grazing land, because the self-mulching soils can't be easily destroyed by hooves. Cattle grew fat and happy here. But grains and cotton make more money. Now it's one of the most intensively farmed, broadacre-cropped, wealth-producing areas of the continent. It's one of the most transformed landscapes of the nation, and its colour is no longer khaki green but gleaming gold.

In *A Million Wild Acres,* his landmark book about the history and ecology of the adjacent Pilliga region, historian and farmer Eric Rolls describes the country beautifully: 'The plains are like flat, black ocean. In the marvellous mirages of hot summers, they often look like true ocean, a surging blue which indistinctly joins the sky. There is nothing else to be seen. Even the trees are drowned in blue light.' This is a land of thin waving stems, of brushed silken fields smooth as Persian carpet. The thin strips of travelling stock routes, still shaded by eucalypts, box, belah and acacia, seem eccentrically messy in comparison. But that scrub is the last of a type of dry rainforest millennia old.

Moree is wealthy, not just a rural hub but a destination, home to artesian baths and a multimillion-dollar aquatic centre. Eastern European migrants incongruously pilgrimage here annually to take the waters. It is also a town of stock agents and silos: the sight that greets those who arrive by road is yards of gleaming new John Deere tractors, ranged by the dozen with their shining green snouts, announcing Moree's practice and its pride. The Moree Plains Shire produces a yearly average of a million tonnes of wheat, worth about $180 million, and many of the wealthy families of the district consider themselves patrician, the makers of the country. Even the footpaths of the town are silky granite. In rain they become slippery. It doesn't rain that much in Moree anymore, however.

The Moree Tourism website puts it sweetly: 'At different times of the year, the wide plains of the Moree district are a natural tapestry as the beautiful differing colours of the bounteous crops flood the land.' One commodity the shire has in abundance is sunshine. About ten kilometres out of Moree, a company called Fotowatio Renewable Ventures runs one of the largest photovoltaic solar plants in Australia. The plains are changing in more ways than one.

But in the summer of 2016–17 Moree had a heatwave that broke all records. It equalled its hottest day ever recorded: 47.3 degrees. And it had fifty-four straight days from December to February in which the temperature rose over 35 degrees. The previous record, back in 1912, was twenty-one days.

There is no shade and less rain because the trees are gone. Once, there were grassy woodlands. Then there was a broad clot of scrub, thick with koalas, wild pigs and prickly pear. That has been vigorously cleared in the past fifty years. Now the land is naked.

*

JUST A FEW HOURS' drive southwest from Moree is Cuddie Springs, where stone tools place First Nations peoples there between 30,000 and 40,000 years ago. The original inhabitants of what would later be Moree Plains Shire had thousands of years of experience in that landscape. They saw it dry and moisten. They probably witnessed megafauna grazing on its plains, stepping through the forests. They walked every centimetre of that land. They knew it; they changed it.

The Aboriginal peoples in the northern part of the district are Bigumbul/Kamilaroi, and to the south, Weraerai. The area is strewn with what's left of their traditional meeting and sacred sites: a grand bora circle at Terry Hie Hie, more at Northcote, Boobera Lagoon, Berrigal Creek and others. And in Boobera Lagoon, the Rainbow Serpent, Garriya itself, is believed to rest.

Most of the people of the plains were 'disposed of in one determined engagement', according to Eric Rolls, when a massed group of warriors challenged the stockmen on a property near Borambil, an hour south of what is now Tamworth, in 1827 or 1828; almost all of the young men died on one day. Those who weren't killed in frontier violence were captured and put on missions, and their descendants have shared scantily in the wealth of the country since.

In the course of millennia, the land consumed the traces of those humans who first stepped so lightly on its surface. That self-mulching soil, says a heritage survey report, has devoured their footprints. What was left has been scraped away by demolition, neglect, ploughing and laser levelling for irrigation. The bora trees were knocked down, sometimes unknowingly, sometimes not.

The old Scott brothers' ancestor came out, like many other Celts, in the 1840s, and settled near Moree in the 1870s. The family took up land, stocked it with 100,000 sheep and built a large homestead. They poisoned dingos, felled trees, dug dams, put in wells and fences. The history books don't mention what happened to the local Kamilaroi. The property shrank, but two small blocks survived in their hands until 2011: 'Strathdoon' and 'Lochiel'.

Ian Turnbull was born in Moree in November 1934. It was the year of a grasshopper plague so bad the insects ate the clothes off the washing line, the blinds off the windows; they shaded the very sun, so the trains halted on the track. Dust storms came booming over from the inland, bringing smothering gloom and clogging vehicle engines, stripping the landscape to the west and obscuring this one. They were caused by erosion, due to farming and pests, such as rabbits and grasshoppers. The legacy of pastoral experimentation was already flailing.

This was the Depression era, when men would come by looking for work and a feed, tearing cooked meat off the bone like dogs. The week Turnbull was born, there was a storm on the Thursday night and heavy black clouds on Friday morning. Those grasshoppers were soon to hatch and, with the oppressive weather and farmers under strain, buyers had to sign a pledge that poison would be applied only to the insects and not used for murder. There were warnings for anthrax, galvanised burr. On 'Strathdoon', the Scott brothers' father was penalised for not killing enough rabbits. A compliance officer came to inspect the block and fined its owner for running an environmental hazard: anyone who owned Australian land was expected to kill wildlife, put up fences and ringbark trees. You were letting the community down if you did not, and the law would make sure you knew it.

Mostly settlers just grazed the country, letting the cattle roam wild in the scrub and pear, bashing it back where they could for roads, settlements and, later, fences, but unable to clear it. This was until ball-and-chain clearing and the cactoblastis moth came along. 'The way was now open for the development of the famous Pallamallawa wheat belt,' a Croppa Creek town history states proudly. 'Development has been most spectacular.'

Long-time resident Robeena Turnbull contributed to that history. 'My happy childhood was spent at "Lima",' she wrote. 'When Dad bought the property in 1931, he camped in the woolshed until the house was built.' Croppa Creek barely existed when Robeena was born. It formed within what was once a run called Bogamildi, which at its prime covered over 220,000 acres, right on the richest little wedge of agricultural country on the continent, the heart of the black-soil plains.

It was a world marked by distances. Local church services were held under a tree, the minister doing the rounds on a buggy. A man called Jacob Haddad came around once a month in a truck stocked with hosiery, boots, sewing supplies and fabric. Kids, a working part of the farming life, were sent off after school to infect prickly pear with cactoblastis moth larvae and chase wild pigs through the scrub on horseback. Landowners grew wealthy on vast properties, farmers struggled on small plots, and bitter power wars between nineteenth-century squattocracy and selectors continued to play out even as a gravel road was put in and Moree built a fine art-deco cinema for the first talkies. By the 1940s Croppa had houses and a railway line. Drays carted wool to town in handsewn bags that were stocked in great towers. But works on the line were lit by slush lamp – a dish of tallow with a string, as basic and rustic as in the 1790s.

'The phone was connected in 1952,' Robeena recalled. It was only a line with twelve parties; anyone could pick up a receiver and listen in. 'We drove into Moree every six weeks for groceries and business which was an all-day affair. My brother Ran and I, being the eldest, used to sit in the back of the 30 cwt. Oldsmobile truck rugged up in blankets.' The winter roads would stick any cart to a stop. For weeks it was impossible to get supplies from Moree. It might have been any time in the previous century. 'Often a storm had been across the road while we had been in town and we would end up bogged, mostly on the road near the place "Yambin".' She could not know then that the property would one day be her home with Turnbull, the scene of his midnight arrest, police in the garden alert for resistance, headlights trained on the front door.

In the mid-1950s Ran, then in his twenties, began to farm 'Leyland', in the Gwydir Shire near the village of North Star, with support from his father, Les. Ran got help to build a wool shed from a trainee carpenter, Ian Turnbull. The two young men built the shed, and a cottage next door. They got on well. Turnbull – who had a little block himself, out near Inverell – married Robeena a few years later. Ran, content to live and work on 'Leyland', began to love his small patch of land. He studied it deeply and understood it to be a gift from God, to be managed in a responsible, nurturing way to the best of his ability. But Turnbull, with his father-in-law's encouragement and a bit of his money, began to buy, clear and sell land.

'Now in 1987,' Robeena wrote comfortably in the local history, 'Ian and I have been married for twenty-eight years, during which time we have raised four sons, Douglas, Roger, Grant and Sam. We have two daughters-in-law and two grandsons, Cory and Nathan.' More descendants would yet be born.

Steadily moving through the decades, Croppa Creek has remained a small, close world. Its proud little primary school still has only a handful of students. The silos, gleaming beacons, rise above the town; inside lie the billions of grains of the people's prosperity. This is *l'Australie profonde,* its mythic colours of gold and green, its timeless ways, its small gods. It was country destined for wheat from the first hopes and plans of the colony, but the endless burnished plains of the Golden Triangle have been a while in the making.

*

THE WEALTH OF THE Moree plains links, unexpectedly, to the musings of white-wigged political philosophers hundreds of years earlier, and their considerations on property ownership and the land. Distant and abstruse though they seem, the ideas of these European and American men directly inform modern Australia, are sensed deeply in its rural communities and were present at the gate of 'Strathdoon' when Ian Turnbull explained to Glen Turner and Chris Nadolny why he had to develop his property. They contour the motivations for this tragedy: why a man like Turnbull could feel such a grip of ownership on land he has fashioned and profited from, whose boundaries he's marked and title he holds, and how a government compliance officer like Glen Turner is charged with reminding him of the responsibilities of that creed.

English philosopher John Locke, writing in the 1690s, was a defining character in this paradigm. Earlier thinkers had posited that God bestowed country; occupation of land implied property, albeit contingent on divine will. Locke adjusted this concept: it was the application of action that conferred a moral right of property. His *Two Treatises of Government* proposed a logic of ownership which begins with the principle that each man (it was always men) owns his own body and his body's labour. Nature is a 'negative commons', a world that exists for all, and when the person applies his labour, the ground on which he does so becomes his.

Unowned land, or *terra nullius,* as it became known, was a 'land of an equal richness lying waste in common'. And if land was virtually unlimited – as seemed the case with the endlessly extending Americas of Locke's day – what could be the injustice in using, and so claiming, it? 'Nobody could think himself injured,' Locke wrote, 'by the drinking of another man, though he took a good draught, who had a whole river of the same water left him to quench his thirst. And the case of land and water, where there is enough of both, is perfectly the same.'

A century later, and only six years after the First Fleet 'discovered' another apparently endless continent, American revolutionary philosopher Thomas Paine riposted that property ownership was in effect theft: it deprived the many of their natural inheritance of God's bounty. '[T]he earth, in its natural, uncultivated state was, and ever would have continued to be, the common property of the human race,' he wrote, presaging the concept of shared human stewardship. 'Cultivation is at least one of the greatest natural improvements ever made,' he agreed, but he insisted only the improvement itself and its profits, not ever the land, could belong to an individual. By taking both profit and property, the landed, entitled gentry had inflicted 'a species of poverty and wretchedness that did not exist before'.

The only redress, Paine insisted, was a property tax, which would redistribute some of the unjustly coveted benefits gained from appropriating the commons. 'I care not how affluent some may be,' he explained, 'provided that none be miserable in consequence of it.'

In the years between Locke and Paine, Genevan thinker Jean-Jacques Rousseau had also proposed a communal concept of property. A civil society, Rousseau thought, existed to protect property rights but curb excessive private property ownership, and to support a shared commons. In *The Social Contract* (1762), he wrote of a fundamental compact between a man and his society. The right of an individual 'is always subordinate to the right which the community has over all'.

Any natural right to own property was on the condition of taking part in civil society, not using it to abuse privilege.

The differences between Locke's concept of ownership and that of Rousseau and Paine are crucial. The first invites an understanding of land as an opportunity for seizure and personal advantage. Today we see Lockean ideas in neoliberalism. The strongest, the first, the most vigorous or powerful take the spoils. Once seized, it is theirs. Anyone who wants something of it will have to pay. Rousseau and Paine agree with Locke that action – the labour involved in improvement of land – is fundamental to the legitimate ownership of property. But land *is* finite, so possession by one entails denial to another. The landholder only profits from cultivation – any farmer, for example, is the owner of his products but not of the earth that made them. If an occupier takes too much from the land, he must compensate the people. This is a horizontal perspective, looking outwards to fellow humans, aware of our shared interests, respectful of our temporary presence on the planet. Action is taken and improvements are made with consideration of their cost. In place of the Lockean pyramid whose summit becomes a fortification, there may be – there was – a village.

The Enlightenment took inspiration from both Locke and Rousseau, but Locke's formulas were immensely influential in shaping the Western view of nature. By the time of Australia's settling, the ineluctable mark of a British citizen was land ownership. It enfranchised him, gave him rights, offered access to authority: he could complain, have restitution, be compensated. Suffrage was only granted to British men with some kind of property entitlement. This excluded about 60 per cent of them, both natives in the old world and free white men in the new.

Land – elemental, foundational – was the desperately prized asset in a new colony. Without it, a man was only an object.

So imagine the feelings of modest people, rural or urban, unskilled or former farmers, who a generation before might have shared pasture but had, since the devastating Clearances in Scotland and the Enclosures of the commons in England over the previous century, been evicted from even that small subsistence. Or those who had never even seen a field or a forest, and were told of boundless land for the taking: thirty, forty, fifty acres, apparently empty of competition, ripe for God's work of improvement. It must have seemed breathtaking. Families could feed themselves. Clans would restore, dynasties be nourished. A man might make a name for himself. He could pass something on to his children, and he could mind his own affairs.

Two hundred years later, it is likely that Ian Turnbull, looking to cultivate the last of the black soil on the Scott brothers' old blocks, felt much the same way.

2

*The good folk say the drought is sent
By heavenly power as punishment—
As punishment to work us woe
For crimes that we have done below—*

**—Francis Humphris Brown,
Songs of the Plains: The River and The Road, 1934**

The dark green of the brigalow at Croppa Creek had been stared at by the descendants of settlers for nearly two centuries before Ian Turnbull's family took possession of some of the last fragments. The township lies at the dwindling tail of the Brigalow Belt, what remains of perhaps 9 million hectares at colonisation, which now extends inland along the Queensland coast from Townsville to mid-New South Wales, covering slightly less than the entire area of Tasmania. The Belt widens, is winched small and fragments as it comes south. The brigalow remnants around Moree and Croppa Creek are some of the largest – and most unprotected – in the nation.

Brigalow, *Acacia harpohylla,* is a tough, ancient plant. First named scientifically in 1864 by Baron von Mueller, the tree is a legume, which produces a phyllode – that is, the enlarged stalk of the leaf forms crescent-shaped, flat blades.

One of brigalow's most remarkable attributes is its resistance to fire in a combustible continent. As Tim Flannery observes in *The Future Eaters* (1994), almost everything about the plant is designed to impede fire, from the way the narrow, hard phyllodes fall to the ground to how the trees are shaped. What brigalow does, moreover, is shelter other species of vegetation beneath it. These plant communities have much of the typical Australian vegetation found in rainforests, as well as mammals like long-nosed bandicoots. The brigalow, in this sense, is a protective haven for an ancient Australia, pre-dating even Aboriginal arrival. It is what's left of an antique and complete ecosystem.

Native plants are not just relics or ornaments. They house biodiversity and represent cultural and heritage values, and many have qualities unique in global biology. But practically, they also protect the land surface. They help retain water and regulate rainfall; they halt erosion and provide windbreaks; they foster microbes, fungi, pollinators and other elements that form the food chain. They store carbon. They provide wildlife corridors. They diminish problems with salinity and acidity. In short, they work on the land as surely as farm labourers. They are removed from a landscape system at a cost that has not often been well explained to landholders, but has been paid by successive generations.

For graziers, who acknowledged its edible young foliage, shade and wind shelter, brigalow wasn't a real problem until clearing provoked the vegetation to thicken so it swallowed whole herds. Anything that interferes above ground (ringbarking, felling, spraying and poisoning, bulldozing) or even with the surface roots (if stock trample the ground, if the land is scorched with fire, if it is repeatedly levelled by a tractor) triggers what expert Henry Nix calls 'a massive suckering response'. Brigalow can produce 25,000 suckers per hectare, and remain like this for thirty years before stirring to its next phase: whipstick brigalow, a barrier of tensile saplings that can endure for more than fifty years, at between 5000 and 20,000 stems per hectare, taller than a man. At the surface the roots are braided and set, firm as ships' cables, and five metres higher the canopy meshes and tangles. Below, the roots, as with other legumes, carry bacteria that fix nitrogen into the soil. Belah does a similar thing, but using a fungus. The two species are drawn to weathered, infertile soils, and over time they restore them. Brigalow encourages a collegiality of other virtuous growth.

But the brigalow is not loved. It stands a dark, muscled fortress on the good soil it has nurtured; it impedes view and passage and progress. The dominant mentality is to reap its gains, and then curse and destroy it.

***

IAN TURNBULL HAD BEGUN his farming life with grazing, but had long since given it up for crops: conversion of grazing to cropping land was where the money was now. There were heavy mortgages on each of the Scott blocks – no time to waste. By the end of January 2012, his son Grant had secured 'Lochiel', about 1500 hectares, for $3.2 million, and 27-year-old grandson Cory and his wife, Donna, had bought the 900-odd hectares of 'Strathdoon' for nearly $2 million. The arrangement was that Turnbull, in addition to taking the profits from the first year's crop, would supervise the clearing and cultivation. Doug and Bill Scott were in their eighties and had wanted to give something to their relatives – the cash would do nicely, and the price was good.

The task ahead wasn't complicated: get rid of the paddock trees and some scrub, and there'd be huge big fields easy to sow and plough. Minimum tillage – a method causing as little soil damage as possible – would put that wheat in on the good soil.

Turnbull knew you had to be clever with money. Shrewd. Had to have a savvy accountant and a good lawyer. The government wanted to stick their fingers in everything; well, they'd never quite get to the bottom of the pot. Turnbull wasn't stupid – he'd protect their wealth, make sure the young ones got their fair share. It took work, keeping track of what was under whose name, for how much, dividing it all up. It had been a life's work, building and building the family's wealth: so many hard days out there, so much to keep track of, what with managing all the staff.

When they stopped grazing, it got simpler. It was a shame to give up the sheep – his dad had been a wool-buyer for years, and Turnbull had grown up when the country rode on the sheep's back. But now the future was big crops.

Things had shifted since Turnbull was born into the penumbra of nineteenth-century farming. In the past few decades, ecologists, scientists, greenies, even some agronomists had come to value what grew above the black soil. Before the sale, Cory had got in touch with the regional Catchment Management Authority to get an idea whether clearing would be allowed: he was hoping to remove the odd paddock trees in the areas already cropped, and clear out what he thought was just regrowth scrub; next door on 'Lochiel', Grant was looking at a block barely ever touched, even more crammed with brigalow. But Cory was told that these blocks were full of native vegetation, either original or regrown, much of it species so rare they were called 'endangered ecological communities'. None of that should be touched, and further surveys would be needed on the rest.

Environmental regulation, too, had flipped. Once it demanded extermination of wildlife, the crushing of trees, the raising of fences. Now if a person wanted to clear they needed to submit a vegetation plan to the Catchment Management Authority, to ensure that native ecologies were preserved. Transgressions involved the state government: the Environmental

Protection Agency and the Office of Environment and Heritage and their team of officials, investigators and compliance officers. Then there was the federal level, the *Environment Protection and Biodiversity Conservation Act 1999*, which protected native elements, some overlapping with those protected at the state level, others not, and landowners were supposed to get permission there too. It was complicated; country pubs had long filled with muttering that no one could explain what happened if the state laws said one thing and the national laws another. So the temptation for a man like Ian Turnbull, directing his family to turn these properties to profit, might have been to do what one could, just have a go and cop the consequences.

A clever man played the odds. The regulators were, it was rumoured, spineless: they rarely tried to prosecute. They mightn't even know about illegal clearing, unless someone dobbed. If they did have a go, you argued your case: you thought it was regrowth, it just caught fire, we had the wrong map. And if it came to court, you got a silk.

Five grand a day, well, you put that in your bank account to begin with, ready. Funds for a fine, too. It could never be as much as the profit on the land: a developer could buy a block now and double its worth in a couple of years.

It was a shame about the koalas. Turnbull liked the little buggers. He had even gone to a local talk about protecting koala habitat earlier that year. They were an icon of the district, and Gunnedah, a couple of hours south, called itself the koala capital of Australia. Someone told Turnbull they reckoned there were a hundred koalas on those blocks. Or forty. But they were in the trees, and the trees were in the way. No one likes shooting koalas, but once they're on the ground you have to put them out of their misery, and then it's best to burn the bodies.

As for the scrub, well, everyone bashes the scrub. The more you cut it, the harder it grew back. No worries about that stuff. People have been bashing that scrub back since the early days, and it's still there.

***

THE STORY OF WHEAT in Australia, those gilded fields that would become the very image of our prosperity, did not begin auspiciously. European varieties of the precious grain struggled in the local soils. There seemed no clovers to replenish the soil: settlers didn't yet know the leguminous properties of brigalow or the similar nitrogen-fixing talent of other species. It proved more expensive to grow and transport wheat even short distances, such as from the Bathurst Plains to Sydney, than to import it from other parts of the empire. Thus wheat, one of humankind's oldest symbols of wealth and now a particular grail of the British imperial project, was one of the hardest-charged items of the whole Australian endeavour.

As with much else, the crop's failure baffled the colonists. They didn't know that Australian soils are formed in the crucible of a very dry, hot environment that annihilates much active soil biology: they are lacking both micro-and macro-nutrients, and tend to be inhospitable to water drainage and plant growth. They don't get much of sea-spray nutrients or dust blown from other continents; glaciers haven't churned old goodness to the surface. Instead, our soils are scoured by desert winds and blasts from the Antarctic.

Of course, the plains had been productive grasslands since long before settlers arrived with their pitiful sacks of seed. Early observers recorded Aboriginal people of the plains eating grains in the hot summer, when other foods were less available. They didn't till, preferring 'the land unbroken', as Major Thomas Mitchell wrote in his account of exploring the northwest plains, but cut Panicum (panicgrass) with stone knives, tossed it to be winnowed by the wind and ground it for flour. They stored seeds in granaries and baked bread. When the people of Jericho in the Fertile Crescent began growing wheat along alluvial flats, Aboriginal people had already been gathering and cultivating grains on country that flooded seasonally for many thousands of years. But the colonists didn't recognise, or allow themselves to acknowledge, Aboriginal husbandry. It was far more important to *not* see it –

to confirm James Cook's scanty impressions from decades earlier that Aboriginal people were few and nomadic hunter-gatherers, and the countryside Edenic, unworked, originary: *terra nullius.* The force of this willed perception was so phenomenal that it has persisted to the present day, allowing Bruce Pascoe's account of Indigenous agriculture, *Dark Emu* (2014), to come as a revelation to most of us. Yet as Eric Rolls observed, 'When Europeans came to Australia, the soil had a mulch of thousands of years. The surface was so loose you could rake it through the fingers. No wheel had marked it, no leather heel, no cloven hoof ... No other land had been treated so gently.'

Aboriginal land management took aeons to find its best expression. In Australia, settlers tried to achieve the same explosive outcome in decades. Many newcomers did their best, but merely standing in boots on the land was a violence. Some were purely incompetent, absurdly transplanted from urban British slums or Irish hillsides and left to farm as they could. Others were humiliated by the perversities of the Australian ecology despite their familiarity with British cultivation techniques, which included careful resting of the soil, alternating stock and crops to replenish nutrients, and ancient firestick farming called swidden. They ignored the traditional knowledge already shaping the landscape.

Native plants could endure only so much: ploughs killed off many, especially the humble groundcover. '[N]o person, to my knowledge,' lamented farmer James Atkinson in 1826, in a handbook he wrote for new settlers, 'has yet tried any experiments to ascertain how far any of the native grasses might be improved, or made more useful by cultivation.' He could see the value of native timbers, but admitted many were unnoticed by his colleagues, 'distinguished by the Colonists by the names of bastard iron barks, bastard box, bastard stringy barks'. Yet his British gaze still saw the plains as vacant: '[N]o traces of the works or even the existence of man are here to be met with, except perhaps the ashes of a fire on the banks of some river.' This made an excellent prospect for properly applied agriculture, and the land was 'easily wrought', he declared.

But that soft and rakeable soil took the hoe for less than a decade, by Eric Rolls' estimation, and then began to compact.

The efforts of the typical 'indolent' settler, in Atkinson's mordant account, extended to felling trees for a raw slab hut and a clearing in which first maize, then wheat was optimistically sown, into unprepared ground feebly chopped by a hoe. The makeshift approach would work initially but '[t]he consequence of this miserable system is that the land in a few years gets exhausted'. 'In the mean time [sic], the Settler clears another piece of fresh land, and with this,' he wrote in dismay, 'proceeds as before.' It was as if agriculture had to be invented.

Settlers tried, but the land bit back. The more they grazed, the more stock trashed the land they trod; the more Europeans tried to cultivate the soil, the more it seemed to harden, desiccate, veil with salt, groove in erosion gullies, blow away, rebuff their crops, fill with weeds. The dreams of reshaping rivers and irrigating deserts came largely to nothing. As the soil degraded under pressure from intensive cultivation, wheat didn't just fail to thrive, but became infested with disease and rust. And all the farmers could see aside from their dying crops was a land green with trees they didn't recognise or know how to make use of.

In the end it was technology as much as climate or philosophy that contoured the continent after white settlement. Modern Australia was made by farm machines and railways. The secret was combination and efficiency. In the 1840s, the stripper machine was invented – not coincidentally, in Australia – and its ease of threshing finally made South Australia an exporter of wheat. In 1843 a 'patented manure', the first modern fertiliser, was invented in England, followed by a factory to make the stuff. This discovery changed everything. No longer would farmers be required to rotate grazing and crops, so stock droppings could replenish the soil. The timeless cycle of animals and agriculture was cracked apart. Instead, farmers welcomed artificial, controllable technology, applied mechanically.

Next were tined seed drills, which cultivated ground as well as sewing seed. The kerosene tractor came to the north in the 1920s. Felling with a ball-and-chain arrangement, strung between two tractors, was a success. Finally, ground could be truly broken.

By the 1960s, the Brigalow Belt was still the largest undeveloped moderate-rainfall country in Australia. This horrified state governments. Incentives were offered to clear it all. A ball-and-chain could flatten 10–14 hectares an hour. And, echoing the warfare descending from the skies to the northwest in Vietnam, defoliants like Agent Orange were liberally poured from aircraft.

For many a family, a weekend wasn't complete without a bit of scrub-bashing. Clearing brigalow was sweaty, soul-blistering work: your skin became scratched and grazed, dirt grimed in your sweat, twigs stuck under your shirt; you had to cut and haul, and then come back to burn. Or you could ringbark and wait, haul it, stack it, burn it. But it often returned, sometimes worse than ever. There were vast acres of this stuff, and it never seemed to understand that you wanted it gone.

***

THERE IS A TALE about Turnbull and his boys, told by someone who knew them when they were young. He would put the little kids on a tractor; their feet wouldn't even touch the pedals. The man would coax them into position, show them how to put their hands on the wheel. Then he'd start the engine and the machine would begin to move, and the child – tiny atop the huge thing – would look beseechingly, and the father would tell them it was for their own good, and leave them, trundling up and down the field for hours, and their father would thrash them if they stopped.

***

GLEN TURNER, A MAN in his fifties with a genial face, a receding hairline and sharp eyeteeth, lanky legs and a passion for home brewing, owned a property outside Tamworth with his partner, Alison McKenzie. It was 150 acres in a valley, much of it untouched bush. For ten years they lived in a cabin. After their first child was born, they began building a house. They did a lot of the work themselves. Once it was completed, the new windows would frame a view of green, all the way down to a creek.

Telegraph Point, where Turner and his three sisters grew up, is a small town between two forests, inland from Port Macquarie. Those forests were, of course, logged for years: the peaceful Wilson River used to jostle with floated trunks. It is a dappled place, and the roads are lined with dry verges and delicate bush. The town has little tidy brick houses, plush green winter paddocks and old gums. Timbertown is a nearby theme park, devoted to the historic curiosity of the region's forestry. Tourists come to the state forests and walk the Bago Bluff National Park.

Glen and Alison, beginning their life outside Tamworth, began to plant trees. A thousand times they bent to dig and scrape earth along the creek line, fit the roots of a sapling to its hole, press the soil back with their palms. The native trees grew to 15 metres, holding the soil in place. They planted another five hundred. They filled in gaps with trees. They were building themselves an ecosystem, a homemade forest, its roots gripping the earth and holding it steady.

'I didn't perceive him as gung-ho; he seemed pretty measured in what he did. I mean, in most ways he was very measured,' remembers Chris Nadolny. 'He was a pretty social sort of guy. Actually, very social. He was always pretty inclusive, and when we stayed together we always made sure we stayed in the same hotel, had meals together and stuff like that. He wasn't just like that with me, he always extended himself to be social with everyone he worked with.' Very much a community guy, Nadolny adds, involved with coaching footy and helping out at the children's school. One notorious fundraising event involved Turner's proposal, 'cow bingo': inviting bets on what marked square a cow would leave a pat on. But first the cow in question had to be chased down the suburban road by Turner and a fellow parent. Out on the road, he'd call his kids at bedtime and speak with them tenderly. 'He was an avid reader of *The Sydney Morning Herald*,' his former colleague recalls, 'which contrasts with *The Daily Telegraph* or the local papers that most landholders read.' But Turner wasn't an eco-warrior, either. Nadolny, himself a modest activist, chuckles. 'He was actually more interested in home-brewing beer than in green politics.'

In late 2011, Turner – formerly a surveyor, then a compliance officer in water, now environmental regulation, based at the Environmental Protection Agency in Tamworth – got the news that Turnbull and his family were planning to buy 'Strathdoon' and 'Lochiel'. The EPA was only just holding onto the native vegetation compliance: it was about to be handed to the Office of Environment and Heritage under a restructure. But for a few more months, the EPA still had it. And, the Turnbulls having come to the agency's attention over questionable clearing before, the sale raised a red flag.

A year or so earlier, Turnbull's son Roger had been investigated for clearing on his property 'Talmoi'. Inspections were made; a minor breach was found; a caution was issued. The experienced officers who delivered it expected some appreciation for the reasonable response, but were left shaken when Roger allegedly reacted with fury. Then in March 2011, someone tipped Turner off about clearing on another of Roger's properties, 'Roydon'. Turner had a look and arranged orders for Roger to do remediation there. A penalty notice came through for Roger in December 2011, along with the news that his relatives were buying the Scotts' blocks and had already asked about clearing them.

The legislation that Turner was being called on to enforce was contentious. In 2003, several state agencies, including the Environment Protection Authority, the National Parks and Wildlife Service, and Resource NSW, had been merged in a supersized ministerial department: the Department of

Environment and Conservation. The *Native Vegetation Act 2003* heroically pulled all forms of native vegetation clearing under one framework, and forbade it unless in accordance with development approval or a regional agreement on management, to be decided by local committees. Building on the *Native Vegetation Conservation Act 1997* introduced by premier Bob Carr, it was a huge flip in paradigm. From 1995 on, trees over ten years old could not be removed from private land (with certain exemptions).

The Act was supposed to be firm but fair, yet instantly the topic glowed red with dispute. Farmers used to hacking back woody vegetation and out-of-control scrub now felt they were being told that it should all be cherished and guarded. The counterargument – that scrub was regrowth, no matter its age – began to cement. To adherents of this position, 'illegal clearing is not degradation, it is restoration', as historian Cameron Muir paraphrases it. Ian Turnbull was firmly in this camp.

In retrospect, supporters of the 2003 Act concede that it wasn't well explained, and the motives for preserving the native vegetation weren't presented. Ecological literacy, they acknowledge, can be the difference between seeing scrub as a messy impediment or appreciating its complex ecology and its role in sustainability. Instead, discussion on the issue often got waylaid by the idea that the heroic pioneer bashing the bush had been committing a crime, which seemed uncomfortably close to the so-called 'black armband' view of colonial history that still rankles conservatives.

Many also felt that a bit of bush was valuable, keeping the wind off or giving shade, but when it began to sprawl across good arable land, it had to be pushed back. Farmers complained, in a persistent misunderstanding, that under the new laws they weren't even allowed to clear invasive weeds, but must watch them storm the land unrestrained. The system of prohibition on clearing certain types of plants was effective, but seemed harsh to farmers used to making their own evaluations, and some grew expert in exploiting loopholes –

for example, preserving trees but digging up grasslands.

Compliance officers such as Turner enforced penalties, but it was so difficult to prove native versus invasive species of grassland that his busy office soon gave up attempting many prosecutions; for other offences, the fines were so small that they didn't balance against the massive profits to be had from developing good cropping country. An offence under the Act also had a statutory limitation of only two years – even if there were compliance officers and ecologists to conduct an investigation, some had to lapse without prosecution. Some farmers waited it out: simply didn't turn up to interviews with compliance staff, or burned evidence. There were cases where farmers were aggressive, threatening, uncooperative.

Meanwhile, for all the frustrations and imperfections, the Act held, albeit with occasional revisions. By 2012, Turnbull and his family would come to know it very well.

*

TURNBULL DIDN'T TALK to Doug or Bill Scott about his plans for the blocks before the sale went through at the end of January 2012. The trust was implicit: they all used the same agent, and Turnbull's lawyer, Roger Butler, was one of the trustee owners of the property, along with Bill Scott. The brothers were even allowed to stay on in the homestead on 'Strathdoon', their niece in the cottage. The place had been poorly managed, degraded. But the properties were bought on the condition, the old men believed, that their legacy would be upheld: there would be no clearing.

Turnbull had already leased some of the cleared bits of 'Strathdoon' from the Scotts the previous year, and Grant had done the same on 'Colorado' next door. Now he had his grandson, whose middle name was Ian, on the land too. The pressure was on, and those forgotten old blocks were in their last summer mornings of peace.

The Turnbulls got the paperwork started. Cory submitted a property vegetation plan to the CMA and applied for approval to clear, on the grounds that the vegetation on 'Strathdoon' was regrowth, and therefore expendable. He didn't realise the application couldn't be granted until the contracts were actually exchanged. While it was still under consideration, and with the contracts awaiting signature, Turnbull moved the dozers in.

It's true that 'regrowth' under the law technically means only what's regrown since 1990 – earlier than that and they call it 'remnant'. But old Turnbull, overseeing the work, didn't bother with that kind of pedantry. When the OEH got him in for an interview a few months later, he told them regrowth is anything that's come back after clearing: 'After the ground was settled ... I say regrowth is what – it's regrown since the land was originally settled.' The blocks had been occupied since 1857, said Turnbull, and overstocked; all the native grass had been eaten out long ago. What was there now was just growth after spring rain. Grant's 'Colorado' next door was all native vegetation – limebush and belah and brigalow, a kind Turnbull called 'boonery': big trees, maybe a hundred years old. But then some of it had been ploughed before, so he was only doing what others had done in their turn. He'd never had to deal with permissions before, he insisted, and he'd had twelve properties in his time; and Roger Butler, trustee part-owner of 'Colorado' (then 'Lochiel'), had an Order of Australia. He hadn't told them they couldn't go ahead. Though it's doubtful Butler had knowledge of Turnbull's plans.

The Scotts weren't so happy. As soon as the clearing started, there was mess on the blocks, and the old men irritably began burning the dried stacks to clear things up.

The Turnbulls seemed surprised when the EPA began to get involved. Many in the community were watching. Some were likewise doing profitable conversion with old grazing blocks; some of those were doing it illegally. They saw Turnbull bring in dozers on blocks known for their protected species: what would happen?

A woman called Alaine Anderson lived next door to 'Strathdoon' with her husband, Lionel. They had crops too, but they liked to replant trees, and

Alaine was mad about koalas. She wasn't from the area originally, but that didn't make her afraid to voice her opinions. She had stood up in the Croppa Creek hall, in that talk about koala protection that Turnbull attended, and told the locals what to do. Even lectured them all in church about looking after nature. She had maps, she said, showing the koala habitat shrinking to almost nothing. Every now and then someone would pull out her letterbox or put drill bits in her tyres, show her how it went. The Turnbulls mostly ignored her. But when some anonymous person sent a letter saying the Turnbulls had a reputation for illegal clearing and the EPA sent someone out to have a bit of a poke around, perhaps they suspected Alaine.

The way the EPA (and later the OEH, once it took over such matters) found its targets was a process of elimination. Satellite images of vegetation cover were run through comparison software to identify tens of thousands of anomalies. These were then whittled down: those caused by fire, permitted cases and so on. Just a few thousand unexplainable instances were sent to each regional office: the office in Tamworth received about 2500 a year. A fraction of these were selected for investigation, based on scale and severity. A former head of the EPA, and Turner's boss there, Simon Smith, explained how the huge potential workload was borne. 'I'd say, how do we break this down to something we can deal with? So we'd put a risk assessment on it.' Looking for systemic issues, problem owners or likely candidates for illegal conversion, they'd winnow drastically. In 2014–15, for example – the year of Turner's death – there were 465 complaints listed in the OEH's public report. Though most of those cases were later found to be lawful, they all required examination. 'One officer can only do two, three cases, maximum.' There were, Smith said, usually two or three compliance officers in his division, and about twenty-four across the whole state, and some of them had other responsibilities as well. About fifty priority cases statewide would be chosen and more fully investigated, Smith explained, and of them, about ten would make it to court.

'And in among that fifty,' Smith said with a sigh, 'was Ian Turnbull. And it just so happened Glen was assigned to see what was happening.'

*

IN FEBRUARY 2012, ON a warm, blue afternoon, Glen Turner visited the two blocks with Stephen Beaman and Chris Nadolny. Turner and Beaman were compliance officers; Nadolny was the ecologist who, should the case proceed to court, could present information about the impact of the clearing on plants and animals.

The three men turned off the highway and entered the landscape of wide, cropped fields and roadside scrub. They parked first on the corner of County Boundary Road and Talga Lane, where there was some phone signal. Turner out got his phone and strolled away from the car, peering through the trees into Grant's 'Colorado'.

'Cory,' he said, when his call was answered. 'This is Glen Turner of the Office of Environment and Heritage.'

The agencies were about to be restructured; the new title was still unfamiliar on his lips. The situation was familiar, though, after years of driving out to properties, greeting wary landholders and establishing the authority of the state agency. For Turner, this was a precautionary routine expedition, likely resolved with a chat in a paddock and a note in his files to keep an eye on developments.

'Oh yeah?'

'I'd like to enter the property "Strathdoon". I understand you have an interest in that property.'

Cory said the gate was locked. That wasn't usual practice in the country. Turner raised his eyebrows at the others watching from the car. 'Cory, I have legal power of entry. How do I arrange access?'

'I'll have to ring one of the blokes,' the young man said. He sounded nervous. Five minutes later, Turner called him back. He should ring Ian Turnbull, Cory said, and gave him the number.

Turner called Turnbull. He said later he couldn't remember the exact details of the conversation, but it was cordial. Turnbull said they'd been clearing lime bush and small brigalow. He was in Moree for the day, but Turner was welcome to go in and have a look. The gate wasn't locked after all.

The old Scott brothers were on site, near the 'Strathdoon' farmhouse. The inspectors introduced themselves and surveyed the clearing. Doug Scott was setting fire to a heap of scrub, drinking a beer. The old man watched Nadolny woozily as he jotted down details in a notebook.

No one answered when they tried the cottage further away on the property, but two dozers and a front-end loader were parked nearby. Turner photographed them. Nadolny, a small, neat man with short-shorn grey hair and bright, thoughtful eyes, walked around, head down, crouching to finger a bit of crushed groundcover. It was a bare piece of land, cleared half a kilometre in either direction. The only trees were near the fence and the building.

'What do you think?' Turner asked.

'It's predominantly native,' Nadolny said.

They spent the next hour photographing and making notes on the felled vegetation. Then they left, and went to Moree for a meal and sleep.

When Turner and his colleagues returned the next morning, one of the dozers was growling as it crunched fallen trees and shrubs into stacks. The ground was grooved raw with tracks. Turner waved for the driver to stop. The man wouldn't give his name or address, but he wore an orange shirt with *Ivan* stitched on it.

'Who owns the dozer?'

'Ian Turnbull,' the man said reluctantly. He was a solid, square figure with a large head covered in thick white hair. Turner jotted a note in his book.

'You blokes know the law inside out,' Ivan said suddenly, 'and I don't know anything.'

'Do you know about the *Native Vegetation Act?*' Turner asked.

The answer was no.

Then Turnbull turned up. A tall man, still handsome, hair still thick. He had a nose rough from sun damage, old man's bushy eyebrows. He explained that he was the financial backer. Cory wouldn't be available to answer questions. They'd had advice from the local Catchment Management Authority, he said, and they were only clearing regrowth anyway.

Nadolny suggested that it was native groundcover; Turnbull said it was just native grasses coming back after destocking and some rain. They were restoring the country, really: that scrub had gotten out of hand, and the grazing hadn't helped. A bit of cross-ploughing and letting the leaf mulch onto the soil would get the nutrients going. They weren't going to clear it all, of course: they were leaving trees down in the gully for the koalas, and those along the fencelines.

Turner said he'd need to be interviewed. Turnbull replied coolly it would have to be through his lawyer. Turner didn't record his response.

After they left Turnbull, the men went on to 'Colorado'. Trees had been felled: bimble box, whitewood, belah, rosewood. There were blade marks from the dozers on the trunks. The officers saw piles of ashes where stacks had burned. Turner took photos and location readings, recorded detail in his notebook, collected vegetation samples.

Nadolny voiced it: some of the clearing was not just native, but of an endangered ecological community. After felling the trees, the farmers would plough, and the groundcover, and the potential for the brigalow to regenerate, would be gone. This was significant vegetation; time was of the essence. The work must be halted to allow for an investigation.

Back at Tamworth, Glen Turner entered Simon Smith's office and shut the door. It was the worst possible moment for an urgent, decisive intervention. The agency was in the midst of having enforcement of native vegetation laws removed from its remit and transferred to the Office of Environment and Heritage, which did important work in protecting state resources, but had absolutely no familiarity with enforcing environmental regulation. National parks officers and ecology researchers did not, some had already made clear, have an appetite for confrontation. And Smith, experienced and confident, was about to leave his position as head of operations. Turner's step sideways into the OEH would be on his own.

The pair talked for two hours, wrestling with options. Smith proposed issuing a rare stop-work order. Turner could see pros and cons. He'd have accepted another option, Smith recalls, but agreed it might work. Smith hastened to the director and deputy director of the OEH and argued hard. 'I had to do a lot of talking. I couldn't in all conscience leave this thing unanswered, leave the degree – the wilfulness – of the clearing.' He knew Turner would be left to enforce the order. 'Glen had all the information, we had all the documents there, we'd documented everything. I just hoped that the OEH coming in would pick up the responsibility and run with it.'

He got the stop-work order approved about twenty-four hours before his position ceased to exist. 'I knew I was being provocative,' he concedes. 'I lit the fuse and I threw it over the fence.'

***

LAND CLEARING IS THE watershed issue for tensions between farmers and environmental agencies. Nothing stokes feelings quite like it. It goes directly to the questions of ownership raised by Locke, Paine and Rousseau. It relates to what we deem shared heritage; to the concept of a common wealth that spreads across private property, despite fences, and down through time; to the dilemma between maintaining land and working it; to the choice between a legacy for your children or the survival of ancient ecologies. It goes to possession and entitlement. When land is cleared, fractures erupt. When land is cleared, agreements explode.

As much as ethics or practicalities, farmers are influenced, like everyone, by their social landscape. What're the neighbours getting away with? Should I have a go? Will someone else do it if I don't? A landscape with a bulldozer on it is an incandescent stage for these questions.

But what influences one farmer to smash down trees and another to hesitate? Those who study such matters identify the anthropocentric, who see nature as there to be used, and the balanced or ecological, who regard it as inherently valuable and under threat from human activity.

There are many farmers of the ecological type in the northwest of New South Wales. There are also a proportion who might be called 'developers', primarily interested in profit, with an anthropocentric, exploitative attitude to the land they buy, work and sell. They, too, respond to what they believe neighbours are doing: brusque clearing for broadacre conversion. Their transgressions don't seem significant to them. Others are doing the same, or worse.

It would be a narrative convenience if Ian Turnbull's psychology was no more complex than that of an ordinary developer. But Simon Smith knew Turnbull in the early 1980s, when Smith was involved in the Soil Conservation Service. He remembers a surprisingly different character. 'He was quite a progressive farmer. He was involved early on in picking up these conservation farming techniques. We had a group of "champions" happy to take people onto their property, show them what they were doing; he was someone I would have regarded as one of my champions in conservation farming techniques.' Turnbull helped Smith form a Moree Conservation Farmers Association, promoting zero-and minimum-till methods, then believed to be the least destructive practice, and educating about the benefits of a healthy farm ecology. He was no radical – conservation farming is more technical than mystical – yet he comprehended the advantages of a more responsive agriculture, and led his peers into new territory.

Thirty years later, farming culture had changed, and Turnbull followed suit. About 80 per cent of people, Smith believes, will comply with regulations. But 'there are those risk-takers'. In 2012, grazing land in the Moree district was there to be converted. Powerful landowners had recently had significant and conspicuous wins over the EPA, and the weaknesses of the system had been exposed. 'People were looking at these cases,' explains Smith. 'They weren't seeing a regulatory response to it; they were seeing a massive amount of money being made in capital value. They thought, *Shit, if they can do it, why can't I?'*

Turnbull, reflects Smith, 'had seen that the benefits were very high'. It wasn't about healthy land, or a relationship with place, anymore. It was about the social landscape around him and the temptation of a huge profit in the short term. And the laws might change under OEH management, 'so what the hell: why not? Why wouldn't you take the risk and clear?'

Turnbull was not insensitive to land conservation, but his focus was on the soil beneath him. He could see ahead, to his grandsons profiting from those blocks; he could see what was in front of him, his neighbours driving dozers over scrub. And he could see Glen Turner standing at his gate, watching him, threatening ruin to the small empire he had built.

*

A WEEK LATER, TURNER returned with a stop-work order. He tried to give it to 'Ivan' to hand on, but the man wouldn't take it. Ivan Maas had worked for Turnbull for many years, as had his son Robbie. Maas, Turner wrote in his notes, watched him resentfully as he noted the refusal to sign for receipt of the order. Turner shrugged and got back in his car.

Years later, when the defence was alleging that Turner had a tendency to make threats, to harass, to stalk, Maas said Turner called his house several times and left menacing messages threatening jail; came to his very home with the stop-work order. 'I felt very confronted by him,' Maas would complain. But that day on the property Turner had gone straight to Turnbull instead, driving back down County Boundary Road and up the long, dry driveway of 'Yambin' to the distant group of silos where the old house was, surrounded by a margin of green lawn in a pale brown world. He found his man.

They met on the verandah in the hot March air. Robeena was there too, but there was no offer of a cup of tea. Turnbull raised the subject of Roger, and accused Turner of harassing his son the previous year. Roger's wife, Annette, had had to call the police, Turnbull said angrily. Roger had had to go on medication for depression. I'm on it for the same reason, Turner unexpectedly confided, according to Turnbull.

Turnbull wouldn't sign for receipt of the stop-work order either. Turner took the order, unsigned, and left. Turnbull's solicitor, Sylvester Joseph at Roger Butler's chambers, wrote to the OEH and demanded that all further communications be through him.

Turner was the man on the ground, but he was only doing as instructed. Turner, insists Nadolny, was diligent, priding himself on being fair and reasonable, on fulfilling his responsibilities. He had an excellent record as an officer, though not all landowners were inclined to admire it – Turner had sustained injuries in the course of his work when one irate landowner seized the keys to his ute and rammed him with a quad bike. 'Glen was just doing his job,' says

Nadolny. 'Doing it by the book. Trying to be as careful as anything.' Turner's work notebooks contain lines of dialogue, precise GPS readings, every photo, records of each catalogue item of evidence.

Meanwhile, Turnbull called Simon Smith in his new office at the EPA, hoping his former conservation farming ally would assist. '"Simon, Simon," he said, "you have to stop this! I'm a good person!" I didn't talk to him,' Smith recalls soberly. 'I left a message saying, "If Ian Turnbull rings, tell him I can't deal with this matter anymore. It's not my responsibility."'

He should have called him back, Smith now reflects: arranged a meeting with Turnbull and the OEH, been a liaison. 'I knew Ian Turnbull, I had respect for him, I knew I could talk to him.' Smith, who'd lived in Moree himself, wasn't scared of an angry farmer; he believed in courteous disagreement and rational argument. And he knew Turnbull was frustrated, looking for someone to talk to. 'But I didn't do that. I sort of...' His deep voice fades. 'I do sort of kick myself:

I threw the bomb over the fence, knowing I wouldn't have to be responsible for it. Hmm. Poor judgement.' A pause. He imagines a conversation with Turnbull, quieter voices prevailing. 'I probably should have done that.'

*

THE BATTLE LINES WERE being drawn. First Roger, now Cory and Grant: it seemed all the Turnbulls were having a go at what looked like potential law infringements. Roger was already fighting from his corner. Cory and Grant were silent or away, but had Turnbull, the old bull, the patriarch, as their spokesman. His word was that they had had a nod from Luc Farago of the Catchment Management Authority, and what they were clearing on 'Strathdoon' was basically regrowth. He wasn't going to have anyone, not even Farago himself, tell him otherwise.

Turner organised another letter for Turnbull, pointing out his legal responsibilities, this time signed by his new boss at the OEH. A week later, Turner and Nadolny returned to take another look at the properties. Turner stood in the same places that Farago had, took photos, compared them. Clearing seemed to have halted, but there'd been some tilling in preparation for sowing of crops, and the precious grasses and groundcover had been ploughed. Where there had been protected native scrub, there was now cleared land. Nadolny and Turner grimaced.

Meanwhile, Turnbull got extra hands to help clean up the place before the stop-work order came into effect. With six blokes working hard, they'd have it done.

Next, the OEH requested to speak with Cory. Turner didn't get much out of him in the formal interview – which was held in the Turnbulls' lawyers' offices, Cole & Butler in Moree – but afterwards he got the young man to admit that his grandfather mostly got his way on the property. 'He's guaranteed the loan, so it's hard to disagree with him,' Cory conceded. Then Turner got Grant in. He didn't get much from him, either. But just a few days later, by the end of March, Turner learned that Turnbull had lodged an appeal to the stop-work order in the Land and Environment Court of New South Wales.

Turner went back to look around the properties yet again at the end of April, when he was in the area. He reckoned there'd been more clearing, ploughing, pushing fallen trees around. It was pouring rain, according to Turnbull's testimony years later. Both he and Grant were there on 'Colorado' when Turner allegedly said to Turnbull, 'I have a strong dislike for your son, Roger,' and, turning to Grant, added, 'And I'm starting to get a strong dislike for you.' According to Turnbull, Turner grew more and more agitated. The rain thrashed harder, and eventually the exasperated compliance officer left.

Turner made no mention of any encounter in his usually meticulous notes. There were no other witnesses to verify events.

In May, Turnbull got the stop-work order revoked on a technical matter. Simon Smith admits it had been 'rushed'. The OEH, new to this kind of enforcement, didn't even try to challenge his appeal, not wanting to waste taxpayers' money on the case and thinking a win unlikely. The department had been distracted: it was a failure of communication in a large organisation in the midst of huge structural revision. Six months later, the state minister for the environment would be closely questioned in parliamentary Budget Estimates on how this happened. But in the meantime, instead of warning the family off further transgressions, the OEH had unwittingly encouraged them. Prosecution, it appeared, would be hesitant.

'I was very disappointed,' remembers Simon Smith. That stop-work order could have been revised and resubmitted. 'I had no power to do anything anymore. I left the whole matter with Glen and his supervisors.'

At the end of May, the stop-work order was lifted. The Turnbulls boasted to neighbours that they'd get a new dozer, to catch up on lost time.

But Turner was back in the district again in June, inspecting another potential case of illegal clearing towards Boggabilla. On his way to a Moree motel, he went down County Boundary Road. Glancing to the left as he passed 'Strathdoon', he could see a new crop. He stopped the ute. He didn't go in, just took photos from the road.

A few weeks later, he got the call from the anonymous tipster. The Turnbulls were clearing again.

3

> Whatsoever, then, he removes out of the state that Nature hath provided and left it in, he hath mixed his Labour with it, and joined to it something that is his own, and thereby makes it his property.
> **—John Locke, 1690, quoted in *The Sydney Morning Herald,* 1839, to justify European possession of the Australian continent**

The first white man to the Moree district was a fugitive. He'd escaped his master and taken to the bush. The local people supposed, very reasonably, he was a ghost.

George Clarke, known as 'The Barber', was young, handsome, clever, charismatic. When he reappeared in Sydney in 1831 with the ritual markings and tattoos of a full warrior, his skin blackened, one of his Aboriginal wives was by his side. For nearly three years he had been outside the white world. In those lands, not yet twenty-five years old to those in the colony, he was a king. He spoke of a great river and fertile lands. Astonished, the colony listened.

Clarke, from Worcestershire, had been transported for petty theft. Life in Australia had begun excitingly, with being shipwrecked on a sandbar for six weeks. Back on solid land, he was assigned to Benjamin Singleton, reportedly a respectful master. But Clarke fled north and was taken into a tribe, initiated and endowed with several wives. He learned language. He attended bora ceremonies, probably at the bora ground near Terry Hie Hie. And he erected a bark hut and a stockyard of saplings and stretched hide to keep rustled European stock at what's still called Barbers Lagoon, on an anabranch of the Namoi River. It was his former master Singleton's cattle he stole.

By the 1830s, the remote badlands were becoming more settled and Clarke turned himself in, along with his tribe. Singleton, showing munificence, had never reported Clarke missing, and put his ornamental convict back to work. But he listened, enthralled, to the tales

Clarke told him of the Kindur river and the rich plains beyond it to the north.

An expedition was arranged. They didn't get far, because Clarke fled once more with his tribe. This time, Singleton reported him.

Things had changed. The raiding was challenging now – the settlers were alert and armed – and conflicts between settlers and Aboriginal peoples were rising hot. Surveyor Major Thomas Mitchell, coming to the area shortly after, would blame Clarke directly for the lamentable situation. But when he was caught, his tribe tried to save him. With a police gun to his head and believing the authorities' threats to massacre, Clarke sent them away.

It was from Clarke's accounts that Mitchell took his direction as he, in turn, set off to open up the north in November 1831, broaching the black-soil plains for two centuries of development. Meanwhile, Clarke was charged with every crime in New South Wales, and was sent to Norfolk Island and then Tasmania (where he briefly escaped for a final time). A celebrity, he told his story to the papers. He was hanged in public on the gallows in Hobart in 1835.

But Clarke had threaded a lure line through the northwest that was soon braided thick by followers. Mitchell's expedition reported rich, open country. Settlers were already massing, surging across the Cumberland and Liverpool plains and then, once that good land was snatched, eyeing the prospects north. And an Act of British Parliament in 1824 had established the Australian Agricultural Company for 'the cultivation and improvement of Waste Lands in the Colony of New South Wales', which at that time was the whole of eastern Australia.

Freed convicts were the first to be granted land; more general free land grants had been made in 1792; by 1825, there were nineteen counties of the colony, and these 'limits of location' were supposed to hold. When the Blue Mountains were broached and the plains 'discovered', the colony's survival was assured; but the government had to keep control of its population of convicted renegades and sharp opportunists. That control was swiftly lost beyond the Divide. In 1829, the boundary was extended; two years later Mitchell took Clarke's lead north. Many of the first squatters were sly-grog men, runaway convicts and unauthorised stockmen. The Europeans, intoxicated by liberty, were rogue from the start.

*

THERE IS A CURIOUS correspondence through history between the discipline of the body and the discipline of the land. As Keith Thomas points out in *Man and the Natural World* (1983), the people of pre-industrial Europe bound and whipped both their children and their vegetation. In the nineteenth century, it was convicts as well. Like renegade social elements, the land was to be controlled. The settlers flogged the scrub, arms raised with an axe rather than a scourge. The bush was 'corrected'. It was 'reformed' and 'improved'.

Indeed, it was convicts who haplessly hoed or cheerfully harvested, showing the earth the redemptive way, the profit of suffering. Clearing the ground of its former errors. Smoothing a new plantation. The crimes and sins turned over, God's green garden once more blooming above.

*

SO THE FIRST FLEET had arrived with a very freighted mission, as well as over a thousand souls, Governor Phillip's greyhounds, hundreds of petticoats, ten thousand bricks, a printing press and seven hundred hoes, though not a single plough for the establishment of a great wheat colony. Australia, with no old institutions to be challenged, no intransigent peasantry or feudal nobility, was for the expectant newcomers a *tabula rasa,* just as John Locke had imagined the human character was at birth.

As the colony took a precarious hold on the distant continent, there must have been a glowing moment of optimism in hundreds of minds in London salons and government offices, in homesteads, hovels and victuallers' headquarters. They were daydreaming of a great, new, distant enterprise beyond the horizon.

It was a grand historical moment of churn. At the time *Terra Australis* was identified as the destination of that First Fleet, both industrialisation and more efficient agriculture were encouraging a general faith in the improvement, through reason and dedicated manipulation, of the human state: confidence ran high. It seemed all the world was laid out to be studied. First step: place imperfect people on imperfect land, and gain in a shared triumph. It was an Arcadian dream, related to the fantasies that had helped establish the colonies of the United States. The Exodus and Eden myths are both to be found in settler narratives: the Europeans in the antipodes were at once exiles, ejected from the green havens of the motherland, and arrivals in a bountiful paradise.

In the wake of the hapless convict entrepreneurs came willing migrants. A William Wingate of Sussex, who emigrated to New South Wales at the age of thirty-seven, wrote to his relatives in England in proud delight: 'if you new what i now nough, you would not stopped in England so long where now you might have been independent the same as i am thank god i can say i am independent of the world for i work when i like and i play if i like this is a comfort to be highly prized blessed be good i can say that this is trugh god being my witness...'

Colonists didn't abandon their relatives and possessions, sail across frightening expanses of ocean, watch their children die on board from dysentery and slip the little bodies over the side for a scenic frisson. Three or four months is a long time to sit on a tiny ship as it rocks precariously on the seas and imagine a future on solid, boundless land. Down on the other side of the globe, a man could be king. The unsettled could become homed.

The colonisation of Australia happened at a historical moment peculiarly suited to exacerbate the collision of cultures that percusses through the Australian environment to this day. Instead of forging a common approach with the land's existing inhabitants and a shared reverence for the eternal return of seasonal change, Europeans arrived at the period in their own history when all of this was being overturned. Tumbling away went 'timeless' agricultural practice, and in its place the ambition to push the land, to demonstrate progress, to elevate humankind upon the mountain of industrial farming. 'Fencing and enclosing land,' wrote settler James Atkinson, 'is the greatest and most important improvement that can be effected upon it.' Just at the time when Europeans were more certain than ever of their superiority and agency, they fell upon a continent that would test these articles of faith to the utmost. Everything they held about the roles of God, land, action, science, human nature and reason was challenged. It could not have been more fraught, or more vulnerable, an endeavour.

Nevertheless, plenty were keen to board those boats. Many of the 1.5 million free men, women and children who emigrated in the nineteenth century had versatile agrarian skills. After brimming at the edges of the Port Jackson settlement on Sydney Cove for twenty-five years, the colony exploded over the barrier of the Blue Mountains and spilled into the plains beyond. Moree district had a dozen settlers in 1832; six years later, more than a hundred.

Stock and grazing were the Australian success story: the Merino wool of the colony had done the job hoped for by its champions, Joseph Banks and John Macarthur, in competing for the British Empire with European fine wool. Frontier after frontier of the interior had fallen under the hoofs of sheep and cattle. Now, too, familiar species were imported: the countryside soon rustled with skylarks, sparrows and blackbirds. Historian Geoffrey Bolton estimates that more than 1300 plants have been introduced to Australia since European invasion. There was nostalgia but also commercial advantage in bringing valuable species here. All the most profitable crops grown in this country are introduced species. So are most of the feral animals.

There was an old saying: 'The Thirties made the squatters and the Forties broke them.' The colony, skewed to pastoralism and stock, had by the 1840s overproduced wool and meat while having to import grain. The prices for wool and stock collapsed, and many squatters went bust. Sheep began to be killed and boiled for tallow instead of kept for wool; the product was bought by Britain to make explosives.

Then the gold rush, with its manic increase in rural population, windfalls of money and demand for meat, restored fortunes or made new ones. Settlers stood at the peaks of the Blue and the Snowy Mountains and saw horizons of forest, tipping away over the curve of the earth. It would surely take centuries to cut them. 'Restraint,' wrote Geoffrey Bolton, 'seemed unnecessary.'

By 1860, the country had 20 million sheep and nearly 4 million cattle. They were almost all in the southeastern corner of the continent. Thirty years later, it would be 100 million sheep and 8 million cattle, spread across the country. All might be remade in the antipodes; instead, the damage came up like retribution.

*

DOWN ON THE SOUTH coast in 1835, grazier John Batman tried to buy land from its Aboriginal owners. The implications of this precedent were horrific to the British authorities, so Governor Bourke proclaimed the momentous assertion of *terra nullius*. It conclusively dispossessed Aboriginal peoples of their land; as it asserted the privilege of the Crown, it was also supposed to intimidate, or at least extract money from, the squatters profiting from Crown land. By 1839, the Border Police and a hapless assembly of commissioners were at work. But now that it paid its tithes, squatting was legal.

Then the booming 1860s saw the famous Land Acts of New South Wales, designed to initiate a new generation of development and occupancy in the interior. Premier Sir John Robertson passed two Selection Acts, in 1860 and 1861. The squatters' vast estates, all held on lease, would be re-appropriated by the state and broken into smaller properties. Selections of land would be offered, including to the squatters themselves. It was a fair idea and an awful reality – squatters naturally hated having their estates seized, protesting that they had opened up the country, taken risks, with only basic tools and convict labour to develop it. They made sure, through tactics such as 'peacocking' (buying up the best patches of land like the eye in a peacock's tail) or 'dummying' (using proxies to bid for blocks) to recapture the land with fertile soils and timber. Those who selected land often got what was left over, and struggled, while amused squatters around Warialda, near Croppa Creek, bought up parcels under names like Anthony Trollope, Napoleon III, Charles Dickens, Henry Parkes and other celebrities.

Selectors had to live on their land. It had to be cleared and made arable. An early form of compliance officer would conduct inspections to ensure this. Wealthy squatters benefited in that small blocks could be bought freehold and leased. But on small blocks with bad access to water and thick scrub, often in the semi-arid interior, where climatic conditions were rough, selectors found life endlessly exhausting. Up the road, mansions were being built. The Land Acts, supposed to distribute land democratically, instead resulted in larger, more consolidated monopolies, with an enormous transfer of public lands to private accounts.

Revisions in 1884 tempered things a little. Runs were again divided, this time into two: one for lease by their owner, the other for selection. It was still unsatisfactory – the conditions of selection meant that what land had been redistributed was now in the hands of often unskilled families, frantically clearing timber and scrub, trying to make the land pay for the cost they had to bear.

The northwest of New South Wales eventually became home to many Scots: tough, traumatised people. Neighbouring New England was originally called New Caledonia, and names such as Glen Innes and Inverell evoked the landscape from which many had been evicted. In Croppa Creek, one block was named 'Lochiel', for the Scottish estate from which its crofter owner had been cleared. More than a century later, the purchaser of that block renamed it 'Colorado'. He was also a descendent of Scottish migrants: Ian's son, Grant Turnbull.

**

THE THIRD TIME IAN Turnbull and Glen Turner met was at the gate of 'Strathdoon', with Chris Nadolny, that day in late June 2012 when Turnbull explained his interest in conversion from grazing to crops. The farmer was still acting as spokesperson for his son and grandson. He said they were clearing because it was prime agricultural land. But Turner was only interested in the compliance issues. 'By doing more clearing,' he warned, 'you're only making the situation more serious.' The OEH was considering recommending that remediation – restoring the ecology – be undertaken for the earlier clearing. Turner added that it wouldn't have to be where the crop was already planted. They'd be allowed to get that harvest in first; the OEH wouldn't make them grub it up. He thought he was being reassuring.

Turnbull didn't enjoy being granted permission to reap his crop. He didn't like hearing that the investigation wasn't going away, or that trees might have to be replanted. The OEH was kindly not going to rip up his crop? He looked at Turner from under his thick brows with a flash of anger that unnerved Nadolny. 'If you've got any respect for your life,' he said, according to Turner, 'you won't.'

Threatening state officers incurs a serious penalty, up to several years' jail. Turner recorded in his notebook his response: 'I interpret that as a threat and if you continue to threaten me the police will become involved.'

'I'm an old man,' Turnbull fired back. 'I don't care. I can do anything I want.'

Now things grew heated. Turnbull wanted to know who'd snitched on him. Nadolny grew fearful for their informant: Turnbull seemed dangerous. Turner, undeterred, showed Turnbull his notebook and the information given by the anonymous caller. He spoke frankly to the old man, warning he knew of a similar case. That individual had been fined $400,000 and had the land locked up for fifteen years until the trees grew back.

Beside him, Nadolny nodded. 'You'd better stop this now,' he said earnestly. 'This is going to be terrible for you. You'll dig yourself into a hole and never get out.' Turnbull began to protest. Quiet Nadolny pressed on. He didn't usually speak up to landholders, leaving that to the investigators. But he had an urgent sense of foreboding. 'I've seen cases like this,' he interrupted, 'where people are absolutely destroyed.' The OEH men knew that many local landowners were watching what might happen to the Turnbulls, and that even risk-averse OEH lawyers now considered this a certain prosecution. It was going to be bad.

The old man shook them off irritably, talking again of regrowth. The distinction between 'regrowth' (recent revegetation) and 'remnant' was crucial; Nadolny thought that perhaps the farmer had misunderstood the difference. But, he persisted, Turnbull was clearing brigalow, which was an endangered ecological community.

Turner pulled out an aerial photograph taken twenty years earlier, on which he'd marked the new clearing he and Nadolny had seen back in April. 'This is part of the evidence I've used,' he said steadily, 'to form the opinion that the trees cleared were remnant.' It looked like about 200 hectares of protected, endangered scrub, brigalow and other species, had been cleared.

Turnbull didn't seem to comprehend.

Could Turnbull show them the supposed regrowth vegetation, Turner asked.

Turnbull grew enraged. 'I had to pay the government a quarter of a million dollars in taxes,' he snarled, according to Turner's notebook, 'and you come here to tell me what I can and can't do.'

'I'm not here to tell you what to do,' Turner replied. 'But there are rules set up by the New South Wales government that you are required to follow.'

Turnbull responded that if Turner wanted to enter 'Strathdoon', he would have to go over the gate with his authorisation papers. Could Turner come and meet Cory, the actual owner of the property, in town? Striding away, he took out his phone and called his lawyer, Roger Butler, to arrange the meeting in the Moree chambers. But there was only a voicemail saying the office was closed for lunch. Turnbull dug in. The OEH would have to send all correspondence to Cole & Butler. And he'd told 'the boys', Grant and Cory, not to take any registered mail. Turner said he'd try Butler again in the afternoon.

Then Turnbull left, driving off south down County Boundary Road in his white ute, as the dust lifted behind him and Turner and Nadolny watched in silence.

*

I HAD TO PAY the government a quarter of a million dollars in taxes, and you come here to tell me what I can and can't do.

Turnbull's complaint was an old, rancorous one. It came from a landscape of ancient abrasions: the long legacies of libertarianism and conservatism. It came from a place of mercenary reckoning that imagines civic responsibility can be salaried away, that recalled the 'robbery by government' that made the squattocracy of the

1860s pay for lands they had sweated salt and blood to seize.

Suspicion has long streaked British attitudes to government. Most nineteenth-century subjects, lacking property, did not have civil rights, including the right to vote, while brutal responses to the Chartism movement and petty crime made for deep enmities. As evicted Aboriginal tribes had discovered, a traditional land could be forfeited or forsaken; their dispossessors brought the advantage of knowing this. From the Clearances in the Scottish Highlands and the Enclosures of England, British settler migrants had learned that land was not the common birthright their ancestors had enjoyed – it could be taken away and it could fail. They had seen whole communities perish or disperse, and rich lands grow pale and barren. It is little wonder, then, that they gripped to their patches of land so tightly.

The apparition of a government man at a station gate had, for nearly two hundred years, rarely meant good news. As Geoffrey Bolton explains, 'Australians inherited the strong British dislike of government interference; but they also formed the habit of relying upon government action.' Such a paradox made for a submerged resentment that still roils. The landholders of the 1840s in the northwest had felt egregiously short-changed by the government in Sydney. In exchange for their dauntless endeavours in the wilderness, they found that authority, normally so quick to mount criminal charges in defence of property, appeared to abandon them. Instead, their efforts to defend themselves against Black reprisals seemed to be chastised. Governor Gipps, in particular, stepped over the line, they felt: lecturing and punishing when he had no idea what it was like up there in the outlying districts.

What was the good of authority, then? It was nothing but oppression – an instinct confirmed two decades later, when in the Robertson Land Acts those squatters were made to pay money as well as blood for their land. And even then, with monies paid, the meddling continued.

Ian Turnbull had spent time in the United States. There he had heard wheat growers and landholders explain their liberal grand narratives of private property and the need for solidarity against state harassment. Without secure protection by law, there wasn't investment, there wasn't wealth. But then the government would come and knock a man's legs out from under him. Where was the proportionate representation if you paid a quarter of a mil in taxes and they still didn't take your calls?

'I'm not here to tell you what to do,' Glen Turner had said. 'But there are laws.' He might have been hapless Gipps, trying to establish a coherent society bound by authority, speaking more in sorrow than anger as squatters fumed and fomented. The government would talk of laws. But, the settlers felt, there was justice, and that was another matter.

***

THERE HAD ALWAYS BEEN weapons in Australia: waddies and spears, lil-lil clubs and boomerangs. The first whites brought flint lock muskets, then revolvers and rifles. Guns came in the arms of the First Fleet soldiers. They were fired at beasts, at Blacks, at each other; native wildlife, Aboriginals and convicts received most of the bullets for decades. Spears were thrown in return.

To be armed was to feel protected, but it was also to feel powerful. For decade upon decade guns were held in the hands of the anxious and angry, were kept above mantelpieces, were slung in holsters at horse-sides. Everyone wanted to hold the gun, no one to have it held against them. To point the barrel was to say: *I stand. You fall back.*

Two hundred years later in Croppa Creek, as everywhere in rural Australia, guns are still part of farming life. They are regulated now, kept in locked boxes, registered and numbered. They are brought out often enough though, to cull pests: feral pigs in the paddocks, kangaroos in the scrub. Rifles rattle around in back trays of utes.

Ian Turnbull had used guns for fifty years. He had licences for two shotguns and two rifles. He was a good shot.

***

AFTER TURNBULL'S UTE DISAPPEARED, Nadolny and Turner exchanged disbelieving looks. At Turner's suggestion, they each noted down what they remembered of the exchange. Then they proceeded with their inspection of the property. They took photographs, examined vegetation and cut samples from felled trees with a chainsaw. The trees were already buried in stacks of dried timber, ready for burning. On the ground was a huge chain, the type that is hooked between two bulldozers to take down trees. They took a photo of a mature brigalow standing in a pile of fallen timber and scrub. It was near sunset, winter dusk, when they left.

Turner wrote up the encounter with Turnbull and his findings on 'Strathdoon' that night. He made meticulous observations of times, locations, file numbers. His crabbed hand recorded every action and statement from Turnbull. Each line of the farmer's speech was introduced formally: 'Mr Ian Turnbull said...'

A week or so later, Turner received an anonymous email with an attachment. It reported 'illegal clearing of Belah, Brigalow and Box Tree which contained 6000 acres koala colony'.

In April 2012, just two months earlier, the federal environment minister had listed koalas as a threatened species in parts of the country, including New South Wales. Numbers in the state had dropped by a third over twenty years. The catastrophic impact of habitat loss and urban incursion had dulled this legacy. Everyone in Moree had stories of koalas ambling down the main road, or hiding in pockets in the bush. But dogs often killed those that straggled into backyards and parklands in search of water. Many locals were proud of their iconic wildlife and kept habitat locations a secret. The trees on 'Strathdoon' and 'Colorado' weren't just some of the last of the brigalow in the district, they were also the home to some of the last koalas.

Killing koalas was a crime, and their presence on the Turnbull properties complicated things.

*

TURNER TOOK TURNBULL'S THREAT to his life seriously. After he reported it, there was discussion with his managers whether he should keep dealing with the farmer. The Turnbulls were powerful and rich: the kind who had QCs over for afternoon tea when an OEH officer was due.

But Turnbull was an intransigent type he'd met before. Turner resented the idea of kowtowing to his bullying behaviour. 'Of course I will abide by your direction not to go onto the properties, but there is no more or no less danger for other people who work for OEH,' Turner wrote tetchily to management on 7 August 2012, as a response was slowly developed. Ian Turnbull had glared at him at the gate of that property with felled trees right behind him. The stop-work order had been swatted away. Meanwhile, Roger was clearing on his property up the road. Years out in the back blocks of the northwest had shown Turner the effects of constant chipping at the small refuges of native vegetation. He spent weekends with Alison carefully tamping soil around sapling and seedling on their property, while out there in the plains, there were would-be developers smashing whole woodlands with their tractors. The emphasis in the regulations was on encouraging voluntary compliance, because, as the OEH website put it, 'most people want to do the right thing'. But if they didn't, people like Turner were charged by the state to make sure they had to. In the end, it wasn't about his feelings for nature or otherwise. Turner was not the kind to shrink from his task of enforcing compliance.

'It is BECAUSE I work for OEH in native vegetation compliance that I was verbally abused by Ian Turnbull,' he wrote with restrained exasperation.

I copped worse from his son Roger (in a separate investigation) and often get a less-than-courteous welcome from farmers just because of the type of work I do ... I understand your managerial responsibilities [with regard to] OH&S of staff, but if I'm not to go onto these properties then Gary [Spencer] (or whomever does the rest of the field work) has quite a few days to spend in Moree and they face no less risk than I ... if

I were to turn up with the support of the NSW Police I'd say we would not have any more trouble.

Turner's senior manager, a long-time resident of the environment department, was newly in charge of the agency's statewide compliance investigations, and managing a thin landscape of officers across New South Wales, travelling between regional offices. He replied to Turner, 'You should not plan to go to Strathdoon or Lochiel [Colorado] but continue to be the lead on the investigations.' He had inherited a situation that involved a direct, corroborated threat to the life of an officer. He made his decision: Gary Spencer, a special investigator at the OEH and a tough former cop, would be a steady presence managing the relations with the landowners; compliance officers Michael Wood and Steve Beaman, already looking at clearing breaches near the Turnbull blocks, would support him. Turner would lead from the rear.

A week later, Turner wrote acceptingly of 'our expectation that if a similar (or more significant) threat is made next time we go out to the properties, Gary's experience and training ... will put him in a better position than I to handle such a situation should it arise'.

The police were not notified of the threat. Turnbull was not relieved of his gun licence. Turner and Nadolny had trusted in official protocol, but something got lost in the process: the OEH was used to dealing with administrative wrangles, not threats of physical violence. In fact, other staff had also received threats from angry farmers, and no one had told the police. Turner could only remind Nadolny to keep detailed notes on everything, *everything* to do with this case, now that it was escalating. Nadolny reflected, years later, that in the final analysis it seemed he hadn't written quite enough.

4

Before farming could operate on a large scale the country had to be cleared by ringbarking and burning. Jack Parker and Les Stevens would light fires early in the day and late in the afternoon would set fire to the heaps. Next morning hot shovels of hot coals were carted to light other heaps. At night these fires looked like fairyland to we children.

—**Gretta Fea Uebergang, *And So the Story Goes: The Croppa Creek District, 1848–1987*, 1987**

On a hot December evening in Tamworth, ecologist Phil Spark sits back in his motel-room chair and prepares to discuss his involvement in the Turnbull story. It has haunted him since 2012.

'My work takes me all around the northwest into all the back blocks.' He sighs. 'So when you get off the main roads and into the back blocks, that's when you start to comprehend the extent of the clearing.'

The thicket of silence, as Spark describes it, is as tight as brigalow scrub itself. 'And it's really, really difficult to break through it. Everyone knows someone, or is related to someone, who's been into illegal clearing. I have good friends out there, people that I consider good friends, who won't say anything to a journalist, won't say anything. And I think, *Why not? You know it's wrong, you know it's wrong as I know it's wrong.* But there's this pressure. This really tight community thing.'

Spark is a burly man in middle age, with hooded eyes and a thatch of sandy hair. Freckled arms, a barrel chest, worn-in Blundstones over seed-pocked socks. A thoughtful, practical individual of apparently unlimited diligence. He was a farmer himself, taking over from his parents at eighteen. 'I was the sort of kid that had lizards in boxes. I've been a nature freak since day one, really.' At thirty-three he began studying conservation, and at fifty handed the farm over to his son. 'I persisted [on the farm] because I wanted it to be there for him to take it on.' Like Turnbull, Spark felt the freight of legacy behind him, the responsibility to land and family. 'He's now running the farm. So that ticked my box.'

Since the mid-1990s, Spark has been conducting biodiversity surveys, a skilled task requiring wide knowledge and close attention. He gets to know local areas in minute detail: the landscape of cropped fields and remnant stands of vegetation, and the secret one hidden in groundcover, nestling amid fenceline scrub or in the middle of paddocks. He loves seeking out the tiny marvels of endurance. One of his current favourites is Belson's Panic (*Homopholis belsonii*), a rare little low grass that grows along verges such as those in Talga Lane. He speaks of it tenderly: it is 'a lovely thing', listed as vulnerable in the Commonwealth and endangered in New South Wales. Groundcovers such as Panics are often overlooked or carelessly ploughed, but they are critical in knitting together an ecological community. It is Spark's job to track these remnants and alert authorities to their existence so they can be protected.

After a lifetime of amateur interest, he began professionally by 'kicking around the bush a lot' during then New South Wales premier Bob Carr's campaign of biodiversity surveying. Gaining some contracts, Spark and a friend would go out for whole summers and examine everything. By the early 2000s, he had contracts to cover the entire east coast, the Tablelands and more. Now he works as a consultant ecologist for the OEH, for National Parks and Wildlife Service, and for Local Land Services, almost entirely with a focus on conservation. He sometimes gives talks on biodiversity at country primary schools. 'The kids are great. All kids love wildlife, especially all rural kids. As long as you want to talk about animals they'll talk to you.'

Spark had work out near Croppa Creek around the time the Turnbulls bought 'Strathdoon' and 'Colorado'. Perhaps 85 per cent of land around the hamlet was already cleared, mostly converted to cropping; the rest was mainly gullies or sandstone, soil too poor for good agriculture. Spark was contracted by Local Land Services – then the Catchment Management Authority – to set up long-term koala monitoring in the scrub areas near Croppa Creek.

Alaine Anderson, on the property adjoining 'Strathdoon', alerted him to potential clearing on the blocks in late 2011. County Boundary Road, three hours' drive from Spark's home in Tamworth, is fairly out of the way. But, 'Yes,' Spark says with a wry look. Since the Turnbulls took over the blocks, 'I drifted up there fairly frequently.'

Spark began to document the activities on 'Strathdoon' and 'Colorado', taking photographs from the road showing the dozers at work. Spark could see koalas on those blocks. It was he who gave the talk in the Croppa Creek hall about protecting the animals in February 2012, which Ian Turnbull and Alaine Anderson both attended. 'The koala population was a really big thing.' He quickly had the Northern Inland Council for the Environment, the Total Environment Centre and the NSW Environmental Defenders Office interested. These organisations exist to monitor transgressions and support conservation. He and Anderson started sending letters to state members of parliament, especially Robyn Parker, the Minister for the Environment, informing her of the dramatic land clearing at Croppa Creek.

The properties, Spark readily admits, were not virgin land. They had been cleared in the past. 'But it's still an endangered ecological community that should be protected to mature! To regenerate itself back to the original community! Whereas Turnbull ignored all that.' He shakes his head. 'That brigalow on that rich soil, there's so little of it left. So little of it.' But the type of farmer Turnbull was, he believes, 'just thinks of their land as a factory'.

Spark, an experienced reporter of infringements, called the OEH and spoke to Glen Turner. Spark was surprised the local Catchment Management Authority hadn't red-lighted the Turnbulls' activities. Turner assured him that the OEH had certainly tried; though the stop-work order hadn't stuck, they were still on the case. The CMA hadn't given approval, even if Turnbull kept implying it had. The two men began to exchange information.

Minister Parker was sent more briefings and photographs. Alaine Anderson was also in touch with the federal member, Mark Coulton. There was no action to stop the clearing, so Spark amplified his campaign. He sent material to the Greens, the Labor Party, the media and conservation groups. He began working with the Total Environment Centre in Sydney. Everyone agreed it was terrible, that someone should be doing something to stop the Turnbulls. But the Turnbulls stolidly went on clearing.

'Well, yeah, you look at all my correspondence with the ministers ... I wrote to everyone I could, and we had the Environmental Defenders Office on the case with us, and they wrote to the minister. We got the feeling all along that Turnbull was being told by someone in a position of power, "It's all right, mate, we're going to look after ya." It just reeks of it.'

*

CHRIS NADOLNY, WHO HAS had plenty of exposure to landholders' feelings about compliance officers and ecologists, gives a faint 'Yeah?' when asked if environmental crime is a concept that means much to farmers. 'I think a lot of the attitude there relates to the fact that the regulators are not seen as local and are seen as a foreign culture.' A local Landcare group's advice might be welcomed, but the arrival of government officers, ever since the days of the Border Police and the Land Commissioners, is not. 'There is that sort of them-and-us attitude, particularly among the big clearers, because that's their way of life: they're aiming to get money by developing,' Nadolny says. However, he emphasises, while many push a few trees, 'it's relatively few people who do most of the clearing'.

But many feel blamed for it. Farmers become antagonised by authorities' implications that they're all potential vandals. As social researcher Frank Vanclay puts it, in a defence of the complexity of farming attitudes, 'Farmers do what they consider to be the "right thing".'

Nadolny agrees. 'I started out assisting with the Landcare movement, and I had a lot of contact with farmers who did have a lot of social responsibility and were very strong on management, whereas more of my later career was involved with illegal clearing, where the attitude was very, very different. In some cases they still held a Landcare-type ethic but a different set of values, a different set of standards. Like, "My clearing wasn't really that bad, I left these paddock trees, I left this and that habitat." And you can have the two coinciding – a person who, on the one hand, does a lot of clearing, but on the other, supports community action, gives money to things like revegetation.' Ian Turnbull had been a champion of conservation farming. Under questioning, he spoke often of 'restoring' the properties and of his progressive agricultural techniques. But he was comfortable with ball-and-chain destruction of thousands of native trees and their habitat.

Farmers are by necessity practical people. Some have inherited the life and the devotion; some have chosen it. A few are 'land miners', scraping what they can from the earth's riches, but most, even if they gaze upon scraped fields and crumbled scrub, adore the land they live on and sense their privilege and responsibility as well as their opportunities. Farmers eat responsibility for breakfast: to their families, to their mortgages, markets, animals and boundaries, as well as to the future. Those who broadacre-crop must spend many thousands of dollars of chemicals; those who use rotational grazing management must constantly adjust their programs and rarely take a holiday; those who pursue regenerative agriculture must study constantly; those who go rogue and plunder the earth despite regulations must prepare for years of legal combat.

After decades of talking with farmers about their attitudes and practices, Vanclay concludes that the broader social context of land management challenges is not duly appreciated. Many of the environmental damage issues they preside over, farmers point out, are the result of earlier regulations, such as mandatory land clearing, or recommended scientific methods, like dry fallow farming. The advice, not the farmers' attitudes, is to blame for the results. Governmental ambitions, agricultural research, market demands, changing climate: they've shaped the land as much as any individual behind the wheel of a tractor. And when push comes to shove for sustainability over profitability, they can baulk at being the ones to make sacrifices. 'Farmers,' says Vanclay emphatically, 'do not believe they are "raping the earth" while driving their tractors.'

But they can be ignorant or naive. 'As an ecologist,' admits Nadolny, 'I think we haven't really done what we should have to explain to farmers the value of native vegetation.' He gives an example of farmers observing shade trees in grazing paddocks. Grasses grow softer and richer under a tree. Stock are tempted to it; they eat it out and trample the stubble. The farmer, Nadolny explains, only sees the bare soil and concludes that trees inhibit grass growth. Thus he pulls out the trees, believing he's helping the environment. 'So a lot of what's driving farmers to overclear is this false perception of the environment. And we just haven't extended that knowledge.'

They want to pass the farm on in good condition. This, Vanclay claims, is more important than any economic decision: it makes all the costs, labour and stress worthwhile. They worry that their children won't want to continue; they feel blood flushes of obligation to previous and future generations. The dread of failure in this special regard is suspected to be the cause of many suicides. The land is one part of farming, the longer purpose and social element are others. 'For farmers,' Vanclay writes, 'sustainability means something along the lines of "we as a family, on our farm, in the future".'

***

'GLEN WAS A REASONABLY experienced officer,' reflects Simon Smith, 'but he did lose his cool a bit. He did get a bit personal; he was invested in the whole thing. Glen would call a spade a spade. He could very easily be offensive, or be taken to be offensive. Yeah, he was emotional, and wore his heart on his sleeve.

'Glen tended to get worked up; he did get fiery. He'd give back as much as he took, which isn't necessarily a good thing if you're trying to be an impartial investigator. Glen was impassioned about the issue [of illegal clearing] and trying to stop it, but at the same time he was also very reasonable, and could hear both sides.' He understood and respected farmers, his former manager says. 'But his view was that the law was designed to achieve a purpose. People make mistakes, he said, but the people who deliberately and repeatedly break the law when they know that's what they're doing: that got up his nose more than anything.'

The next time Turner visited 'Strathdoon' and 'Colorado', on 21 August 2012, he went with his full crew, as instructed. Beaman and Wood were to help collect evidence, Gary Spencer to facilitate access and Nadolny as the expert ecologist. They had entry permits and GPS receivers to map and record locations.

The OEH vehicles parked outside 'Strathdoon' on County Boundary Road. Emerging from a waiting car nearby were the Turnbull men: Ian, Grant and Cory. Spencer asked his colleagues to wait. They watched as he went over to the Turnbulls and spoke with them. There were thoughtful faces, a short exchange. Then Spencer returned and the others watched the Turnbulls drive away.

They entered through the 'Strathdoon' gate. There were stacks of piled vegetation, including mature trees. About 400 hectares had now been cleared since May.

Bill Scott's niece, Anna Simmons, was living in the cottage on the property. She was alone at home, cleaning a deer head for her husband, when Turner and Spencer came to the door. Turner, interested, took a photograph of the head to show a friend. The officers spoke to Simmons about inspecting the property; she shrugged and they left to look at the site.

By the edge of a clearing on 'Strathdoon', Turner and Nadolny found three koalas in trees. There was also koala scat in the shadow of felled poplar box trunks on the ground; they couldn't see what else was buried beneath the heavy wood. It was the first direct evidence they had of the animals living on the property. Turner became very quiet, and headed back to the cottage with Spencer to interview Simmons. He looked, remembered Nadolny, upset.

According to Simmons, Turner raised the prospect that her uncle Bill could be held responsible for the Turnbulls' clearing on the land before the contracts of sale for the two blocks were finalised. He also mentioned darkly that Roger Butler, Turnbull's lawyer in Moree, had been a trustee beside old Bill.

'He was really aggro when he was speaking to me,' she complained later in a statement. 'He spoke with a raised voice. Turner had a harsh and very stern manner. He kept stepping towards me.' Simmons thought he might be recording the conversation. 'I was scared of him because he kept coming at me. I felt he was hammering me with all this personal information and I felt like I was going to jail.' He was out to get the Turnbulls, she said, and he threatened to take her to the Supreme Court.

'Spencer stood there with a really shocked look on his face,' she claimed. 'He then tried to end it. He said, "Alright, I think we've got enough information, thanks for your time, Anna."'

Before the men left, Simmons asked Turner to delete the photo of the deer head.

What Simmons didn't relate in her statement was her fury at Turner's intimation that the matter could become criminal. She 'gave him a serve', Simon Smith marvels, remembering Turner and Spencer's account to him afterwards. 'She abused the hell out of him.'

'You're just a selfish bitch,' Turner apparently flared back. 'You only want the money.' Koalas were being killed just outside her home. But she, just like the Turnbulls and the Scott brothers, seemed more interested in human affairs.

Simmons was on the phone to her landlord, Cory Turnbull, as soon as the officers left, and fled in tears to her uncle's house. Cory told his grandfather. Ian called Spencer, who called the senior manager at OEH. Turner, Simmons had told them, had said he'd keep at the Turnbulls until he put them off their farms. Ian 'didn't like that at all', she said in a court statement in 2016. 'Not at all.'

Within days, Simmons complained to the OEH directly. 'I don't want to get anyone into trouble, but Glen needs to get some disciplinary actions,' Simmons wrote. 'If he had handcuffs, he would have locked me up then and there.'

After they'd left an inspection of Turnbull properties, Nadolny recollects, 'Glen used to say – he said this a couple of times in a joking, kind of half-serious tone – "Well, I bet Ian Turnbull's on the phone to Kevin Humphries right now."' Humphries, National Party star and state parliamentarian, was gearing up to take ministerial power in the O'Farrell Liberal–National government. A former schoolteacher, he had been in parliament since 2007 and presided over an enormous electorate, comprising a massive 44 per cent of the state's landmass. It housed some very wealthy people, including influential members of the NSW Farmers Association. He had apparently met groups of farmers and assured them that land clearing would soon no longer be impeded by the old native vegetation laws. The legislation would, he had indicated, not just be amended but wholly trashed.

*

THAT AUGUST NIGHT in the motel dining room, Nadolny sat talking over the day's events with Turner and the other officers. After leaving Simmons' cottage on 'Strathdoon', the group had continued on to 'Colorado'. On that property, there was a belah pushed over. A bimble box felled nearby. Nadolny found a koala and her baby in one remaining stand of trees, and another koala nearby. He noticed there were no bodies to be found, though koalas had likely died there. The men mulled over their frustration. If the threat of inspections didn't work, then what? Surely there was more than one way to get things done.

Turnbull was probably thinking the same thing as he picked up the phone to his lawyer.

***

THE FRONTIER MELTS INTO the interior and comes out the other side. Few places are hidden in our continent. There are no bushrangers anymore. Getting lost in the bush makes the news. Settlers and convicts wanted property for suffrage; now, in post-colonial democratic Australia, they're tax-paying, subsidy-receiving, drought-assisted, legislated subjects of the Commonwealth.

Laws have changed since Australia was founded partly as a home for gun-flourishing criminals and police. Indigenous laws, a fine lace of iron-hard filaments that lay over every community, every relationship, had held systems in place for thousands of years. They, like the other institutions and axioms of Aboriginal life, were shaken loose by European settlement, though they remain amid modern experience, in First Nations people's sense of relation to country and to the authority of Elders. European law, founded on protection of property, is often as implacable. Modern Australia, inheriting and adapting British jurisprudence, has firm if not consistent ideas about what is and what is not allowed, what is and is not to be protected.

Jeremy Bentham, founder of utilitarianism, used the Enlightenment's computational model of human behaviour to propose deterrence methods: by modulating the costs versus benefits of the transgression of laws, society could make penalties sufficient to outweigh potential profit. This system, still generally adopted through the West, works up to a point. But for many property developers, fines are built into the finance.

'Governance is a behaviour management system, with many cogs and levers that might be deployed to change its outcomes,' note academics Paul Martin and Donald W. Hine. Responses to the idea of environmental regulation are called, in cool behavioural science, 'motivational postures' and are influenced by how much 'social distance' people perceive between themselves and authority. Some citizens are broadly aligned with governmental paradigms and submit to their requirements. Those who, aligning with a narrative of victimhood, feel oppressed or alienated by a system are likely to resist abiding by its laws. They may become what sociological researchers Robyn Bartel and Elaine Barclay, in their research on 5000 agricultural workers across the country, call game-players.

Game-players tend to be older, typical of the ageing population of Australian farmers. They feel that regulations express the values of city-dwellers, and complain that hobby farmers and mining companies aren't scrutinised and imposed on to the same extent. Game-players are invested in maintaining control and independence. A person with a resistant, intransigent posture to authority – like Ian Turnbull – might respond to strong enforcement or generous financial incentives, but he would more likely enjoy finding ways around regulations, might stolidly persist in the face of criticism and chastisement.

The more an authority and its subjects share beliefs and values, the less likely defiance is. It comes down to the building of trust, respect and agreement on the purpose of regulation itself. It depends on what people believe everyone else is doing (as with the celebrated habit of tax avoidance, there's a paradox that if regulations are needed, it signals that someone has been getting away with something). It depends on levels of peer pressure to encourage compliance, and on the potency of shaming, ostracisation, surveillance and social penalties. Criminal subcultures, Barclay and Bartel remind us, are shaped by the same foundations.

***

'THE FEDERAL GOVERNMENT WAS quick to investigate the clearing,' Phil Spark wrote in 2017 in a submission calling for an inquest into Glen Turner's death, 'but in the end they did nothing with it.' He continued: 'A fire spread from a burning heap of vegetation that burnt a large area on "Colorado".' He was writing of a literal fire, which federal inspectors suspected had been deliberately lit to blind their view when they visited a week after the OEH team, making it impossible to determine how much land had been cleared. But it was a metaphor, too. For the Turnbull case would soon ignite the flammable subject of political interference and incompetence in protecting the natural assets of the state.

***

FARMERS, MORE THAN MOST, are formed from the nutrients of the cultural soil in which they originate. Many Australian historians have dug into this humus to explain the national character.

Australia's history is not only of ruthless British imperialists raping and murdering their way to ownership of traditional lands. When the new arrivals are themselves subjects, the effects compound. Libby Robin, in *How a Continent Created a Nation* (2007), proposes that an unresolvable yearning and trauma was brought to Australia by the Irish, still preferring the prelapsarian, uncolonised Celtic landscape of their imagination. Scots, far from feeling colonised solidarity with local mobs, were among some of the most ferocious attackers on Black communities.

Weak relationships with the environment go with strained social relationships. Inland, in small communities and isolated farmstead families, it was a tense social world. Here, a white-collar ex-convict might work for a former agrarian itinerant; the bourgeoisie got just as dusty and leaf-strewn in their crinolines and bonnets as the former lags in their kitchen.

Conceive of the resolve required to take a patch of bush and raze it. To cut down the men, women and children who stood upon it. People were transformed in the colony, permissions given, their latencies erupting. They washed human blood from their palms. In Wiltshire, in Aberdeen, life was not like this. How strange it must have been; how full of relief and even pride a man or woman when, tested, they could find it in themselves to act; what a balm dissociation and denial. '[I]t is no coincidence,' observes historian Cameron Muir, 'that the same society that perpetrated [Indigenous] massacres produced animal and plant extinctions and the degradation of grasses, watering holes and soils.'

The frontier lands of Australia were not a vortex of horror from end to end. But the violence – abrupt, stunning, blood-spilling violence – was a wide-spattered pattern.

From all this endurance, brutality and strangeness came a recognisable type, the Australian character. Anyone who lives in or visits a town like Moree will see him there: blue check shirt and wide-brimmed hat, jeans, dusty boots, a firmness of jaw and squint of eye. He is celebrated in everything from Slim Dusty's music to Patrick White's *The Tree of Man* (1955) to Robert Hughes's *The Fatal Shore* (1986); he is recreated in popular 'rural romance' fiction and Senator Barnaby Joyce's wardrobe. Russel Ward, writing in *The Australian Legend* (1958), suggests that the famous Aussie battler, the Gallipoli larrikin, the twinkling rogue, was born from the rebelliousness of Irish settlers, the antiauthoritarianism of the itinerant pastoral worker and the defiant pride of its native-born generations. We know its branded iconography: R.M. Williams boots, Akubra hats; the celebrated blue-eyed, thousand-yard stare.

In one photograph published by the media, taken years before he committed murder, Ian Turnbull looks the very avatar of the tanned New South Wales farmer, with his square face solid and lined, posing proudly in his check shirt in front of the 'Yambin' silos.

Then there are the furrows of his cheeks, the leaping eyebrows, the averted gaze and the letter box mouth, in a shot taken in the passageway between custody and police transport van.

5

> The wilderness ... came with us, the invaders. It came in our heads and it gradually rose out of the ground to meet us...
> **—Les Murray, Introduction to Eric Rolls'** ***A Million Wild Acres,* 2011**

A week after the encounter with Anna Simmons in late August, Phil Spark rang Glen Turner. 'There's a dozer operating on "Colorado",' he said. He was at the fenceline, waiting for the police. 'They're pushing trees right now. I've got photos of it. The Total Environment Centre is going to contact the premier's office.'

He rang off and called the federal hotline to report unauthorised clearing and risk to protected species. He knew all too well that federal and state environment departments rarely shared knowledge of cases. Koala habitat was being destroyed, he told them, as well as other endangered ecological communities listed in the federal

Environment Protection and Biodiversity Act.

Hours earlier Gary Spencer had called Grant Turnbull. It was just past eight in the morning. 'Grant,' Spencer said, 'we have received some information that some clearing is taking place on your properties.'

They weren't clearing, Grant said. Just cleaning up and tidying the stacks of trees they'd already felled. Then they'd get the tractors into the sheds. 'Just in case anyone says we are clearing, I give you my word,' Grant said. 'There will be no more clearing done.'

'It's very important,' said Spencer, 'that no more occurs until this is sorted out.'

Grant got back on the front foot. 'From the beginning,' he said, 'we've been waiting for someone to come out and sit down with us and tell us what we can and can't do, and we're still waiting. We are not environmental vandals. We just want someone to come and tell us what we can do, so we can get a farm plan. We've been waiting for CMA for eighteen months. We've put aside 500 hectares for land for conservation and made corridors for wildlife.' Again, he said, 'I give you my word there'll be no more clearing.'

But that night, Spencer rang Grant again. There had been reports from neighbours. 'Grant,' he said carefully, 'I just need to clarify a few things. You know when I spoke to you and I told you it was in your best interest to stop clearing until the matter is all sorted out? I have received information that some clearing has occurred today on the property.'

They'd just put the tractors away, Grant said. You couldn't leave them outside or they'd be pinched.

Spencer told him that someone had seen trees being pushed.

Grant had tried to ring Ivan Maas, he explained, but 'he must have had his phone off'. They didn't have radios. 'He had to cross some fields to get over to where the sheds are. One of the tractors got bogged and we had to pull it out, but they're all in the shed.'

Spencer pushed a little harder. 'Was Ivan doing any clearing of trees?'

'He probably was, but as soon as I got off the phone with you I went out there and put the dozers away. I gave you my word that no clearing was going to happen, and as soon as I spoke to you I went out and stopped it.'

*

TWO DAYS LATER, THE Commonwealth sent out investigators from the Department of Sustainability, Environment, Water, Populations and Communities, at the time under Labor minister Greg Combet. These were officers supporting the federal protections, which overlaid the state ones and carried higher potential penalties. They too saw the pushed trees. They saw burning stacks. They gave Ian and Grant warrants authorising their inspections and warned them again of the laws they were potentially breaking and the ways they could check for protected species such as koalas on their properties. They spoke of severe fines and confiscated dozers. They talked of seeking their own stop-work order. One of them followed up with correspondence stating, in the plainest terms, that except for fire-risk management, no more felling or burning should be done without approval.

The same officer also wrote of how, as the inspectors were standing on 'Colorado', someone set grasslands and fallen trees on fire near them. In the middle of the burning grass, a single tree was left standing. The inspectors had just seen a koala in it. Now smoke billowed across the field. 'The lighting of those fires,' he wrote in an email to Grant, 'might be seen as an attempt to obstruct my colleagues and I from carrying out our duties.'

They'd thought the inspectors had gone, Grant explained earnestly. He hoped the officer would contact him personally next time he was on the property and about to leave. And he sent a helpful 'heads up' that they'd have the dozers out again soon, 'to push and spread piles of dead ground wood to be burned'. 'We do want to work with you on this,' he added, 'not against.'

*

THAT AUGUST, SPARK AND Alaine Anderson began writing a series of letters to local member of parliament Kevin Humphries, explaining Turnbull's activity and asking him to intervene. His friendship with the Turnbull family was local knowledge, but they wrote nonetheless. 'We have heard all the political spin,' wrote Spark baldly; 'we now want the facts about what has happened and what you are doing to rectify the situation.' Anderson was still writing to Robyn Parker, the state minister for the environment, about the clearing of koala habitat. Both politicians assured Anderson and Spark that investigations were underway. 'Once adequate information is gathered the most appropriate regulatory response will be determined,' Minister Parker wrote late in September. 'I appreciate you bringing [the allegations] to my attention.'

***

THE LAND'S HORIZON WAS as vast as the ocean over which settlers had voyaged. It swallowed bullock trains, explorers and settler parties; it engulfed ambitions. A person could evaporate in that sky.

Almost all settlers to northwest New South Wales came from green lands with no arid zones. For many, it was the first time their skin had been so dry or felt such heat. A ploughman from Sussex, an accountant from Birmingham, a seamstress from Galway, their eyes screwed up in the glare: what had they imagined, and what did they make of the reality?

To many, Australian nature was eccentric, novel, curious; it was also monotonous, wearisome and melancholy. They voiced bafflement at the apparent 'reversal of nature' in which, in the exasperated description of one settler, 'trees retained their leaves and shed their bark instead, the swans were black, the eagles white, the bees were stingless, some mammals had pockets, others laid eggs, it was warmest on the hills...' It seemed a gnomic metaphor, but there was no poetry in it. Literature faltered here. Reassuring synonyms were sought: a patch reminded someone of the Highlands, another of the Weald. Some loved the new environment. The delicacy of tree ferns and the graceful droop of eucalypts were admired by Europeans from the First Fleet on, including the sensitive Lieutenant Watkin Tench in his wonderful account of the new land. Others were aghast: 'The country is horrible,' explorer Daniel Brock wrote bluntly, 'a Climax of Desolation – no trees, no shrubs, all bleak, barren undulating sand. Miserable! Horrible!'

By Brock's time in the 1830s, distaste for Australian landscape had become a mark of good taste. No longer 'evergreen' but 'ever-brown', the bush was scolded for being unpicturesque, unvaried, lacking ornamentation, untidy, desolate, tedious, too quiet, too loud or, in Charles Darwin's words, 'looking actively *dead*'.

How had the original inhabitants endured it?

The colonial plan was to 'improve' the native people with agriculture. Governor Macquarie sought desperately to make the Indigenous peoples between Sydney and Parramatta into peasant farmers. In 1814, he drew up plans to distribute land and tools to them; two years later, he was still pleading with them to take them up. Traditional cultures were not much interested in an ideology of progress. Others of his fellow settlers weren't so patient, or so inclined to imagine harmony beneath this hot sky. The Kamilaroi people, the second-largest group in Australia after the Wiradjuri, held over 30,000 square miles. In the first years of the 1830s, in the huge, mainly waterless plains, there were few reasons for competition. But by the late 1830s, as waterholes were seized and game taken, there was growing defensiveness among settlers and infuriated pushback from the local tribes. The 1830s and 1840s marked the worst of the violence. A local man put the attitude simply: 'Shoot them all and manure the ground with them.'

Violence between stockmen (many of them convicts or ex-convicts) and Aboriginals reached the Gwydir River, only about 30 kilometres south of Croppa Creek. The ferocious Major James Nunn came from Sydney in late 1837 with a party of about thirty troopers and some volunteers. His two-month campaign killed hundreds: in 1838, perhaps up to 300 Aboriginal peoples were ambushed and murdered at Snodgrass Lagoon on Waterloo Creek, southwest of Moree, on what is now Australia Day.

In the 1970s, a William Henry Weick, who had grown up in Warialda, confessed, 'I often think about "Murdering Gully", about 4 miles east of Warialda. As a boy I was told it got its name because at one time the Blacks were rounded up and murdered there.' There appears no trace in formal history of Murdering Gully, but it is not the only site in Australia to hold that purpose. The last attested massacre in Australia happened only ninety years ago, at Coniston in the Northern Territory. It was in 1928, six years before Ian Turnbull's birth.

Professor of imperial history Ann Curthoys suggests in her essay 'Mythologies' that settlers' inability to acknowledge the humanity of Aboriginal peoples and therefore the magnitude and horror of the violence enacted against them led to a strange reaction. Not only were settlers constantly suppressing their guilt, but they came to identify simultaneously as superior to and victims of Aboriginal Australians.

There is a strange, morbid fixation in Australian myth of just how hard a person has to work on this land. One of the perplexities of Aboriginal life for colonists was how idly the people appeared to exist. Their contented eating of shellfish and game, the amount of sitting and communing – it appeared insulting to the newcomers, who whacked, hacked, lugged, shoved, piled and sliced through their days. Blacks weren't grimed with sweat; their hands weren't scarred from pulverising scrub; they weren't collapsing over a meagre campsite meal of damper and boiled mutton every night. It was as if they had no idea how to earn their place – so they should not have it.

It's a weird kind of heroism that feels braver the harder it's fallen to its knees. But John Locke had placed emphasis on labour to morally justify the owning of property. The more work put into the land, the more settled a man was upon it. So if the axe wouldn't clear for crops, cattle would be hauled across rivers to tread the soil. If the stock, trampling the native vegetation, encouraged the scrub to explode in great thickets, this would be hacked and burned away. If the soil lifted and blew away in vast sails of dust, if the earth was grooved in rain-washed gully erosion, if bushfires flamed incandescent from horizon to horizon as eucalypts replaced more fireproof species, there was all the more work to be done. There would never be any end to the work. A man could sweat for eighty years on this land: how thoroughly, then, he would own it.

By the start of the twentieth century, after a centenary of occupation, 'battling the land' was a proxy for the traditional masculine challenges of hunting and warfare. An actual war, which was waged for 150 years and barely acknowledged, was subsumed by a 'war' on nature. If Indigenous people were mentioned, it was in connection to the settlers' endurance, their suffering. The infamous capture of Eliza Fraser in Queensland and the killing of the Mawbey family in New South Wales encouraged an idea of settlers 'under siege'. White Australians in the nineteenth century, says Curthoys, were able to acknowledge tensions and moral concerns about black–white relations. But as Australia entered a new mood of nation-building in the early twentieth, the idea of settler heroism soaked into Australian historiography. What W.E.H. Stanner famously called 'the great Australian silence' fell.

Understanding ressentiment, the perverse little psychological gambit identified by Kierkegaard and Nietzsche, is fundamental to understanding Australia. Ressentiment is the twist by which inferiority or insecurity is not owned, but externalised to another, who is then called 'inferior'. It allowed white Australia to compensate for its colonial sins by blaming its own victims.

Eventually, the trauma of repressing violence and culpability evaporates the capacity to empathise with others' trauma. In Curthoys' words, '[t]he self-chosen white victim finds it extremely difficult to recognise what he or she has done to others'.

Ross Gibson's brief *Seven Versions of an Australian Badland* (2002) is a psychogeographical study of a stretch of roadway near Rockhampton and its dark histories. Examining photographs of late-nineteenth-century Queenslanders, he notices a pervasive cast. These men had done and seen terrible things, but although they kept silent about them, they couldn't hide the evidence on their faces. 'No matter how much self-conviction or arrogance sheened the faces, many of them were also taut with some deep stun of alienation and doubt,' Gibson wrote.

A cast gets set on European visages that have worked too hard outdoors for too long. The mouth is a serrated horizon-line. Furrows mark a neck and jawline clamped to the rigours of adversity. Eyes are tarped with forbearance. When one encounters the face in bus stations and roadhouses, it is usually not reading or talking. It is persisting, wasting no vigour, wisely, and keeping to itself whatever it knows. It's the right kind of countenance for contemplating the brigalow, and it first took shape during the settlement years. It is in hundreds of photographs from the late-nineteenth century ... No matter how fervidly they might have told themselves the land was there for the taking, many of these people knew in their souls that they were not getting anything for free.

There is another, particularly compelling photograph of Turnbull, taken the week he killed Glen Turner. It is his mugshot, grainy chiaroscuro in the blow-up included in the files of the Supreme Court of New South Wales. His hair is mussed, his mouth clamped, there are furrows on his nose and lines in his forehead. His eyes gaze out like black marbles, lids pinched a little as if looking into bright light. Turnbull wears no expression on his face but a composed steadiness. It is the face of someone who has acted, and has nothing more to say.

***

ONE OF THE MECHANISMS of ressentiment is that, in the deft sheeting of responsibility to another, it gives licence to shed inhibition, social norms or obedience to the law. The weaker the person feels, the less they can suppress their reaction. A person feeling vulnerable will speak bitterly. They will fixate on blaming another. They will imagine a system ranged against them. They will pause their vehicle on a winter road on the way to meet an unsuspecting, unarmed foe, and slowly get out their gun.

At some time that year, according to his son Roger, Ian Turnbull began talking of killing Glen Turner. Roger said his father would often complain to family, friends and even local shopkeepers. He might have spoken with a laugh, but he would say, 'If I go to jail, I won't be there long. I may as well take Glen Turner with me.'

6

> We toiled and toiled clearing those four acres, where the haystacks are now standing, till every tree and sapling that had grown there was down. We thought then the worst was over – but how little we knew of clearing land!
> **—Steele Rudd, *On Our Selection*, 1899**

'Spirit of place' and 'place attachment' – or *eutierria*, the neologism coined by Australian ecological philosopher Glenn Albrecht – all suggest the same basic thing: love and feeling for a place with which a human has a nourishing relationship. For Indigenous Australians, 'country' has manifold and profound associations with family, culture, mythos, support and responsibility: 'my mother', as poet Ali Cobby Eckermann puts it. For Australian descendants of European migrants and settlers, things are more complicated.

On her property outside Croppa Creek, Alaine Anderson is trying to explain her passion for the land. A trim, vigorous woman in her sixties, with fine blonde hair and a capacity to talk without pause for an hour, she is the first to concede it's an instinct, not something easy to articulate. 'I haven't got an underpinning of science studies, I haven't got that. The only thing I can say is that that we four girls were brought up in the real bush, on horseback. Dad would come home with a feather or a leaf and Mum would look it up. In most country areas, the people who have their roots in the country are instinctively caring of the environment. Because we know that if we look after nature, it will look after you.'

She mourns her children's lack of connection to the country, living in a city. 'They're not connected to the land anymore. They don't realise that my grandchildren would love to come home and feed the little wallabies. It is good for our souls. It is good for us. And it is very healing.' She'd recently had a group of disabled young people come to touch the koalas in her care. 'Nature,' she says certainly, 'is there for us to support us, make us happy, make us laugh, make us cry.'

In their work on farmers' attitudes and values, researchers Nicole Graham and Robyn Bartel, like many before them, point out that place attachment fosters a healthy investment in those sites. People with strong place attachment feel protective of and connected to the wellbeing of a place. They may also, however, be parochial, resistant to change, NIMBYish, uncaring of the wider consequences of protecting their patch or devoted to the preservation of damaging practices. It might be observed that this can be said of traditional owners as much as treechange greenies or intransigent farmers, though the deeper that attachment to place, and the more comprehensive the understanding of its qualities, the more a wise and equable relationship is possible.

For non-Indigenous denizens of Australia, place attachment is often associated with private ownership. The pride of a suburban gardener is as keen as the rapture of a devoted bushwalker.

For farmers, the instinct is even sharper: property means privilege. That privilege, argue landholder rights groups to this day, bestows a special relationship to a piece of land. The famous multigenerational familiarity and expertise, pride and custodial sensibility of farmers is the return for decades of hard work. The land loves the hand that tills it. For many farming families, it is that sense of legacy and responsibility that forms their fierce attachment to place. To grow up, enter adulthood, work upon and pass on a single patch of land is a powerful experience few of us will know.

Landholder rights groups argue that freehold title, still a minority option in New South Wales despite the reforms of the Selection Acts, guarantees the best investment in long-term landscape health. Virtually all of western New South Wales, like most Australian grazing lands, is still Crown leasehold, originally on short-term leases. Agriculture, on the other hand, is generally founded on freehold, and that puts a landholding farmer in a position to invest in and cherish a productive property. Others see in the idea of private property a hyper-separating, deracinating abstraction. Here farmers consult lawyers, and those lawyers, in rooms far from the country, speak a strange, occult language. Documents and digital binaries are more important there than root systems, migration paths, nitrogen levels. Landholders arguing a special privilege on land are simultaneously claiming an intimate, metaphysical relationship and casting their relationship in the most material terms.

Property means both agency and liberty. Liberty to generate profit, liberty to act on the land and freedom from interference in doing so, at least up to a point. The United States' libertarian ideal, derived significantly from Locke, limits the extent that any agency, including the government, may interfere with an owner's entitlements without incurring what is known as 'takings'. 'Takings' means the reduction of rights and entitlements – just as in Locke's axiom, he who has 'subdued, tilled and sowed any part of it, thereby annexed to it something that was his Property, which another had no Title to, nor could without injury take from him'. Here Locke won out over Paine or Rousseau. The assumption is that a landholder owns – has 'annexed' – rights over the soil. Anything that reduces that ownership is an affront, a grievance requiring redress. The government, in 'taking away' a right, can only legally do so by 'just terms' – that is, compensation.

The concept exists in Australian law, but as American political trends penetrate Australian discourse, the limits of the Australian application are being tested. Does country belong to all of us, and is its legal ownership an appropriation from our common wealth? Or can land be taken, so we must pay to maintain an interest in its bounty? It seems a long time since our ancestors enjoyed a commons to which all were automatically entitled: since some mythic Eden with fruit for all to pluck.

The idea of 'takings' isn't really about property. It is about state versus individual. It distinguishes between and polarises the public and the private.

Land law in Australia is divided into two arenas: property rights (advantaging an individual) and environmental responsibilities (usually seen as a burden). In New South Wales, the Local Land Services or Catchment Management Authority governs use of property, including granting permission for development and clearing, and the Office of Environment and Heritage covers environmental regulation and its enforcement. 'Takings' can be the battleground between these two related but sometimes opposing principles: a pushing and shoving over boundaries like the rope in a tug-of-war. In the Turnbull case, the slippage between the two agencies made for some of the abrasion.

Property Rights Australia is an illustrative Australian lobby group. Its website states that 'property owners are entitled to the basic rights of exclusive access, use and the opportunity to profit. Legal recognition of those property rights is in the best interests of a fair, just and prosperous community.' Their motto is 'STAND YOUR GROUND', and they run a 'fighting fund' to prosecute legal test cases and 'other strategic causes'. The site features heroic images of men, of cleared land, of handshakes, wide-brimmed hats, sheep; silhouetted forms of adults and children holding hands beside the iconic windmill water pumps that signify rural Australia. It is typical of strategic branding in its admixture of patriotism, tradition and ownership.

But farmers and graziers cannot be kings of grass castles altogether. A freehold or pastoral lease implies that a landholder is responsible for management of that land, including its environment. This means cooperation with neighbours and agencies – reciprocity and obligations as well as rights. In times of natural disaster, floods, droughts and fires overrun those meticulously defended borders and boundaries. What then of absolute property rights and proud independence? What then of defiance?

***

MURRAY FISHER WAS ONE of the Commonwealth investigative officers from the Department of Sustainability, Environment, Water, Populations and Communities. Like Gary Spencer and Robert Strange, he was a former cop. He had stood beside Turnbull on the land and talked with him about koalas and clearing their habitat. The family, said Fisher, had to observe the rules, the law.

Turnbull, according to Fisher's account, raised his eyebrows. 'I'm an old man,' he said, as he'd told Turner. 'I'll do what I want. What are you going to do with me?' He'd bought the block for the black soil there, the last of it. It needed to have a crop on it, and that's what he was going to do.

***

IN NOVEMBER 2012, NEARLY a year after the Turnbulls began their clearing, Grant finally submitted a completed application for a property vegetation plan for 'Colorado' to the local Catchment Management Authority. 'Improvement of land' is still a criterion for development. Ten days later, he duly signed a 'referral proposed action' for review under the federal

Environment Protection and Biodiversity Act. As the federal investigators and the state-based CMA had reminded him, both permissions were required. He was absolutely prohibited from clearing without them.

The federal application was later withdrawn. Six months from its submission, the CMA application would be rejected. Ian Turnbull and his family, having first not sought permission, then having had it denied, cleared protected land at various periods from 2011 to 2014.

Above them, rippling in the winds of political change, was the mesh of state and federal legislation. It is not wholly surprising that Turnbull pleaded ignorance of some of it, whether he really was oblivious or not, because it is a tangle, overlapping a network of state-level regulations with further weavings of national laws, different supervising ministerial departments and various authorities.

In April or May 2014, Turnbull wrote to Kevin Humphries, the newly minted Minister for Natural Resources, Lands and Water. 'Because,' Turnbull told his defence lawyer in the Supreme Court in 2016, 'the situation seemed to be becoming completely absurd with their demands and whatnot. It was just a simple – we bought the place and we were just converting a grazing property into a broadacre farming property, which all the other farms around had been converted some 20 or 30 years ago.'

Humphries, a son of Tamworth, came out to Croppa Creek. Turnbull and Grant drove him around the farms. The minister 'just shook his head', Turnbull said.

Turnbull was still operating under the belief that Humphries, as a Nationals minister, would maintain his loud enthusiasm to change the landclearing laws. But on taking power, the Liberal partners of the coalition demurred on such a plan. The New South Wales Liberal Party had a perhaps surprising history of pro-conservation legislation, along with pro-development enthusiasm; the Askin and Greiner governments had introduced protective laws. The user-pays ethos extended, for them, to 'polluter-pays', and damage to the environment should, in that tradition, come at a cost. This put them at variance, even decades later when that ethos had somewhat waned, with the 'agrarian socialists' of the National Party. Changes to the native vegetation laws were in the works, but not the annihilation that had been touted.

Few would say the state and federal laws complement each other adequately. Conservative ideology, unenthused by centralised authority, dislikes national laws. The state system, in which wealthy and influential landowners have even greater prominence than in a national context, has, in Queensland and New South Wales under conservative governments, been increasingly accommodating of rural development for private profit. For landholder-rights advocates, the gap between state and federal laws is not simply unwieldy – it demonstrates that the federal laws, less sympathetic to land clearing, are superfluous: ignored at best and barely enforced at worst. Their protections of endangered nature and their insistence on a common wealth of natural resources and bounty must be dissolved. Conservationists agree that inconsistencies are dangerously exploited by developers.

While the details of the law are finicky and often disputed, the principle is clear: individuals are subject to the state's mission to protect its assets. Transgressions are penalised. Compensation is due to the state when its riches are stolen. There is bureaucracy, protocol, judiciary. There is an established system, and it is run by adults.

*

HERE ENTER THE LAWYERS. There is the restricting of environmental harm, and there is the prosecution of those who cause it. So long as an act is not completely morally repugnant – for example, the poisoning of protected wedge-tailed eagles – environmental crime has traditionally been seen as 'victimless'. Most environmental offences are strict liability offences, in which the severity of the action, not any mitigating circumstances of the offender's intention or mental state, is weighed. Financial penalties, rather than jail time, are the custom. However, public attitudes are changing.

Much depends, it seems, on the object of a crime. If it's a person or property, the full weight of the law comes down. On an ecology, it's more diffuse: is it a crime against the small mammals who sleep in that scrub, the protected plants in it, the soil beneath, the firebreak it represented? If it's against the future potential of an ecological community, the damage is more vaporised still.

How you weigh such issues depends on who you are and what you assume. Many people, not only farmers, might be classified as 'anthropocentric', seeing the environment as a setting for human life, to be protected in order to safeguard, above all, the human habitation of it. Researchers Robyn Bartel and Elaine Barclay, who identified 'game-players', found that one of the most commonly recognised environmental crimes is trespass. Someone's aerial chemical spray drifts carelessly over boundary lines (organic farms are especially sensitive to this), or fire explodes out of unkempt scrub across fencelines, or polluted water churns downstream, or someone's son comes furtively hunting on private property. The hermetic seal of property rights can't stop these things, and the crime is often perceived as against the landowner more than the place itself. In the informal courts of the pub and golf club, intention is judged in two tiers: deliberate contamination is harshly condemned in those who should know better, but ignorant negligence is as bad in those who don't. 'Social norms will strongly influence farmers' perception of what jeopardises environmental management,' write Barclay and Bartel, 'and accordingly what should and should not be defined as an environmental crime.' In the real world, unlike the legislative, it is still humans, not the ecology, who seem to matter most even in assault against other living species.

Asked by the researchers if they felt like victims of crime, many participants hesitated. Some were uncomfortable with the implied sledge to their masculinity. Others calibrated it pragmatically. Actions that dramatically impacted the function of a farm were crimes, such as deliberate polluting, water theft or sabotage – and illegal land clearing. Others were written off as accidents, non-malicious or once-offs. In the study, more than 80 per cent of farmers agreed that deliberate pollution was as bad a crime as stealing – perhaps this goes back to the idea of 'takings'. Many felt strongly about water theft. But in New South Wales, the hottest topic was management of 'woody weeds' and restrictions on clearing them: restrictions that were soon to change.

*

ONE REASON WHY ONLY a fraction of landholders join Landcare groups, why they agitate so fiercely against regulation and why many continue to clear illegally is because for two centuries Australians were told to bash the bush. Why, suddenly, should they stop? 'They think it looks better cultivated,' Phil Spark says with a shrug.

Barclay and Bartel rather bravely focused their research on land clearing because it is such a nightmare for compliance. Nearly 60 per cent of landholders in their survey agreed to some degree that illegal clearing was wrong. But at the same time, most believed in absolute property rights, with some confusion between American and Australian laws, and saw clearing as 'improvement'. A quarter said they were unsure or neutral on the criminality of illegal clearing. Sometimes regulations were themselves regarded as encouraging damage to the land.

One farmer said it would be a crime if he flattened *everything* on his land. Another respondent, an agronomist, claimed it was important to distinguish between a man cutting down one tree and another felling acres. A second agronomist denied there'd been any damage in the previous twenty years in New South Wales from clearing, legal or illegal: he saw it all as improvement. It was pointed out that some woody weeds increase erosion, so restrictions on cutting them seemed to worsen the situation. Another farmer said most farmers would think illegal clearing wasn't a good idea, but not really a crime compared to assault or theft. 'I think it's a funny world we live in,' he told the authors, 'when we are starting to look at environmental crimes as such – when cutting down a tree is a bigger crime than abusing a woman or breaking into someone's house.'

You work your land. You pay for it. You plant an oak tree, and you stoop one day to pick up its acorn: your acorn. It's bitter, then, to be told your oak is a mistake, your acorn is unjust, that you must chew on your loneliness until, like raw acorn in your mouth, it poisons you.

7

> The tree which moves some to tears of joy is, in the eyes of others, only a green thing which stands in the way ... As a man is, so he sees.
> **—William Blake, letter to Reverend John Trusler, 1799**

There is a fable by Australian author and artist Shaun Tan called 'Stick Figures'. It is a dreamlike illustrated tale, in which frail, spectral figures, made of dead branches and grassy clods of earth, haunt the suburbs of modern Australia. The stick figures loiter uncertainly in this melancholy landscape, revenant and watchful. Boys, Tan explains, like to idly smash the figures. 'It becomes boring, somehow enraging, the way they just stand there and take it. What are they? Why are they here? What do they want? Whack! Whack! Whack!' The images show figures silhouetted on front lawns, hesitating behind an empty bus shelter; spindly shadows extend across the dry concrete of a car park. 'It's as if they take all your questions and offer them straight back: Who are you? Why are you here? What do you want?'

The uncanny rises when we are most complacent. Repression is anxious and imperfect: sometimes the bodies of murdered Aboriginal peoples were simply thrown in rivers or over cliffs. The bodies were buried lightly or not at all. The bones bleached in the sun after the dogs had had at them. Millions of native animals, too, have rotted before their time. Evacuating the land of its original inhabitants meant it became spooky, spectral. It was empty of what should have been there and full of the emptiness. Two hundred years of heroic settler mythos has not quietened those bones.

***

LATE 2012 AND THE paperwork continued. Glen Turner began chasing Luc Farago at the Catchment Management Authority, who had met with the Turnbulls back when the properties were first purchased. Phil Spark was in touch with the

Environmental Defenders Office about launching his own prosecution under the principle of 'open standing', which seemed possible if Turnbull could be shown to have knowingly destroyed endangered species under the *Environment Protection and Biodiversity Conservation Act.* Spark thought he had a strong case, since Turnbull had been spotted at his koala workshop in Croppa Creek in the early days of the clearing.

Spark began haunting the fencelines of the properties. He documented the steady clearing, the species remaining, the crops going in. The cleared areas were being ploughed. He took photos and video and sent them to everyone who cared or should: the media, the authorities, conservation groups. There was an urgency: the Turnbulls weren't just felling trees, but would soon plough more too. 'That was always our cry,' remembers Spark sadly, 'you know: you've got to stop him now, you've got to stop him now, because when he gets the plough in all that regeneration's just going to be annihilated. But they still couldn't stop him.'

In the New South Wales parliament in early October 2012, the Greens' Cate Faehrmann and Labor's Luke Foley asked environment minister Robyn Parker why the clearing, which appeared to be of endangered ecological communities, hadn't been stopped. The CEO of the Office of Environment and Heritage, also in attendance, took the question. Whether the Turnbulls had permission, Sally Barnes said, was still under investigation. In fact, no permits had been issued. She admitted that the OEH hadn't reissued the stop-work order because they didn't want to waste the money.

Faehrmann asked why, if there was evidence in February 2012 sufficient for a stop-work order, still nothing had been done to stop the work, eight months later.

The investigation, Barnes said stolidly, should be finished by Christmas. There was no problem, she insisted, with the department's execution of investigating and halting illegal land clearing. 'We need to go through our procedures to make sure, as I said, there is procedural fairness—'

Faehrmann cut her off. 'With respect, how long does that process take?'

The Environmental Defenders Office helpfully wrote to Barnes the next day, pointing out that she had the discretion to issue a stop-work order again. Faehrmann seconded the suggestion in a media release. The EDO noted that the federal minister, too, had powers to 'cause to be taken' any steps required, including prevention and remediation orders. But the federal investigation appeared to have ceded to the state one, believing they had a better chance of success.

Spark's patience was wearing thin. 'We had everything, but everything we tried, it was just going nowhere.' He laughs incredulously. 'It was unbelievable!'

The Environmental Defenders Office kept up the hard work. Alaine Anderson continued writing letters to the federal member, Mark Coulton. The Greens, the Nature Conservation Council and the Total Environment Centre all issued media releases about the issue. A few environmental reporters at Fairfax were kept alerted. An article appeared in *The Sydney Morning Herald,* featuring an interview with Spark. Jeff Angel of the Total Environment Centre, deeply involved in the campaign, was quoted decrying the ongoing clearing. The OEH, under pressure now, told reporter Ben Cubby that a prosecution was imminent.

On 13 December 2012, a year after he began clearing on the two blocks, Ian Turnbull was charged for his part in and directing of the first six weeks of what would become nearly three years of illegal clearing.

*

THE OEH LAUNCHED THE prosecution in the Land and Environment Court for 'an offence against s12 of the *Native Vegetation Act 2003,* in relation to the unlawful clearing of native vegetation on "Colorado" and "Strathdoon"' between 1 November 2011 and 18 January 2012. It had taken a while, but was the beginning of a sliding avalanche of suits, as the OEH progressively prosecuted Turnbull, then Grant and Cory, for various phases of land clearing on the two properties. The chronology becomes slippery – one case was concluded even as another was being answered; an appeal was being launched while a new investigation began. The family was ordered to replant on properties even as they were still clearing them; they were newly accused and convicted as they appealed the previous charges or penalties. Each member of the family had his own thread of legal matters – and in the middle of things, new investigations of Roger Turnbull's clearing at 'Royden' were begun. The whole horrendous mess commenced in December 2012; nearly ten years later, matters are still unfinished.

Meanwhile, the trees were still being pushed. The ground, with native grasses and remnant seeds, was ploughed, grinding out the potential for healthy regeneration. The crops continued to be sown.

By the time Turnbull received his summons in December, neighbours were reporting to authorities that trees were being torched on the properties. The biggest ones, which couldn't be pushed, were set alight, Alaine Anderson wrote to her federal member; levees banked up around piles of felled timber had a match put to them. The fire jumped. The Rural Fire Service was called; they were refused entry; the police had to be sent for. They were allegedly seen to burn stacks on days of total fire ban. In the high summer weather of January 2013, Alaine Anderson was frantically hosing the vegetation along the fenceline shared with 'Strathdoon' to save eucalyptus for koalas as flames chased the animals into her property.

Another day, Anderson was putting water out for koalas on the fenceline with 'Strathdoon' when, as she described it to Mark Coulton, a dozer came crunching through the scrub beside her, clearing all along the fence only a hundred metres away. No one was checking for koalas resting from the midday sun in the shade, though Cory's uncle Grant had been seen, she claimed, at a Moree talk about koalas only two months before. Disoriented animals were regularly huddling in Anderson's trees, and wandering onto County Boundary Road and into the main roads of Croppa Creek itself, she said.

A reply arrived in her postbox, the one sometimes torn out by neighbours: Coulton shared the good news that koala numbers were up. His office apparently didn't understand that the animals were visible because they were fleeing, their habitat being burnt; didn't read Anderson's descriptions of koalas found starved to death. 'Having unmanaged forestry is also a danger to Australia's fauna. Thank you for taking the time to write to me about your concerns,' he finished. 'All the best for the coming year.'

*

FOUR MONTHS LATER, IN April 2013, Grant, Cory and Cory's wife, Donna, were given directions to conduct remedial work on 'Strathdoon' and 'Colorado' due to the clearing in late 2011 and early 2012, for which Ian had been charged. They were not being prosecuted yet: this was a shot across the bows.

Remediation meant first causing no further damage to a site, and then the careful replanting and sustaining of new growth, ideally of the same native species that had been destroyed. All exotic species, commercial crops and non-native species had to be removed in designated areas. The Turnbulls had to allow native species to regenerate as much as they could, and encourage this with ground preparation, seed stimulation and monitoring. If the ground was too damaged for scrub to regrow alone, they would have to plant it, including choosing the right species and density, digging the very soil to plant in and looking after the saplings. They had to maintain records of all their efforts, and keep the OEH informed all the way. The directions would usually be in place for fifteen years.

Remediation orders are issued by the OEH and legislated by the Land and Environment Court. Soon after receiving them, the three landowners appealed the extent and conditions of that remediation.

The law concerning remediation is notoriously, as Simon Smith puts it, 'weak'. It is often used when the OEH doesn't feel confident in a full prosecution, or as a courteous compromise; it hopes to achieve some restoration to damage, and it allows, in some readings, the convenience that cleared land may yet be utilised while the net ecological value is maintained. Smith sees it as 'a very poorly designed piece of legislation' that is 'very easy to get around'. Complicated technical arguments about tree coverage, species variety and maintenance can be spun out in court for months or years. What's more, the time required for an appeal, and the redrafting and issuing of new directions, could be well used.

The same day in May that Grant, Cory and Donna's appeals were heard, Turnbull was entering a guilty plea for the clearing – but only grudgingly. He disputed the extent, the amount and the harm he had done. This meant it had to go to a sentencing hearing in which that harm could be evaluated. It guaranteed some time.

*

A MONTH LATER, IN June 2013, Turner was again on his way back from Boggabilla when he came down County

Boundary Road. As he had a year earlier, he took photos from points along the fenceline. He sent them to the department's solicitor, Rasheed Sahu-Khan, for the records. 'Crop extends,' he wrote in his notebook, 'to the fence running North–South through the centre of "Colorado".'

Nadolny, Turner and another compliance officer, Terry Mazzer, headed back to Croppa Creek in September, but were halted at Moree by news that the Turnbulls had lodged an objection to the inspection. Calls were being made in Tamworth and Moree, lawyers were frantically emailing. Nadolny read a novel in the park beside Moree Courthouse while Turner and Mazzer filled in paperwork for a hearing. Optimistic, they set off in the afternoon, and made it as far as the fence of 'Colorado' before another flurry of calls ended with one from their regional manager. Turner answered; the hearing had gone well, he told Nadolny, but the department was concerned with adverse publicity. They were not to enter the blocks. The ecologist took notes from the fence, gazing at huge fields of wheat where a year earlier there had been a tangled mess of fallen trees, with a few still standing.

Turner and Nadolny returned to the properties in December. This time, the gates were locked.

'I drove along the County Boundary Road,' Turner wrote in his notes, 'and then along Talga Lane. I parked the vehicle on the road reserve adjacent to the northern boundary of "Colorado".' This was where he would park with Robert Strange eight months later, on the winter road.

The Turnbulls' lawyers were still challenging the OEH's access to the property. The two officers had permission to enter, as far as they were concerned, with an Authorisation of Entry onto Land document in hand. So they decided to climb the fence.

'I felt pretty exposed,' remembers Nadolny. 'Before we went on, I said, "Glen, Glen, let's talk about this threat."' He was referring to the threat on Turner's life that Turnbull had made the year before. 'And we did – we had a good ten-minute discussion about it. Glen's point of view was that he didn't think the Turnbulls were criminals. He felt that the threat was bravado. And the other thing was they'd obviously spent a huge amount of money on legal defences, so if they took [matters] into their own hands then that'd all come to naught. So anyway, he convinced me at that time that any threat would be unlikely. But I still felt pretty worried about going in.'

They were limited by how far across the property they could get on foot, so they walked through the cleared land collecting koala scat and vegetation samples and taking photographs. There was a raptor nest in the crown of a brigalow, remnant brigalow and belah, some brigalow regrowing its suckers.

The country was dry, though not yet in drought. The groundcover was parched, and there were kangaroo corpses lying here and there, gunshot wounds still visible. There were no workers to be seen, no roar of dozers. But it was a very different landscape to that the Turnbulls had purchased two years earlier.

Turner wanted the full picture. He arranged for a light aircraft belonging to the National Parks and Wildlife Service to survey from the air. He was preparing for a new prosecution – in January that year, his notebook recorded phone calls from Croppa Creek locals. Someone had been asked to work for the Turnbulls on 'Colorado'; they'd felt nervous, and didn't want to give their name. And a neighbour of Grant's, Brenton Whibley, had seen some clearing. The work was back on.

***

THREE MONTHS AFTER TURNER and Nadolny cautiously walked across 'Colorado' on that hot summer morning, in early March 2014 Turnbull was tried in the Land and Environment Court in Sydney for the illegal clearing of 2011–2012.

It was stuffy in the court, the air-conditioning broken. Judge Sheahan removed his robes and suggested the other legal figures did too. Turnbull was represented by Queen's Counsel Todd Alexis, a handsome, alert man with white hair and dark brows.

The old farmer sat listening staunchly. First up was what advice the family had sought from the CMA about clearing those blocks. Luc Farago testified that he'd visited the site to meet Cory and Ian and do a preliminary assessment. He saw that some of the previously cleared areas had a fair amount of regenerating native grass; where there was over 50 per cent it couldn't be cleared at all. He advised, he insisted, that there'd be no permission granted to clear remnant trees, even if they were in the middle of regrowth areas; the brigalow and belah and poplar box there were potentially protected. After further consideration, he told Cory that he thought continuing use provisions might cover some of the cleared land, as the Scotts had done a little cropping in their time, but Cory shouldn't do anything until he legally owned the property. 'Continuing use' meant a restricted allowance for activities, such as cropping, that had been in train before the state laws had been revised in 2003. A month after the conversation, Glen Turner, on behalf of the EPA, sent Cory a letter explicitly reminding him of the need for permission and of the force of the law. Six weeks after that, the Turnbulls began clearing the block.

Cory informed Farago that he'd begun clearing, but 'it shouldn't be a problem', he said, according to Farago's evidence, 'as I've only been clearing regrowth and areas where the groundcover is less than 50 per cent native'. Farago told him to stop until he had approval. By the time Farago was supposed to inspect, Turnbull had the dozers out and the EPA was already investigating illegal clearing on 'Strathdoon'.

Much hinged on whether the Turnbulls were clearing regrowth; how much native grass cover there had been; and whether any endangered species had been on the blocks. The Turnbulls had engaged an ecologist, Peter Hall. He spoke bluntly, making a case that the scattering of vegetation on the two blocks meant the koalas had already had to cross grass from one tree to another; walking on wheat crops or stubs wouldn't make much difference. In fact, having only a limited number of trees could make mating more convenient. In any case, Hall said, you had to consider the clearing of koala habitat in the context of the whole landscape. There were other places they could go.

The prosecutor, David Jordan, was incredulous. 'Are you saying that the clearing has done the koalas a favour?'

Hall retreated; no, but the Turnbulls hadn't cleared everything. He conceded that ploughing prefers long, clear lines for the tractors, and paddock trees or clumps of vegetation impedes that. But the Turnbulls, he said, wanted to protect the koalas; they'd left trees in the gully (overlooking the fact that these couldn't be cropped anyway). There was, he estimated, still 200 hectares of fragmented koala habitat left on the blocks – never mind that they had to cross 100 metres of open, cropped land to reach the next. The brigalow was too thinned to be considered an endangered ecological community. The endangered species, he said, were actually coping well with change – as you could see because they were still there. On the Turnbulls' blocks, most of the felled trees were young, not the hollow-bearing habitat ones.

Hall's evidence went on and on. He argued that the clearing was minimally damaging; the land, he seemed to imply, was already too compromised to be worth protecting. His opinions were echoed by another consultant ecologist brought by the Turnbulls, who agreed that the felled trees had probably not been good koala habitat anyway.

Then it was Chris Nadolny's turn to give his evidence. In his soft, steady voice, he gave a detailed assessment of the vegetation he'd seen on the blocks, including native trees, shrubs, vines, mistletoes and groundcover. The brigalow, he said, definitely qualified as endangered; other species had already been reduced by two-thirds in their catchment management area. There was significant loss of habitat on the properties, including for several threatened species such as the koala and the grey-crowned babbler.

'I was on the stand for a day and a half,' says Nadolny, 'and Ian was listening to what he would have regarded as all the rubbish I said about the environmental impacts of the clearing and all that sort of thing, and how it was native vegetation and how it was altered. The trees that he felled were large old things with hollows – in that part of the country, they would have been a couple of hundred years old.' Those trees had probably pre-dated white settlement. But they'd been felled by the modern inheritors. 'He wouldn't have liked to hear that even if he knew it was true.'

The Land and Environment Court had to consider various aspects. Had Turnbull meant to damage the environment? Did he understand the consequences of the clearing? Was he aware that it was not permitted? Did he think pushing native trees was wrong?

'Your Honour,' Turnbull's silk said, 'when one looks at this, this is not a man who wilfully engaged in a deliberate endeavour to contravene quite deliberately the law.'

'We never intended to clear it all,' Turnbull told a different court – the Supreme Court – years later. He'd known, he confessed to the room then, that there would be restrictions and permission needed, but the land had been rung before. Turner, he explained, had said they could only farm what they'd already cropped, and lightly graze stock on the rest. 'I don't know what he thought you would lightly graze, because it was heavily timbered,' he said. 'Unless there was a lot of summer rain, there was no grass, and a lot of erosion among the trees.' He could tell it was eroded because of small white pebbles that usually lay a few inches underground. He'd been a conservation farmer: it wasn't a thoughtless enterprise. 'We thought those factors would all be remedied with broad-acre farming, with competent [soil]banks and zero tilling, leaving all the crop residue on the ground to protect [it].'

The Crown prosecutor leaped on this. 'So you're suggesting, are you, that by clearing it all you were going to make it better for the environment?'

'Exactly,' Turnbull agreed. 'Exactly.' But then he thought again. 'I had better put that right. We never intended to clear it all.'

That discussion about erosion and tree coverage, permit applications and tilling techniques occurred as Turnbull was in the dock being tried for murder. And still he was protesting that he'd been in the right.

Back in March 2014, Turner was in court for the three days of the hearing. He and Turnbull exchanged glances. Turner was keeping his feelings to himself, but he must have hidden a weary grimace. On the first day of the hearing he'd been sent some photos by Phil Spark. They showed dozers at work on 'Colorado', pushing trees. Two days later, 6 March, with Turnbull sitting grim-faced beside his lawyer as Alexis rose to speak, Turner had his colleague Robert Strange, recently returned to the native vegetation division, drive the three hours to Croppa Creek to have a look. The view was as expected; Turner duly made the familiar notes. Meanwhile, in the court, Todd Alexis QC was attempting to mitigate the penalty. Turnbull's age, he'd said, meant that he was unlikely to reoffend.

***

JUST WEEKS LATER, IN April 2014, there was big news in the district. The largest wheat grower in Australia, Ron Greentree, was selling up some of his holdings in the Moree area. A jowly man with dark brows, usually photographed in the obligatory Akubra and check shirt, Greentree co-owned the Boolcarrol and Milton Downs stations at Bellata. His business partner was Ken Harris, of the huge Harris family, which had holdings in New South Wales and the Kimberley. They had bought the stations – 47,500 hectares of luscious black-soil country – in 2008 for a total of about $75 million; they put in 300 kilometres of roads, built accommodation and 'increased both the area of plantation and the productivity of the farms'. 'Improved', that land was now massively increased in value.

Wheat sales had been deregulated in 2009 after the Australian Wheat Board scandals, and Greentree, a former chairman of GrainCorp and the Grain Growers Association, had profited from higher prices. But prices turned, and a few years later he was ready to sell to fund managers, who were investing in

Moree. 'This is succession planning,' Greentree announced to journalists. He had the welfare of local farmers in mind: 'I really want to make sure that young farmers get a chance to get hold of these properties,' he told Matthew Cranston at the *Australian Financial Review.* 'I am a first-generation farmer myself.'

In April 2014, Greentree and Harris put the property on the market. The asking price for Milton Downs was $200 million.

Turnbull would have read all this in the papers, heard it at the Croppa general store. He hadn't even started farming until he was nearly thirty, and had begun with just one property. Now, he was friends with the right men, had the right kind of attitude. He had respect in the community. With 20,000-odd hectares in the Turnbull name and a shed full of dozers, he had begun the running. If only Turner wasn't there, simply wasn't there.

That month, Turnbull told Roger he'd dug two graves, one for Turner and one for a colleague, somewhere on the

Turnbull farms. His son thought, *Fuck, Dad, what are you saying?*

'But I never imagined,' Roger said, 'he would actually do it.'

PART TWO
MURDER

8

> To provide suitable conditions for shallow-rooted, annual crops, farmers must apply industrial devices each year to replicate catastrophe.
> **—George Main, *Heartland,* 2005**

In 1896, blood rain smothered Melbourne. A dust storm had carried dirt all the way from the Red Centre. The land had been flogged and, belatedly, people realised it. Joseph Jenkins, a Welsh immigrant farmer who worked as farmhand, travelling around Australia in the mid-nineteenth century, came to a conclusion: 'There are three characteristics peculiar to the farmers of this colony,' he wrote. '[E]xhausting the land, abusing the horses and exploiting the labour.'

Drought, inevitably, had hit before, in the 1870s. Almost everything declined – including pests. But crafty, hardy native flora crept back, even into new territories. The brigalow especially prospered. Clumps became scrub. 'It came up so quickly it was cast like a protective net over plants, birds, mammals, insects that would have disappeared for ever in the disasters of the next seventy years,' Eric Rolls writes of this late insurgence.

This didn't put a stop to the clearing, of course. By 1884, a total of 4 million acres had been authorised for ringbarking across New South Wales; a few years later, permits were granted for the same again, with permission only required to clear big old trees. The countryside was now a spectral landscape of white, dead stalks.

Pastoralists realised that they would simply have to accept fluctuations in the climate and make the most of good years. So when the soil was wet again, rather than reduce stock numbers, they sunk artesian wells as a back-up and went for broke. If they felt uneasy and vulnerable, how good, then, the glee of action. Swinging axes, dragging trees, clearing acres – it must have been immensely satisfying. Much masculine literature was devoted to paeans to the axe, the dauntless frontier bushman, the passing of antique forests to the radiant horizon of the new. 'The stump, a symbol of nature subdued,' writes William J. Lines in a mordant history of the Australian environment, 'became an enduring image in Australian history.'

But wool prices fell from the 1870s; by the mid-1880s, the rabbit plague reached the Darling River and leaped across. Shearers' strikes in 1891 and again in 1894 brought the wool industry to its knees. By 1895, with another drought coming on, there was economic chaos, with banks closing and food shortages in the cities. Stock was fed mulched native vegetation and prickly pear. The compacted soil that blew off in dust storms went flying away under their hoofs, unable to soak in moisture when it did rain. Many believed the productive capacity of the plains was finally exhausted. The chief botanist of the New South Wales Department of Agriculture, Frederick Turner, appealed to pastoralists to at least keep native grasses so seeds could replenish bare earth, but they did not. Nor would they set aside fodder for bad times, but used it to expand their flocks. Most seemed to think there would always be somewhere else, some new frontier on which to bet their fortunes, and they assigned the drought and failing land to the spite of an unjust Providence.

***

ON 10 JUNE 2014, there was an incident on Roger Turnbull's property 'Royden', just south of Ian Turnbull's homestead off the Croppa Moree Road. Roger and his wife, Annette, owned several properties in the district: they'd had 'Wallam' for twenty years, north across that road from his parents' 'Yambin', and they'd also had a couple of others up near North Star. They'd bought 'Royden' in 2008 for nearly $4 million, and moved in in late 2010, when the previous tenants moved out.

In April 2011, the same year Ian Turnbull went guarantor to help with the purchase of the Scott brothers' blocks, Glen Turner had visited Roger to investigate reports he had illegally cleared 97 hectares on his property. He'd moved farm equipment onto the property and begun to farm wheat, barley and chickpeas, according to Turner's report. Roger had had some kind of altercation with Turner. There had been remediation orders and a small fine of $3700 issued. Now, with his family under serious investigation for similar offences, Roger wasn't in the mood to show patience. When two OEH officers, David Minehan and Wendy Illingworth, visited in June 2014 to inspect the remediation works, Roger allegedly lost his temper. There are accounts that he locked them in a room, and someone in the house called the police to report them as intruders, although the officers held an authorisation of entry document. 'There were words or something,' Chris Nadolny recalls.

The officers, according to the story, called their manager for help and were released after about fifteen minutes. No charges were laid. The agency seemed to take it as just one of those situations where feelings had run a bit high. 'Roger wasn't formally indicted or anything,' says Nadolny, but the encounter 'would have upset Ian'. *Fuck the bastards,* Ian Turnbull must have thought. His family was being persecuted; this was personal.

That June day was a hectic one for the Turnbull family. As Roger was shouting at compliance officers near Croppa Creek, his brother, son and daughter-in-law were in the Land and Environment Court in Sydney for two days of appeals hearings against the remediation directions issued by the Office of Environment and Heritage back in April 2013, even while the judge was considering what penalty to hand down to Ian Turnbull for his part in the clearing.

Grant and Cory seemed to think their penalty unjust. Grant argued that he honestly believed he was clearing regrowth on 'Colorado'. Cory told the judge that his grandfather had acted without his authority. Cory, like his father and uncle, lived much of the time away from Croppa, either in Moree, in an apartment owned by Robeena, or across the border in Toowoomba; he worked regularly but not full-time on the properties. It was the old man, with his interest in the first year's profits, who doggedly worked the blocks. 'My grandfather is eighty years old and I can't control him,' pleaded Cory. 'If he has something set in his mind, that is what he does.' Once the clearing began, Cory said, they had to continue to clear it all for crops, so they wouldn't be financially ruined. After the family had borrowed heavily to buy the properties, the wheat price had gone down and drought had arrived.

The Turnbulls had initially claimed that the blocks were too expensive to fence to keep stock, so they had to be cropped, hence the clearing. In fact, the boundaries were already fenced, even if not robustly, and the costs of fencing had dropped dramatically. Now they argued that the remediation would cost them $5 million over fifteen years. The family had already lost $300,000 that year – and they were awaiting a sentencing and a possible fine for Ian's charges. They were nearly $2 million overdrawn.

The OEH lawyers protested that the Turnbulls couldn't be allowed to get away with a wilful breach of regulations. The department had put significant resources into this prosecution: not least, an overworked Glen Turner had committed much to the investigation, visiting the properties six times, in the face of threats.

The OEH was under public scrutiny to stop the clearing. It was a high-profile case, and had been mentioned in state parliament. Morale within the OEH was declining after some promising prosecutions had been pulled. To have the Turnbulls' illegal clearing conspicuously punished would be a big win. A failure would send a very dangerous message to the New South Wales farming community.

Turnbull felt the family was being scapegoated. 'There's every farm in the 30 kilometres from "Yambin" to "Colorado" has had a bulldozer on it pushing trees,' he would tell the Supreme Court in 2016. 'They were honing in on the Turnbull family to make an example.'

The OEH suggested that the cleared land be restored. But the fact was that the Turnbulls had been thorough: they'd felled, repeatedly; they'd raked and sprayed, to kill emergent weeds and regrowth from the stricken vegetation; they'd ploughed and cross-ploughed, to grind the remaining native seeds and seedlings. And then they'd planted crops. Could the land ever be 'restored'? Soil erosion and degradation, edge effect and other kinds of intrusion would be felt not only in the cleared areas but all around.

The Honourable Justice Brian Judge Preston, who has a record of publishing thoughtful pieces on the problematics of environmental law, ruled that a bankrupted Turnbull family wouldn't be able to restore the properties, so they could continue cropping the land already cleared. They could 'offset' in other areas, by planting native vegetation as compensation. This was essentially a win for the family. The commercial operation could remain intact.

The Turnbulls were allowed to keep the roads carved into the remediation areas. They were meant to dismantle their stacks of felled timber and spread them out over the cropped areas to let the seeds distribute – but those stacks had already been burnt and sprayed. They disputed how hard they should work to keep non-native weeds out, how many, which species. Preston, reading advice from Chris Nadolny and the Turnbulls' ecologists, Peter Hall and Sinclair, carefully considered the distribution and density of the replanted species, the ratios, and the risk of a weird uniformity if every hectare had to have at least twenty trees of brigalow, belah and poplar box, as the OEH suggested – a prescription of 100 live stems per hectare. He noted that 'recolonisation of the area' was likely to be 'very slow and uncertain', pointing out that brigalow often seeds only once in fifteen years. The family had killed some prestige vegetation. The Turnbulls, he ordered, should tend the regrowth as carefully as a garden, with mulching, watering, weeding and tree guards. The Turnbulls asked for a period of five years for monitoring and reporting on the regrowth; when this was queried, they argued that it was a typo and was meant to be fifteen. Preston agreed to fifteen.

Preston's ruling runs to fifty-five pages. When the Turnbulls began pushing trees, they began a process that would devour countless more trees in some other, unknown place, in the reams of paper representing hours of time, thousands of words, meticulous legal consideration. Whole forests might be pulped in order to defend and condemn the felling of native vegetation.

The decision came on 25 June 2014. That July, a shaken but resolute OEH charged Ian and Cory Turnbull with the second lot of illegal clearing on 'Strathdoon' in 2012. They would be back in court within months. But by then Ian was already facing charges for murder.

***

THE LAST YEARS OF the nineteenth century brought a reckoning in New South Wales. Pastoralism seemed finished. It had ruined the plains.

An inquiry in the 1880s, following the devastating drought, illuminated landholders' attitudes. The commissioners' questioning drew complaints for focusing on the lack of grass for stock, rather than acknowledging there was not enough water to grow grass. The connection seemed to elude the graziers. They still kept increasing stock. By 1891, there were about 13.5 million sheep in western New South Wales. These animals were stamping and eating the country to stubble.

It began to seem to many that agriculture could save the day. Only 2 per cent of freehold land in New South Wales was under crops; Victoria and South Australia, having had more luck with breaking up squattocracy holdings under their own land acts, had already surged their agricultural efforts, encouraging interstate rivalry. The moral qualities and machismo of agricultural labour had not been forgotten, and as a nation-building project on the eve of Federation, it seemed apt. The analogue to the improvement ethos was a dread of going backwards. Wheat would feed and build the country.

Though the endeavour had largely failed the first time around, technology and society were different by the later part of the nineteenth century: the criminal element was much reduced, the Aboriginal peoples mostly dispersed or dead, the urban bases were stable. A brisk utilitarianism resumed, in which landscape would be parsed almost totally for its suitability for agriculture.

Technology and scale converged on the fields, and landholders realised that small estates simply weren't sustainable if they were to use the straight-driving new machines. The big runs, divided by the Selection Acts, were set to recohere. And wheat finally came in a big way to the plains of New South Wales.

Those lands seemed made for grains; indeed they had been formed for them, by the traditional owners. The country west of the Divide, especially the basalt plains around Moree, was some of the best on the continent. Aeons of erosion had sifted minerals through the soil and skeins of big rivers, and creeks had the water. The problem, as settler James Atkinson had noted back in 1826, was erratic rain, unpredictable floods and haphazard droughts. Gambling on 'good years' meant relying on the rain falling at the right time. But if it did, and you could get rid of the scrub, then what prospects!

Wheat was made for a strange kind of national romance. Governments and farmers alike loved the popular ethos of golden plenty. 'Where golden grain is golden gain,' cooed a promotional pamphlet by the newly invented Country Promotion League in 1920, 'there is a welcome for you.' Historian Cameron Muir describes its ascension to an exalted place in our national mythos: wheat, with its biblical associations, its satiny fields, its satisfying ceremony of sewing, harvesting, threshing and milling, its European heritage and even its blondness, fitted wonderfully into the racist, nationalist, agrarian culture of white Australia on the eve of Federation. It was celebrated as the food of the homeland (although, as Muir points out, the British mostly ate rye, barley and potatoes) and a proper form of nourishment, unlike the rice cultivated by the non-whites to the north. Renowned scientist Sir William Crookes baldly claimed in a famous speech in 1898, 'Wheat created the white race. It did not just shape white civilization, but gave white people their intelligence and biological characteristics.' Wheat production duly and patriotically soared.

But Australia's wheat took a long time to find its fittest habitat. The international supplies of nitrates were running out; the coastal plains of Australia were already exploited. Limits were reluctantly set on expansion; limits were overrun; those who attempted the dry inland soon met with disaster or fell back. The great continent began to feel like a trap.

***

AS TURNBULL PREPARED TO finish his clearing, he knew that the New South Wales land-clearing laws were also on the brink of a reckoning. A review was being prepared, and all over New South Wales clearing was accelerating in anticipation of the loosening. If Turnbull could be patient, perhaps he could fall under the shelter of new regulation.

But legislation can be a long time in the offing, he couldn't afford to wait years. His profit share was only of the first year. He needed time to let the ground wet down over the season, aiming for a winter crop. There were only eight weeks left in summer to work: eight weeks to get it ploughed, levelled, stick-raked and the sticks picked up. It was a race against the clock. The future of his family was at stake.

'He had this belief,' psychiatrist Dr David Greenberg later testified, 'that he was the head of the family and had to pass on his heritage, the farm and that lifestyle, to his family.' International consortiums come and go, but family dynasties endure, homesteads are kept, surnames mean something. The Turnbulls looked the part, but they'd only had land for less than a century. Sydney Turnbull had settled lightly with sheep; Ian Turnbull had ploughed the ground with his appetite for purchasing. Roger and Grant were the seedbed for the future. Grant, too, had a young son hoping for life on the land. It was Cory, and Grant's teenage son, who could make the Turnbull name cover a map, like an empire.

There was one thing in the way: the OEH, and an officer named Glen Turner.

*

TURNBULL'S REFUGE FROM THE vexation of his family's trials was his brown recliner, in the lounge room at 'Yambin'. His life had a rhythm: the hush of Robeena sleeping beside him in bed as he, unable to sleep, lay awake and watched dawn creep across the ceiling; the grunt of the dozers starting up every morning and rumbling to a stop each evening; the sight of the smooth, sweet land he'd cleared.

He was taking a lot of medication for this and that. Every morning was a tray of pills. He had angina, indigestion and reflux, skin cancer on his nose. Osteoporosis. Peripheral neuropathy, a condition where the nerves in his legs were shot. They would ache and twinge. Sometimes it was all he could think about, the pain; it was part of what kept him awake.

He was overheard saying he was willing to do something to help overturn the laws that so frustrated him – to be a 'martyr to the cause'.

Although Turner hadn't spoken to Turnbull for more than two years, his name was on an affidavit in the file that came along with the summons for the second lot of clearing when it was delivered in June 2014. Now Turnbull and his grandson were accused of more illegal clearing of protected vegetation on 'Strathdoon'. The old man held the papers in disbelief. 'The fact that Cory Turnbull was indicted,' reflects Nadolny, 'would have made Ian see red. He would have been absolutely mortified.'

Ian knew that Grant was intelligent and robust, a fighter, a manager of complex business affairs. He could look after himself. But to have young Cory sent through the trial process again seemed to injure Turnbull's sense of justice. Cory and Donna were only just starting a family and didn't need this. It was all threatened because of the interfering OEH. The face Turnbull saw when he imagined his bureaucratic enemy was that of a tall, serious man called Turner.

Turnbull should have been expecting a new prosecution, given the first one had been successful. The family had cleared not just between November 2011 through to January 2012, but again and again; they were clearing again right at the moment. But he was completely dismayed by the new charges. 'This will finish us, it is not going to be stopped,' he apparently told Grant.

'He was at a point of despair, is how I'd describe him,' Grant later said. 'He was down.'

And it was Turner who had had Strange out there to have a look back in March; had sent a file about the clearing to Local Land Services.

Turnbull instructed his lawyer to file a complaint, his fourth, against Glen Turner. 'Our client has a particular discomfort,' Sylvester Joseph's letter to the OEH said, 'dealing with Mr Turner. He feels he is victimised by what appears to be a personal vendetta.' The OEH, according to Joseph, responded by issuing another notice, demanding Turner be granted access to inspect 'Colorado'.

In mid-July, Ian and Robeena hosted their old friends the Cushes, as they did every year. As usual, Turnbull drove Ian Cush and his wife around the properties on a proud tour, showing off the winter crops. They headed out from 'Yambin' and up County Boundary Road. A right turn to 'Buckie', on the far side of the Croppa Creek township, where Grant lived at times. A stop at the friendly little Croppa Creek general store, with the big robot on the front fence made from old plastic milk crates, the dim store interior stocking books on mental health (*Taking Care of Yourself and Your Family,* ninth edition), a menu consisting mainly of bacon-and-egg rolls, and a noticeboard with advertisements for horse acupuncture, the mobile preschool, someone seeking a partner to sharefarm.

They sat and had a coffee, in view of the stream of white four-wheel drives pulling up outside. Turnbull mentioned that the remediation order meant installing fences, which they couldn't afford. Turnbull did not mention – perhaps he did not understand – that the court had said they needn't fence: they could decide how best to protect the vegetation. Turnbull grumbled to his friends, who'd had their own issues with land-clearing permissions, that they hadn't had any stock since 2002. The Cushes were struck by his gloom. There had been a change in the man. He seemed vexed, rubbing his aching legs, his mind alight.

'If by shooting Glen he could overturn that,' Nadolny says of the pressure to remediate, 'it would have been quite possible that OEH's reaction might have been to drop the clearing charges.'

If only the OEH could be deterred from their prosecutions; if Cory could be spared; if there needn't be all the effort to defend his family; if he could just get on the dozer a few more times, just get on with pushing trees and raking them up. If everything didn't have to be such a bloody battle, if no one got in the way, if Glen Turner didn't exist, how soon Turnbull might put down his burden, might finally rest, his duties done.

That month, Turnbull cancelled his lifelong subscription to *The Land* newspaper. He gave Cory his $600,000 crop-planting machine, and told him, according to Roger, 'If anything happens to me, make sure you look after your nanna.'

***

DESOLATE GROUND CAN BE fertile. In the 1890s, the bare fallow technique, which involved leaving fallow ground stripped of weeds so water could soak in, was used in the Wimmera, where it produced wonders. Its first thirty years saw yields across the country return to the levels enjoyed by early settlers. Fallow periods, to extend their good effects, were employed for longer, with more and more ploughing to increase the fine tilth of the soil. This churned away the weeds that otherwise bound the soil together, and left the tilth to blow away. No matter: 'If it blows, it grows,' farmers intoned, and they watched lovingly as the membrane-thin remnant of topsoil gusted over the few treetops left.

It was true that bare fallow worked up to a point, but the nitrogen in the soil soon depleted. This issue was solved, luckily, by Fritz Haber and Carl Bosch, who invented a method of synthesising nitrogenous fertilisers to create superphosphates. The incantation 'fallow, Federation and phosphorus' was taken up. By 1914 the wheat industry was the nation's biggest employer.

Then the precious new Federation wheat began to take the fungal disease of rust. Scientists worked, tweaking and trialling new varieties. In 1946, Dr Walter Lawry Waterhouse released Gabo, especially suited to high-fertility zones with low rainfall, such as the black-soil plains.

The black-soil plains are a fussy environment for grain. Environmentalist Eric Rolls tells the story of agronomist Jim O'Reilly from Gunnedah, south of Moree, driving to farmers' meetings in the 1930s with a piece of string hanging out of a bottle of sand and another from a bottle of marbles. Robeena Turnbull's father, Les, might well have met him at one of his displays. O'Reilly would explain that however much nutrient was in the soil, if it didn't touch the plant roots, the grain would wither. The black soil was like marbles rather than sand: conventional techniques of cultivation were hopeless. Instead, farmers should adapt their technology, work shallowly with tyned equipment and consolidate the soil. With this knowledge, the settlers who'd nearly sold off scrubland as useless 'put their black plains under wheat and found it the richest of land'.

There were good years and setbacks. Wheat rust adapts too, and even today varieties are still being adjusted to race ahead of it. The timing of rain relative to the state of the ripeness, the optimum length of the stalks before they start to bend and break in the wind, the point at which a grain should desirably germinate: these are all fractious issues, dependent on very specific locations and conditions. The vast blankets of wheat, barley, oats and rye that cover the Moree district plains under the direction of farmers such as Ian Turnbull look smooth and uniform and simple. Their growing is not.

Technology exploded the field of possibilities. A wheat farmer called Headlie Taylor collaborated with H.V. McKay, inventor of the Sunshine harvester, to produce 'headers', machines that could even reap crops flattened in storms. Diesel-engine tractors with rubber tyres, hauling wide machinery and fitted with lights, could suddenly work hundreds of thousands of hectares in all types of weather. Some of the best wheat quality and yield was the result; but more importantly, it was comfortable. Decades later, improvements were still being made: farmers could not overstate the revelation of air-conditioning and heating in tractor cabins. There could be hours more work in a day. Rolls gives a dreamlike description of himself and his colleagues in the Pilliga, each alone in their cabin in the pre-dawn toil as, '[s]tupefied by noise and cold, we sat and spiralled round our paddocks sowing wheat'.

The year 1929 was the official 'Grow More Wheat Year'. In the Mallee, people obeyed the call, digging superphosphates and crops into the soil. For every gain there is a price; again, the exposed soils of bare fallow farming gusted away in dust storms that could make a man go blind.

Then the Depression crashed the wheat price. The soil gave out once more. Diseases got to the crops and erosion continued. It was a scene of devastation from horizon to horizon.

This, with all the vicissitudes, was the agricultural landscape into which Ian Turnbull was born.

There was pensive discussion among agricultural scientists, politicians, landholders and public intellectuals about what had gone wrong. The phrase 'balance of nature' was in people's mouths. Some, such as nutrition expert Sir Stanton Hicks, observed that industrial farming had perturbed the 'balance'. Others said that a hectic Nature had failed to maintain her balance, and it was up to humans to restore it. The concept converged with an ecological idea of 'equilibrium' to provide a scientific basis for environmental management. This evoked a regime reminiscent of Isaac Newton's clockwork universe in which variables could be removed, elements isolated: it was a matter of 'getting the balance right'.

There was a moment in the early decades of the twentieth century, as Ian Turnbull was born, in which the projects of science, conservation and agriculture aligned to redress imbalance in an unexpected manifestation of 'ecology': the industrial farm.

The factor that makes the difference is humans: we have the power to make dramatic changes to whole ecologies, and we get to choose how much our demands for food and other resources determine where the 'balance' should fall. 'Nature', in this scenario, is the Nature that suits humans best.

Subterranean clover, like brigalow, fixes nitrogen in a plant's roots. In the years after the cataclysms of the 1930s, 'sub and super', along with herbicides and pesticides, radically renovated farming across southern Australia. Good seasons boosted confidence, the price of wool rose, the cactoblastis moth had the prickly pear on the retreat at last, and the energy of the postwar period kicked Australian agriculture to a new level. Turnbull's father, Sydney, rode the wave of the new farming with his small grazing holdings, and the son watched him prosper.

On the western slopes of New South Wales, the area devoted to cereal crops increased almost fourfold between the end of World War II and 1980. The mid-point of this expansion, the early 1960s, is just when Ian Turnbull and Robeena bought 'Yambin', their first farm at Croppa Creek, in the very heart of the richest agricultural land in Australia, the Golden Triangle, and entered the universe of industrial farming.

***

TURNBULL CONTINUED TO WAKE before dawn. For nine days he worked on the dozer, in the winter weather, for six hours a day, despite insomnia, despite the pain in his legs and his angina. 'Strathdoon' was already cropped. He wanted to finish the clearing on 'Colorado'.

Turnbull and his hired help, Ivan and Robbie Maas, worked hard. The trees were pushed. They were raked and stacked, and the stacks were set on fire. When they burned down, the land would finally be prepared. After that, it was just a matter of ploughing ashes into the waiting soil. They would have made it in time for the winter crop.

Come the weekend, Ivan and Robbie were off. Turnbull kept going on his own. His legs were killing him, tingling and aching. 'I just wanted to get that [clearing] all done and over,' he told the Supreme Court. 'It was to be my last year on the farm.'

The prosecutor in the murder trial, reflecting on the lead-up to Turner's death, suggested that Turnbull had pressed on so urgently because he knew a final judgement was due on which parts of the blocks were to be replanted for remediation. Justice Preston's decision came on 25 June 2014. The final details of the orders, the exact locations of the offset areas, would be given on 31 July 2014. That month, Turnbull was not just ploughing, spraying and cropping areas that were soon supposed to be regenerated, but intently pushing what native vegetation still remained.

Grant, Turnbull said in his murder trial, had given him a map to work off, showing what was supposedly safe to go ahead and clear, and Turnbull just followed the instructions on the tattered piece of paper on the passenger seat of his ute. Grant might have been around, or on the Gold Coast – Turnbull couldn't remember. Cory was in Toowoomba, working with his father, Roger. But Turnbull was there, every day, working on their land, the blocks he'd taken the lead in buying and clearing. He had an interest in getting it cleared, didn't he? To establish them on it. 'The second and third generation on to the land before I retire,' the old man said stoutly.

He had no map for what was coming. Turnbull drove the dozer to clear the offset areas. There would be no regeneration. No restoration. Soon it would all be under crops.

9

Cuius est solum, eius est usque ad coelum et ad inferos: Whoever owns the soil, it is theirs all the way up to Heaven and all the way down to Hell.

In the Supreme Court in 2016, several psychiatric experts testified as to Ian Turnbull's state of mind in July 2014. Dr Olav Nielssen, a consultant psychiatrist at St Vincent's Hospital in Sydney, who assessed the accused just over a week after the crime and again eighteen months later, testified that the Turnbull family shared a history of depression. Ian's mother, Beryl, had been so stricken after his birth that she was hospitalised, and two of his sons were taking pills to alleviate the stress of being on the land.

During his first evaluation, Turnbull told Nielssen that he'd been feeling low in recent months. At his age, friends were dying off. He didn't want to travel, watch television, go out. Repairs seemed too difficult. He didn't like to drive in town anymore, and his truck licence had been revoked. It was hard to make decisions, somehow. No, he hadn't mentioned any of this to a doctor, just got the prescriptions, had the usual chats. His memory was going, he said. There was a persistent sense of growing weakness, an instinct of an approaching end. 'I had the feeling that I had to get things done before I died,' he told Nielssen. 'All I wanted was to get this farm developed and pass it on better than I took it.' Then, 'just pull out'.

He'd had suicidal thoughts in adolescence. In the 1960s, when the drought was bad, he'd taken antidepressants for two years. But that was all. After that he'd been growing a family, growing the business. No more trouble, he told Nielssen.

By 2014, the Moree district had been in drought for three years. Drought is considered a stressor for farmers, whose livelihood, home and heritage are all implicated. It is particularly associated with a reduction in the seeking of professional help. There had been floods in Croppa Creek in late 2011 and February 2012, as the

Turnbulls were beginning the clearing. Properties were cut off, as in the days of Robeena's childhood, by the waters and the mud. Then some called the parching of 2014 the worst drought in the northwest in a century, but state subsidies ceased in June.

Robeena claimed Turnbull grew convinced that Turner had a vendetta against him, and became more and more obsessed. In late 2013 and early 2014, she affirmed, her husband grew quiet. For a man previously very sociable and popular in the community, he was unusually withdrawn, repetitive in conversation and compelled only on the subject of Turner, on which he'd talk for hours. Grant agreed. The Cushes and neighbour Garry Colley, too. They described Turnbull as dishevelled, distracted, ponderous, with a morbid turn in his thinking. Their descriptions supported the idea that Turnbull was depressed and his capacity inhibited: the crux of his defence for murder.

When he slept, he would awaken at dawn, he said, with 'Turner in my mind. Turner. Turner.' More often, Robeena would find him awake in bed at

3.00a.m., or he would rise in the winter dark and go to the kitchen. After fifty years of marriage, they woke separately.

He didn't have words for feelings. Farmers in remote areas rarely do, explained another psychiatrist, Dr David Greenberg, who met Turnbull after eighteen months in remand. 'They have to be resilient and stoical because they've got to be able to do everything for themselves. They've got to be plumbers, electricians, mechanics ... I mean, they've got to be self-sufficient.'

'I'm virtually finished,' Turnbull told Nielssen in 2014. But he denied being depressed. And before the trial two years later, in jail and facing a murder charge, he still denied it.

***

TURNER HAD NEARLY COMPLETED his house with Alison. His children, ten-year-old Alexandra and eight-year-old Jack, were his joy. 'Glen was happy,' Alison wrote in her victim impact statement. 'Glen didn't want any more. He had me, he had our kids, he had his farm, he had a job he enjoyed and he had a life full of friends and fun and music and laughter.' He played piano. When his daughter was a baby, he'd prop her up on a cushion atop the instrument. He loved bluegrass.

***

THE FRONTIER IS FULL of renegades. The squatters, careening carelessly over the official bounds of settlement; the escaped convicts who skirted the margins for decades; the researchers on remote experimental farms where soil loosened into sand; the soldier-settlers, told to make the best of flogged land on the margin; the industrial farmers, knocking down the odd paddock tree: they were all far from the authorities, who were in a different world, down there on the coast.

Today, a 'countrymindedness', as political scientist Don Aitkin puts it, persists in the stories rural people tell about themselves. Many of the wealthy landowners of Moree might live some of the year in Sydney's prestige Potts Point, winter in Bali and holiday in Italy, educate their children in boarding schools and stream Netflix in their living rooms, but they keep their hard-bitten squint, their blue check shirts, their love of local boy John Williamson and the instinct that they are misunderstood, living on the thin edge of survival.

Urban populations often don't comprehend or value complex histories of agricultural landscapes, or the architecture of agribusiness finance, or the compression of trade policies. They see native vegetation trashed, monocultures maniacally imposed, bull-headed attitudes rewarded, political corruption; they see consequences, but not connections.

Farmers complain rightly that they are maligned by people who have no clue. The ones who gobble the grain, munch the cereal, pour the oils, spill the milk. Most of us feel we've paid our price at the supermarket checkout. Any cost more – to the environment, or to the harmony of the countryside we glimpse on our travels – feels a price too high. We take, but we do not give. Victorian and New South Wales coast-dwellers logged out their forests and cleared grasslands for more than a century. Now they tell Queenslanders and those on the New South Wales border country to pull back, leave good soil unused, because they would like to keep those forests, that scrub. Those who have worked so bloody hard are expected to give up their future wealth, not pass the farming way of life onto their grand children – because someone down on the coast won't like it?

And the food. The food has to come from bloody somewhere.

The scientists and the government caution and regulate, some farmers grumble, but only a few decades ago they said the opposite: they said clear. They said the country must be taken, must be worked. They said 'you're our heroes'. And now they say knock down the fences, empty the vats of chemicals, let the bush grow over your crops, let the trees engulf your home, they're more important than you.

Country people's injured reaction to city folks' criticism widens the divide, of course; attitudes dig in, are defended with palisades. Slick lobby groups present, in historian George Main's words, an 'oppositional, exclusive position for rural landholders', undermining 'what sense remains of common interests between rural and urban sectors'. They rouse with martial talk of a 'clash' of opposing interests, a 'call to arms'.

Ian Turnbull's entry into farming in the mid-1960s was during a historical moment of almost psychotic belligerence towards native environments. *Silent Spring* (1962), Rachel Carson's landmark work about industrial farming in the United States, described how postwar technology and science once more tilted the 'balance of nature' question: across the Western world, wild spaces were seared with chemical weapons and crushed by machines. In that period, still percussing with the effects of the mid-twentieth-century's immense violence, there was a reprise of accusations of the 'uselessness' and inconvenience of the scrub even as nationalism evoked a gumnut arcadia. Turnbull's father could wash his hands of the poison he'd laid for wallabies and koalas, and wipe his hands on a tea-towel printed with them. Stealthy and sterile were the weapons of this psychopathy, and an apocalypse was the result.

Neoliberalism, with its insistence on dehumanised market rationales, removes ethics of care, community or responsibility. There is no room in a broadacre field for contamination: paddock trees are obstacles, native animals are pests, indigenous plants are weeds. Chemicals guard against and eliminate interfering vegetation and wildlife. Yellow crops fill the centre, green natives are edged to the periphery. It is efficient: 'agriculture', in Carson's words, 'as an engineer might conceive it to be'. Or an economist.

For Ian Turnbull, 'Strathdoon' and 'Colorado' were worksites. Alaine Anderson, next door, feels differently. Some people, she says sharply, 'have a lot of money, and they have technology. They don't hop out of the airconditioned cab. They have a pie warmer and a DVD player and remote-controlled robotic tractors. So they're not getting down smelling the earth; they are not counting seeds.' From the lofty position of a tractor cab, the earth may be merely a surface, as abstract as the screen full of numbers when they go home to do the accounts.

*

'DEPHYSICALISATION' IS A LEGAL term signifying the privilege of human over private property. 'Land law' is now 'property law'. This flinty, abstruse vocabulary is part of the process by which land has been appropriated, not because 'land' is actually abstract but our culture prefers it to be so. The matter was as blunt for Lord Coke in seventeenth-century England – 'For what is land but the profits thereof?' – as, four hundred years later on the other side of the world, for Moree MP Kevin Humphries: 'If the community wants farmers to set aside productive land ... they should be paying for it.'

Turnbull bought the blocks with the last of the black soil and determined they should be cropped. All qualities of that terrain apart from the potential of the soil were irrelevant to him. In Turnbull's rights over that land was manifested a monomania, founded on purpose, principle and privilege.

Exclusion of and separation from other interests is an axiom of ownership. That might include not just trespassers but ecological interests. Contemporary agriculture includes constant vigilance and the maintenance of order.

In fact, farmland is no longer the place for yeoman idylls or squatter dominion, but an economic and material base for an industrial system of production and export. Huge investment consortiums, able to survive on one good year in five, devour smaller holdings on thin margins. As American environmentalist Wendell Berry reminds us, industrialisation has always been about replacing people with machines. 'If you've got a neighbor, you've got help,' Berry points out, 'and this implies [a] limit ... You have to prefer to have a neighbor rather than to own your neighbor's farm.' An industrial farming landscape is unpeopled. And aerial chemical spray, used to kill insects or fungus, drifts over the land and across those stern boundary lines, sheds poison over the remnant vegetation, weakening birds' eggs in their nests, contaminating eucalyptus leaves as they grow, sifting into water reservoirs and running off through the soil towards the coast and all the way to damage the coral reefs far out to sea.

But there are ravines between farmer and farmer, too. Political ideology loves the craggy landscape of extreme postures: coast-dwellers against country folk, greenies against black-soil battlers. The contours of difference between farmers are as important as that between clay soil with eucalypts and black soil with brigalow. Some farmers cleave to the old ways. Some are exasperated by them.

And in the jostling, abrasions rub raw at times. The family farm is overshadowed by a massive agribusiness; spray drift contaminates an organic farm; untreated pests pervade a carefully sterilised boundary. One farmer might quietly illegally clear scrub. Another might dob him in. Another yet might, as was rumoured to have occurred in Croppa Creek, send in a gang of workers with an earth-moving machine to trespass on a neighbour's property and forcibly clear his remnant woodlands. Phone lines will be cut.

Crown lands might be bulldozed and farmed over. Frontiers will be erased and redrawn.

A Glen Turner is charged with responsibility for maintaining the tiny incursion of public interest in private land: the overlap between broadacre-crop zone and fenceline vegetation, or the minute dotting of ecological communities across a landscape otherwise assigned to private profit. This is a tricky, subtle practice. Boundaries are not easy to maintain. Palisades have gaps. Weeds, roots, dust pass across and between every borderline; sorrow, concern, judgement and ghosts follow them.

Thoughts may thicken, too, in the margins of the mind. Resentments can become embedded. An idea may wriggle under the fence of resolve and, once broken into clear ground, make havoc.

***

IN OCTOBER 2018, ALAINE Anderson was on her way to pick up antibiotics. She had seven koalas in her care, needing medical attention and nutrition. Another three had recently come to her after suffering chemical burns from the aerial spray of pesticides and herbicides on farms around their habitat. 'They're in the tips of the trees, where the aerial spray happens,' Anderson explains. 'They've got so little protection. Our treelines are only about 25 metres wide. It's not enough cover for them.' Two of the three had neurological damage.

Down in the waterways, the eucalypts grow in the clay soils, seams of refuge from the basaltic soils coveted by the broadacre farmers. There, in the remaining scrub, the koalas live. But the nutrition isn't high. 'Pretty paltry out here,' Anderson confides. 'Like cornflakes, really.' She goes out every day to cut three lots of leaves each for her koalas. But trees are being taken out of the waterways too now. Above those gullies, the trees have been mostly cleared: a few sentinels left in vast broadacre fields, and the thin margins of fenceline vegetation. 'One or two trees aren't going to last with exposure and chemical spray and drought and all the rest of it.' Once those refuges are gone, Anderson worries, 'There's just nowhere if we haven't got those good waterways.'

The koalas are 'all but gone from this district now', Anderson says bluntly. 'We can't release them here. Even down on the Mehi River, there's a whole stretch near Moree of kilometres that's been burnt by chemical, all those big red river gums.' The koala colonies are isolated. The travelling stock routes, long strips of bush alongside the highways, are being grubbed up and planted by farmers despite being Crown lands, and the fenceline scrub is being knocked down. A few trees are left here and there in gulches and groves, but they're often surrounded by field stubble or waving crops.

The last of the brigalow on 'Strathdoon' and 'Colorado' was home to some of the last koalas. Chris Nadolny had seen six koalas on 'Strathdoon' in August 2012, before the third lot of clearing, and others had seen evidence too: scratch marks, scat. But as the fragments of habitat disappeared, many of the animals were kettled, like protesters hemmed in by police. When developers want to clear koala habitat, it's said, they run the dozers in a tightening spiral. The outer trees fall. The animals flee inwards and upwards. As the dozers close in, crashing the vegetation, the animals begin to scream. It is a terrible sound, people say. And, others will tell you, the best thing then is to put the beasts out of their misery.

***

'WASTE', BRITISH WRITER JAY Griffiths tells us, comes from an Italian word *guasto,* connoting 'ravage, damage, injury'. The scrub-covered land that greeted the waves of white settlers was seen as 'wasteland': a legal term that indicated undeveloped Crown land. In the utilitarian paradigm of colonisation, the unused is either the yet-to-be-exploited or the expendable.

The word itself connotes abrasive, messy, compromised vegetation. The plants are imagined low and stunted, even if they're not. Scrub infiltrates, but at the same time is also diminished.

Scrub, thickened and tangled, waving its strange low, hard phyllodes and shaggy leaves, with its fused canopies and dense undergrowth, growing on slants and obliques, blocks the eye. Straying sheep are hidden. Sightlines are compromised. A man cannot see to pursue, or what stalks him. Confections were made of the dark scrub, the dark people who lived in it and the shadowy presence of mythic beasts both local and transported: bunyips and bogies, banshees and marsupial devils. It became a metonym for what thwarted and disappointed the great project of improving Australia.

Historian Ross Gibson uses a patch of brigalow scrub up near Rockhampton to describe a landscape haunted by the consequences of the past: massacres of Aboriginal communities, murders of tourists, assaults on the land. It is 'one immense crime scene'. The scrub was a space into which things might disappear, 'a lair for evil' where the delinquent, the fugitive and the outlawed could be stowed or stow away. It has associations with criminality and concealment: murder victims' bodies are still abandoned in shallow graves to the stoic watchfulness of the thickets of forest and freeway strips. A writer for

The Bulletin in 1895: 'No man who disappears mysteriously in Australia can be safely set down as dead until the scrub-country has been raked for him.'

When Ian Turnbull spoke of digging graves, he sometimes mentioned a hole large enough for a four-wheel drive, too. A chasm that capacious might go unnoticed, even in 2014, even in the scraps of scrub that remain.

Miasmas might lurk in the scrub. Bushrangers. Devils. Murderers.

***

ON THE MORNING OF 29 July 2014, Turner kissed his children goodbye as they ran to catch the schoolbus, and he and Alison drove into Tamworth together. He had packed an overnight bag for an inspection trip he was taking with his old colleague Robert Strange. Only one of the three properties on the day's list was Turnbull's, but the compliance officer supposed to attend those with Strange had a sudden family situation, so Turner had been pulled in. They were all in the Golden Triangle area, and one was in Ian Turnbull's neighbourhood.

Turner hadn't spoken to Turnbull for two years – since that meeting at the gate of 'Strathdoon' in June 2012 – despite the legal cases. The new court case was a long way off being heard.

As he hugged Alison goodbye, he said, 'I wish I wasn't going to Moree. I'd much rather be at home tonight, sleeping in our bed, with you by my side.' It was typical of him, she thought. A beautiful thing to say.

By late afternoon, Glen Turner was in the Croppa Creek area, on his way to Moree for the night. He and Strange had got as far as Pallamallawa when, having a bit of time to spare before twilight, he decided to turn north and show Strange the properties in Talga Lane they would be inspecting the next day.

Strange was up for the ride. He was generally pretty cheerful. He had been with the OEH for a while, having moved over to land management from the water division, and he'd been coupled with Glen Turner for the past six months. He liked Glen: the two of them had played touch footy when working together in the water division ten years earlier.

The detour took them north up County Boundary Road, right past the gates of 'Strathdoon' and 'Colorado'. Strange knew this stretch from an inspection a few months earlier. He'd even visited Anderson and seen her koala patients.

Turner's mind was on the inspection he'd inherited. Although he probably knew that Turnbull had lodged a fourth complaint against him just weeks before, he didn't mention this to Strange. Perhaps he had bigger thoughts: just four days earlier, Anderson had emailed him yet again to say the Turnbulls were clearing. The last of the trees on 'Colorado' were falling.

The sun was setting at the end of the lane, far into the west. It had been a nice day for winter, the sky now clear and pale.

As the officers approached 'Colorado', they could smell smoke in the late-afternoon air. They stopped. When they drew level and glanced across, they could see a great raft of timber alight in the middle of a cleared field, like a funeral pyre. Others, too: there might have been thirty beacons of fire in the middle of newly cleared ground. The open grassy woodlands were gone.

There was prickly pear and myall beside them on the roadside, then clear space until, far across the field, a line of trees remained, so thin the sky could be seen in threads among it. Turner narrowed his eyes.

Strange pulled off to the side. He hopped out to take some photos while Turner dialled Arthur Snook back in the office. 'Arthur, we're on the road at "Strathdoon" and "Colorado". All that area that is on the remediation map to be retained has now been cleared. They're burning the piles now.'

A white ute appeared from a gate ahead of them. Turner watched it turn onto the road as he asked Snook for an authorisation document to get onto 'Colorado' to get some samples from the wood stacks. His boss said he'd have it to him by the next morning. 'Have you been onto the property?'

'No. We're on the road,' Turner said. Outside, Strange was checking GPS readings. 'They've just lit the fires and you can see them flaring up.'

'What are you doing there, anyway?'

Strange climbed back into the driver's seat and closed the door.

'I've had a few concerns about some of the information lately,' Turner said, 'and I just wanted to check it out.'

'Leave it for now, and ring me in the morning.'

Turner had his finger over the button on the hands-free. 'Okay. Talk to you in the morning.'

As they headed off to Moree, they overtook the white ute, which was dawdling by the roadside. Strange could only see a bulky silhouette inside, but Turner recognised Ivan Maas. 'He's on the phone,' said Turner, with a knowing look. Strange turned left towards Moree, into Talga Lane.

Smoke rose in the clean winter air to a fading sky.

They stopped the car.

10

> Featured saying: Gandhi, 'An eye for an eye will make the whole world blind.'
> —***The Crooble Chronicle*, Croppa Creek's newsletter, August–September 2014**

Turnbull was already walking towards his ute as his phone rang. It was Ivan Maas. 'They're on County Boundary Road,' he told his boss. Turnbull got into the cabin and started his engine.

In Talga Lane the car had dawdled, the men peering out the window into the side of 'Colorado'. They went a bit further up the lane, then Turner asked his colleague to pull over.

They got out of the car where a thin wire fence stood at waist height. Turner had his GPS location reader and was jotting the coordinates in his notebook. Strange took out his camera and took a series of pictures. As he clicked, he heard a vehicle pull up behind him.

Strange looked around and saw an elderly man in a blue check shirt get out and stop between the cars. He raised something to his shoulder. He put his eye to a barrel.

In that moment on the road there were birds above, heading to nest for the night. The soil under the scrub was rich with tiny life; in cover of the undergrowth, wallabies and koalas might have been watching. At 'Yambin', Robeena was turning on the lights. In Tamworth, Alison McKenzie was driving the kids home to make dinner.

There was the sound of a shot.

Strange looked over at Turner. He had fallen to one knee. He looked up, a hand to his jaw. 'Ian,' Turner said, 'what have you done?'

Perhaps it was a BB gun, was Strange's first thought, and this guy is just trying to be smart. But there was blood on Glen's face.

Turner rose. They walked quickly towards their car.

There was another shot. Strange saw blood on Turner's shirt.

Turner ran towards the vehicle and Strange followed. Turner got to the passenger door, Strange to the front headlights, but the gun barrel followed them, and the man advanced. Turner crouched beside the door. The man said, 'You've ruined the Turnbulls! You're here crucifying us. You're going home in a body bag.'

Strange could hear Turner's hoarse breathing. Strange spoke with a dry mouth, hands up in surrender, eyes on the man. 'Sir, please, put the gun down. Put the gun down, please, sir.'

The man wouldn't look at him. 'No. No, no, no. Turner, you've taken this too far. You've taken us to court.'

Strange tried to move and the man moved sideways with him, around the car.

'You've ruined the Turnbulls, you sent us broke.' He spoke firmly. The words fired forth. 'We're in a drought, you know. You're constantly persecuting us. You're out here all the time. You've got planes flying over here. What, what am I to do?'

'Sir, he's, you know, he's hurt. I need to get him to the hospital. Please, put your firearm down. Let us go.'

'Move back,' said the man, 'or you'll get one in the heart.' His hands, gripping the .22 rifle, holding it steady, were black with engine oil.

Every time Strange asked Turnbull to put the gun down, the man raised it defiantly. Evidently he was a crack shot: the first bullet had nearly had Turner right in the head. He told Strange to drop the little camera; Strange dropped it. He told him to move back; Strange moved back.

'Glen, just keep down, keep down,' Strange murmured. When Turnbull edged around the car he muttered, 'Move to the back.' He kept pleading with the man. 'Sir, put the gun down. There is no need for this.'

Turner said hoarsely, 'Let us go, Ian, let us go.' His hands left bloody smears on the side of the car.

'Don't move,' the man told Strange, and trained the gun at him. 'Or I'll fucking shoot you too.'

And Turner wept, 'Please. Please get us out of here, Rob. Get us out of here.'

Minutes had passed; Strange didn't know how many. It was getting darker, the sun soaking away beyond the trees. Strange kept moving around the car.

The beam of the headlights shifted across him. He edged out of them, thinking that the dark would give them cover to get away. But he knew the man would be alert to this. The man would want to get it finished before the light went. He could hear the thought in Turner's voice too. He was getting frightened of the dark.

There was a moment when the man focused on Turner, and Strange was able to get his hand into his pocket, to his phone. Thank god, it wasn't locked. He glanced down quickly and dialled triple zero and pressed the green call button. The phone light glowed in the lowering dark and he tucked it further in, eyes on the gun, hoping the man wouldn't see the light, hoping someone was already answering and would hear him say, 'Sir, you've got to put the gun down. We are unarmed. You have to put the gun down.'

Choking on his words, he said, 'Sir? We're here to do a job. We're only doing what we're told to do.'

'You're not here to do a job,' the man spat. 'You're here to ruin us, to take us to court. It's not enough that we've been in court. You don't leave us alone.' He jerked the gun forward. Strange felt the implacable eye of it. 'All you want to do is just ruin, ruin the Turnbulls.'

Strange could tell the call hadn't got through. It was maybe twenty or thirty minutes by now since the horror began and still no one knew about it. No one was coming to help.

Turner got the passenger door open. Strange edged over to give him cover; the man noticed the movement and Turner backed away. But the door was open.

Strange thought, *If I can get to the driver's side, get the man's attention, Glen can get in.*

He made to move, but the man aimed the gun straight at his head and said, 'I fucking told you, I'll fucking shoot you. Now get back.'

He flinched. He thought, *I'm going to get shot. I'm gone.*

Turner was by now crouching around the back of the car, bleeding from the chest. There was a red stain on his upper breast. The man moved back there, saying, 'You're going to die, Turner, you're going to die.'

Strange thought, *I have to get the gun off him. I have to, I have to hit him – get the gun –*

He moved and Turnbull swivelled the barrel once more, fixed him with one furious eye. 'I fucking *told you.*'

'We need to go,' Turner panted. 'Rob? We need to go.'

Strange forced his voice to stay calm. 'Mate, it's okay. I'll get you out of here – just, just bear with me.' He turned to the man: 'Please, he's hurt, he has a family and two little kids. We're unarmed. We're only here doing our job, doing what we have to do to earn a living.'

'Well, we've got to earn a living too, but you're fucking here crucifying us.' The thin little rifle clutched in his hands. The harsh, steady voice. 'You'll just be back again and again, and I'm putting an end to it.'

'I won't be back, I can assure you,' Turner gasped.

The man looked at him. 'You're going home in a body bag, is the only way you're going.'

Turner somehow got his arm in under the fibreglass canopy at the back of their ute. His fingers found the yellow EPIRB and pressed it. A light showed it had activated. He dropped the thing. Hesitating on the far side, Turnbull fired twice through the window of the glass canopy and shattered it. A bullet grazed Turner's chest.

Another shot went past Strange's head. He shouted to Turner, 'Glen, Glen, get down.'

Turner gasped, 'I know!' Then he said, 'I can't do this anymore, I can't.' He broke from his crouch and ran to the darkness of the trees. And Turnbull raised the gun.

Bang. Turner dropped to the ground, face first. Strange spun around to look at the man. Turnbull let the gun fall to his side and said, 'Right, you can go now. I'm going home to wait for the police.'

*

ANDREW UEBERGANG'S GRANDFATHER HAD a station at Crooble, 15 kilometres south of Croppa Creek, and Andrew had been working there all day. There were two ways the young farmworker could go home; he took the Talga Lane way a bit before 6.00p.m. On the way north, he saw Ian Turnbull's white Nissan Patrol heading south down County Boundary Road. He knew Turnbull, and his grandson Cory – he had worked for them occasionally. He turned left into Talga. The sun had almost set – just a glow on the horizon ahead, the trees a black wall on either side of the road. And about a kilometre along, in the shaft of his headlights, he saw a man standing in the road, his hands up, eyes closed.

The man was plump, with glasses and a pale face. He opened his eyes and stared at Andrew. He said something about Ian Turnbull. He said his mate had been shot. He needed to use a phone, his had no signal. Asked where Turnbull lived. Uebergang told him: 'Yambin'.

Uebergang got out in the dusk and saw the dark form of a man lying in the grass, motionless. He didn't know what to do; he stood, shaking his head, freaking out while the other man used his phone in his car. Then he hopped back in and took off down the road to get help. He called his uncle, thumbing the phone in the dark cabin, heart racing, watching the fenceline scrub for the gate of the next property, 'Talga'. Turned in; up the drive. The door opened and Brenton Whibley came out.

Already the words had been in his mouth once: 'Someone's been shot.'

'Shit. Who shot him?'

'Ian Turnbull.'

'Oh, shit.'

Brenton's wife, Felicity, had first-aid training. She snatched up her medical kit and took her ute. As Uebergang drove out the gate, he recognised a work vehicle from Turnbull's place coming past.

*

ROBBIE, IVAN MAAS'S SON, was working for Grant on 'Buckie', shooting wild pigs, that day. The pigs were wrecking the crops. He stayed until it was dark, his gun beside him in his ute, then finally turned the headlights on and made for home. He was on the way back up County Boundary Road when he heard Ian on the shortwave frequency the Turnbull staff shared. 'Are you there, Scott?'

Robbie heard the Turnbulls' farm manager, Scott Kennett: 'Yeah, Ian?'

'I just pumped a couple of shots at Turner. I think he's dead.'

In the dark of his cabin, Robbie heard these words but couldn't understand. What had happened? Who was Turner?

Turnbull said, 'I'm going home to wait for the police.' His voice was steady and gave nothing away.

The transmission ended, and a moment later his phone rang. It was Scott Kennett, asking where he was. They had to go and see what had happened. Robbie's heart was thumping.

*

SCOTT KENNETT, WHO'D WORKED for Turnbull and Grant for more than twenty-five years, had had a normal day. He was at 'Buckie', working on a planter all afternoon. It wasn't surprising he was still there: 'I don't really work to clocks,' he would later tell the court. 'If there is enough light I just keep going.'

Close to dusk, he got a call from Ivan Maas that Glen Turner was in the area, checking things. Ivan had been working with Turnbull in the field all afternoon, until one dozer got a bad leak. Turnbull couldn't fix it and took it back to 'Buckie' for some tools. Now the farmhand had tried to call his boss, but the signal was bad. Ivan mentioned to Kennett that as a caution he'd locked the gate, by now their common practice when anyone was around the properties. Kennett made a mental note to watch out for the government men.

He came upon Turnbull in the shed, looking for an oil filter and oil. He mentioned that Turner was around. Turnbull gazed at him. 'I thought he would be about at some stage.' He took the oil from Kennett's hand and walked out. Kennett heard him checking his voicemail as he walked to the car, then Ivan's voice over the phone. Kennett called out after him that Ivan had locked the gate; Turnbull nodded, put the equipment and can in the tray of his ute, and left.

It was just on 5.30p.m. Kennett's farmhand, Henry Martin, finished up and filled his ute with petrol before leaving. About ten minutes after Martin left, Kennett drove a tractor to the fuel tank, spent about five minutes filling it, and got in to drive it back to the shed.

Turnbull called on the radio's private channel. 'I just pumped a couple of shots at Turner. I think he's dead. I'm going home to wait for the police.'

*

ROBBIE GOT HOME AND quickly put the gun away. Then he sped to a dark paddock on 'Buckie'. Kennett got in and they drove along Talga Lane. Kennett called Turnbull's son, Grant, who was in Queensland. 'Have you talked to your dad?' he asked. 'Your old man just said he shot Turner.'

Grant sounded shocked. Kennett said he and Robbie would go and see what was happening. Grant could barely reply. 'Just let me know,' he said, and rang off.

Robbie dipped the high beams for a car coming towards them. Then they passed another car, parked on the side of the road, its headlights shining into the trees. They slowed, staring, but did not stop.

'He's done it,' Robbie said.

'Looks like it,' Kennett replied.

They went on a bit past 'Talga', then did a U-turn and headed back to the HiLux with its lights on and, now, the two other cars, and the body on the ground, a woman kneeling over it.

*

NICOLA KENNETT RANG HER husband after the two-way call came through on the receiver. 'What the hell did I just hear?' She was getting dinner for her daughter, her kitchen warmly lit in the house they lived in on the property next to 'Yambin', the lodgings part of Scott's job. He said he didn't know. He rang off. Nicola kept making dinner; got some texts from friends about ordinary things; paced nervously. Scott rang back. He said there'd definitely been a shooting – it was out on Talga Lane. He was on his way with Robbie; the Whibleys were helping. Nicola texted Felicity to see if she was okay.

*

FELICITY WHIBLEY HAD BEEN home all afternoon with her family, as usual. She too was in the kitchen cooking dinner when the phone rang; at the same time, a car she didn't know came down the driveway. Felicity picked up the phone as her husband went to the door. In her ear, her neighbour Michael Coulton was saying that someone had been shot. At the door, Andrew Uebergang was saying that someone had been shot. He looked terrible.

Someone has been shot. Everyone saying the same thing. Those words, in her kitchen, in her hallway, in front of the kids.

Should she or Brenton go? Someone had to stay with the children. 'I better go,' she said. 'I don't want to see someone die.'

She got in her car and drove east, along with Andrew Uebergang. The quiet road, empty for the past hour, pounded now.

Felicity followed her training. In the dark she found the man and knelt beside him, joining Strange. He was lying on his left side. There was blood and water on his face, blood all over his shoulder, a hole in his back. She rolled him onto his back. Pumped one, two, three, four, five times. Blood gushed from his mouth. He was dead. If she pumped any more, it would only push more blood out.

*

UEBERGANG WAS TRYING BOTH torches in his car. He shook them, but the batteries were dead. He swore; he started his car and nosed it forward to shine the lights where Felicity was on the ground with the two men.

Another car pulled up, making it four pale vehicles in the dark now. Scott Kennett and Robbie Maas got out. They stood and stared; then Kennett said they'd guide the police when they arrived, and drove off again.

Felicity and the man were busy, so Uebergang stepped back a bit. He was scared, kept glancing around. Stood in the dark of the road with Robbie's taillights floating away and the sound of two people gasping over one who wasn't making any sound at all.

*

ADAM BAXTER, A SPRAY-RIG operator, collected his car from a property west of the highway just after dusk and drove home eastwards along Talga Lane. He was most of the way down it when he saw lights ahead and three vehicles parked on the side of the road. There was a white dual-cab HiLux parked at 45 degrees, facing into trees. A white Toyota Prado, facing east. A white Landcruiser nosed in, with lights on. He knew Grant Turnbull's property had had issues with land clearing; he guessed this was a chin-wag. But as he passed, the headlights revealed a body on the ground.

He reversed and stopped. There was a woman kneeling over the body; he recognised Felicity. He recognised Andrew Uebergang. In Uebergang's ute there was a man he didn't know on the phone.

Uebergang walked over. He was distressed, talking fast. He had come across a man in the road whose mate had just been shot, he said. Baxter began worrying that the shooter was still nearby or might return, and he turned back towards his car.

Ian Turnbull was the shooter, Uebergang said. Then, 'Have you got a shotgun?'

Baxter shook his head. 'Not here. Why?'

And he understood that Uebergang thought Turnbull might return and kill them all. He could see the fear in the young man's eyes – Uebergang didn't want Baxter to leave.

'Do you need help?' Baxter said.

'I don't know what I'm supposed to be doing,' said Uebergang.

And then Felicity rolled the body onto its side and walked away from it. 'He's cold,' she said. 'I can't feel a pulse.' She was crying. 'He's gone.'

The ambulance service was calling Uebergang. He handed the phone to her. Lights were coming from both directions down the road.

Strange folded Turner's hands on his chest. It didn't matter now how dark it was. He said to the silent man on the ground, 'Glen, Glen. Alison and the kids need you. Glen? Glen, they need you.'

*

SCOTT KENNETT AND ROBBIE Maas were out on County Boundary Road, looking for the police. Kennett rang Grant again and explained what he knew. Grant said, 'This won't be good. Do you know where Dad is?'

*

THE AMBULANCE SERVICE WAS out there, bolting through the winter dark towards the GPS from Turner's EPIRB, but unsure where exactly to go, calling Robert Strange as they went. The police radio was live, the police were ringing the ambulance supervisor at base; Tammy from the ambulance service was on the line to Australian Search and Rescue. The GPS signal from the EPIRB was slowly becoming exact. There was a discussion among emergency services of trying for a helicopter from Canberra. And in the middle of this, a call from the Croppa Moree Road, requesting an ambulance for a distressed elderly person.

*

FELICITY BEGAN TO PANIC. Adam Baxter – she hadn't noticed him arrive

– handed her a phone. A woman's voice from the ambulance service stuttered on the line, dropping out. Felicity clutched the phone: should she keep doing CPR? 'He's cooling down already,' she heard herself say.

She could see headlights coming from each end of the road. The police? The lights weren't flashing. A scorch of fear came over her. The ambulance staffer told her to get in her car. 'Get in your cars!' Felicity screamed, and everyone leaped out of the dark into cabs, slammed the doors. Only Turner stayed, lying out there. 'I was so scared,' Felicity said later, 'but I managed to hold it together.'

And then there were more lights down the road, red and blue ones this time. There was the sound of tyres on gravel and the police and an ambulance arrived.

*

THE ROAD HAD BEEN empty when the gun was raised at Turner. Now it seemed everyone in the world was pelting towards them. Robert Strange said later that he felt guilty for thinking it, but he was glad it wasn't just him anymore, that there were others to look after Glen, that he wasn't alone on the winter road.

*

KENNETT AND MAAS RETURNED along with the police. The locals huddled as uniforms surrounded the body.

'Ian said he shot him,' said Kennett, 'over the private channel on the two-way.'

'I can't believe it,' Uebergang said.

Felicity was shaking. Uebergang insisted on taking her home. She didn't want to leave Turner, but eventually agreed. He and Baxter dropped her off. She walked in the door and said to her husband in a strange voice, 'The man is deceased.' She didn't even know his name.

Her face wore her shock. She tried to describe how she'd tried to help him, but CPR wouldn't work. Nothing would work.

She calmed a little later that night, but she was frightened for a long time afterwards. She understood now how easy it was to die, how she too could be shot to death, could lie on the grass with blood on her face and a smudge of earth on her brow.

*

HUNDREDS OF KILOMETRES AWAY in Dubbo, Arthur Snook was holding his phone, listening to nothing. It had rung less than an hour earlier: the Australian Maritime Safety Authority, with news that an EPIRB allocated to Glen Turner had been activated. Glen had told him, not long before, he was looking at the Turnbulls' clearing. For ten minutes he'd tried Turner's and Strange's phones over and over again. He'd got onto Robert Strange finally. 'Talga Lane, Talga Lane,' the man had gasped. Then, a few minutes later, Snook, in his nice, normal, lamp-lit office far from the cold country lane, got through again.

'He's dead,' said Strange, from the cabin of Uebergang's ute.

'Who did it?' Snook asked, aghast.

'Ian Turnbull, and he's gone.'

Snook, left to picture what was happening, couldn't do a thing. He rang triple zero again, made calls to colleagues, paced the office with the phone in his hand as he waited for news.

*

IN THEIR HOUSE OUTSIDE Tamworth, Alison McKenzie arrived home with Alexandra and Jack. There was a message on the machine for Glen: it was search and rescue in Canberra, confirming that his emergency beacon had gone off. Could he please call as soon as possible.

Alison rang the police to explain it was a mistake. Glen was in Moree that night, doing a job out there tomorrow. The police said, yes, there's been a shooting. Glen's been shot. That was all they knew. The police said they'd let her know when there was more information.

Alison kept calm; she began to think of getting to Moree, to the hospital. She rang her sister-in-law to come over and take care of the kids.

To the west, now the earth had turned away east, people were spinning into action. Phone calls were furiously seething in the airwaves. Cars were bolting all over the countryside. Only the trees were still.

*

ALAINE ANDERSON AND HER husband, Lionel, were at home at 'Strangford', beside 'Strathdoon'. A neighbour rang her; did she have an ecologist staying the night? Enough people knew that Alaine and Turner were in contact about clearing in the area. No, said Alaine, but rang her ecologist friend Phil Spark, who was working in the area. He answered, thank god.

Wait till morning, Spark said, we'll find out then.

*

SCOTT KENNETT CALLED GRANT again on his way home a couple of hours later, around 8.30p.m. Grant had located his father at home. Cory had been there – he'd heard Turnbull on the two-way and gone straight from Roger's property to the homestead to tell Robeena. Minutes later, Turnbull had walked in through the laundry, washed his hands and entered the kitchen. Cory had fetched him a chair. He had taken his shoes off, gone into the living room and sat down in his armchair. Cory had left his grandparents to have some time together.

Kennett met Nicola at home and they went straight over to the Turnbulls' place next door. Robeena let them in.

Turnbull was sitting in his brown recliner in the lounge room under a doona, his socked feet showing. Kennett hesitated. It was a shock to see the old man just sitting there. Nicola knelt beside him and touched his arm. 'Why?'

Turnbull gazed at her. 'I had no choice,' he said. His arm was trembling beneath her hand. 'He was ruining my family, and it was never going to end.'

'You did have a choice,' she said.

He looked away. 'I am sorry to all of you.' He shivered under the doona. Scott took Robeena into the kitchen. Ian, the elderly woman said, was not sure if Turner was dead. 'I hate to tell you,' Scott said, 'but he is.'

And in that silence, everything changed.

From the lounge room, Turnbull spoke again. 'The gun is still in the back of the ute. It's still loaded.'

Nicola called an ambulance for Turnbull, saying there was a distressed person who needed attention. She helped Robeena make beds, to keep her occupied. Robeena asked, 'Do you know what's happening with the police?' In the end, Nicola called them and talked with a detective, giving him Turnbull's mobile number. The two men spoke.

Scott knew by now that the police were at the gate. The ambulance hadn't arrived. He went down in Robbie's ute 'to see what was taking so long'. It was now five hours since Turnbull had lifted his gun.

The ambulance was waiting at a distance from the house. Beside it were police officers and detective senior constables, their sharp shooters stationed behind trees, and, in a police car, Robert Strange. He knew one of them and explained what was happening in the house. The police asked him to wait with them. His wife was still in there; Robeena; the gun in the car.

*

AT 8.30P.M., ALISON MCKENZIE rang the Moree police. She was put on hold for long minutes. Tinned music playing down the line as her heart churned, watching the kids' anxious faces, trying to hold back her alarm as the reassurance that Glen was okay did not come.

Then she was put through to a detective who told her that Glen was dead.

The children saw her face, heard her voice. They rushed to clutch her. They all screamed. They wept and shrieked.

*

OUTSIDE 'YAMBIN', ROBERT STRANGE knew he was probably safe in the car, with three or four other officers, but he didn't feel it. And Glen was still out there, back in Talga Lane.

Arthur Snook rang again. 'I'm sitting out the front of the defendant's house,' Strange told him. He voice was strained; agitation was kicking in.

'Whose house?'

'Turnbull's,' said Strange. 'I'm in the back of the police car outside his house. I don't feel comfortable here. Arthur, get me out of here.'

*

PARAMEDICS CAITLIN MURPHY AND Daniel Perram had been at Talga Lane, seen the body, confirmed Turner dead. Then they'd had a call to attend a man suffering emotional distress. It was only on the way they realised it was probably the killer; they rang the operations centre, and when they got to the address, joined the sharp shooters and the police cars waiting outside, until they were sent away again.

*

NICOLA AND ROBEENA KNELT and put shoes on Turnbull's feet. He stood and walked to the door.

He stepped onto the porch, then onto the lawn. He turned around on the spot, to show he had no weapons. Detective Senior Constable Timothy McCarthy and Detective Brent Falkiner moved forward. 'Ian,' McCarthy said, 'you're under arrest for the murder of Glen Turner, which happened about 5.45 this evening.'

The old man said only, 'Yeah, well, just before dusk, anyway.' Turnbull faced the wall as directed; he said 'yeah' when asked if he understood his rights. His hands were cased in paper bags, taped at the wrists, not too tight. They would be swabbed for gunshot residue.

In the house, Nicola and Robeena were looking for his medication bottles. The pills were in daily dispensers, but the police couldn't dose them without the information on the packaging. Detective McCarthy asked if he'd changed his clothes. He pointed at the pair of runners in the kitchen and told the women that they weren't to touch them. There would be a search warrant for the house.

It was nearly midnight. Eventually, Turnbull was taken off without his heart medication.

Robeena's brother Ranald came from North Star to pick her up. Scott Kennett was taken to Moree to make a statement; Nicola drove one of

Robeena's cars home. The police seized Robbie Maas's ute, to test the pigs' blood in the back.

Robert Strange was now on his way on the hour's drive to Moree. Ian Turnbull was in a police van on the same road, just ahead. Glen Turner was still lying in Talga Lane, where he'd remain until morning, as dew collected on the grass in the cold winter night.

11

The principal task of civilization, its actual raison d'être, is to defend us against nature.
—Sigmund Freud, *The Future of an Illusion*, 1927

Early hours. There was work to be done at the fluoro-lit police station. Robert Strange gave a statement at 1.00a.m. Sylvester Joseph, the Turnbull family lawyer, arrived, talked to Ian Turnbull. At 2.00a.m., Turnbull was briefly interviewed. At 3.00a.m., he was swabbed. His clothes were taken off and bagged; he was put in prison greens. By 5.00a.m., he was asleep, and when custody officers woke him two hours later he was calm and uncomplaining. A photograph was taken around 8.00a.m.: that steady, shuttered gaze, that closed mouth.

Turnbull's daughter-in-law Justine, his son Sam's wife, had rung Scott Kennett on his way to the station. Then Sam called. They urged him not to say anything without a lawyer. Grant was on his way down from Queensland. He got to 'Yambin' just before 2.00a.m. to find police standing at his father's door. Inside, Robeena was with her brother Ran and his wife. The three old people sat at the kitchen table. They did not discuss what had happened. A police officer was in the room. By 2.00a.m., the elderly people left for North Star. Twenty minutes later, Grant watched as police searched the house and took photographs of a bloodstain beside the white basin.

Roger, away in the United States with Annette, barely knew what to feel when he heard the news. He had gone to the police a few weeks earlier to report his father's muttered threats about Glen Turner. But the police had believed him unreliable. They had just shrugged and made a note.

Meanwhile, in Tamworth, Alison McKenzie was holding her children as they cried. Glen's sister, Fran Pearce, had been away from home in a hotel when Alison called her. Now, at 3.00a.m. Fran woke her parents in Port Macquarie to tell them Glen was dead. Glen's mother, Coral, began screaming,

'No, no!' His father shook. 'Who will look after the kids?' he cried.

The morning came too soon. In the early light, the coroner's van came to get Turner, but the body wasn't removed until nearly midday.

Detective McCarthy took Arthur Snook to the Moree morgue. Snook had got in from Dubbo and not had much sleep. He had to be there: an officer of the OEH had been killed in the line of duty. They met the van at the entrance. The back doors were opened and an assistant unzipped the body bag from the top. 'Yes, that's Glendon Eric Turner,' said Snook, and the body was taken inside.

Records detail every movement of its handling, every location and pause. A Life Extinct Form had to be completed; a Report of Deceased for the coroner, a Certification of Search of Deceased Body, a Deceased Identification Statement. Ian Turnbull had not yet finished generating paperwork.

In Armidale, eating breakfast in his kitchen, Chris Nadolny heard the morning news bulletin: an environmental officer had been shot dead near Moree. Nadolny knew immediately who it was, and who had killed him.

*

IAN TURNBULL WAS LED into Moree Courthouse that afternoon. His eyes were red: filled, the local media reported, with tears. He sat immobile in the courtroom as Sylvester Joseph said the family, after a sleepless night, wasn't ready to discuss bail, but would reserve the right to apply for it another time. Ian Turnbull was charged with one count of murder. His lips were seen to tremble. He was taken away. Media outside the court clustered hopefully as Turnbull's older sister and her husband walked from the courtroom without comment.

*

THE FOLLOWING AFTERNOON, 31 July, Robert Strange did a walkthrough for the police out at Talga Lane. Arthur Snook was there. So was Detective Timothy McCarthy and two colleagues. The crime scene was undisturbed, apart from the removal of Glen's body. The

OEH's, Andrew Uebergang's and Felicity Whibley's vehicles were still parked; the little work camera, dropped to the ground. Strange felt bad that Uebergang hadn't got his car back yet. He'd only been passing by.

The police asked Strange to tell them exactly what had happened.

'I saw a, a man raise his arm and what appeared to be a rifle in his hand, and then I heard a, a shot fired and I ... Glen, I looked over at Glen and I could see him, and Glen was going, and said, "Ian, what have you done?"'

The police filmed him for an hour. Later, they closed the crime scene, drove away the vehicles and left the road to the scrub and the fields.

At the morgue, Glen Turner's body was autopsied by Dr Rexson from the Newcastle Department of Forensic Medicine. The autopsy report lists Turner's clothing. He was wearing: blue jeans (blood spatter on left thigh), blue underpants, brown socks, brown leather shoes. He was wearing: a white-and-blue check shirt with blood around the collar, chest and left shoulder; a white T-shirt with blood in the same areas; a brown leather belt. He was wearing: a police tag around his left ankle.

There is a list of all the parts of his body. Hair, eyelids, eyebrows, ears, lips, gums, teeth, penis, scrotum, testes, anus, thorax, abdomen, upper limbs, fingernails, lower limbs. The report observes that 'the toenails were long'.

His measurements were taken. In death, height is measured as length.

He had a little coronary artery atheroscolerosis, some lung damage from smoking. Some THC in his bloodstream.

He had grazed the left side of his forehead as he fell under the final shot, as well as his knee.

Turnbull had a .22, which fires small bullets. The first shot went through the side of Turner's jaw, out the back of his neck. The second hit his chest, up near his shoulder. The third didn't penetrate his body, only grazed his skin. Then Turnbull fired a bullet that lacerated Turner's aorta. He bled out into his chest. Four litres of blood.

***

A WEEK AFTER THE killing, Robert Strange was at Tamworth police station, flicking through images of twenty men, one of whom was Ian Turnbull. He signed the image of Turnbull, formally identifying the man who'd raised the gun and killed his colleague. In the black-and-white mugshot Turnbull's face is grained and marmoreal, mouth steady, eyes steady, staring straight out. Strange had already been questioned about Turnbull's demeanour during the killing. He was 'focused and determined, in all honesty', Strange said. 'He understood everything I said to him and dismissed everything I said to him.'

Meanwhile, Detective McCarthy drove to Turner's office in Tamworth. It had been locked since his death. McCarthy got Arthur Snook to open it; he took Turner's compliance notebooks, an external hard drive, a folder containing Turner's affidavit about Turnbull's threat on his life. He already knew about the death threat. Turner had mentioned it to Strange: 'Glen told me on at least one occasion, as he had a habit of repeating himself. It was common for

Glen to tell me a story he had already told me previously like it was the first time he told it.'

Similarly, Robert Strange would be condemned to repeat the story of Glen's death over and over. He told it to the police on the night of the murder; he told it to the detectives at Talga Lane; he would tell it in the witness box. It was the longest story he'd ever tell.

*

ALISON MCKENZIE COULD not see her husband's body until ten days after he died. It took that long for his body to be released. 'Ten days of wondering where he was, what was happening to him and what would he look like when I saw him,' she said. She spent the time imagining his death, without her there for comfort; his body, alone in the dark. 'This is something that haunts me to this day,' she would one day tell a court. 'I cannot bear the thought of him being out there in the cold by himself. I should have been there to hold him.'

During that period of intense grief, she and Pearce lay awake each night, crying and comforting Jack and Alexandra. They worried about funeral costs. They made list after list of things to be done. The two would drive into Tamworth for appointments. McKenzie suppressed her tears before the children, but wept all the way in the car.

The day they learned that Glen was killed not with one clean shot but several, they collapsed. He had been stalked for forty long minutes, he had pleaded for his life as he crouched behind his work vehicle. They fell to the floor, clutching each other.

Glen Turner was cremated at a small service, attended by his friends and family. The pathologist had dissected his jaw, where Turnbull's bullet had hit him. For the funeral service his face was covered with wattle leaves, to hide the injury.

Alexandra needed cremation explained to her.

The next day there was a memorial service. Hundreds came. Stories were recounted. Glen had been president of the primary-school parents and citizens association, as well as volunteering at the school canteen and starting up a scheme with native gardens. He coached kids in touch rugby. Alison and the children planted a jacaranda in their garden, in front of friends, in his memory. Watered it with Turner's own home brew.

Jack Turner cried in his bed that night. 'But mummy,' he mourned, 'I'm only nine.'

***

IAN TURNBULL HAD TOILED on the bare fields of 'Colorado' for weeks. Now he had the long days of incarceration to sit and rest, and contemplate his deeds.

The traditional legal definition of crime is 'the combination of a harmful act with a guilty mind'. Out on the land, in those bare paddocks, farmers might see no 'crime' even when a law has actually been broken. Or a grievance can occur, beyond the capacity of any lawyer to articulate.

Country communities talk. Shame is their instrument. 'A quiet word' or 'keeping the peace' is preferable to bringing in the authorities. A little gossip is judiciously applied to send a message. Or the traditional Australian indulgence of a whinge behind someone's back, and a compensatory shrug that you don't always do right yourself.

Sometimes, silence descends. The wry nod and momentary hush at the pub counter. The raised eyebrow and shrug; the turning away. And if pushed for a response: 'I couldn't possibly say', 'I'd rather not comment', or 'Oh, well, you know.'

In Croppa Creek, they didn't speak of clearing. The white utes and four-wheel drives drove up all day long to the little general store for bacon-and-egg rolls and toasted sandwiches, clustered in the golf club car park in the evening, parked along the road at the school fete on the weekend. The men got out of their vehicles, washed clean of twigs and dirt, of blood from their scratches and tractor diesel oil, of smoke from burning stacks. They nodded and drank and muttered together. They talked about grain and crops and drought. The women spoke of drought and school and taxes and their husbands' moods. But few spoke of the clearing.

Now they had to learn how to do it, in their familiar sitting rooms and club foyer, the courtyard of the general store, from ute window to ute window stopped in the road. To speak of the death of Glen Turner. To parse the distinction between guilt, the acknowledgement of a true accusation, and guilt, the inhabiting of remorse. How might they speak of the guilt of Ian Turnbull, who had been one of them, sitting in these same rooms, and now taken far away?

Years later, these people were still unable to talk of it. *You have to understand,* they pleaded. *It's too painful. It is just too difficult.*

Ian Turnbull never pleaded innocent to any of the charges brought against him: not for the illegal land clearing, not for the killing of Glen Turner. He never denied he'd done those things, but he couldn't say he was guilty of crimes, either. He had his reasons. He wouldn't concede that he knew his acts were wrong. He'd been pushed into them. He was the victim; he'd been harassed.

Turnbull couldn't imagine himself culpable. It was the rest of the world who hadn't understood.

*

IN THE WEEK AFTER he raised a gun to Glen Turner, Ian Turnbull was moved to the recently refurbished Cessnock Correctional Centre, north of Sydney, among 750 other inmates either on remand or serving sentences. His cell was shiny and white. Its chair and bed were fixed, glossy, the walls laboratorial. Outside the thick-walled, heavily surveilled building, thousands of native seedlings had been planted for some softening green.

Turnbull was in custody there on 5 August when his lawyers walked into Moree Courthouse to announce that the family would offer more than $5 million for bail. His barrister that day, Hament Dhanji SC, offered a ten-point proposal for Turnbull's bail. The defendant could stay with relatives at secluded Castle Cove on Sydney's North Shore, the lawyer said, and could appear daily at Mosman Police Station.

Five million dollars was the amount that Grant Turnbull had said in the Land and Environment Court would bankrupt the family.

Magistrate Darryl Pearce refused bail. The crime was serious, the likelihood that the defendant would, if convicted, serve out the rest of his life for murder. Turnbull was charged, additionally, with the detaining for advantage of Robert Strange. He peered down the monitor of the video link from Cessnock, but said nothing.

*

THE DAY BEFORE TURNBULL'S bail application, Phil Spark had taken a journalist down County Boundary Road. There was a large yellow dozer, with a wide-toothed blade at the back to scrape up trunks, trundling in the soil, kicking up dust below the blue winter sky. The clearing was finishing up on 'Colorado'. The journalist took photos. In the foreground, short, fresh green crops; in the background, a duller smudge, the native vegetation. The dozer went around and around.

12

The first Chief Judge of the Land and Environment Court of NSW, Justice Jim McLelland, described the role of the Court as being to 'balance the aspirations of those who wished to turn Pitt Street into a rainforest and those who wished to turn a rainforest into an industrial estate'.

—**Nicola Pain and Sarah Wright, 'The Rise of Environmental Law in New South Wales and Federally', 2003**

They are all thinking of you.
They hope you are okay.
Keep strong and do your prison exercises.
I hope he's warm and he has something to eat.
Please tell Ian to stay strong.
Yes, I've been telling them that all the family's strength is funnelling through me to Ian.
I've received 40 letters, it's all just support.

We just want you to know that your family have our support.

You look after that man, he's a special person to me.

If there is anything I can do to help, I'm only too willing.

In Moree Courthouse, preparations began for the trial for Glen Turner's death. There was discussion about whether a fair trial could be held in Moree, given the high public feeling in the district.

As long as you [are] keeping strong there's people behind you.

They think of you every day.

They'll send you a birthday card.

You keep strong and keep well.

I saw two people in town and they both wanted to know if they can write to you.

Saw them in the street and they shook my hand and they said they have been thinking of you.

She said Mum wants to ring you but she's afraid she'll cry.

She said we think of Ian every day.

He's thinking of you.

He just wanted to know how you were.

Sylvester Joseph quoted transcripts from phone calls Turnbull received in prison, as well as the encounters Robeena reported as the rural community reacted to the news. They were, he said, simple messages of 'general concern about his health and welfare in custody at eighty-one years of age and reflects their feeling that the shooting was and remains an inexplicable event, in light of Mr Turnbull's age and prior good character'.

'Give Ian our best, tell him we're thinking of him and we're praying for him,' and he gave me a hug and got emotional.

Would you please give Ian our love.

They just want to give their best to you and tell you their [sic] thinking of you.

*

IT WAS ONLY TWO days after Glen Turner was killed that the New South Wales Land and Environment Court gave the final directions for Grant, Cory and Donna to remediate their blocks. Travelling to court in Sydney, they were all still in shock. The directions issued to Grant ran to twenty-nine pages, many of them blank, for Grant to fill in details of weeds removed, seedlings planted, native vegetation remaining. They would remain blank, as the Turnbull family turned its energies to protecting their patriarch.

*

MEANWHILE, THE MURDER OF Glen Turner and the land-clearing saga was splashed across the news. Both *The Daily Telegraph* and *The Sydney Morning Herald* ran major features on 31 July. Reporters had flown into Dubbo and Brisbane and clambered into hire cars, got talking to locals. Moree's wealth was remarked on, the quiet aristocracy of land developers up there in the Golden Triangle, and its welter of more agitated citizens eager to comment on Turnbull's deed.

The small community where Turner died was, a Croppa Creek citizen told a journalist, 'ripped apart' by the crime. 'We just want some good to come of it. We didn't know him very well, but he'd been in this district on and off for some time and everyone would have known of Glen.'

Bec Morrissy, who was involved in the local Landcare group, began a fund to help Turner's family. 'He has done different work with different landholders in the area,' she was quoted saying, 'but it's really a case of the Croppa Creek community being shocked at what's happened in their own backyard and really wanting to rally and help Glen's family.'

The New South Wales environment minister, Rob Stokes, near tears, offered his sympathies to Turner's family and the OEH in parliament, saying, 'Glen was clearly a beautiful man who led a beautiful life and leaves a beautiful family and legacy. We thank him for his service, we grieve his loss.' Flags, he added, would fly at half-mast on all department buildings that weekend. Along with OEH boss Terry Bailey, he would later hand-deliver a book of work colleagues' memories of Turner to his parents in Port Macquarie.

Meanwhile, the NSW Farmers Association and the deputy mayor of Tamworth expressed sentiments of sympathy. Kevin Humphries put out a statement offering his condolences. 'This is a terrible tragedy,' he wrote. 'It is distressing to think there are young children who will grow up without a father after this incident, and I hope the community will rally around them during this difficult time. This is a devastating and traumatic time for many people.'

Someone else in Croppa Creek spoke to the media anonymously:

> That millisecond has affected so many people. It's total sadness. I've known the family for a long time and we're good friends. I just can't put the jigsaw together. It's beyond belief. The environmental laws didn't cause this. Road laws don't cause accidents. I feel so sorry for him and his family, but there's no reason for it to have happened. People have to respect the law ... There is just so much pain on both sides, for everyone involved, for those that knew them or didn't.

Others emphasised the pressures Turner had personified, even as they condemned the killing. *What could you expect,* they said. *A terrible business. They pushed him too far.*

The Telegraph interviewed Moree Plains Shire mayor Katrina Humphries. She was troubled by the case – she took pride in Moree and its prosperity, its local advantages and its recent development; it was she who'd obtained the glossy granite paving for the centre of town. Humphries is hands-on in the district, accessible to all from her fish-and-chip shop in the Moree main street. 'Ian is a well-known and respected member of the community,' she told the paper. 'He has been a part of the community forever. I'm horrified that things have broken down so badly.'

As mayor, Humphries had to speak for both the landholders who were friends with the Turnbulls and the individuals sharing their distress at the violence. 'Violence was always going to happen,' she said. 'I thought it would happen over coal or gas or water ... the frustration is so great but obviously to have an outcome like this is so horrible. What are we doing as communities, as Australians, what are we doing that a tragedy like this happens through absolute frustration?'

She spoke of the 'toxic well of anger' between government, miners, farmers and environmentalists. Native vegetation was a hot-button issue, as was coal-seam gas, water rights and the whole concept of government regulation on private property. Humphries was trying to reflect the concerns of her constituents, but her words sounded partisan, as Turnbull supporters pushed the image of a hounded man – as *The Daily Telegraph* put it in a headline, 'pushed to despair' by a 'feud' that 'consumed a hardworking man of the land'. Everyone now recalled radio broadcaster Alan Jones having fulminated, back in 2010, that supposedly oppressive enforcement of the *Native Vegetation Act 2003* was 'the kind of behaviour that leads people to murder'.

Within days of raising his gun, Turnbull was a martyr. Suffering rose around his reputation like vapour. He was harried, persecuted; an elderly man relentlessly pursued, prosecuted and broken by government authorities who spied on him with surveillance and came onto his property constantly, sometimes with no warning. He'd been provoked into the act. Members of the Turnbull family gave interviews, under condition of not being specifically named, about how 'Dad', in between collecting trampolines for school fetes and delivering Meals on Wheels, had been driven to the brink of despair.

Quickly, the idea circulated that Turner had been trespassing on 'Colorado' when accosted; that he'd been in the process of serving yet another prosecution notice to the family in an unannounced visit. It took a week before Fairfax papers got confirmation from the Moree police that neither of these rumours was true.

Others pushed for a more complete picture of what had happened. 'It makes us look like rednecks,' a Moree businessowner told *Sydney Morning Herald* journalist Rick Fenely. That was the apprehension he was hearing voiced by customers in his cafe. 'We understand the *Native Vegetation Act* can be harsh, but I haven't spoken to anyone today who thought it was inevitably going to lead to violence.'

Fenely went to Humphries for comment. 'No one, but no one,' she said to him, 'is condoning what's happened, but my goal is to make sure it doesn't happen again. We can't stick our heads in the sand and pretend there isn't a problem because there bloody is. I'm fed up to the back teeth with politicians who won't stand up and talk about this ... We've all got some blood on our hands. We've all known this has been an issue for quite some time, and it's not been addressed.'

As the coverage gained momentum, politicians, state and federal, hastened to explain the scenario. 'It's a tragic event that I think has been brought about by bad legislation,' Coffs Harbour MP Andrew Fraser told *The Daily Telegraph*'s sympathetic Ben Pike, who, despite lamenting the loneliness of Talga Lane as a place to die, added that the law required 'strict and cumbersome consents'. The Nationals state leader, Andrew Stoner, was eager to use the moment to prise apart New South Wales' land-clearing laws, 'enforced by

Big-Brother-style satellites', as Pike put it. Federal minister for agriculture and prominent Nationals MP Barnaby Joyce characteristically appealed for 'commonsense' justice for ordinary individuals enduring the authority of the state – overlooking the fact that he himself embodied such authority. 'You have this crazy situation where you don't own the vegetation on your land, the state government does,' he said, 'and many people have had enough.'

***

THE TURNBULL FAMILY, BETWEEN them, ran more than half a dozen properties, as well as other financial interests. They managed staff, maintained expensive machinery, purchased huge quantities of chemical fertiliser and pesticides. They had houses, frequently unoccupied while they visited other residences, and gardens to keep trim. There were fleets of vehicles, shedding, roads to maintain. Portions of interest in family companies and projects had to be negotiated, contracts signed. Actual farming practice needed devising: what to plant, a choice of fertiliser, the timing on each of the properties; which harvests to collect, silo and sell each year. Regulations required all those permissions. Lawyers needed to write letters. There was personal family business, too: the school fees, the normal household bills and projects. Tax returns were a nightmare. The farmhouses had offices crammed with paper.

The mythos has largely gone from Australian farming now. Too much talk from cityfolk of 'extraction', 'resource management', 'exploitation': rapacious terms that turn noble labour into pillage. Farming landscapes are blanks of hedge-fund investment, belonging to diffuse shareholder ciphers embodied on digital screens, or processing plants full of mutilated animals manipulated through their lifecycles according to economics, or the relic endeavours of family farms staggering in the gusts of market demands. There is so little room for 'non-essentials' such as dialogue with the landscape or sentimental instinct for biophilia, intergenerational heritage of native ecologies, stewardship of the scrappy scrub. Anyway, why would anyone need a relationship with a landscape as dull as asphalt?

There is a melancholy to it now, even the victimhood narrative souring, pesticide cancers and suicide quiet killers where once there were spearings, falls from horses, bushrangers and snakebite. In marketing, affable, squinting and behatted farmers are more and more often portrayed against setting suns.

Some farmers – busy clearing remnant native vegetation and spraying the soil, inserting seed with needles, watering and tending to crops, reaping silofuls of grain and cereals – do not often notice the progress from 'vulnerable' to 'threatened' to 'critically endangered' when it comes to the animal and plant populations on their blocks. They do not perceive the blank and denuded land they've made. The vision they see is that printed in high-saturation on cereal packets, tourist pamphlets, annual reports and investment prospectuses: wide, wonderful fields of grain worked by glossy tractors, building 'wealth', feeding the nation, continuing the work of usefully occupying this country.

It took a long time for things to flip, but in the past fifty years the Australian state has inverted – or at least complicated – its traditional roles. Now government encourages industry, even while it has a responsibility to protect the land from the very incursions of industry. This leads to strange alliances, like farmers and conservationists equally opposed to development, mining or the despoliation of the country's natural assets. Citizens are as likely to barricade themselves against government-authorised coal-seam gas exploration licences, dozers relentlessly pushing trees on behalf of the state, as government compliance officers who are there to safeguard the native life of the country.

We are in a long moment when all parties are trying to do two things at once. Governments and the civic institutions within them want development, and they want to protect from development. The population want agency over the government: some of us desire freedom from regulations;

others, freedom to strengthen regulations. It appears our relationship with the land is as binary as ever. Does it owe us its wealth, or do we owe it?

*

TREE FELLING BY EUROPEANS in Australia began on 27 January 1788, the day after their arrival in Botany Bay, as Tim Bonyhady points out in his elegant *The Colonial Earth* (2000). Shelter and fire had to be made, and ground cleared, on the orders of His Majesty's authorities. A few years later, Governors Hunter and Collins ordered some tree felling prohibited, on the basis that it polluted the valuable fresh water. But their concern was for their own resources.

If Ian Turnbull's destiny was shaped by the compression of historical and cultural legacy, so was Glen Turner's. One story of country in Australia is what we have done to change it. Another, less known, is the story of how we have loved and protected it.

The root change in paradigm, to the concept that Australian nature was worth state protection, was a long time forming. Like the Australian colony, its soil was in Europe. It was 1856, more than half a century after decades of booming settlement, that one of the first environmental harm cases in Australia was brought by a landowner, Thomas Power, against a tenant farmer who stripped valuable trees from a property without gaining any cultivation. The tenant argued he was just doing things in the Australian custom, rather than the English way. That custom was to cut down a tree.

The English way, ironically, was to adore a tree. Notwithstanding felling for industry and war, fashions back in the old country in the eighteenth century, historian Keith Thomas relates, were to cultivate exotics and cherish British species; to convert frightening forests to cosy gardens; to give trees 'an almost pet-like status'. Poetic manifestos were published in great masses to protest tree-felling: 'To future ages, may'st thou stand/Untouched by the rash workman's hand', and so on. Under the influence of Rousseau and others, trees, like 'natural man', were encouraged to grow in pleasingly 'wild' ways. 'Everyone who has the least pretension to taste,' wrote one man in 1776, 'must always prefer a tree in its natural growth.' The foliage of Britain formed part of mystical and religious sensibility, and suggested eternity, fecundity. People knew their trees.

Despite the confidence of bewigged Whitehall masters, not everyone still assumed that humans had a divine mandate to dominate nature. Instinct drew people to plant for beauty and comfort, rather than simple utility. As the population became increasingly centred in cities and the threat from dangerous beasts receded, many grew nostalgic for the authenticity and plenty of the countryside. From protests against tight trimming of hedges, voices began to condemn tree-felling altogether. These shifts were, as historian Keith Thomas identifies, 'aspects of a much wider reversal in the relationship of the English to the natural world'. Though it might seem very distant from the grim antagonism of many Australian colonists, that reversal was the seed of the modern environmental and conservationist movements here.

The British Empire, taking possession of the enormous continent of Australia, had an unprecedented opportunity (notwithstanding the Indigenous inhabitants and the insolent convict population) to impose a vast order of land management. But the limits of authority were very quickly made manifest. Governor William Bligh in Sydney was trying, even in 1807, to regulate land use as the township expanded hugely, hoping to preserve open space and give some order to the density of habitations. He was notoriously defeated in this and other reforms, first by the political agitation of his enemies and then by the Rum Rebellion; it was an ill omen for the authority of the state in environmental regulation. And the colony was not here to admire a botanical garden. It was a commercial, administrative and imperial project required to demonstrate its viability.

By the end of that century, Bonyhady says of the irresolute, hypocritical or ineffective legacies of governmental authority, 'it was a commonplace that colonial governments were incapable of implementing their environmental ideals because of their vulnerability to electoral pressure from colonists concerned with short-term advantage rather than their long-term collective interests'. Little has changed in 220 years. Even before Australia was federated, there were tensions between the mandate of the state and the desires of its citizens. 'In a rising colony,' wrote the exasperated Bligh, 'it is of some importance ... that individual convenience should sometimes yield to general regularity and public utility.'

Many settlers mischievously tested the limits of authority. But equally, individuals began to challenge the government when it was incompetent or corrupt. There was even a claim tried, in 1895 in the New South Wales Land Appeal Court, in regard to 'the people's inheritance' of a healthy environment. These first protests were rare and rarely successful, but they were a beginning.

***

THE MOMENT NEWS OF Glen Turner's death came through to Arthur Snook, the OEH thrummed with shock. Some compliance officers were reluctant to leave the office, and voices in the media claiming the death of a state officer was inevitable didn't help. In the days following the crime, all compliance field operations were suspended in New South Wales. The federal department also put everything on hold. What had been a challenging job had become a deadly one.

Environment minister Stokes and the OEH's executive officer, Terrence Bailey, met with the Armidale team that Turner had worked with in the past. Chris Nadolny was there, and Turner's former colleagues from the Environmental Protection Authority were invited in from their adjacent office. Stokes and Bailey spoke sombrely to the shaken staff. They had to acknowledge that one of their number had been killed for doing his job, the same work they were doing.

The OEH considered giving up on continuing to prosecute Ian Turnbull and his family. The man had killed one of their officers, a public servant in the line of his duty, and had explained to witnesses that he was motivated by stopping the investigation. He was claiming his crime was a reaction to persecution, the atrocity a measure of the provocation. He was claiming he had been singled out unjustly. He was banked with Queens' Counsels, supported by his family. Could the department afford to continue a case against a man who was attracting support as a martyr to its 'oppressive' investigation? Could the office afford to continue sending staff into a work environment where their lives could be at risk? Many officers' field trips involved meeting a landholder who owned a gun.

'We all put to our OEH chief executive that we have to go ahead with prosecutions,' says Nadolny. In that meeting, he was still numb from the news. But, as one of the few who knew Ian Turnbull, he spoke up. 'I said in particular that they were regarding Ian as a mad person, that there was no justification in it. I said, "Well, look, there is justification in it if he could get off the charge."'

Simon Smith from the EPA spoke up too. The agency, he felt, had contributed to the escalation of hostilities; now it had to respond. '"This is basically anarchy,"' he remembers saying. 'If you stop now and pull out of this, you're just condoning anarchy. You're pulling back so anyone can just threaten an EPA officer or OEH officer, and we'll run away. That's not regulation. That's not a proper response.'

If the OEH had decided not to continue with the prosecutions, the Turnbulls would have cleared their land with impunity. Turnbull would have a stronger case that Turner was a rogue bully; he might go down for manslaughter, instead of murder. Turner's professional reputation would be injured; the staff would be further demoralised; Turnbull's neighbours might be encouraged in their illegal clearing. The cycle would continue. The way Chris Nadolny tells it, the urgent commitment of Turner's colleagues steadied Terrence Bailey's resolve. Glen had died but his work must be finished. It would be his legacy.

Less than two weeks later, the OEH went ahead with its prosecution of Grant Turnbull for the second batch of clearing on 'Colorado', over the latter half of 2012. Six weeks after that, on 19 September, the OEH was in court, seeking remediation orders for that clearing, and an injunction to stop Grant from entering and clearing the parts of 'Colorado' that hadn't yet been pushed. In between the court appearances, Bailey approved yet another inspection of the properties, five weeks after Phil Spark and a journalist had seen the continuing clearing. They got the interim injunction against Grant 'to restrain any further unlawful clearing or further damage being done to the cleared land'. With the patriarch in jail facing a murder charge, an avalanche of the law was belatedly falling on the Turnbulls.

*

IN DISTANT SYDNEY AT the same time, policy writers and lobby groups, senators and consultant ecologists were poring over documents that would be another legacy of the encounter between Glen Turner and Ian Turnbull on that winter road. They were notes towards a complete overhaul of the native vegetation protection laws of the state.

When Turnbull faced Turner over the gate at 'Strathdoon' back in late 2011, the government was a new Liberal–National coalition under Barry O'Farrell. By the time Turnbull was clearing the last remnants of native vegetation on 'Colorado' three years later, Mike Baird was premier. His leadership bid had been supported, according to Phil Spark, by the NSW Farmers Association, allegedly on an understanding that he would help pass legislation to undo some regulations against land clearing. On Baird's retirement from the premiership in 2017, certainly, NSW Farmers thanked him for the changes to the laws. O'Farrell had helped to establish the Office of Environment and Heritage to administer protections for ecologies. Glen Turner was a compliance officer authorised by a government that had, for most of its history, been on the other side. If Turnbull had cleared fifty years earlier, he would have been legal;

if Glen Turner had been a compliance officer then, he might have been urging the pushing of more trees.

***

THE ROVING, HOMESICK, WEIRD colonial brain wanted connection. Dissociative appreciation of the bush was one method. Australian flora and fauna, those perverse phenomena by which colonists were so embarrassed, came to ornament a continent that boasted of its exceptionality and its youthful zest. Kangaroo and emu were chosen for the Commonwealth coat of arms even as bounties encouraged their killing; Henry Lawson, Banjo Paterson, Rosa Praed, Marcus Clarke and Adam Gordon Lindsay evoked a rural world that actually frightened many of their readers. But plenty of Australian people did love the bush – at least the idea of it, if not the reality.

Gigantic old-growth trees were discovered as felling penetrated deep forest. Such majesty and evident antiquity evoked some of the awe for the past that Europeans felt was miserably lacking in this cathedral-less and castle-less continent. Language began to show a sense of belonging and investment in the land: some did sense they were the watershed for the future. The term 'heritage' came to be used.

And if the empire taught that its subjects were backwards, imitative, derivative, provincial, barbarian and marginal, Australians embraced this renegade status. It was *our* heritage. As Rebecca Solnit muses in her work on emigration and identity, *A Book of Migrations* (1997), the outlier-ness of imperial colonies is claimed and flipped by postcolonial nationalisms: 'A nationalist movement or and independence movement is an assertion by its promulgators that theirs is a center, not a periphery.'

Colonists, Solnit suggests, emphasised the 'wildness' of the territory they worked upon. 'They were ultimately producing another first-world fantasy: the uninhabited "virgin" wilderness that still exists in many wildlife and nature documentaries ... and in the fantasies of would-be discoverers then and now.' This potent and enduring fallacy also abides in the foundations of Australian environmentalism.

In modern times, many a tourism campaign has photographed white Australians standing on rocky outcrops, gazing rapturously across a chasm of red rocks or green peaks into a radiant distance that dissolves like an epiphany. The forests of Tasmania and Far North Queensland, the epic central deserts, rushing rivers and bush-covered mountains, are our glory, the kind of thing we boast about to European cousins sitting miserably in Birmingham or Catania. We have deserts you can die in before you've finished walking a tenth of their span; forests as opaque and menacing as anything in a German fairytale; we have droughts and flooding rains. Our wildlife can make you gasp at its wonders or kill you in an instant. Australia, with its 'beauty and its terror', we teach ourselves, is exceptional. Our wilderness, we like to brag, is *wild*.

For some, the wilderness was the stage that set off the gallantry of its humans, the cast of a patriotic national saga. For others, the wilderness was, in its defiance and endurance and vulnerability, our secret treasure, a mystery to be unlocked; a vast, quiet patrimony.

We killed and ran off the first inheritors of that patrimony. We demolished much of the work they had done, and devastated much else. Could the rest be salvaged, and would it welcome our protection? Might it ever forgive us? These were the questions that gradually emerged over the twentieth century, in what very gradually evolved into environmental and conservation movements.

There are countless conservation groups in Australia today. They all cherish the idea of wilderness and work devotedly to protect nature under threat. The people who support those causes try to conceive of intricate relationships of ecologies; they may work in offices and meeting rooms, or out in the field, researching, safeguarding and even blockading; some live in natural environments or remote areas. The great majority, like the general population, are non-Indigenous. And they sometimes forget what Jay

Griffiths reminded herself: that indigenous peoples 'have a different word for wilderness: home'.

The Indigenous Australian continent was not self-willed. It, too, had been shaped, maintained, curated. It was not wild, but it was not domesticated, either. Non-Indigenous Australians sometimes struggle to parse the difference. A humanless landscape may not be pristine but evacuated; ecstatic fecundity may actually be damage; quickly, one's assumptions become tangled as weed. We love our wilderness distant not only for its romance but the remoteness of its questions.

Are 'we', mostly non-Indigenous Australian descendants of settlers and colonists and migrants, the new custodians of Australian nature? Are we culprits or their repentant opponents? Do we want to be – should we be – custodians, diligently repairing damage done, or, wary of causing further inadvertent harm, should we leave nature to fix itself? Is nature in need of our support, or is it the fierce and enduring legacy of millions of years of evolution, battered but ultimately impervious to our pathetic attitudes? And the biggest question of all: should we think of European settlement as a good thing or a bad?

13

To those people who put immediate utilitarianism in front of everything, let me remind them that we are pioneers of a continent – a continent which possesses a remarkable and in many respects a unique vegetation; and the pleas of those who ask that the specialised vegetation should not be destroyed unnecessarily is worthy of some regard.

—**Joseph Maiden, *From the Useful Native Plants of Australia,* 1889**

On 10 September 2014, the OEH sent Chris Nadolny and fellow ecologist Terry Mazzer to inspect the latest bout of clearing on 'Colorado'. With them for protection were the New South Wales police. Nadolny was reassured by their presence, but it had come to this: government officers protected by firearms, a vision of the old colonial days.

They could see now what Turnbull had been doing the week Turner was killed. Since Nadolny had been there the previous December, 'Colorado', including the areas reserved for remediation, had been vigorously cleared. It seems the last of the clearing had gone on for nearly a month after Turner's death.

Grant was supposed to be following the final directions on remediation on the property. But the remnant endangered ecological communities of brigalow and box, the native grasses that had begun to return, the koala habitat: it had all been pushed.

The officers walked over the ground, silent with feeling. There, to the north, was the boundary fence, towards which Turner had run for shelter before the final bullet caught him. On the far side of that fence was the road, the soil he'd bled into. There were the ashes of the stacked timber that had been burning that night, beacons that made him stop the car, that flared in Robert Strange's photographs below the last twilight Turner saw. There were the invisible marks of the trees that had been felled, the unmappable sites of vanished vegetation, koalas' obliterated tracks and fertility blanched from the soil. This was where their colleagues had worked so hard, and for so little. This was where Turner had stood to take GPS readings of his observations. This was where he had to stand and watch the dozers. This was the place the OEH itself was being tried. It was a great blank now, a fenced space, churned smooth of all its history, ready to be sown with the staff of life.

*

JUST OVER A WEEK later, on 19 September, Ian Turnbull was given sentence for the first lot of clearing on 'Strathdoon', and what had still been called 'Lochiel'. For his own actions and his direction of others to clear, Turnbull was fined $140,000 plus costs to the prosecution. The court found that Turnbull had been aware that approval was required and hadn't had it. For seven months after being issued with a stop-work order, he had continued to clear. Justice Sheahan found that over 3000 trees had been felled – an environmentally 'significant' number, leaving the dislocated fauna without enough habitat. 'I find that the level of the environmental harm caused was substantial,' said Sheahan, and that 'Ian's conduct was reckless breach, a factor that increases the objective seriousness of his offence'. Indeed, the judge said, he'd 'flagrantly disregarded the consequences of his actions'.

The old man heard this. Had he been expecting it? He had been described by a friend as 'devastated' years earlier when charged: his community was watching. His son and grandson were implicated. Everyone in the district was converting grazing land to cropping: why had he been singled out? The Croppa Creek golf club would be talking. The media was outside.

Even so, facing a possible fine of up to $1.1 million and costs possibly up to $340,000, he had got off lightly.

***

THERE ARE THOSE WHO believe we inherit the earth. For them, nature is a gift. There are others who see humans in a stewardship role. As elders need the assistance of their children, so

Mother Nature needs our help when enfeebled.

There are others still who can only perceive humans as a metastasising cancer consuming its host, best removed or contained. The healthiest places in the world are those unpolluted by human presence.

A stateswoman of American conservationism, Margaret 'Mardy' Murie, described this sentiment as she composed the founding ethos of the *Wilderness Act 1964,* which covenanted 9 million acres of federal land in the United States for wilderness reserves. 'A wilderness,' Murie wrote, 'in contrast with those areas where man and his own works dominate the landscape, is hereby recognised as an area where the earth and its community of life are untrammeled by man, where man himself is a visitor who does not remain.' Her definition has become famous for its precision and its cogency.

But humans 'attribute qualities to a landscape which it does not intrinsically possess', according to British nature writer Robert Macfarlane. 'We read landscapes, in other words, we interpret their forms in the light of our own experience and memory, and that of our shared cultural memory.' A dream of wilderness is a necessary emollient for those who feel humans do damage to the land. Its unruliness is what we feel has been lost from the modern human sphere, where maintenance and control are our habit: erotic Dionysos to chilly Apollo.

There is a final tribe, often a mix of Indigenous peoples and Western philosophers, who hold faith in an Earth able to maintain itself – animals, rivers, gardens, humans all. 'We were born wild to a wild earth,' believes Jay Griffiths. 'To me, humanity is not a stain on wilderness, as some seem to think. Rather, the human spirit is one of the most striking realizations of wildness. It is as eccentrically beautiful as an ice crystal, as liquidly life-generous as water, as inspired by air. Kerneled up within us all, an intimate wildness, sweet as a nut.' Humans and nature are not separate but one whole. Systems decay and recompose, energies braid in currents that cannot be stopped but must continually change course: nature as a rhythm, not a particle but a wave.

***

IN CESSNOCK CORRECTIONAL CENTRE, Turnbull was keeping in touch with his family by phone. He knew he was being recorded, but he spoke freely. In phone calls in September and October 2014, he made what a judge would term 'strong critical comments about the OEH and its officers ... indicating a strong dislike by the Accused of that agency and its officers including the deceased, Mr Turner, and Dr Christopher Nadolny, an ecologist'. He agreed with his wife: Nadolny was 'just a nasty piece of work', a 'sneaky snipy bloody snake in the grass'.

On 2 October, Turnbull was transferred from Cessnock to the Supreme Court in King Street, Sydney. He was again applying for bail. Robeena told the court of her husband's ill health, stoicism through pain, debilitating weakness due to peripheral neuropathy. He could barely walk ten steps, she said, before collapsing. She was also suffering, doing weekly twelve-hour round trips by plane from Grant's place in Brisbane to Cessnock to visit her husband.

The shooting was an isolated incident, Robeena told the court. The night he came home from Talga Lane, he said he'd simply cracked. 'I didn't mean to kill him,' he'd told her. He looked 'wretched': 'His face was blank, it appeared as though he was somewhere else.'

But the court also heard of Turnbull's angry descriptions of Turner and Nadolny. He'd told a prison psychologist the crime was 'the deceased's' fault. It heard how the Turnbulls sat in armchairs for five hours, stolidly waiting for the police to arrive, while Glen Turner bled out in the dark.

Bail was refused. Turnbull, the judge said, was rich enough to flee, and, faced with murder charges, had considerable incentive to do so. It was likely that his hostility to authorities had been noted in his community. He was a danger to the OEH staff, and to the public in general.

*

IN THE MOREE DISTRICT, the talk continued.

Turnbull was still being sent messages from supporters. Many stopped short of praising the murder itself, though some did not.

He was pushed too far, people continued to mutter in the pubs and supermarket car parks. The government picked on him; they pushed him to the brink. By picking up the gun he'd only showed the desperation many others felt. When Turnbull cleared his land and when he was investigated for it, when he was told that weeds were more important than his family's survival, and when he fired his gun at the man representing the authorities, he stood on the soil of Talga Lane for many.

The September verdict in the land-clearing case on 'Colorado' came just at the right time for those who saw him as a scapegoat. Turnbull's acts became the hinge on which big things swung. He was used as an example by supporters of farmers' rights. His became the back that had been broken for them all.

On the other side, Glen Turner joined a numberless list of those who have died protecting the environment. The Thin Green Line, it is sometimes called. Turner wasn't patrolling the jungles of Colombia, protecting gorillas against poachers in the Democratic Republic of Congo or protesting mining projects in Turkey, but his was the first recorded death of its kind in Australia since the infamous 1975 murder of journalist Juanita Nielsen in Sydney for opposing the Victoria Point development. It was shocking because, for all the grousing, authority is generally respected in Australia. While disputes over land management, resource extraction and conservation run hot, few people since the massacres of First Nations peoples have died directly from them. In 2014, at least 116 people – 'the defenders', as they are sometimes memorialised – were murdered across the globe for their resistance to environmental damage, and the number would only rise further in coming years. They would include indigenous peoples, rangers and activists. But it was shocking that a father of two would be gunned down outside a wealthy town like Moree.

The death of a martyr is the beginning of a story. Glen Turner's murder was mourned for the loss of a man discharging a public duty. Only later was it publicly decried as a death in the cause of protecting nature. Turner's official role was emphasised in media reports, and his stunned colleagues and peers across the country felt the impact of his death on morale and protocol. His name was added to the International Ranger Federation Honour Roll of those killed on the job.

But the victimhood narrative endowed on Turnbull was stronger. The image of the man holding the gun, defending his right to the land, is a composition we have been encouraged to honour. 'Pushed to the brink on the land' is an old story. 'Authorised to protect the scrub' is not.

*

WITH BAIL REFUSED AND the court case some way off, the Turnbulls coolly made new plans. At some point in 2015, Ian sold his various property holdings to his wife for a dollar each. It was, he told the Supreme Court a year later, only so that Robeena could keep the farm running while he was in jail, awaiting trial.

Roger saw how things were heading. His father's situation was inhaling all the family energy, the assets, the entitlements. The elder son had been on the outer with the family before the shooting, and the feeling now was that he wasn't being loyal enough to his dad. He had supposedly warned the police that the old man was dangerous. Roger and his wife had even been in contact with Alison McKenzie, to express their condolences.

For twenty-six years, Roger would maintain in a statement of claim to the Supreme Court in 2016, he'd helped his parents with their properties. This was, he alleged, despite his father's bullying and frequent apportioning of blame for everything that went wrong; despite the phone calls demanding his urgent presence on the farm for what turned out to be a trivial task; despite taunts of his divided loyalty and insults to his wife and his children.

There was an understanding, Roger reminded his relatives, that whoever committed to the family business in this way had been guaranteed its inheritance. There was a legacy: millions and millions of dollars of agricultural investment over fifty years, the prestige and power his father had amassed, a dominant Turnbull presence in the district. Roger had done what was asked. For the first few decades of his adult life, the statement claimed, he'd worked unpaid, unthanked. For his devoted toil, the inheritance was to be his. Instead, his father called him 'stupid'. He was blamed for spells of drought.

He'd had his own troubles, with the OEH looking into business on his properties 'Talmoi' and 'Royden', and that incident with detaining the compliance officers, but he'd kept going, even with his son Cory dragged into all the mess, his boy devastated by what had happened and liable for absurd fines, convictions even. His grandfather had wrecked the boy's future before it had even begun.

Roger and Annette had other children to look after, two of them with special needs, and there was sour blood in the mix of emotions: Turnbull had always taken against Annette. She didn't come with land when she married Roger; Turnbull told his son, 'You've made a bad choice in wife, you're getting what you deserve.' He blamed her for the boys' condition. 'You have disabled children,' she says he told her, 'because you have rotten eggs.'

Then there was Roger's own little brother, Grant, dashing onto the scene during the clearing, and then off again to Queensland, leaving his eighty-year-old father to do all the work. The brothers had barely talked since the late 1990s, when they'd had a falling-out. There was a partition agreement drawn up then to silo parts of the Turnbull money to the sons on Turnbull's retirement, and Roger had stopped working full-time for his father based on this understanding. It was twenty years ago now, but Roger assumed that the agreement hadn't changed. Even when Turnbull kept shifting his retirement age back. Now the brothers were having to deal with each other, with their father in the middle of it all, still controlling them.

Roger was alert to the dangers to his entitlement. The lawyers' fees – Cole & Butler, a QC and the rest of the team – would consume a fortune. If Turnbull was found guilty, Turner's family would probably sue for damages. Robert Strange would sue for damages. The wealth of the Turnbull family would be chewed away.

Roger got a letter from his father in jail. It was the last one he'd get. Turnbull informed him there was no inheritance for him yet. They would need to keep hold of the estate because they'd need the money to defend him on a charge of murder – though they were hoping he would be convicted of manslaughter at worst. If so, there would be some kind of reduced sentence. He was an old man. He was a pillar of the community. Now look what had happened. In a way, he was a victim too. So they'd also need cash for when he got out of jail.

Then Turnbull goaded his son, accused him of sympathy with Turner over his own father. 'Your second best friend Turner has got me in jail for more than likely the rest of my natural life,' he wrote. 'And it will take a lot of mum's money to even get that over.'

Roger went to his mother. She confirmed that she now owned the properties.

A silence fell within the Turnbull family. It was the silence of an inhale.

14

> And in all the land of your possession ye shall grant a redemption for the land.
> —**Leviticus 25:24**

The history of environmentalism in Australia has faded somewhat, along with the old Wilderness Society posters of the Franklin Dam, and its current resurgence in the face of annihilating threats can feel amnesiac. But its story is as formed by cultural compression and shove of circumstance as that of agriculture and settlement.

We forget that dismay is an old feeling. After initial confidence in an eternal frontier, the scale of destruction as ringbarking took hold in the mid-nineteenth century took people aback; the apparently infinite forests showed gaps. The plains turned out to be finite after all, and there was no sight of the inland sea. The 1860s are called the decade of environmentalism: by then, already, less than a century into white occupation of Australia, the degree of change alarmed many. From the rich soil of the Romantic period and the stems of science in the Enlightenment grew a surprising bloom – a care for nature. In 1864 George Perkins Marsh published *Man and Nature* in America, which, along with the impassioned writings of Henry David Thoreau, had a galvanising effect on concerned types. 'With the disappearance of the forest, all is changed,' Marsh intoned. His work showed how the physical environment had altered: soil health, vegetation types and amounts, rainfall, temperature and weather patterns. The book was avidly read here, and the government of New South Wales, heeding Marsh, decreed the first timber reserves in 1871; that 100-foot-wide strip of vegetation left along the coast helped create Australian beach culture.

The world's first national park, Yellowstone in the United States, was created in 1872, and seven years later the second was established: Royal National Park, south of Sydney. This was one of the first major instances of a government authority acting to protect the environment against development, and a new momentum took energy, which would eventually be realised in departments of the environment, in regulations and the enforcement of protection of ecological communities.

New South Wales had formed a branch of the Royal Society in 1866; the Linnean Society of NSW arrived in 1884. These precursors to the CSIRO were research bodies devoted to practical concerns: scholars pursued nascent agricultural science, studying soil health and vegetation prospects for potential cultivation. There could be no question of sacrificing industry to nature, but perhaps a compromise could be attained.

And in the unlikely setting of Bendigo, Victoria, possibly the world's first conservation group met in 1888. Rural citizens, says historian Tim Bonyhady, could be more preoccupied with conservation issues than the louder voices coming from cities through the press and political stages, where economic and cultural prestige were shouted about and fashions on the subject of native vegetation vacillated.

Bendigo had just had a drought and floods, exacerbated, locals felt, by clearing. Now people began to coordinate their concerns.

In New South Wales, too, there had been a terrible drought, and the government launched a commission into water conservation. Historian Cameron Muir tells of how an alert, thoughtful researcher called Robert Peacock explained to the commission his revelation that the problem wasn't the recalcitrant scrub, but bushwhacking, which had violently disturbed some equilibrium. In 1900 he published an article condemning the state of the land. Its degradations, he wrote urgently, were 'too familiar landmarks, resulting from the mistakes of the past, and calculated to teach valuable lessons to those willing to listen to the voice and teachings of Nature'.

There were those willing. Groups continued to cohere, like-minded doubters of the progress ethos gathering and sharing their theories. Furrowed brows bent over pages of minutes. A bifocalism was opening between those on the land: between those who, looking backwards with long vision, foresaw trouble ahead, and those who, gazing a short way ahead, ignored the present and the past.

Late in the century unfederated Australia still lacked a central authority for issues like basic sanitation or the distribution of water. Almost from the start, people, sceptical of government and remote from the bases of authority, had had to solve problems on their own. The impulse was still colonialist: even among naturalists, the attitude was often exploitative, manically sourcing specimens for natural history collections and tramping across fragile ecosystems in eagerness to be the first to describe a species. Then the 'bushwalking conservation movement', those hardy souls led by Myles Dunphy who bashed around the scrub for fun, began to push for more authenticity in the urban surrounds. The amateurs were mobilised. They were, in a way, as selfish as the settlers who wanted to use land for other purposes. But their intentions marked a turning point.

*

IT WAS A COMBINATION of scientists and writers who pushed the environment into a brighter foreground in Australia. In the 1940s two men, scientist Francis Ratcliffe and broadcaster Philip Crosbie Morrison, both made calls for nature that were too loud to ignore.

Ratcliffe's writing on the derelict interior put an end to dreams for populating those landscapes. In the 'Dirty Thirties' he had looked down a railway track north of Broken Hill: on one side, untouched scrub with clear air; on the other, a stock-compacted 'yellow asphalt' blowing away. Australians, said Ratcliffe, have 'every reason to be intensely proud of their record in settling the great spaces of the inland'. They were only to be chastened, he quipped, 'in that they seem to have done the job too thoroughly'.

Crosbie Morrison was a radio journalist, and editor of the magazine *Wild Life,* which later also had a hugely popular radio program. His mission was to engage the general public and amateur enthusiasts in love for, and then conservation of, the natural Australian world. As World War II raged, he proposed nature as a balm to the spirit, as consoling as religion.

Although there had been conservation agencies since the early twentieth century, they focused on 'resource conservation', not 'nature conservation'. The point was to support the land so it could support agriculture and grazing. The federal research agency CSIRO was invested in problems like soil erosion, rabbit plagues, irrigation, dust storms and fires. State departments managed some issues around fauna, but usually licences around hunting or fishing; wedge-tailed eagles, galahs, cockatoos and kangaroos were all evaluated not for their vulnerability but in terms of the threat they posed to human endeavours. It was community groups, field naturalists and bird-watching leagues that took up concern for the wellbeing of native wildlife and vegetation. In Victoria, Crosbie Morrison drew focus for many people worried about the nature under pressure from development. Dunphy's campaign promoting walking maps and information, and his belief that the best scenery should be reserved for public use and benefit, and later Crosbie Morrison's idea that if you show people the natural world they will instinctively respond with sympathy and protection, encouraged human relationship with nature. Humans must trudge in heavy boots over fragile ecosystems, must disturb Eden. Better we enter it, find presence, find our human scale against its immensity. But soon campaigns focused on the idea of protecting nature by keeping it separate from humans in parks and reserves.

Public defence of nature, too, began its identity as separate from, even opposed to, authority. In the subsequent years this would twist strangely, so that Ian Turnbull, descendent of settlers, could find himself defending his idea of 'conservation' against Glen Turner, agent of government, charged with the same mission that began in opposition to the authority he now held.

The areas initially selected for reserves were not necessarily those most in need of protection, but the most convenient or inexpensive for the government to put aside. Their boundaries were frequently, haphazardly, defined by more important projects: golf courses, mining sites, arable areas. They enclosed land previously cleared for plantations, or were located atop landfill sites, in former Aboriginal missions, or on old sewage works. Their value as natural assets was perversely determined by their lack of material wealth.

Then along came 'gap analysis', which used broadscale vegetation mapping to find 'gaps' in order to plan for future reserves. The Australian Academy of Science, founded in 1954, pioneered these projects. Gap analysis was an early union between the worlds of resource conservation and nature conservation, because it gave quantifiable evidence of changes in the physical environment. 'The scientific approach cooled emotional pleas about saving bushland and provided a way to make pragmatic choices,' Libby Robin explains. 'Nature reserves were no longer just a matter of personal taste or aesthetics, nor would they be limited to the "leftover lands".' At last, biological resources would be given the dubious distinction of economic value.

The science was horribly eye-opening. The gaps were enormous: biological diversity was at dreadful risk from development. So began, in earnest, conservation biology: what Robin calls the 'science of crisis'.

Partly this was driven from the cities, from where 'the countryside' felt more and more remote. The nationalist interest in landscape shifted focus from the battler on the land to the more distant and evocative deserts, oceans and wildernesses. Thus by late in the twentieth century, agriculture and rural scrub, in the middle zone, seemed more and more 'other', devalued, even quaint.

In the cities we still don't really know or care about agricultural lands: on the map, as we drive out into the countryside, many places are marked as blank, what Val Plumwood called 'shadow places', those 'we don't know about, don't want to know about, and … don't ever need to know about'. Most of us are ignorant of whatever nature remains there. We drive fluidly past kilometre after kilometre of farmland, oblivious, seeing only picturesque cows or sheep, pleasant meadows, colourful crops; some more lovely, some less.

We do not map silence, where frogs once croaked or birds called. We do not map movement, of wildlife at night, migration paths, seeds blowing in the wind, the places where shadows used to lie beneath trees, or animals and people who are no longer there. We do not map ghosts.

***

TURNBULL WAS PLEADING, IN the pre-trial hearings in the Supreme Court, not guilty to the murder of Glen Turner, but guilty to the lesser charge of manslaughter, on the grounds of substantial impairment.

Others were also preparing for the trial. Over at 'Talga', Felicity Whibley looked over the statement she had written by hand after that terrible night: 'I was at the stove cooking dinner. Brenton and our son Matthew were watching TV in the loungeroom.' She had carefully inserted 'adjoining' before 'loungeroom'. 'At the same time the phone started ringing,' she wrote, and told the story. She had hesitated over how to phrase the need for someone with first aid; she crossed out the phrase 'And I was trying to both process and catch what both men were saying', referring to Michael Coulton on the phone and Andrew Uebergang at the door. Both men were saying 'almost the exact same thing': 'Ian Turnbulls [sic] had just shot someone, multiple times, I think he said chest & back and that it was bad.'

Felicity had trouble sleeping after the crime, she wrote. Her statement concludes, 'Since that night I have been in shock ... I have not been myself.'

***

IN THE MIDDLE OF the twentieth century, after a hundred and fifty years of Australian agriculture violently slamming from triumph to disaster, optimism to apocalypse, and back, thought was given to the idea of balance.

The 'balance of nature' extolled in pious seventeenth-century Europe was echoed by modern science with the emerging doctrine of 'wise use' – the judicious application of technology to use the land, but not abuse it. Industrialists and primary producers liked this concept, as it allowed them to continue farming with, in fact, the promise of more growth. Politicians and historians liked that it fitted with the narrative of progress, improving the land. And would-be conservationists liked that it chimed with the ecological system of 'equilibrium', imagined as a kind of zen state of perfect functionality.

There was a moment when ecology was seen as a close companion with wise-use agriculture. With time, the popular concept of ecology became more and more identified with the side defending nature against industry. But ecology itself is science, neutral.

In her examination of the galvanising Little Desert campaign of the late 1960s, Libby Robin identifies a difference between ecology and 'ecological consciousness', a form that engages attitudes in 'individual, collective and political senses', and emerged over more than a century. It wasn't until 1949, when American biologist and conservationist Aldo

Leopold published his celebrated *A Sand Country Almanac,* that modern ecological consciousness found popular expression; thirteen years later, Rachel Carson's *Silent Spring* confirmed its worst fears. The seeds were sown for the environmental movement. But the full harvest of ecological studies, and its political or metaphysical consciousness, wouldn't be reaped until the 1980s and beyond. By the 1960s, Marxist and postmodern critics were applying structural critiques to feminist, race and labour issues, but the science that guided conservation was respected: a practical, utilitarian way of looking at nature, for both a farmer with an ag scientist by his side or a bushwalker keen to access scrub. Nature was not yet political.

It was, ironically, the workers of the industrial world who introduced a political element. In 1970, Jack Mundey and the New South Wales Builders Labourers' Federation began 'green bans' on construction work on urban bushland at Kelly's Bush in Sydney. This radical instant, which attracted the impulsive support of many, came at a time when people began to perceive an acute finitude to resources. Talk of population pressures, oil supply politics, the rapid disappearance of bushland due to postwar development, the increasing salinity and aridity of the Australian interior and the rise of private interests grabbing at public assets – sand-mining proposals on Fraser Island or the flooding of Lake Pedder in Tasmania – irritated and worried people in a new way. New Age mysticism, folksy nostalgia and worship of Gaia collided with pragmatic concerns over resource capacity; wistfully, people looked for wilderness.

The 1970s were ferocious times for conservationists. Huge amounts of energy and discussion were expended on multiple causes: commercial whaling, sand mining, hydro-electric schemes, old-growth logging, nuclear proliferation, chemical pollution, desecration of Aboriginal heritage, overfishing and other threats to Australia's ecologies. On the other side traditional interests were pressing for cheaper power and dams, and expanded resource extraction, and against the concept of

Aboriginal land rights. There were calls for 'limits to development' and to 'think global, act local'. People began to think of themselves as stewards of the planet and to feel they had agency in preserving it. Much of the energy for environmentalist campaigns came from cityfolk, drawing on international connections and calling meetings in suburban homes and inner-city pubs. The neighbourhoods rang with arguments and chants, the streets thrummed with marching feet and Roneo presses whirred with newsletters. Mining magnate Lang Hancock had to yell to be heard when he snarled about 'these people, whose numbers are swelled by a great mass of unwashed, unspanked, dole-bludging dropouts'.

Somewhere, forgotten in all this, were the back blocks of rural country – the unspectacular scrub, the quiet animals, softly being sprayed with DDT, mutely witnessing the soil wash away.

*

FEW NATURE-LOVERS MAKE PILGRIMAGES to the brigalow copses in Croppa Creek. Alongside the Newell

Highway, which runs north from Gunnedah to Moree, are some of the travelling stock route reserves still used by both grazing stock and koalas; they are only a few metres deep, pinned between roaring trucks and cleared paddocks, the rest stops littered with cigarette butts and yoghurt squeezies. But 'west of the highway', says Alaine Anderson, 'you can do a 360-degrees and not see a tree'. The besieged patches of native scrub are the last of this land as it was before Europeans arrived, the last of a fully functional ecosystem; but they are a cause taken up by few. The words 'native vegetation protection legislation' do not get hearts racing.

There is a term in biology, essential to understanding how we relate to nature: 'shifting baseline syndrome', coined by a fisheries expert, Daniel Pauly. We calibrate the health of nature around us according to what we knew as children. We may faintly credit our parents' and grandparents' accounts of an unrecognisable world before we were born, but each generation defines a new baseline for normality: what the weather is like in summer, how forested the hills are, how many fish makes a typical catch from the ocean. We can lament but barely comprehend the massive changes that preceded our awareness. We don't really understand that the baseline, after two centuries of occupation, is already in 'a state of extreme depletion'.

We still have May Gibbs's stories of flannel flower babies and Mr Lizard in our children's libraries, but that world already feels like a fairytale. A third of all mammal species have become extinct since Europeans invaded. Almost half of the 3.7 million hectares of native grassland in western New South Wales at white settlement has been destroyed or replaced; less than 1 per cent of the temperate grasslands in all of eastern Australia is 'unmodified'.

Within two hundred years Australia had arrived in a situation where only manic discipline of activism and research seems able to safeguard the natural. Australia now has nearly thirty major conservation organisations, plus several state and federal departments of environment, official research bodies such as the CSIRO, and tangential research projects across universities and private enterprises, as well as countless local enthusiast and activist assemblies. Keeping nature natural takes a lot of work.

Our faith in science has become ambivalent. Some historians believe nature conservation, rationally supported by research, is, ironically, a legacy of the same Enlightenment that created its requirement. Science authoritatively describes for us now the benefits of human contact with natural places: how the heart rate slows, respiratory issues decrease, vitality is restored, peace and happiness increase, depression may lift. Research consistently shows the need for deeper conservation, yet policies don't reflect this in practice. The manipulation and vacillations of conservation science, with its failures to predict environmental consequences, impractical solutions to perceived problems and ill-conceived support for projects such as flooding Lake Pedder, has made some people sceptical.

We have dug deep holes in the earth with our foundations, and rather

than learning to skirt them, we are somehow still falling in.
***

JUSTICE PETER JOHNSON DECIDED against holding the murder trial in Moree. There was too much hot feeling there; locals were mortified by the crime in their district, while the Turnbulls were apparently overwhelmed with supporters to pitch in complaints about Turner in support of Turnbull's defence that he'd been harassed. Detective McCarthy, who'd attended the crime scene and arrested Turnbull at 'Yambin', attested that it would be hard to find an impartial jury in Moree given the small pool of eligible populace, and that police had concerns about maintaining security in the courtroom.

McCarthy told the court that Robeena had met with Moree mayor Katrina Humphries, who was hearing a lot about the Turnbull case from all sides. Robeena told her husband about the meeting later, in recorded phone conversations, reassuring him that 'everyone' she spoke to in town supported him – though whether this meant support for his actions or his wellbeing in jail was an open question. Turnbull confided in turn that even a corrective services officer in Long Bay had voiced his approval. 'What you've done has done more for the cause than you could imagine,' the officer had apparently said.

Despite solicitor Sylvester Joseph and barrister Todd Alexis QC arguing forcefully that Turnbull should be tried by his peers in his own community, McCarthy's argument, in which land management was part of a murder trial, held sway: 'Beliefs regarding the policing of land protection laws have been formed over many years, even generations. It is a contentious issue in Country New South Wales. It is questionable if the court could find an individual who would be prepared to attend jury duty, who does not opine one way or the other.'

The Crown prosecutor agreed. It was hashed out in diligent discussion until eventually, 'for reason of local prejudice or by reason of widespread prejudice among the class from which the jurors are to be selected, or because local prejudice might be thought to exist', Justice Johnson decided the trial would be held in Sydney, at the Supreme Court. The date was set, finally, for April 2016.

*

THAT SAME MONTH, NEARLY two years after the horror of Talga Lane, Robert Strange submitted documents to the Supreme Court, filing for damages for negligence, false imprisonment and assault. His lawyers were seeking up to $1.85 million for the injuries to his mental health from Turnbull's actions that winter night. But they would find that Ian Turnbull's worth was reduced. This was even as the value of the land on 'Strathdoon' and 'Colorado' was booming under their bloom of crops. Turnbull owned virtually nothing by 2016; all the properties and holdings belonged to Robeena. And Strange's lawyers would be blocked from even tendering to the court the transcript of audio files of Turnbull and his family arranging the transfers.

The farmer did not deny he'd forcibly detained Strange in order to kill

Turner, but his QC Alexis told the court his client couldn't summarily plead guilty to the other counts, of negligence and assault. Strange would have to be content with the detaining, or fight for the rest.

Meanwhile, Alison McKenzie made arrangements for Ian Turnbull's murder trial. She scheduled four weeks off work. She would have to travel to Sydney, leaving Alexandra and Jack to be cared for by relatives and friends. It would be one of the most awful months of her life, but at the end of it, she hoped, there would be justice for Glen.

But the trial preparations dragged on. Turnbull's lawyers argued every point; they wanted a trial as early as possible, they said, but disputed issue after issue.

'Eight weeks,' McKenzie lamented later. 'Eight weeks away from work, eight weeks commuting back and forth to Sydney so I could spend weekends with the children, the huge monetary and emotional expense of being away from home for that amount of time.'

She was speaking to documentary filmmaker Gregory Miller, who was following the case. McKenzie had agreed, along with her sister-in-law Fran Pearce, that he could accompany her throughout the trial and record her reactions, in hopes that any publicity would help raise public attention to the issue of illegal clearing and the cost to Glen Turner's life.

Pearce, too, had had her ordinary life pulverised. She now spent hours a week on the road, travelling the four hours between McKenzie's place in Tamworth and her parents' home in Port Macquarie, where she was now the elderly couple's primary carer. Her partner, Rob, had had to take unpaid leave to help out; she had declined promotions and opportunities, dropped to part-time hours, sacrificed time for her friends and hobbies. She was, she would later say in her victim impact statement, 'consumed with Glen's death and its consequence'. She was the contact for all media, police and justice matters, so also had to take extended leave for the trial.

In Toowoomba, where she was living with Grant, Robeena packed her suitcase. Into the case went thick skirts and a jacket, hairclips for her elegant white chignon, a shiny handbag. Her presence would be dignified, stoic, impassive. Perhaps she tucked some handkerchiefs into a corner, just in case.

15

Someone once congratulated Thomas Cullen, one of the pioneers of this district, upon his long life. The enquirer asked the old man why he had lived so long. He replied that in his youth he had always kept a loaded gun.
—**R.J. Webb, *The Rising Sun: A History of Moree and District 1862–1962*, 1962**

At 4.00a.m. on 21 April 2016, Turnbull was woken in Long Bay Hospital Wing, where he was being kept because of his various health issues. By 10.00a.m., trundled around for hours on a bus delivering prisoners to various sites in turn, he was expected in court.

He'd already been there for the pre-trial hearings earlier that month, in which legal allowances and technical arguments had been discussed. The days had been long: court adjourned in the afternoon but the circuitous transport meant he didn't get back until ten at night. A few days earlier, Justice

Johnson asked if Turnbull could be given special direct transport to and from the court, to get him home earlier. It wasn't compassion or coddling but so that Turnbull, eighty-one and in poor health, would be fit for the administration of justice.

The Supreme Court edifice is grand arcades and handsome red brick, but the courtroom in Sydney's King Street, where the trial convened, was smaller than McKenzie and Pearce expected. Just after 10.00a.m., Turnbull was led in by the court officers, and he seemed very close. It was the first time the women had seen him in person. 'That was a difficult moment,' McKenzie told Miller afterwards. 'He had no emotion on his face whatsoever. I found it hard to look at him.'

Robeena was there too, looking composed in an expensive white jacket, her hair up. She sat by herself in the courtroom. Pearce didn't want to like her. She didn't feel inclined to respect her: the woman had sat in a lounge room while Pearce's brother died alone in the dark. But then, seeing the elderly woman, she felt sorry for her, and went over to introduce herself. The warmth wasn't reciprocated; Pearce retreated, rebuffed.

Ian Robert Turnbull had been charged on two counts: the murder of Glen Turner and the detaining of Robert Strange. This second act was done 'with the intention of obtaining an advantage, namely, the killing of Glendon Turner'. When he appeared by videolink in December 2015 to be arraigned, Turnbull pleaded guilty to the Strange charge, so no trial would be required there. But Turnbull would not plead guilty to murder. His defence team, despite the eyewitness and the autopsy proving the victim's death by multiple gunshot wounds, would hold out for a verdict of manslaughter.

Murder comes under Section 18 of the *Crimes Act 1900.* It is a state crime. Murder occurs when someone voluntarily (with the intent to cause grievous bodily harm or kill) or by deliberate omission (with reckless indifference to human life) causes a death. Voluntary manslaughter includes the same definition of taking life, but, in the words of the Criminal Trial Courts

Bench Book of the Judicial Commission of New South Wales, 'the culpability of the offender's conduct is reduced by reason of provocation or substantial impairment by abnormality of mind'. The result is death, but it is under circumstances where 'a reasonable person in his or her position would not have considered a lethal response was reasonable'. Two of the partial defences available to invoke a verdict of manslaughter are extreme provocation and substantial impairment – partial because they go some way to exoneration, but not all the way. These defences require consideration by a jury. Turnbull's team used them both.

A defence of extreme provocation could be used if the killer had acted in reaction to a serious indictable offence performed by the victim, and if the deceased's conduct would have caused an 'ordinary person' to lose control. The loss of control is key: for a conviction despite a defence of extreme provocation, the prosecutor has to prove utterly that the killing was *not* due to provocation. It was an intimidation tactic by the defence team. The slightest implication that Turner's behaviour had pushed Turnbull to his response would mean the charge of murder would fail. As it happens, the law concerning these extenuations had been tweaked a month before Turner's killing, and the Turnbull case was the first in which the new definition of 'extreme' rather than plain provocation would be tested.

Substantial impairment, a new term for the old concept of 'diminished responsibility', required Turnbull's lawyers to prove that while Turnbull had 'cracked' under provocation from Glen Turner that afternoon, he had a long history of mental health deterioration due to the impact of Turner's investigations: he had 'abnormality of mind'. Turnbull's defence team was claiming that during the time period he stopped the ute, took out his gun, confronted Turner and began shooting, he was not in sound mind. For this defence, the impairment must have been so severe it might 'warrant liability for murder being reduced to manslaughter'.

A conviction of manslaughter would imply that Turner had, in a sense, brought his death upon himself, and that Turnbull was a kind of victim.

The Crown prosecutor, Pat Barrett, made his opening address to the jury. The Crown did not accept the manslaughter plea, he said. Turnbull had been motivated by a 'personal hatred of Mr Turner' and had convinced himself he was being persecuted in the face of investigation over his own illegal landclearing.

Barrett reprised Turnbull's words to Turner at the gate of 'Strathdoon' back in 2012 – that if Turner had 'any respect for' his life, he wouldn't recommend remediation. 'I interpret that as a threat,' Turner had said, 'and if you continue to threaten me the police will become involved.' Turnbull had replied, Barrett told the jury, 'I'm an old man. I don't care. I can do anything I want.'

Glen Turner had been advised to have no more contact with Ian Turnbull as a result of that encounter, but due to staff shortages, had been kept in the background on the case. A new prosecution had been looming, with Turner's name on an affidavit. But he'd never spoken to Turnbull again until July 2014, when he dropped to his knees and said, 'Ian, Ian, what have you done?'

There was a brief sketch of the killing: the encounter, the details of Turner's wounds, Turnbull's radio call, the late-night arrest at 'Yambin'. Nicola Kennett kneeling by Turnbull's armchair and asking 'Why?' Turnbull's reply: 'I had no choice. He was ruining my family. It was never going to end.'

Alison McKenzie and Fran Pearce began to comprehend what lay before them. After leaving the courthouse that first day, they would go to buy waterproof mascara. By the end of the second day, they would be cautioned not to be too emotional while hearing testimony, in case their tears and groans disturbed or led the jury. That might require the jury to be dismissed. They had to keep their faces unflinching, assume the same distant impassivity as Turnbull on the other side of the room: the settler face that Ross Gibson remarked on in old photos of those who repressed awful images in their minds. But tears could be shed quietly.

Barrett presented the affidavit Turner made in June 2014, a month before his death, prepared for the next hearing against Grant, Cory and Ian Turnbull. Turner described himself as an authorised officer under the *Native Vegetation Act* and the *National Parks and Wildlife Act 1974 No.80.* He'd been with OEH, or its former manifestation, since 2004; before that, he was a surveyor. He had training in compliance investigations, investigation management, global positioning systems, aerial photographic interpretation, geographic information systems, Aboriginal cultural awareness. He held a Certificate IV in government investigation and was studying for the diploma. He wasn't trained in botany or ecological conservation, but years of accompanying experts meant he could identify most common native plants, such as brigalow, belah, western rosewood and poplar box. Turner went on to give a detailed account of his inspections and investigations on

'Colorado' and 'Strathdoon' beginning in January 2012.

Turnbull sat through all this. He heard the long story of their relationship. He heard again his own words: 'Are you there, Scott? I just pumped a couple of shots at Turner.' Of Robert Strange holding Turner's head in the dark, telling him to hold on for the sake of his family. His own arrest. His apology to his family.

The Crown presented the crux of its argument: 'That the Accused fired his rifle at Mr Turner with the intention of killing him in revenge for Mr Turner's investigation into the Accused's land clearing activities in the Croppa Creek area.'

That night, despite the judge's request, Turnbull didn't get back to Long Bay until 9.00p.m.

*

THE NEXT DAY, A juror had to excuse herself for personal reasons. After some debate, the whole jury had to be dismissed. It would take a few days for the case to resume. All the tension would hold a little longer.

But by the Thursday, Robert Strange was in the witness stand. He had been preparing for this moment. 'I needed to talk about it, to get justice for what had occurred,' he recounted later. It was a responsibility, to tell the story right, for Glen.

He spoke of the burning stacks by the side of the road, and of stopping so they could take photos. He spoke of Turnbull appearing with the gun. He spoke of the strangeness of blood on Glen's face. He spoke of the cat-and-mouse pursuit around the car, of his hopes to talk Turnbull out of it, of Turner crouching behind the car, trying to grab the EPIRB in the growing dark. There was one moment when his composure broke. 'I said, "Glen, I have to be fit to get us out."' His voice cracked. '"It's no good us both being shot."' He remembered telling Turner it would be all right.

Todd Alexis suggested to Strange that Turnbull hadn't conversed with him, only seemed intent on hunting Turner. Turnbull had behaved impassively, hadn't he, spoken in a flat monotone?

No. 'It was said with some feeling,' Strange insisted.

Alexis also wanted Strange to concede that Turner had had a fixation on the Turnbulls. Strange wouldn't have it. Turner hadn't mentioned any specific 'run-in' with Roger Turnbull. The family's name hadn't been raised at all on the trip from Tamworth, not even on the detour near Croppa Creek and down County Boundary Road. It was Strange who had observed aloud, having visited earlier that year, that the properties belonged to the Turnbulls. But Turner had not mentioned Ian Turnbull until they saw the stacks of trees on fire.

Surely, suggested Alexis, Turner expressed strong views on the frustrating Turnbull situation? 'No stronger view,' said Strange, 'than any other matter that Glen investigated.' Turner had not spoken of the Turnbulls with dislike. He was always, said Strange, 'a professional officer'.

He tried to make eye contact with Turnbull. The old man wouldn't meet his gaze.

'I wanted him to know that Glen and I went to do a job that day, and

I had to finish it,' Strange told Channel 7's *Sunday Night* later that year. As he spoke, he bulged with the suppression of feeling. 'That's what I said to Glen. I'll get us justice. And I knew all along that I had to give my evidence. And he [Turnbull] had to be accountable for what he did.' He paused, prompted to think of Turnbull in jail. 'Yep. Yep. That's the cross he has to bear. I need to put him away. He's done what he's done, and he has to deal with that.'

Strange walked out of the courtroom and exhaled. The story was told. He'd done the last thing he could for Turner. He needn't hold it back anymore. He needn't carry the story in him like a bullet. He walked out of the building into the autumn morning, his son Joshua at his side, nearly two years after his life had stopped. Now it might begin again.

***

TWO WEEKS LATER, ON 13 May, the defence got to present its case. Todd Alexis maintained that Turnbull had a major depressive illness at the time of the shooting, and this had compromised his behaviour and reactions under duress. The 'feast and famine' of farming life had been endured for decades, but Turnbull had always managed to provide for his family, Alexis said. But in the months leading up to July 2014, it had all been too much. The $5 million put into 'Colorado' and 'Strathdoon' – the latter mortgaged against a guarantee on his own property – was at risk from the OEH prosecutions. 'Their livelihood was on the line because of what he [Glen Turner] had done,' Alexis said. 'The potential for financial ruin was very significant indeed.'

He went on, gesturing to the craggy-faced man in the dock. 'You might think he is made of tough stuff, and I think he was, but until his dealings with Mr Turner in 2012 and the Office of Environment and Heritage brought proceedings against him in the courts, he had never had to deal with this sort of thing before.'

Alexis summoned witnesses who agreed that Turnbull's state had changed over that winter. Turnbull was 'totally obsessed with the situation', family friend Robyn Cush said. 'I think he had come to the conclusion that he was not going to win the case.' He told another friend that Turner had threatened him, saying, 'I will break you.'

The witnesses to the aftermath of the shooting were questioned. They told of the chaos of seeking help; the cars crisscrossing the roads around Croppa Creek; the police arriving at the scene. Andrew Uebergang appeared in the witness stand to tell how he came across a frightened Robert Strange waving him down in the dark of Talga Lane, and how he'd quietly feared Turnbull would return to kill them too. Fran Pearce felt sorry for the young man: he lived in that community, and here he was testifying at the trial of one of its richest members.

Roger Turnbull offered to testify, but wasn't called. Robeena was. 'We didn't feel like we were doing anything wrong,' she explained. 'So why were we being targeted?' Ian had never, she insisted, expressed any intention of harming Glen Turner. But he had returned home on the night of the killing looking utterly wretched, 'like everything had drained out of him'.

Expertly, Todd Alexis created a picture of a farmer harassed by an officer going to extremes: it wasn't Turnbull who was obsessed with Turner, but the other way around.

It had already been put, in the pre-trial hearings, that Turner had a 'tendency' to harass; that he had 'provoked' Turnbull. The 'tendency' was based on a proposed pattern of excessive inspections and aggressive behaviour. Under Section 97 of the *Evidence Act 1995,* Turnbull's team claimed that Turner had a 'tendency to act in a particular way', 'engaging in persistent contact with or stalking persons connected with investigations he was conducting', including coming onto properties without consent or warning and behaving in an aggressive manner. He allegedly did these things knowing they were 'likely to cause a person to fear mental or physical harm'.

The incident with Anna Simmons, who testified that she was in tears after his visit to the cottage on 'Strathdoon', was central to the defence's attempt to establish this pattern. They also summoned testimony from Turnbull's staff and family, as well as landholders who had dealt with Turner. Ivan Maas said Turner had left messages on his phone and turned up at his house to deliver the stop-work order even after Maas asked him to desist. Turner, Maas said, 'was loud, abrasive, aggressive in questioning'; he used 'standover bullying tactics' and threatened him with jail. Maas, a heavyset man in his sixties, noted, 'I felt very confronted by him.' Turnbull, his longtime employer, was a 'champion'.

John Kennedy was a landowner at 'Kurrajong Park', on the Liverpool Plains, south of Tamworth, and had encountered Glen Turner, Steve Beaman and Chris Nadolny in 2009 after reports that he had poisoned regrowth and sunk dams in an eroded area. Turner, he said, had inspected, then congratulated him; later, he sent a remedial direction and a letter threatening a fine. They'd met again: Turner was 'very abrasive', said Kennedy. 'From this time I found Turner a very difficult man to deal with.' They had further encounters: Kennedy was investigated for illegal clearing, and claimed Turner spoke of fines and jail, and was seen driving on his property without permission. Once they met when Kennedy had been shooting rabbits; when he saw the rifle, according to Kennedy, Turner dropped the documents he was serving on Kennedy and began to shake. 'Maybe you should get a different job,' Kennedy supposedly taunted him, and Turner left, saying, 'I'll get you, Kennedy.'

In 2012, Kennedy had pleaded guilty in the Land and Environment Court to unlawful clearing of native vegetation under the Act and was fined $40,000 and prosecution costs.

A month and a half before the shooting, Judith Grills was issued a penalty notice by the OEH for unlawful clearing on her property, 'Wongalee'. She had had a 'fractious' encounter with Turner during an inspection and was left upset and unnerved, she said.

Lynn Hudson described Turner as 'arrogant' and 'heavy-handed'. Her husband, John, was convicted in February 2009 of unlawful clearing of native vegetation and failing to comply with an OEH notice; he appealed, had his appeal dismissed and was re-sentenced, with fines of $318,750 for the clearing and $1275 for his failure to comply.

There was no evidence that Turner had trespassed on the Turnbulls' land, though in media interviews the family referred to him frequently coming onto the properties without authorisation; they'd installed cameras and begun locking the gates, they said, because of this. They'd been unnerved, too, by news of Turner commissioning a flight to take aerial photographs, although this was a standard technique in the years before drones were commonly used. Turnbull testified that he'd once or twice glimpsed Turner on the property, measuring trees, but that he'd 'scooted off' as soon as he was seen; these alleged encounters were not logged by anyone. Under the *Native Vegetation Act,* officers were empowered to enter land for the purpose of determining contravention of the Act, if either the landowner consents or the OEH director-general gives authorisation. On the visits he documented, Turner's notebooks showed he was always in possession of an official authorisation of entry.

Alison McKenzie and Fran Pearce listened, appalled, to the litany of complaints from the subjects of Turner's investigations. It didn't sound like the man they knew, who loved nothing more than going out chatting with farmers, having a cup of tea on the verandah and patting the dog. He'd enjoyed his work; they'd had any number of reports from his colleagues of the respect with which he was held. He had to be tough at times: that was his job, dealing with people potentially breaking the law and being caught doing it. But he was a friendly, professional officer. The defence was acting more like a prosecution.

The Crown riposted that Turner's supposed tendency to harass was in fact a function of his duties: to repeatedly inspect a property over time, especially when faced with a recalcitrant alleged offender; to diligently pursue his enquiries and gather evidence. All compliance officers did this, as well as they could, covering multiple cases over a huge territory.

In the end, the attempt to prove tendency was unsuccessful. Turner hadn't had a tendency. He'd just had a job.

More compelling was the argument around provocation. Extreme provocation in cases of murder is invoked if the dead person had committed a serious indictable offence – for example, stalking – that would cause an ordinary person to lose control sufficient to kill someone. It does not apply if the accused began the process of provocation. It *can* apply even if the perceived provocation was not immediately before the crime – for example, if Turnbull hadn't set eyes on Glen Turner for two years before he shot him.

The defence team had subpoenaed all of Turner's OEH notebooks and files to support the case for provocation. Todd Alexis argued that Turnbull had shot Turner because Turner was on Talga Lane, taking photos of 'Colorado' without notice, and that Turner's conduct from August 2012 (when he'd gone to the properties with other compliance officers) to the day of his death had amounted to harassment enough to drive an ordinary person to lose control as far as killing or grievously hurting him. He alleged that Turner had a fixation on 'getting' Turnbull – for example, he allegedly told Anna Simmons of the clearing, 'We're going to get them for that. It's clear that they are doing this for the money.' His 'persistent contact with the accused and his family and their properties may properly be described as harassment' because it was done with 'hostile intent', causing the accused to 'fear mental harm to himself or a family member, or at least in the knowledge that it was likely to cause such harm'.

After hearing the evidence, Justice Johnson released a decision that had grave impact for the Turnbull defence. The jury, he said, would not be evaluating the partial defence of 'extreme provocation'. If the accused did not prove any of four elements of 'extreme provocation', the defence would not go to a jury determination. And Justice Johnson 'did not accept the submission of the Accused in this respect'. He had concluded that Turner's conduct hadn't constituted a serious indictable offence.

In Johnson's view, Turner hadn't breached the *Native Vegetation Act,* but followed it. He had not trespassed. Aerial inspections were routine and justified. 'It was,' he said, 'the ongoing activities of the Accused and his family with respect to the properties and land clearing which attracted the ongoing, regular and understandable attention of the OEH'. Rather dryly, he continued: 'It may be the case that a person who is being spoken to about possible breaches of the *Native Vegetation Act* (let alone being prosecuted for such alleged conduct) may feel harassed or under pressure or will experience other negative feelings towards the officer whose task it is to ensure compliance with these laws.' The statement Turner made to Anna Simmons, said Johnson, indicated that he was going to act on breaches of the Act. That was exactly what had happened. 'In due course,' the judge observed, 'the Accused pleaded guilty to this offence.'

The Turnbull camp digested this turn in the case. It had seemed obvious to them that Turner was rogue, a dark shadow upon their lives that they hadn't deserved. Where to from here?

***

PAT BARRETT, CROSS-EXAMINING, RECOUNTED the first bullet and the last, and asked, 'You aimed to kill him both times, didn't you?'

'Yes.'

It was 16 May, and Turnbull was in the witness stand. It was not going well.

Earlier, Todd Alexis asked how he felt after he fired the first shot. Once he lifted his gun, pointed it at a man's head and fired. Turnbull reimagined the road, the twilight, the expression on Turner's face as he fell to one knee, clutched his face. *Ian, what have you done?* 'When he fell I thought, *I've killed him,* and I didn't want to kill him,' he said. 'I don't know why I thought a bullet wouldn't kill him, but that's the way it was.'

Turnbull had a hearing aid by this time. He could hear the reaction of the onlookers. He could hear his own voice saying it.

He told the court the familiar story. Ivan Maas had seen Turner in a car and told him. Turnbull had gone down County Boundary Road to find them and couldn't. He'd guessed they were down Talga Lane. He wanted to make contact with them.

'Why?' asked Alexis.

'Well, he hadn't notified that he was coming and he seemed to be continually there.'

And then he got his rifle from under the seat, drove in behind Turner's vehicle and stopped.

'I was thinking that I was going to shoot him.'

'Had you decided?'

'Yeah, I think so, yeah.'

'Why?'

'Because he'd been plaguing the family for two years, just in Grant and Cory's situation, and...' – he said something about Roger too, got a bit muddled. 'Glen Turner was in the paddock and Mr Strange said, "There's somebody here with a rifle", and Glen put his hand on the post and hopped over the fence and he ran past me, as I fired, fired for his head. I was very ... I didn't know whether ... I was extremely nervous at that stage.' He gazed at Alexis, remembering the thoughts rushing through his mind as he gripped the slender rifle. It was a .22, kept for shooting pigs. 'Will I or won't I?'

Those in court listened soundlessly. They could all see the dusk of Talga Lane.

'The calmness came over me like I couldn't believe,' said Turnbull. 'And that was it, it was finished.'

Barrett rose. He made Turnbull go through the tale again. He got him to remember that he hadn't drawn the rifle out from under the front seat as he drove, had he, but had stopped, got out, put the rifle – which he knew was always loaded with an empty shell in the breach – in the open back tray, and then driven further along Talga Lane to reach the men. Then he had stopped, got out, fetched the rifle from the tray and walked over.

This was the first time Alison McKenzie had heard that Turnbull had prepared the gun before he arrived on Talga Lane. She listened, writhing inside. In a moment she would hear the man who had killed her Glen tell of the moment before he did it. Tell these strangers how he did do it.

Turnbull insisted Turner had been in his paddock, on the wrong side of the fence. He told how Turner had put his hand on the top of a post and hopped back over the fence, run across towards the road; how he had sworn at the two men and said, 'Turner, you bastard, you wanted to put the Turnbulls off their farms and you've done it.' And how he had fired a shot at Turner's head. He'd fired again as Turner ran for the cover of the car.

'You aimed to kill him both times, didn't you?' said Barrett.

He thought, he told Barrett, that Turner might be going for a gun when he reached into the vehicle. 'They go out on to farms there, they must have some sort of protection, yeah.'

'And you knew when you went and took that rifle,' said Barrett carefully, 'that he was a law enforcement officer trying to enforce one of the laws of this state, namely the *Native Vegetation Act?*'

'Well, I maintain that the bulk of what we cleared was regrowth,' said Turnbull, 'and he wouldn't have a bar of that.'

Barrett reminded him the issue was not whether he was guilty of illegal clearing, but that Turner was an officer of the law. Turnbull said he thought that if police had guns, a compliance officer might.

Inevitably, they did get into a review of the land-clearing contretemps. 'You didn't like the effect of the *Native Vegetation Act,* did you?' Barrett put to him.

'Well,' said Turnbull drily, 'the answer to that would be no.'

Yet again, it was all rehashed: the Turnbulls purchasing the properties to convert to cropping, that they knew there would be restrictions, whether they believed those restrictions would apply to them. Turnbull repeated that he had believed much of it was regrowth that could be cleared. He was reminded he'd still have needed to get permission; he hadn't had that permission; he'd begun clearing regardless. He clung to his defence that he believed it was clearable under the law. Todd Alexis listened, impassive, to arguments he had heard for years now in the New South Wales Land and Environment Court sitting, as he was now, beside a Turnbull.

They came to the last days before the shooting. Turnbull was, he said, working on 'Colorado' from a map Grant had given him, designating what areas were to be cleared. Barrett suggested the intense work was because the Turnbulls knew those orders were coming. Turnbull said there were still 800 acres left unfelled on 'Colorado' at that time, out of 3900. 'The way we have left it there now it can be farmed as a broadacre farm,' he said. 'There is hope there for the environment.'

Barrett raised Roger Turnbull's run-ins with the OEH after he'd cleared without permission. He was incredulous that Turnbull could have remained oblivious to the stringency of the laws. Turnbull replied that Roger had been clearing paddock trees; it was quite different. Besides, he said sharply, every farm from "Yambin" to "Colorado" has had a bulldozer on it. The environmental officers had ignored all that, he said, 'and they're not silly. They know what's going on, so they were honing in on the Turnbull family to make an example.'

They returned to the last shot, into Turner's back as he ran to the trees. Turnbull sensed it was fatal. He told Strange, 'You can do what you like now, I'm going home. You can tell the police, they'll know where I am.' Why hadn't he called an ambulance? He'd thought Robert Strange would do that, he said. He'd forgotten there was poor mobile coverage in Talga Lane. 'I wasn't in a state of mind to think like that.'

The clearing, said Turnbull, had been finished on 'Colorado' that day. 'Strathdoon' was already done. 'We left areas for the habitat,' he said. 'We left the corridors for the habitat, and fire breaks and wind breaks, and spray drifts also play a big part in crops, spray drifting, stopping the crops with spray drifting.'

Was it true, then, that Turnbull had been the victim of a misunderstanding?

Preoccupied, elderly, he had been given the maps to clear 'Colorado' by his son, and those maps, the son would later claim, had simply been incorrect. A piece of bruised paper fluttering on the passenger seat of a farm vehicle. He knew nothing of the intricate native vegetation laws, their clauses and caveats, but he did know about habitat, something of conservation farming. For such a man, pursuing the ethos of improvement he'd inherited, Turner's accusations might have seemed manic, preposterously hostile. How was Ian Turnbull, born in 1934, expected to comprehend the difference between one kind of regrowth and another; one polygon of sacred scrub from another fit to be crushed?

But, Barrett put to him, he'd kept clearing even after he'd been convicted. He knew it was illegal. He'd been caught again, hadn't he?

'I would have done it in any case.'

'You would have done it in any case?'

'Yeah.'

'You would have done it regardless of any action taken against you under the *Native Vegetation Act?*'

'If we would have done nothing, we would have walked away. If we did this, we've got a chance of growing some crops and being able to get some sensibility into the system ... We cleared in a responsible manner. They weren't doing it to anybody else around. There was clearing going on, and they never saw an environmental officer.'

A man had been killed. It seemed Turnbull could think only of his resentment, the clearing, the land. It was the last of the black soil and it had to have a crop on it.

16

And he said, What hast thou done? the voice of thy brother's blood crieth unto me from the ground. And now art thou cursed from the earth, which hath opened her mouth to receive thy brother's blood from thy hand; When thou tillest the ground, it shall not henceforth yield unto thee her strength; a fugitive and a vagabond shalt thou be in the earth. And Cain said unto the LORD, My punishment is greater than I can bear.

—**Genesis 4:8–13**

In August 2014, a psychologist asked Turnbull if he felt remorse for Turner's death. 'Well, I do, of course I'm remorseful for the man and his family. I have remorse. I do feel sorry for what happened, and for the bloke who was with him I feel sorry. I could have shot him too, but I didn't know him. I think maybe I should have shot myself, but I just wanted to see Rob one more time.'

He'd driven home from the scene just to be with her for a few hours. 'We've had a good life together,' he said. 'And then the police came.'

*

GRANT TURNBULL STEPPED INTO the witness stand the same day as his father. A tall, trim, dark-haired man with glasses, he wore a suit. Recalling the night of the tragedy, he spoke confidently. When he'd heard that his father had killed Turner, he felt, he said, 'complete and utter disbelief'.

Scott Kennett, driving through the dark towards Talga Lane, had called him in Toowoomba after the radio call from Turnbull. 'Dad would not do anything like that,' Grant told the court he'd thought at the time. He'd been aware of his father's tension, and the stress of the mounting legal cases. 'Was he really that bad? How did I miss the mark? It was a numb feeling I haven't felt before. It was complete disbelief,' he tried to explain. 'Just numb.'

His father had been feeling down, Grant said.

'You didn't suggest that he go and see a doctor or suggest that he get treatment?' Pat Barrett asked.

'No,' said Grant. 'Unfortunately now – no.'

*

THREE DAYS LATER, ON 19 May, the defence made the case for Turnbull's substantial mental impairment. Three psychiatrists – Olav Nielssen, David Greenberg and Adam Martin – had assessed Turnbull's mental state in the period between 2014 and 2016.

Nielssen, a consultant psychiatrist at St Vincent's Hospital in Sydney who had examined Turnbull in custody for three hours a week after Turner's death, and again two years later, opened. He told the court that in 2014 he'd found Turnbull wandering in his conversation. Cognitive function tests suggested mild dementia, but Nielssen thought it might be 'pseudodementia': symptoms similar to dementia but temporary, brought on by depression, not permanent degradation of the brain. Turnbull had the 'rigid and inflexible thinking' typical of an elderly man, but also displayed 'melancholic features' pointing to a severe illness.

Nielssen had taken into account Turnbull's family history of depression, as well as Turnbull's bout of depression needing medication in the 1960s. Melancholic depression, a form of major depressive disorder, he explained, would be characterised by a negative worldview and a miserable outlook; problems solving dilemmas or making decisions; morbid preoccupations. Turnbull's issues with insomnia, weakness and loss of appetite, he judged, were not explained simply by old age and stress.

In the initial evaluation, Nielssen listened to Turnbull raving about Turner. He seemed obsessed with explaining. He went on with a singular focus – 'I mean, literally constantly, repeating his name,' Nielssen emphasised, 'constantly complaining about things that he'd done.' He was surprised, later, to learn that the two men hadn't met for years; from Turnbull's telling, Nielssen believed the harassment Turnbull claimed he'd experienced was recent. 'It was almost a fantasy in his [Turnbull's] mind that

Mr Turner was persecuting him. He became fixated with it.'

The symptoms of melancholic depression, according to the current edition of the *Diagnostic and Statistical Manual of Mental Disorders* (DSM-5), include lethargy, sleep disturbance, loss of appetite, loss of ability to enjoy activities, loss of energy, problems concentrating, feelings of hopelessness or worthlessness or guilt, suicidal ideation, loss of libido, no emotional response to even dramatic events; instead, agitation, including wringing hands, or else the opposite, immobility, withdrawal. The symptoms have to persist for a reasonable length of time, at least two weeks. It is debilitating: a person with melancholic depression cannot function. It would be highly unusual for that person to be able to get out of bed and work. But the obsession with Turner, Nielssen believed, led Turnbull to overcome the enervation of major depression in order to drive a bulldozer for nine days straight. It was 'remarkable'. 'It almost seems like a coping style to force himself to go to work ... His obsession with work in those six months I think was just a way of coping with how he was feeling.'

Dr Reid, a neuropsychologist, had found no evidence of cognition impairment, and Dr Sim, a geriatrician, had scored Turnbull 30/30 on a cognition test. Nielssen explained that the tests are complicated and address cognition and dementia, not depression. They had been done, he pointed out, just after the shooting, and were limited in diagnosis to the moment of the test itself.

Alexis asked about abnormality of mind, the key phrase required for a defence of impairment. Had an abnormality of mind affected Turnbull's capacity to understand events, his perception and his ability to judge the morality of his acts at the time? The court listened attentively. 'Yes,' said Nielssen, 'by normal standards.' Depression had affected Turnbull's decision-making and thus his self-control.

Pat Barrett stood to cross-examine. He proposed that it was unsurprising that Turnbull, in jail on murder charges, seemed depressed in the week after he committed a violent crime. The man had sought no treatment for depression before the shooting, Barrett pointed out, nor afterwards. Dr Hearps, the staff specialist psychiatrist at Long Bay Prison hospital, had examined Turnbull and found no major depression. There were other explanations for the insomnia, tiredness, anxiety, weren't there? For example, the peripheral neuropathy in his legs, which tingled and ached or went numb in the night.

Nielssen replied that insomnia is very typical of melancholic depression. He referred to the sociable world traveller Turnbull was formerly and the decline since.

Barrett reprised the lucidity Robert Strange had reported at Talga Lane. The apparent determination and resolve.

That afternoon, Dr David Greenberg took the stand. He had also examined Turnbull after eighteen months on remand and diagnosed him as suffering major depression. He believed Turnbull also suffered a background 'adjustment disorder' – a group of physical and emotional symptoms caused by multiple severe stressors. Greenberg listed some of the stress factors for Turnbull. He'd been in drought for three years. He'd mortgaged his own property to help his son and grandson, and that investment was at risk. He had large legal bills; significant fines, and more to come; huge piles of paperwork; impending court appearances; mortgage repayments. He spent long hours working in isolation, a general risk factor for mental health issues in the farming community.

Greenberg conceded that in their conversation, Turnbull had denied he'd been depressed at the time of his actions. Greenberg said this was an argument against any kind of deception or exaggeration. There had been some discussion, in a pre-trial debate over admissibility of the recorded phone calls, of jokes Turnbull had apparently made about misleading the health professionals. But, 'he's not trying to fake that he's unwell. He's doing the opposite. He presents himself as coping, and not having anything wrong with him mentally.' As for not seeking treatment, his cohort doesn't traditionally seek out medical help for mental or emotional problems.

Turnbull was 'distressed', not just obsessed, by Turner. 'He's not a stupid man, he's a highly intelligent man. I think he can understand it.' However, Greenberg went on, 'emotionally, I don't think he's really in touch with his feelings or what was internally happening to him'.

Dr Adam Martin, consulting forensic psychiatrist, was commissioned by the prosecutor rather than the defence. He had been asked to prepare a report on Turnbull's mental health. To assist, he was given police statements; material from the New South Wales Land and Environment Court cases; Dr Nielssen's report from a week after the shooting; Dr Greenberg's report; the assessments by Dr Reid, Dr Sim and Dr Hearps; statements from Turnbull's personal GP in Moree; and other material provided by the Turnbull legal team. He also twice interviewed Turnbull at Long Bay in February 2016, just two months before the trial.

By that time it was nineteen months since the crime, and Turnbull had been held in Cessnock, a regular jail, as well as in the hospital wing of Long Bay. Martin said that in his interviews with Turnbull he did not perceive symptoms of melancholic depression. The old man had done those nine days' bulldozing: he'd risen early each morning, checked conscientiously on his sleeping wife, driven to the site, worked for six hours and come home tired. On balance, there just wasn't enough evidence to support the idea that Turnbull had gross mental disturbance at the time of the crime. 'He appeared to be functioning pretty well,' attested Martin. 'It just wasn't consistent with a person with major depression or a melancholic-type depression.' Perhaps there was a mild adjustment disorder: that is, an exaggerated or greater than expected emotional response to an event. Reactions under an adjustment disorder do continue beyond the event: stay with a person, inflated and enduring. But it is not usually possible, he explained, to have both an adjustment disorder and melancholic depression at the same time.

There was nothing to demonstrate a lack of self-control, said Martin. Turnbull's imperviousness to Strange went against the idea that he was affectless and depressed. He had refrained from shooting a stranger: this showed he could make decisions. His comments about waiting for the police suggested he knew he had committed a crime and that there would be consequences. The long duration of the attack, building to the final shots, wasn't typical of the impulsive mania of a mental health breakdown. He was calm at arrest, calm in custody.

Dr Hearps, Dr Sim and Dr Reid had had no concerns over Turnbull's mental state; a CT scan had shown no issues. His own GP hadn't assessed him as disturbed or depressed. He had had no treatment, despite constant monitoring and several assessments, for mental health problems while in custody. His composure, said Martin, was good. He did not appear suicidal or hopeless, even after nearly two years isolated from his family in remand, facing a serious charge. Martin had been given recordings of over a hundred phone calls made by and to Turnbull in custody after the crime; all seemed normal. 'So to me,' said Martin, 'the weight of that suggested that he probably hadn't been suffering a major mental illness. He may have been unhappy; he may have been stressed. My view is that it didn't really support that he was significantly mentally ill beforehand.'

Todd Alexis pushed Martin on cross-examination. He questioned him about the evidence he'd read: how thoroughly had he digested it? He recited a string of statements Turnbull had told the other psychiatric experts, and got Martin to concede he hadn't heard them directly. 'He didn't tell you that...' Alexis said over and over, and Martin kept admitting, 'No.'

'Your conclusion that Mr Turnbull was functioning pretty well ... is based on nothing more than the fact that he was working during the months and weeks before the shooting, isn't it?'

'Yes.'

Alexis probed Martin on whether he'd read with scepticism an affidavit from Robeena about her husband's behaviour in the lead-up to the crime, alert to the possibility that Turnbull was faking his illness and looking for inconsistencies. He hammered the point of Martin's possible bias. He pointed out that Greenberg had been Martin's teacher at university, implying that Martin was junior in experience and qualification.

Martin had put a note in his report that he saw the violence as 'instrumental', not 'planned' as such but considered beforehand. Alexis challenged him: by that, did he mean to imply premeditation? Martin had to retreat.

Dr Hearps hadn't had access to the affidavits from the Turnbull family attesting to their concern for Turnbull before the shooting, Alexis observed. The accused, he suggested, was stoical and not quick to show emotion to Hearps, though he might have been more candid with his family. Dr Hearps, Martin insisted, was an experienced professional and would have been alert even during a protocol check, and would have absorbed the subject's history.

Back and forth it went. Alexis pushed the case for his client's severe mental health issues back in 2014, in contrast to his client's lucidity now, after months spent in custodial care.

There was a strange parallel with the Turnbulls' land-clearing court cases: the varying analyses, the dramatically divergent interpretations, the vying experts. Todd Alexis, adroitly probing, testing inconsistencies, asking ingenuous questions. The subject, the flattened landscape, the silent man in the dock: so much talking about them, so much peering at the damage, arguing what it means.

Dr Martin testified that Turnbull had spoken to him about his feelings now. 'I can't undo what I've done.' The old man had gazed at him across the videolink. 'I don't know. I'm sorry about it now, but I'm at the end of my life. I'm just about buggered.' He expected, he said now, to die in jail.

*

ON 26 MAY, JUSTICE Johnson summed up matters for the jury to consider. He said the onus was on Turnbull to prove he'd been substantially impaired; the jury had to credit that his capacity to understand right and wrong and control himself had been impaired, and to believe the impairment was so severe that his criminal responsibility should be reduced from murder to manslaughter. He told the jury to think of community standards, of common sense; to make a 'value judgement'. 'It's the state of mind of the accused at this time which is the central point of this trial,' he said.

The jury shuffled out to deliberate. In the observer seats, Alison McKenzie and Fran Pearce looked at each other nervously. It was eight weeks now since the start of the pretrial hearings. They had flights booked for Tamworth the next afternoon, a Friday, but Pat Barrett warned them they might not make it: a jury, they learned with surprise, might stay secluded until late on Friday, and through the weekend. Turner's mother, Coral, had been in Sydney for the gruelling week; she had to leave.

Stay close by, Barrett told McKenzie and Pearce on Friday morning, when they turned up to the court to be told the jury still hadn't returned. It might be any minute.

'I just want it to be justice for Glen, I want a guilty verdict,' McKenzie told Gregory Miller. 'Because that's what it is and there are no, there are absolutely no excuses.' She shook her head vehemently. 'No excuse.'

Chris Nadolny was there too. He wasn't part of the cluster around McKenzie and Pearce but sat alone. He had escaped media attention; an unobtrusive person, he wasn't the sort to leap before a camera. But he had felt threatened by Ian Turnbull, and had met the man more often than most others in the room. He might have joined Robert Strange, but the two men, indelibly linked by Turner and Turnbull, barely knew each other. Nadolny sat alone, and felt it.

And then, abruptly, it was announced that the jury had returned a verdict.

McKenzie and Pearce, Nadolny and Strange returned to their seats in the courtroom. The jury filed in.

The verdict was announced. It was murder.

Turnbull showed no emotion. Watching him, McKenzie was shaken.

But she and Pearce couldn't hide their relief. They sobbed.

Turnbull glanced at her for a moment. Then he was taken away.

The women's faces, as they walked out of the building to face reporters, wore a different kind of composure: the taut, pressed-lips dignity of vindication stretched tight over brimming distress.

'We expected the trial to be about the murder of Glen Turner,' Pearce read from a statement. 'A good man, doing his job on behalf of our community. Instead it was hijacked by the defence into an attack on Glen's character and a platform for the Turnbull dynasty to continue their grievance in regard to the native vegetation laws.' She drew breath. 'The murderer was portrayed as the victim, a poor, depressed, respectable farmer driven to despair by the Office of Environment and Heritage. In reality, he is a wealthy property developer who simply refused to accept that the law applied to him.'

The children would have to live the rest of their lives without their father, she continued. 'Glen didn't get a chance to go home to his family.' And she summoned Turner for the mash of reporters and camera crew. 'Glen was a man that was full of vitality and he had a passion for life. He was a loving husband, father, son, brother, uncle, friend and colleague. He was a respected member of the community.'

They'd chosen bright colours that day: McKenzie, orange; Pearce, a luminous blue. Each also wore, proudly, a long necklace suspending a large Tree of Life image, made for each supporter of the family and worn by the women every day in court in memory of Turner.

Lastly, they thanked Robert Strange and his crucial evidence. Many knew what it had cost him to speak. 'We are very honoured,' Fran Pearce read out, 'that he had the strength to give his testimony, because we know that's what got the conviction.'

That night, the Turner supporters all went to a restaurant to celebrate. There were dozens of people. There were toasts to the legal team, to Strange; to Glen. McKenzie and Pearce sat together, and the two women pressed their faces into each other's necks to hide the tears.

PART THREE
INHERITANCE

17

> A forest shares a history, which each tree remembers even after it has been felled.
> —**Anne Michaels, *Fugitive Pieces*, 1997**

The torn envelope that now homes the victim impact statements in the court archives has a sticker: *R v Ian Robert Turnbull (2014/223920)/Sentencing Hearing Trial Exhibits and MRI Lists/(15 June 2016-ROP42)*. Inside is an A4 sheet of paper with an adult's handwriting – large, clear, well-formed letters. 'Something terrible happened in my life,' it begins.

Beneath is a little fragile sketch by a child: two blocky cars, a stick figure holding a stiff dark line with dotted lines dashing from its opening and two other figures. One of them appears to be lying down. This page is green-stickered: *Supreme Court of New South Wales Exhibit F*. A Post-it identifies the illustrator as Jack Turner.

Another sketch shows Jack hearing about his father's death. It is dinnertime: the boy in the drawing is holding a plate.

There is also a drawing by Glen, a very detailed sketch of two billycarts, one large and one small. The smaller is 'Jack's billycart. Max. speed 7 ¾ miles/hour.' The large one is labelled 'Daddy's billycart' and has 'special extra features – home brew cooler – blasters – boosters'.

It was 15 June, two weeks after the verdict, and Alison McKenzie, Fran Pearce and Robert Strange were back in court. They were there to read their victim impact statements at the plea hearing.

One of the aspects to be considered in Turnbull's sentencing was the damage his crime had done to the community. The statements, said Justice Johnson, helped to illustrate how 'the harmful impact of Mr Turner's death on the members of his immediate family was an aspect of harm done to the community'. There are no victim impact statements made by microbes, by koalas or flowering groundcover for the harm done to them. But because Turnbull killed a man, he had, for the first time, to hear of the damage done.

Alison McKenzie's statement was carefully composed. It opened with a scene: a family dinner, celebrating Jack's ninth birthday. The next morning, she recounted, she and Glen kissed the kids goodbye as they ran to the schoolbus. The parents drove to town, chatted, parted ways.

She told the court of that evening: her thoughts as the emergency calls came through, the realisation that her partner was dead, the children listening to it all unfold. She spoke of her horror that his body was left on the ground in Talga Lane all night. 'I should have been there to hold him,' she wrote. 'You expect to be by their bedside holding their hand as they take their last breath. I didn't have the chance to do that for Glen when he needed me most, and he won't be there for me.'

She spoke of the loss to the children. The cruelty other kids showed towards them, their lack of understanding. Her daughter having no father to dance with at the school formal. Her son clinging to his visiting uncle when he tried to leave.

Her partner had been a valued person, she said. Their lives together were severed, the family's future blown to smithereens. 'My husband,' McKenzie told the listening court, 'was taken from us by the actions of a selfish, arrogant man who thought of nothing but his own greed and desire to own more land and make more money. His wife spoke the words that should have been mine. Glen and I worked together on our farm, we loved being together, all he ever wanted was to own his farm, and Ian Turnbull took that from him, he took that from us. And there is only one answer to the question of "Why?". Because he wanted more.'

Turnbull 'took ... from Glen and me and our children and our friends and family because he wasn't happy with what he had'. She paused. 'The only thing Glen wanted more of was time.'

On the hard copy in the files she had written and crossed out whole paragraphs. Victim Support Services advises, 'Don't directly express your anger toward the court or the offender.

Your goal is to express your hurt and your pain, not to blame. The blame has already been placed on the offender, so now is the time to talk about what you have been experiencing through your loss.' The statements must not contain anything that is 'offensive', say the court's regulations.

The defence team, given its due preview, had objected to some of those paragraphs in court. 'It is submitted,' complained Todd Alexis, 'that parts of them go beyond what is the "impact" of the death of Mr Turner upon Ms McKenzie.' Justice Johnson overruled the objection. But McKenzie had still crossed out some of the things she had wished to say.

Fran Pearce read her statement next. She explained, with dignity, the enormous personal cost of the aftermath of her brother's death, and the responsibilities that had fallen to her and her partner. She spoke of her brother's good character. She recounted various memories: telling her parents their son was dead; holding the weeping children; sharing a bed with McKenzie, worrying about money for a funeral and the mortgage repayments; enduring the revelation of how Turner died; sharing the ordeal of the trial. Her emotional health was shot now, Pearce said. 'I drink too much to get through the things that are unbearable, and to dim the picture of my brother's body in my head. I have panic attacks. I cannot watch TV or movies where people get shot.'

The trial, she said vehemently, could have been avoided if Ian Turnbull had truly been remorseful and had pleaded guilty to murder: 'We have had the life force of our family taken from us in horrendous and callous circumstances because of one person's greed and arrogance that the laws do not apply to him.' Pearce paused and, when she resumed, spoke deliberately. 'He chose to pick up a gun. He chose to murder my brother. He chose to take Glen away from us.'

Robert Strange told the court how his life was entirely ruined by the events of that night on Talga Lane. There were slow signs of recovery – he no longer had troubling thoughts that someone might shoot him through a window – but he had been emptied by the shock that came from the mouth of Turnbull's little .22. He wore an air of enormous sadness. There wasn't much to say, really, except how wrecked he felt; but he said it.

***

THOMAS HOBBES, IN HIS work *Leviathan* (1651), believed nature was chaos. A mother bird may lament the eating of her chicks, a scavenger scared from a carcass by another might howl in protest. But there are no penalties in nature except natural consequence. Nature operates without the idea of crime. There is little concept of revenge. There are no courts of arbitration.

Humans have laws to remedy these entropies, and to maintain our relations with one another.

The evolution of laws to govern human actions over nature is, in the Western world, comparatively recent. In Australia, our environmental laws, like our assumptions, have their origins on the other side of the planet.

In early-nineteenth-century Britain, faith in time-honoured institutions such as feudalist aristocracy and in the idea of a 'balance of nature' wavered in the face of increased manufacturing and a decline in agriculture, leading to a more individualistic mindset. Wealthy landowners were concerned about protecting their assets, especially, in the new age of steam, against straying pollution. At the same time, a respect for 'natural law', melding with the elemental logic in Locke's popular model of property ownership and Bentham's pragmatism, informed a utilitarian response to the consequences of what we now call environmental harms: they became crimes.

Crimes against nature were also crimes against the future. Perhaps surprisingly, it was poet Samuel Taylor Coleridge who was often credited with developing the idea of 'land as ideally held on trust across generations' and who helped inspire the political will to protect it.

Locke had proposed a kind of 'sustainable development' that worked to promote economic growth within certain constraints, including environmental parameters; the market would rule, inside a reasonable structure that recognised physical limits. Coleridge, an adrenalised devotee of mountaineering, opinion, poetry, risk, opium and political agitation, spoke of 'higher needs' in less tangible rudiments: beauty, virtue, mental health – and healthy land was the foundation of this. In Bristol in 1797 and 1798, young Coleridge met an extraordinary assembly of scientific talents: Humphry Davy, James Watt, Erasmus Darwin and other 'sons of genius'. The result was some truly innovative conclusions about the place of humankind in the natural world. His was what might be called a 'deep green' attitude, which considers humans to be nature's stewards, with the same privileges, dependencies and responsibilities of habitation as private estate owners.

Coleridge put his finger on one of the crucial challenges of modern ecology. 'The two antagonist powers of opposite interests of the state, under which all other state interests are comprized, are those of PERMENANCE and PROGRESSION,' he wrote in *On the Constitution of Church and State* (1830).

Nearly two hundred years later, the farmer and the environmental officer facing off over a gate would be arguing the same dilemma: must progress destroy its own foundations – and future – as it goes? Or must everything be maintained as it has been, forfeiting the potential of change? And who decides these questions?

Later in his life, Coleridge felt that the inheritance and protection of heritage of private estates was what enabled a state to exist at all. For Coleridge, the Westminster parliamentary system came to represent both permanence (hereditary aristocracy, trusted with ownership of land to be passed through generations in good health) and progress (the executive, enacting change for the good). But he proposed a third chamber, a clerisy made of scholars and representatives of the church, as 'the beam of the scales', to moderate the paradox. It would exist, he argued, to 'preserve the stores, guard the treasures of past civilization, and thus to bind the present with the past; to perfect and add to the same, and thus to connect the present with the future'. His proposal for what we might call an independent commission is still worth consideration.

Historian Ben Pontin argues that Coleridge and his followers, under the name of Romantic conservatism, played a significant and neglected role in the emergence of environmental law, even helping to slow Britain's industrialisation. It is a quiet legacy, interrupting modern assumptions about liberal and conservative politics that eventually made their way to the other side of the world.

When Australia was federated in 1901, there was no direct provision for the Commonwealth to regulate environmental issues. Small restrictions were placed in later years. By 1938, the New South Wales *Soil Conservation Act 1938 No.10* indirectly forbade clearing on both private and public land around water catchments. The state government did restrict ringbarking on Crown leases, though not on freeholds. The landmark *Hunter Valley Conservation Trust Act 1950* meant that clearing on 'declared lands' required a permit, and it was backed up by successive legislations through the 1970s that put more and more regulatory thresholds between landholders or public agencies and the bare soil. But it took decades before conservation movements began to seriously impede the carefree felling of vegetation. When the Hawke government passed a law to protect the wilderness area threatened by the Franklin Dam in Tasmania, they had to use Section 51 of the Constitution, about respecting international obligations to protect World Heritage sites.

In New South Wales, town planning and environmental law weren't merged until the *Environmental Planning and Assessment Act 1979,* following Jack Mundey's green bans movement in Sydney. Then came the establishment of the Land and Environment Court of New South Wales, which had the status of a 'superior court', to enforce the Act. It is composed of judges and trained commissioners who are experts in the fields of environmental science, town planning, heritage, architecture, engineering and land valuation. As a recent institution dealing with relatively new legislation, it often sets precedents that have far-reaching significance.

Of the eight aims of the Act, seven concerned the administration of public submissions and advice. It revolutionised landowners' reckoning with environmental consequences, and opened the door for members of the public to pursue action ('open standing') in the case of a breach: anyone could 'bring proceedings in the Land and Environment Court for an order to remedy or restrain a contravention of this Act, whether or not any right of that person has been or may be infringed by, or as a consequence of, that contravention'.

There was a fear that people would go berserk, dobbing in their neighbours, but for the most part that hasn't happened. It is difficult, however, to pursue cases under open standing because, as in criminal law, an accused is innocent until proven guilty, and an accuser can find it difficult to provide evidence without doubt that environmental harm has occurred.

Phil Spark, when asked why he and Alaine Anderson didn't mount an open standing case to stop the Turnbulls, shakes his head and exhales. Why not indeed, he wonders. He had been very busy at the time, he admits, including with a protest against the proposed Maules Creek coalmine; Alaine had both a farm and koala conservation on her hands every day. Both were preoccupied, tired. They had hoped, even as the prospect began to sag, that the government authorities would step in as they were supposed to. But they might have mounted the case, he concedes. The business with Turnbull, the clearing of those blocks, the life of Glen Turner, could have ended differently. But 'the point', he notes sharply, 'is how far do the public have to go, doing what the laws are supposed to do?'

In one version of reality, Spark would have been correct to trust the laws of the land, state and federal. In the other reality, that trust would have been naive.

In 2000, the federal *Environment Protection and Biodiversity Act* came in to comprehensively renovate all existing legislation. The Act has to cover a wide landscape, literally and metaphorically, because it deals with the Great Barrier Reef and the health of inland waterways; endangered species and uranium mining; water table assessments to do with coal-seam gas exploration and local wetlands; World Heritage properties and conservation programs for small native mammals. At its birth it was praised as a triumph of synthesis, a coherent, broad-scale system to integrate the best expertise and administration to guard the largest range of national natural assets. But critics also immediately spotted its flaws: rather than viewing a landscape in its entirety, it concentrates on threatened entities, so by the time an ecological community is declared endangered it's already virtually gone. And the minister of the day has almost total concentration of decision-making. Since the election of the Coalition in 2013, the Act has been used to stop developments such as wind turbines on Lord Howe Island, deemed visually 'intrusive', and a wind farm in Queensland. Farm activity referrals form less than 3 per cent of assessments.

And in 2019, a joint study by academics from the University of Queensland, the Australian Conservation Foundation, WWF Australia and the Wilderness Society calculated that between 2000 and 2017, approximately 93 per cent of land cleared across the continent had never been referred to the federal government for assessment at all. Those cleared lands included more than 7.5 million hectares of potential habitat for threatened species. An estimated 1 million acres of threatened species habitat had been cleared in New South Wales and Queensland alone within thirteen years.

***

ON 23 JUNE, JUSTICE Johnson was ready to deliver the sentence for murder on Ian Turnbull. He had weighed up all the relevant factors and composed them in light of the law. Turnbull was elderly, and it seemed he had had a degree of mental impairment at the time of the shooting, perhaps a mild adjustment disorder. But he'd killed a government officer doing his job. There was deterrence to be considered – both so that Turnbull wouldn't offend again, and so that no one else would think they could commit the same act without significant penalty either.

Alison McKenzie had low hopes for the sentencing. The defence team had been unremitting, mounting every objection or special plea they could. Turnbull was supported by his respectable family, and they had such wealth on their side. They could afford silks and solicitors to string out the trial for those extra weeks. 'I just want justice for Glen,' she told Gregory Miller's camera. She was tired and tense. She wanted it to be over, so she could go home and grieve.

There were the politics, too. The nation was horrified by this crime. Anger had inexorably mounted among environmentalists and greenies at the events in which a man had died protecting the bush. Then there was the flush of feeling in support for Ian Turnbull, the farmer 'pushed to the brink'. The trial had been reported in all major media, as well as contested in comment threads and forums. Everyone had a reaction to Ian

Turnbull's actions. What would be the outcome?

At the bench, Justice Johnson began: Turnbull's crime was as serious as it could be. Turner was a public servant. He was also 'a loving and caring husband, father, brother and son'. He had much to offer the community, 'not only in his family role, but in his service as a public official exercising duties in an important public capacity'.

Johnson reprised the facts of the case, as agreed by all parties: the purchase of the two vegetated properties; the conversion to cropping land by clearing; the Office of Environment and Heritage's statutory obligations to investigate; the general attitude around Moree towards the *Native Vegetation Act.* 'It is fair to describe the offender,' he observed, 'as an old-fashioned farmer, with firm views about land ownership and use of the land. It may be inferred readily that the offender, and members of his family, did not look kindly upon the level of scrutiny, accountability and regulatory action required under the *Native Vegetation Act,* and the extent to which it may slow down, if not stop, the planned conversion of the two properties to broadacre farms.' Turner, said the judge, had behaved with 'diligence and persistence' throughout the chronicle of the investigations and prosecutions, and this had made Turnbull hate him.

Government officers such as Glen Turner and Robert Strange often had to go out to isolated sites to confront hostile landholders who owned firearms, the judge observed. Compliance officers in Australia, unlike their colleagues in the United States, are unarmed.

'I accept,' Johnson continued, 'that the offender was and is a stoical type of person and an old-style farmer. I accept that, in the period before 29 July 2014, he spoke frequently to relatives and friends about action being taken by the OEH. I accept that he manifested a single-minded approach in this regard which focused upon Mr Turner, although he had not had physical or telephone contact with Mr Turner for more than two years before the murder.'

The tale was told again: the scene at the car, Glen dropping to his knee with a hand to his face. *You've ruined the Turnbulls.* Strange desperately trying to call triple zero. *I'm going home to wait for the police.* The midnight arrest.

Then the court rose. 'The aggregate sentence,' announced Johnson, 'will comprise a head sentence of thirty-five years and a non-parole period of twenty-two years.'

Justice Johnson was satisfied that Turnbull's motive 'involved a desire for retaliation or revenge'. Turnbull had told a psychiatrist he was sorry about killing Glen Turner, but it didn't amount to remorse. In addition, Turnbull had left it late to plead guilty to the count of detaining Robert Strange. As such, there would be only a small concession on that conviction, which usually received fourteen years.

The sentence would date from July 2014, when Ian Turnbull had been taken into custody, meaning he had already served nearly two years. But Johnson noted, 'I have taken into account that this sentence will almost certainly constitute a de-facto life sentence, with the offender dying in custody before the expiration of the non-parole period. I am satisfied that no lesser sentence is appropriate in all the circumstances of the case.' There was a unit at Long Bay especially for elderly male inmates where he could be housed.

In the dock, Turnbull showed no emotion. The settler gaze was firm. He only nodded once, and raised a hand to Robeena, sitting in the front row of the court.

The families walked out of the courthouse to a pack of media. Alison McKenzie and Fran Pearce stepped forward. The verdict was a good one, McKenzie said. It would never bring Glen back, but they were glad that justice had prevailed.

Pearce lifted her face to reporters. 'It's a hard emotion to describe,' she said. '"Pleased" doesn't really cover it. It's very relieving. It's probably more than we even hoped for. We hoped he'd die in jail, to be honest. Glen didn't get a chance to go home to his family, so we think that's fair.'

Grant cleared his throat in the midst of a media scrum and spoke again of farmers' frustration, of native vegetation laws, of the government and the Act.

'The politicians need to listen,' he told the microphones. 'The ways this Act is administered: that's what needs to change. Otherwise this tragedy will happen again. And there'll be two families torn apart forever – over a piece of paper.' He shook his head. 'A legislation in parliament.'

A reporter pointed out that problems with the *Native Vegetation Act* are not justification for murder.

Grant nodded. 'That's correct. But the frustration that's out there: it's not just one farmer. It's many people out in rural New South Wales that are extremely frustrated – extremely frustrated – with the way it's administered, and the Act itself.'

Robeena was photographed leaving the scene in her necklace and cream jacket, wiping her eyes. Her husband, like his victim, would never come home. Turner's death, as Johnson had said, 'diminished us all'.

18

A noble tree is in some measure a matter of public concern; nor ought its proprietor to be allowed wantonly to strip his country of its fairest ornament.
—**John Ramsay, landlord of 'Ochtertyre' in Scotland, 1736–1814**

Conservation movements and farming advocates both are fond of the idea of timelessness: the ancient pastoral traditions of harvest; the eternal composure of nature. But they, and their landscapes, are very much formed by the historical. Colonisation was one such historic moment in Australia. Glen Turner's death was another. Events occur. And, like harvests ripening, cultural movements have their own forms to take. By the last decade of the twentieth century, Ian Turnbull was busy buying farms and Turner had begun his professional life, but in the world beyond there was huge interest in programs of social justice.

During the decade, popular books by John Ralston Saul, Camille Paglia, Naomi Wolf, Germaine Greer, Toni Morrison, bell hooks, Umberto Eco and others helped to interpret the covalency of gender, race, culture and class within personal politics. Feminism of the time felt almost triumphant, powered by punk and by political achievements. Meanwhile, Vandana Shiva, Gary Snyder, David Suzuki, Tim Flannery and others mined the histories of human destruction of the land, suggesting variously 'deep green', 'emancipist' or custodial relationships for the future. The Rio Earth Summit in 1992 inspired many; conservation agencies such as Greenpeace, Friends of the Earth and The Wilderness Society were household names. The exploitation of traditional lands such as the Amazon Basin and the Pilbara brought Indigenous issues into the mix, and threats to rainforests were highlighted. In Australia, as Libby Robin says in her detailed history of the time, 'the "green" and the "black" began to negotiate shared ground'. The environment was now a moral cause.

There was actual political effect, too. In 1989, Bob Hawke had launched the One Billion Trees program and another, Saving the Bush, to enhance native vegetation cover, though neither ever fully achieved its aim. Landcare was established that same year by the Australian Conservation Foundation and the National Farmers' Federation. It seemed the central authorities and popular enthusiasm were converging.

Focus finally expanded from deforestation of public forests to the less-glamorous clearing of bush. The NSW Farmers Association asked a committee to look into historian-farmer Eric Rolls' 1981 account, *A Million Wild Acres,* of scrub infestation in the interior, and of how the removal of Aboriginal managers and overgrazing had provoked the overgrowth that now seemed to require such drastic clearing. Rolls fractured the idea, taken up by remorseful conservationists, that European colonisation had ruined a pristine Eden; but he also chronicled 200 years of devastating misjudgement by settlers. The Association was impatient with Rolls' careful distinctions.

Its chairman, Ian McClintock, grumbled that 'the green movement wants to take the Australian landscape back to some point in the past that may never have existed'.

At the same time that conservationists were using cultural history to reify their campaigns, agricultural and mining companies began to use the conservationists' own strategies to build social support. While their lobbyists in Canberra pressed causes, their advertising aimed to instil community support for continued resource exploitation, such as BHP's famous campaign featuring true-blue actor Bill Hunter extolling, in a broad accent and hard hat or Akubra in turn, how the kindly, patriotic company was advancing Australia's wellbeing.

Both sides, increasingly agile in using state authority and moral argument to promote their respective causes, were supported by public feeling. Both now had a history of achievement to draw upon. Both had the ear of government. The thing now was to put it all into forms that couldn't be undone: to have it drawn into law.

*

CONSERVATION ACTIVISM OFTEN OCCURS at a local level. People respond to threats to their neighbourhood. Campaigns are mounted to protect waterways or groves or vulnerable animal populations, funds are raised from local sources, parochial pride is engaged. This form of conservation plays to the privilege of place, in the sense of a location that holds meaning, is visible, personal.

The risk with the local conservation paradigm is that it is anatomical. A frail indigenous flower might be protected from the starving native mammal that needs to eat it. One species soaks up attention, but this may lead to neglect of another, or come at a cost to an ecological community further down the creek, outside the council boundary or at the other end of the migration range. Place is precious, but when it is too lovingly fenced, a garden becomes a jail.

The contrasting approach is conservation at the landscape scale. Broad overviews of a situation, recognising whole scenarios, whole bodies of ecology, give a sense of perspective. Patterns are perceived. Systems are sensed. An ecology is made from relationships. The shrinkage and fragmentation due to broadacre cropping are dramatic in the comparison of historical maps. The mass migration of plants and habitats with the shifts of climate change will happen on a landscape scale.

Yet the landscape view can make for hazardous complacency, especially politically. A decline in habitat in one place is dismissed because there is 'still' so much of it on the other side of the state. The fine detail of change is invisible: a species of fish in the coastal waters failing to breed as normal seems unrelated to inland landclearing that is loosening soil and allowing silt to flow to the sea. Conservation management at landscape scale is subject to dispute: just as overfocused locals might jeopardise the wellbeing of ecologies outside their remit, those with irritable interests can protest the personal cost and make assurances that, when considered on a large scale, their actions are granular, insignificant, affordable.

From landscape-scale thinking comes the crucial and contentious concepts of 'offsetting', 'set-asides' and 'land sparing'. Offsetting, the better-known strategy, equalises loss through allowing the clearing of ecological communities and re-establishing them elsewhere on 'extra' vacant or degraded land. The companion strategy, set-asides, occurs where a land holder, desirous of clearing one area, agrees to not clear, and maintain, another. This seems reasonable – except that where there were two areas of biodiversity, there is now only one. Often implied is the idea of land sparing, by which the most productive parts of a landscape are devoted to agriculture so as to free 'spare' land for other uses, but it works on a separating principle, devoting the very land probably preferred by wildlife to farming instead, and can distort a landscape by allowing the removal of paddock trees or waterways, whether they're required by the wildlife or not. 'Alley farming' – alternating strips of cultivated crops and native vegetation

– can go partway to addressing these issues, but still inhabits this confidence that separated elements can remain distinct.

Offsetting, popular with conservative administrations, places a value on native vegetation and considers that value transferrable. Vegetation is evaluated as an asset, accounting is performed and, as with the transfer of money for goods or services, an equivalent value is imposed elsewhere. The values are blunt: the amount of vegetation is assessed, but not its function in the original location, the relationship it has with other elements of an ecology, the lifeforms that live in or depend on it in that location. Native vegetation on this model has two qualities: it is vegetation and it is native. All else is occluded, emptied of texture and history.

In the landscape view – or the mechanistic model of our Enlightenment ancestors – this might make sense. One could grandly shift ecologies from here to there, maintaining tree density or carbon sequestration, numbers and distribution of wildlife. The proportion of brigalow remaining in New South

Wales could, theoretically, stay the same, only sited in different places. Or even increase: if the management of an offset is put out to tender and ecologists are employed to oversee the regeneration, the result may be more copious and higher-quality vegetation than there is today. But the reality is that the ecological benefits in an offsetting scheme often vaporise across a landscape.

Conservationists like to attend to the particular even as they direct attention to broader relationships and literal landscapes. And farmers appreciate the perquisites of local knowledge and personal property, while promoting landscape-scale mechanisms to displace local responsibilities. Modern law, caught between conservationists and landholders, has it both ways: it allows general destruction of wildlife habitat while offering funding for specific salvations. The *Native Vegetation Conservation Act 1997,* which preceded the current Act in New South Wales, established a provision for BioBanking, a market in conservation credits that could be sold or transferred. It is now under a different name and expanded into a larger system. Particular animal species are singled out for preservation even as the plant species in their habitats are reduced. But government regulation *must* be broadscale, even while effects are felt at the local level. A more particulate system would be incoherent and ineffectual, whether applied to governance, conservation or compensation.

Does it matter if one community group loses a campaign to protect remnant vegetation if two groups elsewhere wins theirs? If a patch of endangered ecological community is bulldozed, but the owners increase their wealth and so pay more tax, and the government ultimately has more money to spend on restoring native vegetation?

Does it matter if habitat is fragmented and separated by baking, shadeless fields many kilometres wide, covered in tough stubble or grains soaked in herbicide; if one side of fenceline scrub is deafened with highway traffic, and the other is full of tractors sowing seed; if spray drift is careening and the soil beneath the scrub is weakened by nearby fracking activity; if the rain is infrequent because of clearing-associated rainfall reduction; if the eucalypt leaves are not as nutritious as they used to be; if the summer is hotter and drier for longer than ever before – but there is still a proportion of native vegetation, a certain number of koalas to be seen, giving a percentage likelihood that others have survived so far?

Landscape models are a Ponzi scheme of transferred risks and penalties, the damage hidden by shifting baseline syndrome, their philosophy appealing to fans of permeation metrics and ecosystem epistemology, but hazardous to the real lifeforms and geographies.

Offsetting is included in the current New South Wales legislation as a provision under 'equity', a partner to the idea that public interests in 'taking' from private property should result in reimbursement for the owner. Here equity means that the community should be reimbursed *by* the owner for 'taking' away from a common wealth. But while this seems just, even refreshing, it comes at a cost for the particularity of what is offset. It vacates its meaning, leaves only an outline, a value dispersing across a landscape to condense in some meaningless elsewhere.

The Turnbulls were ordered to regenerate scrub and, if that failed, to plant trees. But a sapling is not a mature tree. It will not house a koala or hollow-nesting birds for many years, if it survives. The distances of range between one habitat and another will not be precisely recreated. The lizards and insects, microbes and small mammals killed in the clearing will not be magically reanimated.

Under the current law, a property with a thousand hectares of native woodland can clear up to a hundred hectares in one three-year period, and another hundred the three years after that. The set-aside areas must be at least double those cleared. There will be, however, a gross diminution of vegetation. Habitat will be weakened. The networks will be partially cut.

If a restoration project might cost $95,000 to regenerate 30 hectares of scrub, down the road farmers might be smashing down 600 hectares for broadacre crops. 'You can destroy what you've got,' Phil Spark explains, 'if you go and plant somewhere else. So the whole time lag and loss of habitat's just massive. The idea is that you're going to recreate the same community, but...' He scoffs.

Years of effort to disprove offsetting have failed, and it now forms the structural rationale of two-thirds of approvals across the country even when they're not properly acquitted or monitored. The impervious accountancy of it persists, the convenience of its equations. In a 2016 report, the Nature Conservation Council of New South Wales examined eight case studies involving offsetting. Environmental outcomes ranged from 'adequate' (two), 'poor' (five) to 'disastrous' (one). Spark says wearily, 'It's like it has some kind of credibility that it just doesn't have.'

***

A WEEK AFTER THE murder trial began in May 2016, Grant Turnbull had another appearance to make, this time in the New South Wales Land and Environment Court. It was to hear the decision on the third lot of clearing on 'Colorado': the clearing his father had been doing on the day he shot Glen Turner.

Grant must have felt he was perpetually being pulled back in time. That July week, the week of the winter road, was here again.

It was the familiar cut-and-paste information from previous decisions. The clearing from early January 2014 to 31 July 2014 was deemed unlawful. The OEH demanded that Grant remediate the areas unlawfully cleared. He hadn't done the remediation from previous convictions for unlawful clearing; instead, his father had cleared the bits supposed to be regenerated. He hadn't, Grant said, realised he was supposed to tell the OEH about that.

The OEH wanted a restraining order on Grant, to stop him clearing any more land. Grant protested. He'd contravened the Act but gave an undertaking that he wouldn't again. That statement of present intent, noted Justice Craig drily, 'must be understood in the context of the events', which is that the OEH had been telling Grant his clearing was wrong since 2012, that he'd had no sign any approval would be given for the clearing and that he'd already been prosecuted for clearing on the same property. 'The circumstances I have identified do not satisfy me that, without a restraining order in place, Mr Turnbull will adhere to the provisions of the NV Act in conducting his farming activities on "Colorado",' said Justice Craig. He slapped Grant with the order.

Grant had to pay the OEH's costs. He had to do the original remediation, and the new. Grant again protested: it would cost him $4.5 million, including fencing.

Outside his father's murder trial a few weeks later, when Grant spoke to the media, he attempted to explain his father's reasons for feeling provoked by the OEH. 'I've never been to any meeting,' said Grant, 'where anybody's said, "Let's go back to the old ways of doing things." It is simply, "Let's get something that is workable. It has to be workable."'

Ian Turnbull had also commented on the situation to his family. 'How are we going with the bloody thing as far as fighting these bastards and paying the bloody fines and whatnot?' he'd said in one of his phone calls recorded from jail. He had apparently been advised not to pay any of the fines – the penalty for not paying them was that Turnbull would go to jail, where of course he already had. His listener murmured in understanding. 'The main thing,' continued Turnbull, 'is to get the bloody [OEH] off our bloody back so the boys can go ahead and farm.'

***

THE 1991 CHAELUNDI CASE, in which the New South Wales government's own forestry commission appeared to have harmed native wildlife in the Chaelundi forest, established that even inadvertent killing or taking of native fauna was a crime. This included the disturbing of habitat and breeding, feeding or nesting; anything, indeed, that jeopardised habitat and led to even a gradual reduction in numbers of an endangered species was a crime.

More laws emerged in the following decade, addressing fisheries, threatened species, land contamination and water, and finally produced the *Native Vegetation Conservation Act.*

Australia, like many nations, had adopted the protocol of ecologically sustainable development in 1992, following the Rio Earth Summit. Its ethos is in 'using, conserving and enhancing the community's resources so that ecological processes, on which life depends, are maintained, and the total quality of life, now and in the future, can be increased'. Embodied in both the current federal and the state environmental legislation, it has four main planks: the precautionary principle, advising caution in activity that may pose a threat to the landscape; intergenerational equity; conservation of biological diversity and ecological integrity; and improved valuation, pricing and incentive mechanisms. Its principles are to be applied, in theory, to all legislation on any kind of development, at any level of governance, for all time.

The *Native Vegetation Conservation Act* was the work of Bob Carr, premier of the state from 1995 until 2005 and architect of some of the most robust environmental protections in New South Wales. Carr introduced the world's first carbon trading scheme, created 350 new national parks, ensured continuous water access along the state coast and enacted laws to control the clearing of native vegetation as part of a program to curb carbon emissions. He also suffered mightily at the hands of infuriated landholder advocacy groups. A variety of interests, including the Ecological Society of Australia and Indigenous representatives, were included in stakeholder consultations for the Act. Its gestation was typically fraught, as committee consensus was vetoed by government, or farmers' advocacy delegates, having agreed to proposals, were opposed when they returned to their communities. Rural communities felt disenfranchised and truculent, and conservation organisations were clenched in frustration.

When the law was passed, rural lobbies protested. The premier was jostled at Walgett Airport and farmers mounted roadblocks to stop compliance officers coming to inspect properties. There was some cause for their unhappiness: farm values plummeted up to a third, and the administration of approvals became agonisingly slow. Yet the law, though inflammatory and difficult, held.

Phil Spark was out at Walgett at the time, working on a regional vegetation plan, one of the Carr government's ideas to allow communities input on regulation. 'It was,' Spark gives an amused puff, 'a bloodbath.' Exasperation colours his face. 'We thought, after four years, that we were just about to get somewhere, and the NSW Farmers completely pulled all their representatives out, out of all the committees that were operating right across the state, and there we were.' He shakes his head. 'We'd just wasted four years.'

Chris Nadolny, too, had been involved in consultations leading to the Act. He'd been assisting the Native Vegetation Advisory Council, established in 1998, to help direct and liaise consultations with community groups, government agencies and landholders. He co-authored a paper explaining the ecological importance of native vegetation; he had had decades of experience in both practical ecology and fractious relations with authority by the time he walked beside Turner across the stubble of 'Strathdoon' and 'Colorado' to see what the Turnbulls had done.

That advisory council published a report in 2000, outlining the crucial benefits of keeping indigenous flora in landscapes. In 2002, the Wentworth Group of Concerned Scientists offered Carr documents that suggested only an immediate end to broadscale clearing would suffice to restore environmental balance. Yet the *Native Vegetation Conservation Act* had come at huge political cost to the Carr government and antagonised landholders and farmers' groups into obduracy. After various interpretations and refinements in the courts, judicial reviews and merits proceedings, the 1997 Act would be revised.

Contemplating the evolution and future vistas of environmental law at the time, co-authors Sarah Wright and Justice Nicola Pain of the New South Wales Land and Environment Court commented, 'There is no doubt that environmental law is becoming more complex. The judgments in the first 10 years of the court's operation were generally shorter and simpler. Judgments now deal with issues of more complexity.' They quoted the then chief judge Peter McClellan, presciently: 'It cannot be assumed that environmental law and the role of the Land and Environment Court will be free of controversy in the future. The court must contribute to the task of balancing the immediate needs of the present generation with the trust we hold for those who will come after us.'

By the time the Turnbulls bought the blocks in Croppa Creek, the pace of land clearing had slowed, down to about 60 per cent of its previous levels, and the proportion of vegetation that remained was beginning to stabilise – though only about 10 per cent had been truly undisturbed. In 2014, the year of

Turner's death, WWF Australia released a report by ecologists Dr Martin Taylor and Professor Christopher Dickman claiming that more than a million animal deaths had been avoided over a decade. The preservation of habitat alone had saved 100,000 animals a year.

But the same year that report was released, clearing accelerated massively, as landowners anticipated a long-desired change of laws.

*

'WHAT I HAVE DONE,' Turnbull said in a recorded phone call from jail, 'is dropped a bomb to wake people up to what's going on, that's the way I look at it.' In a later call, he said, 'I hope they – even if they alter the law because of the shock treatment. I didn't do it for that reason, but yeah.'

A terrorist act, says Chris Nadolny now of the killing of Glen Turner. A terrorist act with political effect.

In 2011, when Turnbull and his family contemplated buying 'Colorado' and 'Strathdoon', New South Wales was still running the version of the *Native Vegetation Act* that prohibited clearing on most rural land in the state without a property vegetation plan. Clearing would only be allowed when, under the ecologically sustainable development protocol, it 'maintained or improved environmental outcomes'. Some reforms had been made to the Act: farmers were able to conduct some clearing for activities specific to farming, such as keeping roads available, and the approvals process was improved. There were farmers who were happy with the regulations, but complaints persisted. The Labor minister for the environment, Robyn Parker, invited submissions for a review of the law aimed at streamlining the approvals process, removing ambiguities and maintaining environmental standards.

An Independent Biodiversity Legislation Review Panel was formed, chaired by Dr Neil Byron, who had previously chaired the Productivity Commission's inquiry on native vegetation regulations. He was a known critic of the Act. Another member was Dr Wendy Craik, an eminent policy figure known from the Productivity and Murray–Darling Basin commissions. The ecological representative was Hugh Possingham, a respected scientist experienced in biodiversity management and 'ecological economics'. The panel wrangled their way through the apparently paradoxical aims of supporting environmental standards while removing obstacles for landholders to clear ecologies. Fundamentally, an evaluation had to be made as to how well conservationists could trust landholders to clear responsibly, and how much farmers might concede to nature. There would be, threaded through the debates, the dilemma between the virtues of local, site-specific ecology and landscape-scale priorities.

Up for revision were not only the *Native Vegetation Act,* but also the *Threatened Species Conservation Act 1995,* the *Nature Conservation Trust Act 2001* and, tangentially, the *Natural Resources Commission Act 2003.* The parts of the *National Parks and Wildlife Act* concerning animals and plant provisions were due for review too, as well as the native vegetation management elements of the *Catchment Management Authorities Act 2003.* It was to be a comprehensive clearing and regeneration of the law.

Momentum for change had come, not just from years of irritation among farmers, but due to a push from the Nationals and the Shooters and Fishers Party for more landowner rights. Farming is a tricky, expert business; how insulting to be patronised by out-of-town 'experts' and chastised by urban greenies. Where was the trust, where was the respect? Inspectors flew drones overhead, spying to catch farmers out, or encouraged neighbours to dob one another in. Communities were deliberately set at war, mortgages grew inflamed, and meanwhile all the work by grandfathers and great-grandfathers was being undone as the scrub grew back.

'It's all part of the disconnect,' Phil Spark reflects. 'That's my big thing – the government's approach to all these land management issues. They don't come out and seriously put up the science and seriously explain to people why we need to be managing land in a particular way. They just put it out there, and they actually talk against their own regulation rather than go the other way and justify it. And I see that all the time, and it's been that way for years.'

Conservationists, meanwhile, felt that biodiversity laws weren't strong enough. The laws focused on primary producers but overlooked other parties, such as mining companies and urban developers, and farmers, unable or unwilling to work with the laws, were clearing regardless of law. Then there were concerns over the implications for carbon pollution. Hoping for improvement, conservation alliances agreed to participate in a review.

In 2011, a preliminary review suggested amendments to the approvals process, and that more 'routine agricultural management activities' should be permitted. In 2013, as the Turnbulls were clearing, there was a recommendation that more types of clearing could be self-assessed. In March 2014, four months before Turner's death, the OEH published two reports. One confirmed that rates of clearing woody vegetation were generally decreasing.

The other report offered provisional guidance on how farmers might self-assess the clearing of invasive native species and paddock trees, and thin existing native vegetation. No one liked these drafts: conservationists saw the worrisome lack of oversight; landholders thought them too technical, impractical. 'We reviewed all the legislation leading up to this point,' remembers Spark, 'and wrote massive submissions about all the flaws of it.' He was with the Northern Inland Council for the Environment at the time. 'And I think even *we* underestimated the potential of it.'

Two months later, the Shooters and Fishers Party introduced a bill into the New South Wales parliament to fully renovate the old laws. Social and economic factors, according to that bill, should be in the mix, instead of the test on maintaining or improving environmental outcomes.

Finally, in December 2014, five months after Turner's murder, the Independent Biodiversity Legislation Review Panel delivered its first report on revising native vegetation laws, with

Chapter 1 titled 'A Clear Case for Reform'. Existing regulations had 'created mistrust', it said. '[E]ducational, suasive and incentive measures' should be used more often, and 'a risk-based approach be taken to regulation', emphasising voluntary compliance while 'still giving regulators the tools to take strong enforcement action'. The report suggested that a site-specific focus on protecting biodiversity be replaced by landscape-wide outcomes. There were forty-three recommendations, and the balance between environmental and landholder needs could only, *only* be kept if all of the recommendations were taken up. Implicit in the plan was a philosophy that the community should pay for the long-term shared benefits when farmers had to set aside productive land.

Maintaining and improving an environmental state on a particular property was, as the Shooters and Fishers Party had hoped, no longer to be a test of any proposed development. Losses of biodiversity could happen. But there would be more support for private land conservation; now there could be both set-asides and offsets. New agricultural projects, such as clearing old grazing blocks for cropping, would be rigorously tested, instead of written off as simply a continuation of earlier land management. There would be significant funding for detailed maps to help landholders divine biodiversity quality and location. And there would be compliance with the protocol of ecologically sustainable development, even up to consideration of social outcomes and needs.

By late 2014, self-assessable codes were introduced to cover woody invasive weeds, vegetation thinning and isolated paddock trees. Landholders could also self-assess the wildlife present on a property, perhaps with a consultant ecologist, and judge if it was robust enough to survive clearing. Landholders had to notify of what they were doing, and their assessment might be checked, but they did not need a property vegetation plan or a permit. No approval or expert evaluation was needed before bringing out the dozer.

The koalas up in the trees of 'Colorado' were oblivious, but they had lost some of their protection. Things were a long way from restoration, and a thousand animal species were still threatened with extinction in New South Wales. But it was only in areas the OEH judged to be 'sensitive' that an inspection was needed before a landholder was given approval to clear.

When the new legislation was proposed, Spark and his colleagues presented the Turnbull case to the state environment minister as an example. They asked if the clearing done by the Turnbulls, so painfully investigated and prosecuted, convicted and appealed, fined and argued about and paid for by a man's life, would be legal under the new law. The minister, by their account, said yes.

'So.' Spark pauses. 'Yeah.'

If Turnbull hadn't been elderly, if he hadn't felt an anxious urgency, if he could have just waited a couple more years, if he hadn't felt it was the last of the black soil, if he hadn't felt it was the last of his strength, he might have got away with it. Turner would have lived. Grant and Cory would have had their investments intact. The blocks would still have been cleared, the koalas homeless, the brigalow and belah splintered and burned, but Talga Lane would have remained quiet.

'What greater slap in the face could you have for Glen's family, you know? They lost their father and husband and then the government's admitting that it [would be] all legal.'

19

Ill fares the land, to hastening ills a prey,
Where wealth accumulates, and men decay...

—Oliver Goldsmith, 'The Deserted Village', 1770

In July 2016, yet another court case cascaded onto Sylvester Joseph's overloaded desk at Cole & Butler in Moree. Roger's patience had cracked. He was suing his parents for that inheritance.

Like Robert Strange, Roger submitted documents in support of his claim to the equity division of the Supreme Court. His father had bullied him and his wife, he said. There had been a clear understanding; he had sacrificed other opportunities to observe that understanding, and had invested 'substantial capital' back into the family business. And now his dad was stiffing him.

Ian denied it all. There had never been any promise, he riposted. Roger had been paid, in food and board, a car and fuel, and he'd had a share of profits. Ian had never bullied him or Annette. The only thing he did concede was that there'd been a partition agreement: a complete severance of all interests between Roger and his parents' business. It had been a waiver arrangement. He was entitled to absolutely nothing.

Meanwhile, the administration of the Turnbulls' assets was in Grant's hands. Grant, from where Roger stood, was clearly the favoured heir.

Roger pursued the case for months, awaiting a court date. He and Annette continued to live on 'Royden', across the road from 'Yambin'. Robeena was now living with Grant in Toowoomba, but she came back to visit occasionally. The situation was difficult for Cory, caught in the middle. He still owned 'Strathdoon', and he and his uncle Grant were linked by the prosecution cases still spooling out of the OEH for the clearing.

The lawyers' bills mounted. Ian Turnbull's health wasn't improving in jail. And in the end, in early 2017, Roger gave up the case. It was just too much grief. The inheritance was passed from the patriarch's possession to Robeena's. His mother wouldn't see him right, he felt. Everyone was loyal to his father – a convicted murderer, and the man Roger saw as a bully and Annette called 'an arrogant, disgusting pig'. Roger was on his own.

***

MORE THAN TWO YEARS on from Turner's murder, it seemed the OEH was still cautious about provoking confrontations with farmers or taking on cases it didn't feel it had a certainty of winning. In late 2016, the ABC's *Lateline* program sent reporter Kerry Brewster to country New South Wales to investigate what was happening with land-clearing laws.

One curious case, Brewster noted, was the abrupt dropping of the investigation into twelve farmers near Wee Waa, ninety minutes' drive southwest of Moree, known for its intensive cotton farming. The farmers had been told that their properties were soon to be inspected by the OEH due to alleged illegal land clearing. Then nothing happened. No inspections. No further investigation. No explanation.

There were rumours that department staff were discouraged from using surveillance technology to confirm illegal clearing and that they were told, at times, to ignore reports of it. Brewster got hold of a May 2015 email sent by Kevin Humphries, in whose electorate Wee Waa sits, to other members of state parliament, including premier Mike Baird. He'd bluntly suggested all agencies back away from the case: 'It is too explosive and not warranted.' Farmers, he explained, were already agitated and ready to begin blockading their properties from the OEH. 'It will be the start of something,' he warned, 'that will escalate very quickly between farmers from around the state and the authorities.'

'They're driven by this little core minority,' says Phil Spark, 'that seem to have all the political clout.' Humphries, Spark recalls, put the news of the closure of the investigations in Wee Waa on his website.

Brewster asked Humphries about his email to Baird and others. Was it warning of a threat of violence, as had occurred to Glen Turner? Humphries reminded her of conflict in the Macquarie Valley in 2007, when police were sent in to protect compliance officers. He explained his email as sincere concern. 'We don't want to go back to the stage where we need police to protect the authorities to go out to investigate things.' Under Brewster's persistent questioning, he denied he had perverted the course of justice.

The field operation in Wee Waa was suspended, Brewster explained to viewers, because the OEH feared there was an 'extreme risk' of another catastrophe. Apparently frontier violence was still an issue in the twenty-first century. One OEH officer had, in internal documents seen by *The Guardian,* considered that 'the comments of Mr Humphries amount to a threat which cannot be adequately assessed in the available time'.

The official OEH explanation was that a decision had been made 'to postpone' the investigation for 'operational reasons'. It was simply a matter of priority and evaluation, the agency said. In the year to June 2016, the OEH had overseen '520 advisory letters, 320 warning letters, 78 penalty notices, 42 remedial directions, 14 native vegetation prosecutions and secured penalties exceeding $1m'.

The Nature Conservation Council and the Environmental Defenders Office were among the bodies that sprang to call for further probing: an investigation into non-investigations. The connection between the Nationals, big agribusiness and regulation authorities must be examined, they said. There was a clear implication of political interference in the application of native vegetation protection laws.

Those native vegetation protection laws were due to be changed in state parliament that very week.

*

'THE CURRENT NATIVE VEGETATION law puts the onus of biodiversity entirely on farmers — it doesn't share the responsibility across society,' Kevin Humphries said in August 2016. He had worked to repeal the *Native Vegetation Act* since he'd been elected in 2007. He spoke of farmers who didn't want to clear. He explained that many of them understood the importance of native vegetation for soil health. He used the word 'balance'. He did not mention that in the Golden Triangle — which sits, of course, in his electorate of Barwon — cleared land can sell for more than $6800 a hectare, making it the richest cropping country in the continent. At least two farmers would later testify that Humphries, around this time, was pledging to landholders that the laws would be overturned and so they could soon clear with impunity.

In March 2015, the government had adopted all of the Independent Biodiversity Legislation Review Panel's forty-three recommendations. Then in May 2016, a draft package of legislation was released. At first glance it looked like a victory for conservation but, as Chris Nadolny puts it, 'the devil was in the detail'. There were exploitable gaps between the revised *Local Land Services Act 2013 No.51,* which managed natural resources, and the new conservation law; the legislation definitely did not, Nadolny and many others judged, comply with the principles of ecologically sustainable development. Neither the precautionary principle, intergenerational equity nor the preservation of ecological integrity appeared to have been applied.

Submissions were invited from stakeholders and the community. Debates were once more thrashed out. By February 2016, the conservation groups asked to contribute to the draft laws had had enough; they walked out of consultations with the OEH. Now they constellated as the Stand Up for Nature alliance, with the Nature Conservation Council of New South Wales, WWF, Humane Society International, NSW Wildlife Information Rescue and Education Service, and the National Parks Association of NSW all contributing their authority and resources. The NSW Farmers Association declared that they were persisting with negotiations and accused the conservation groups of pique.

Again, the submissions poured in, the concerns, the frustrations. The state environment department reported just over 1000 submissions to the panel in 2014. But more than 7000 were received by the second round, in 2016: the Stand Up for Nature alliance of conservation groups had mustered more than 5000. A mere 150 of the total were identified as being from the farming sector, which fumed over 'click and submit' urban-oriented campaigns. The majority, by far, wanted stronger laws and more environmental protection.

*

NEVERTHELESS, SOME LANDHOLDER ADVOCATES were pleased with the direction things were heading. 'The take away message for developers and landowners alike,' wrote Paul Vergotis, an environment lawyer specialising in appeals against the New South Wales Land and Environment Court, 'is that the Bill proposes a regulatory system that is ostensibly flexible, permissive, and market-based. The suggested changes will reduce red tape and unnecessary regulation, and make land clearing easier.' Others weren't satisfied. The NSW Farmers Association pulled out of consultations for a time in mid-2016 – despite their disparagement of the conservation groups for doing the same. Their problems were ambiguity about the rate and scale of allowable clearing, and obscurity on the subject of vegetation mapping. Members were concerned that the government, having tempted them with full reforms, might end up making concessions to the other side. 'We believe many farmers will not engage or participate in a system that is over regulated, complicated and riddled with restrictions,' said Mitchell Clapham, soon to become the association's president. The organisation passed a unanimous motion withholding support for the new law unless the government agreed to pay them for all the cost associated with upholding environmental restrictions. They said they were being asked to act as park rangers, but without pay.

In August 2016, an OEH report on land-clearing rates was released, taking into account the impact of the self-assessment codes that had been introduced in 2014. The previous report had assessed rates as stabilising or even diminishing; now, updated data showed an increase, and almost two-thirds of that was 'unexplained', possibly illegal, like the Turnbulls'. It was possible, the report said, that the government data was underestimating clearing by six fold. Now that landholders could decide for themselves what might be 'protected' or not, a disastrous trend was forming.

Koala habitat and wetlands, said Kate Smolski, chief executive of the Nature Conservation Council of New South Wales, were not guaranteed protection in the new laws. The Gwydir Wetlands, approximately 60 kilometres west of Moree, already had only 20 per cent of the ecological community that had existed fifteen years earlier. And there was no accounting for indirect environmental damage, such as silting of waterways once riverine trees were logged or billabongs filled in.

Only the previous month, a report in the international journal *Science* revealed the devastating likelihood that human activity had destroyed biodiversity to the point where ecosystems might stop functioning properly across 58 per cent of the planet. Elemental processes such as nutrient cycling, pollination and growth were in jeopardy. The significance of biodiversity health could not have been more clear.

In New South Wales, the Independent Biodiversity Legislation Review Panel was divided, with ecologist Hugh Possingham increasingly worried that the draft legislation was encouraging the most damaging forms of clearing: broadscale and of threatened species. The draft had been reshaped since his participation in the report two years earlier. His concerns were being overridden. In November 2016, he resigned from the panel.

That month, the amendments and repeals were, after years of discussion, passed in the parliament. The debate was closed; the new laws were official. They would come into effect within a year.

The legislation came in two parts. There was the *Biodiversity Conservation Act 2016,* which concerned protections for native ecology and supported conservation, mandating penalties for offences. Then there was the *Local Land Services Amendment Act 2016,* which oversaw land management such as agriculture, handled permissions for clearing and assessed exemptions. Chris Nadolny, asked by *The Sydney Morning Herald* for comment, tried to be equitable. The *Biodiversity Act,* he said, had liabilities: it didn't include issues such as greenhouse gas emissions, and had, troublingly, lost the imperative to 'improve or maintain' the environment. But it was mostly well intentioned and did include some conservation science. However, the *Land Services Act* was concerning. This is where theories of environmental stewardship were actually practised, and he couldn't see any conservation science in any of the codes, only potential for dangerous practices. It could, Nadolny said, 'threaten the most significant remnants of native vegetation in overdeveloped landscapes'.

The Liberal minister for the environment, Mark Speakman, assured the media that farmers would now have incentives to 'do the right thing by the environment'. This included the money for private conservation. And there were safeguards against massive clearing. 'What happened in Queensland simply cannot happen here,' he said. Across the border, the rates of clearing had tripled to 300,000 hectares under the Campbell Newman government.

But opposition spokesperson Penny Sharpe said the new law in New South Wales would increase land clearing, as well as erosion, salinity and carbon emissions, and harm wildlife. She promised a Labor government would 'overhaul' the laws if elected in 2019. Mehreen Faruqi, the Greens environment spokeswoman in the state parliament, also condemned the new law. It was, she said, 'the biggest act of environmental vandalism we have ever seen in New South Wales'.

Alaine Anderson, Turnbull's neighbour, just wondered if things had to be so complicated. Was it too much to ask that a patch of green was left on every property? 'If we all did a little bit,' she said plaintively, 'even on a four-acre place you can bring the little birds.'

***

LONG BAY CORRECTIONAL COMPLEX, opened in 1909, is home to the Kevin Waller Unit for elderly male inmates. The buildings are brick, with watchtowers and barbed-wire fences; Christmas decorations are put on the severe exterior every December. There are great Norfolk pines for the inmates to gaze upon in their outside time.

It wasn't a comfortable place for an old farmer. Inmates were generally two to a cell. In January 2017, one man in his seventies smashed his cellmate to death with a sandwich-maker. The younger of the elderly customarily helped others with bedwetting or mobility problems. The bunks didn't have railings. There wasn't room for mobility aids in the cells.

Days went by. Days went by.

In November 2016, the month the native vegetation laws were passed, Ian Turnbull had a stroke and was taken to the Prince of Wales Hospital in Randwick. Four months later, he had another. Again, he was taken to hospital. He was diagnosed with heart disease, then possible sepsis. He was put gently on palliative care. His family was there at his bedside.

On 27 March 2017, Ian Turnbull died of kidney failure and heart issues, at the age of eighty-two.

There was a post-mortem – external only. He was spared the intimate examination made of Glen Turner's remains. The coroner's report optimistically extolled the dignity of recognising the life lived before a death. 'Unfortunately,' wrote magistrate Derek Lee, the deputy state coroner, 'in this case, very little is known about Mr Turnbull's personal life.'

Reporters following the murder had solemnly presented the Turnbulls as squattocracy stalwarts of the district for 200 years, but that wasn't true. Ian's contributions to the Croppa Creek community were affectionately remembered by residents, but his name doesn't appear in the district papers. Locals in Moree had recently been heard describing him as a 'crank', still dismayed at the attention he'd brought the town; locals in Croppa Creek said nothing to anyone, but some continued to murmur that Glen Turner had harassed the family, that he'd trespassed, that he'd pushed the old man to the brink.

Roger felt differently. 'He's always been a mudguard,' he would tell a reporter. 'Shiny on top, shitty underneath.'

Ian Turnbull was buried in Moree Cemetery. He had been in custody since July 2014, but had served less than twelve months of the 35-year sentence for Turner's murder. The Turnbull family had, in fact, been preparing to appeal the penalty in May.

Alison McKenzie said she'd been spared the anguish of seeing Turnbull protest his sentence. 'We will never have closure, it's just something we are learning to live with,' she told journalist Breanna Chillingworth from *The Northern Daily Leader,* who had covered the case from the start. But, she added with relief, 'he died a convicted murderer'.

For Robert Strange, the fact that Turnbull had served only months of his sentence for the killing was upsetting.

'It didn't sit well with me,' Robert Strange told SBS's *Insight* program. 'It still doesn't.'

A death notice was placed in the paper at the time of Turnbull's death. Ian Robert Turnbull, Late of 'Yambin', Moree, it read. Passed away on 27th March 2017 aged 82 years. Beloved husband of Robeena. Dearly loved father and father-in-law of Doug and Anne, Roger and Annette, Grant and Jacci, Sam and Justine. Much-loved grandfather and great-grandfather of their children. Ian's funeral was held on 6th April 2017. 'Will Always Be Loved and Remembered'.

20

No one argued that we should accept this poor, old continent for what it was. It was ours to improve, to manage. We were to take what was and use our knowledge to make gain for our nation and humanity.

—David Smith, Australian agricultural scientist, circa 1960s

'Dear Premier and Minister for the Environment, I am writing to you today to voice my concerns about the land-clearing laws proposed to come into force.'

It was August 2017, and the new legislation was due to take effect within a week. Alison McKenzie had written an open letter to the state government to share her feelings on the subject.

McKenzie, Fran Pearce and two of Turner's former colleagues, now ex-OEH, had asked to preview the draft legislation and meet with Local Land Services staff to discuss its implications. They were grateful for the opportunity.

his life upholding the laws of our state to preserve habitat for future generations. With the diminishing of those laws, the value of his life is further diminished.'

Environment minister Gabrielle Upton responded to McKenzie's letter. 'Glen Turner was a highly valued and experienced environment officer who was murdered just doing his job. Our state lost a good man,' she reassured his widow and supporters. 'I can assure them that the new codes and laws in no way diminish Glen's work or life.' But, she added, '[t]here will be no delay to the codes' introduction.'

'You can't help thinking,' muses Phil Spark, 'about theories of extinction debt [the number of species in an area likely to become extinct] and island biogeography [biodiversity in isolated natural communities], looking at remnants becoming unviable and population decline. And one of the stupid things with this legislation is there's no consideration for the landscape issue with their clearing. This continuing use code, if you've cleared it once before, or your grandfather has,

'However,' she wrote, 'the meeting did not dispel our concerns.' It was apparent that Turnbull's clearing would soon be considered legal. She mentioned liabilities and contradictions in the proposed scheme. She mentioned Turner's experience of farmers' intransigence with regulations. 'It appears the new regulations have been written to satisfy farmers/property developers like the Turnbulls,' she wrote frankly, and asked the government to delay the laws until they'd been reviewed again by environment experts. 'The regulations are clearly not based on the principles of conservation biology.'

She had never wanted her husband's death to be politicised, she wrote. 'Ian Turnbull was overheard to say that he was willing to be a "martyr for the cause" and murdered Glen in an act to force the hand of government to change the laws to suit large property developers such as himself.' She'd hoped, hearing of the law changes, that they would increase conservation efforts, not lead to more destruction. But, '[i]t seems that he was successful. Glen lost then you're allowed to clear it again!' Farming need not cede any prerogatives. Regrowth and recuperation would not be encouraged, and land bared back to 1950 could be denuded once more. Except for the most critically endangered communities, environmental impacts were not relevant. 'So there's no overriding planning on how we're going to improve the viability of all species. Science just doesn't come into it.'

An emerging theme, as criticism of the new legislation grew, was the suppression of research and expertise. Politics and economics, some said, had nobbled evidence-based policy. 'Science is just forgotten,' Spark says. 'It's just relegated. I think that's partly because most of the people involved in science are now gagged in their occupation; they don't seem able to speak out like they should be or could be.'

Alison McKenzie, too, had word from those in the field. 'From what we have heard,' she said in her letter, 'the expert knowledge of staff was not included, nor were environmental scientists and conservation groups, or their submissions, which also appear to have been ignored.'

The OEH was due to administer the legislation, but when those in the organisation discussed its workings, there was a stifled whine of frustration. Occasional news articles emerged with hints of a department beset by funding issues, high turnover and vexed staff negotiating demanding obligations. The office was pained, with apparent fractures between its divisions, including tension between the science division and other groups of the organisation, which had soured into secrecy and lack of trust. Since Turner's murder, staff had been tried by trauma; by tests of their resolve, as some went out into the field to face potential conflict; and by murmurs of political pressure, which only grew with the revelations of suppressed investigations at Wee Waa.

Investigative resources were insufficient. The small staff was overworked, sometimes inexperienced, and unsupported to manage the intense workload of field inspections, administration of warnings and stop-work notices, and preparations for prosecution, which had to occur within the two-year statutory period for bringing an offence to court. Officers were shuffled from department to department. A staff member takes a redundancy and is not replaced. Another takes leave. A prosecution falls apart because the person who was in charge has moved on.

Phil Spark shakes his head when asked about the situation, saying that even good people are caught up in the department's culture of caution. 'It's very, very big. It's really big.'

When Alison McKenzie wrote her letter, Spark had been hunched over his computer for weeks. He was doggedly compiling a dossier on the events that led to the death of his ally. It was wrong that the process to address Turnbull's land clearing had been so inadequate. It was wrong that questions remained unanswered. It was tremendously wrong that Turner had been put in a position that led to his death. Each night Spark sat up late, after a day in the field, working on a request for a coronial inquest to investigate how Glen Turner came to be unprotected after a threat was made against him in the course of his professional duties. This is what Spark did in his spare time. His wife called it him 'playing golf'.

By May, he had a file. He'd collected all the correspondence between himself, Alaine Anderson and the authorities from the years of the Turnbull clearing. He had copies of his submissions to the state and federal agencies; he had the letter from the Environmental Defenders Office advising him on what terms in the native vegetation protection legislation the Turnbulls may have violated back in 2012; he had a timeline that itemised every single development, as far as he could tell, in the sorry tale of efforts to uphold that protection and their failure. He wrote a polite, infuriated letter to accompany his submission to the NSW Coroner's Court.

He had a strong relationship with Alison McKenzie by now. Her grief had transmuted into an adamantine commitment to continuing Glen's environmental defence. He was requesting the inquest on behalf of

Turner's family: Alison, Fran, Glen's parents, the kids. They wanted someone to address all sorts of failures. The OEH was compromised, the staff unable to do their work properly; the legislation they were supposed to be helping enforce wasn't being applied. According to Spark, shortly before his death Turner made a statement describing his work situation and outlining his concerns.

Spark had a litany of questions, starting with how, in light of a memorandum of understanding between the OEH and the New South Wales Police Force that gives compliance officers access to information about the police history of any property owners before an inspection, the threat to Turner wasn't reported. Turnbull had no prior record of convictions or trouble with authorities. But Turner – who had previously been injured by a hostile landholder with a quad bike – had reported the incident to his managers. Where had the police been, after a government officer was threatened by another man who owned guns?

Meanwhile, up on the Gold Coast, Grant Turnbull's father-in-law, Leslie Slater, who'd worked on Grant's properties from time to time, was starting his own fat file of correspondence. He wrote to SafeWork NSW, to the state government and later, like Spark, to the Coroner's Court. He had, he said, evidence of 'a great injustice' and 'an immense cover up'.

Glen Turner and Robert Strange, Slater asserted, were seen in Talga Lane that afternoon. A person, unknown to Robert Strange, and whose identity had apparently been suppressed by the Supreme Court, had witnessed the men standing across the fenceline on 'Colorado' that evening. As the court had summarily rejected the defence's 'tendency to harass' argument about Turner, this witness had never been called. The implication was that, though trespass didn't justify murder, it informed the pattern of supposed harassment. In addition, the OEH, despite having removed Turner from the investigation, didn't tell him to stay away from the Turnbulls when he called in to Arthur Snook that night:

Mr Glenn Turner from the OE&H was illegally trespassing on Mr Turnbull's property well out of his working hours after being instructed by his superiors to not proceed on that day, on being confronted by Mr Turnbull, Mr Turner threatened to bring down and destroy all the Turnbull family farms. Mr Glenn Turner was at this point highly affected by drugs at the time of his death. Mr Ian Turnbull was at the age of 81, charged with murder and given a 34 year conviction with a 24 year non-parole period, clearly extreme by any judicial standards.

'Ian Turnbull would not hurt a fly and [is] an ultimate gentleman,' Slater wrote to Peter Dunphy, the executive director of SafeWork NSW. He claimed that Turner, having made threats against the Turnbulls, had been taken off the case and Gary Spencer forced to intercede. He complained that the OEH should have prevented Turner from nearing the Turnbull properties, but he'd continued 'on a frolic of his own'. 'Therefore Mr Glen Turner and more importantly his superiors knew there was a risk and did nothing about it beforehand.' That inaction, he concluded, 'is partly to blame for the tragedy that has befallen the Turner family and the Turnbull family.'

In another letter, he expanded on this proposition: '[I]f this employee had been following his workplace procedures he may well be alive today and another man not be in jail, and possibly if the relevant department doesn't change its ability to control their employees this may not be the only death in relation the native vegetation act.'

In Slater's view, Turner's well-attested provocation had not been given due weight, and the 'habitual' use of marijuana Slater alleged not considered relevant. Nor, the provocation defence being denied, was a verdict of manslaughter permitted in the judge's direction to the jury. 'This is all on record. Is this democracy in action?' Meanwhile, 'the persecution continues as Mr Grant Turnbull is still being prosecuted from the OE&H ... [s]omeone in Government has been pulling strings in many areas.' The OEH, the Land and Environment Court and the Supreme Court of New South Wales had all concealed or denied crucial evidence exonerating Turnbull and his family from their crimes, and protected the reputation of Turner, 'a rogue employee doing as he wanted bullying the farming community without managerial responsibility or restraint'. Slater was only further persuaded of this collusion when SafeWork replied with a lack of enthusiasm for reopening concluded investigations, and the NSW Coroner's Court with no interest in the information he claimed to have.

'It is hoped,' Phil Spark wrote measuredly to the NSW Coroner's Court in the same period, 'recommendations could be made to make the role of compliance staff more safe, and the process from field investigation to court hearing streamlined, to enable a speedy resolution in court that would be better for all concerned.'

Slater could not have been aware of Spark's words. But there was some overlap in ambitions between the victim's colleague and the relative of the killer. '[S]ome accountability is required,' he complained, 'and it is a matter of "public interest" for the facts, not just what they want us to hear, to be laid bare and be properly investigated.'

*

A MONTH AFTER THEIR patriarch's death, Grant and Cory Turnbull were back in the Land and Environment Court to discuss the second bouts of clearing that had taken place five years earlier. It was April 2017 by the time this matter was addressed before patient Justice Preston, with the usual reprise of background history, seriousness of the charges, pleas of misunderstanding, definition of polygons cleared, heated disputes about how many and what kinds of trees removed, disagreement between ecologists' testimonies, mathematical additions of estimated area cleared, passing concern about koala populations potentially affected, quotes from authorities' advice given … It was all done first for Grant, and then for Cory. The verdicts and sentencing wouldn't happen until October.

The discussions themselves, though they ended in guilty pleas, took five days.

Chris Nadolny had had to prepare his notes, his memories, yet again and travel to Sydney. Out came the lists of trees now long since felled and burned, the possibility of crushed native grasses almost no one had noticed, the deaths of koalas known only from their scat and their silence. Nadolny stood and gave his testimony. The courtroom was a chamber of weary ghosts.

***

THE ASSUMPTION IN LANDOWNER Australia, as it has been since Europeans declared it *terra nullius* and took it, since squatters ignored government boundaries but cried for protection in frontier war, since the Land Acts and their obligations faded into historical memory, is that owners own. 'If government continues to restrict and compromise farmers' agricultural production with environmental regulation for the benefit of the wider community,' said an aggrieved Mitchell Clapham of the NSW Farmers Association, 'then government has to be prepared to pay for it, not farmers.'

Who is responsible for the environment? Not the landowner who exploits it, apparently. The government ended up squeezed between the demands of landholders and the pressure of conservation agencies. There should have been less bureaucracy as self-assessment entered the system, but compliance and consultation and arbitration were still the government's remit. They were also paying off the effects of the damage wrought by the landholders. Mining companies usually must pay royalties to access the assets of the earth that belong to the nation. Farmers, some of whom strip the earth just as effectively, do not have to do the same.

In the spirit of equity, the new New South Wales environmental legislation carried not only greater encouragement for farmers to clear vegetation, but more money to counter its environmental costs. Part of the package saw the New South Wales government pledge hundreds of millions of dollars over the coming years for conservation and rewilding. Native vegetation and its wildlife could be destroyed, and others would fix it up.

Meanwhile, only *critically* endangered species of ecology were protected, and not necessarily their habitat. Paddock trees, those isolated sentinels, gnarled and riven, were not. They are cities of insects, spiders and reptiles, as well as being havens for birds and mammals. Paddock trees shelter, and their deep old roots enrich the earth, drawing nutrients back to the surface, regulating salinity, circulating water, stabilising the soil. The trees exhale oxygen, the roots attract nitrogen-fixing bacteria; the manured grass beneath a shady paddock tree is sweet. And as landmarks and stepping stones for animals, they form connectivity with other scattered trees. Ecologists propose protecting them from grazing as part of integrated landscape management, as they were treated by First Nations people.

The early settlers found clumps of trees in open country to be 'picturesque', and the sight still stirs nationalistic affection in many of us:

great twisted river redgums or ironwoods, elders of the country. They are monuments to endurance and grandness.

They are mostly mentioned in agricultural literature as an obstruction. Modern farming equipment runs best in straight lines, and 'tramlining' techniques abhor an impediment. The New South Wales Department of Planning, Infrastructure and Environment website says that paddock trees could be lost entirely from southeast Australia within the next hundred years. It does not mention all the dozers pushing them over, fifty a day and counting.

In a decade of work as an ecological surveyor, Phil Spark has seen several extinctions from the local area. Rock wallabies, once prolific, are vanished from this side of the Range. The booloorong frog population, much reduced. The yellow-spotted bell frog on the Southern Tablelands, the hooded robin, almost gone. He noticed little plant species too, medics and panics and grasses, vanishing from the roadsides where they'd once been crammed.

For the brigalow, in shrunken belts and miserable pockets, strung along travelling stock routes and espaliered along fencelines, the margins of farmland have been some of the last refuges. Now they too were open for clearing, virtually to the fenceline, under the exemption for routine farm maintenance needs. 'So that landscape,' says Spark, 'that's already down to probably 5 per cent native vegetation, they can now clear it.'

Many of us probably imagine that there are nature reserves full of scrub somewhere, old bushlands preserved and safeguarded, stocked with all types of native flora. Spark is blunt. 'There's no reserve. Or a fraction of a reserve. So as far as some kind of adequate reserve system that covers all the vegetation communities, there's next to none. So yeah, we're down to what's left on private properties and travelling stock routes.'

Almost everything else is already gone.

*

'SOLASTALGIA,' EXPLAINS GLENN ALBRECHT, an Australian philosopher, 'has its origins in the concepts of "solace" and "desolation".' Solace, he writes, is associated with comfort against distress; desolation is a distress associated with abandonment and loneliness. Albrecht conceived the word by contemplating the relationship between environmental change, ecosystem distress and human distress, and coined the term in 2003 to describe the phenomenon, perhaps ancient but certainly modern, of a sense of 'homesickness', a skewed nostalgia, that may be felt not when one is far from home, but when home itself has become unhomely and strange.

It was invented to express the feelings of people living in the Upper Hunter, not far from Moree, where, over twenty years, rich farming land was gouged for open-cut mines and power stations. The landscape was changed utterly, and people felt not just melancholy, but powerless. Their grief wasn't new in that place: 150 years earlier, First Nations peoples had seen their homeland pounded out of shape, their totem animals bloodied, their own care of country broken. Sickness, madness and despair come from such sorrow.

As then, not all of us react with concern to the phenomenon of rapid, voracious development across the globe. For some, it is the mark of progress, a triumph. For others, it appears God's work. For yet more, it represents the glory of personal profit. There must be people who gaze at the prospects of the Earth in the twenty-first century and feel confident and good. Their horizons gleam bright beyond fields as golden as those of Elysium.

***

IT WAS 7.30A.M. ON Alaine Anderson's property. The air was clear on a Friday morning. Then, with no warning, a helicopter appeared, bashing through the trees, whipping the air, with rapid gunfire coming from it. *Bang, bang, bang.*

It was neighbours, though not the Turnbulls. They were shooting for feral pigs. The old landowners have been succeeded by 'a young generation who don't give a stuff about anyone else: everyone for themselves'.

Kangaroos are also fair game around there. Country people believe they ruin the crops, though a 1992 CSIRO report found the extent of their impact hard to determine. If shots are fired from a helicopter or a moving vehicle, locals consider the hunting to be outside regular restrictions.

Now live fire spattered from the helicopter doors. 'The noise was unbelievable. It was just like Vietnam,' Anderson says. 'It was so scary, and I was in tears.'

After comforting a backpacker who was working on their land, Anderson rang the neighbour. 'I said, "It was so scary and you gave us no warning: what's happening? I could have been riding my horse over there."'

The neighbour was unapologetic. 'I'll do what I bloody well like,' he said, and slammed the receiver down. Anderson rang the police. 'I was shaking like a crazy thing.'

Then the neighbour's wife called. 'She said, "Oh, we are so responsible."

The self-righteousness: "My husband would only ever shoot the other way."'

Anderson and the neighbour agreed they would let each other know in future if there would be shooting. She took the backpacker outside. 'We walked the boundary there and we saw only one dead pig: they probably only got a couple of pigs.' They found a live koala, too. 'How would they know if they had shot that koala or not – they wouldn't.' In the past, her husband has had to euthanise a kangaroo with a rotting gunshot wound, and they've found roos shredded by plunging through wire fences in panic at the sound of hunting sirens. She has a little graveyard on her property for the animals that die in her care.

Between landclearing and changes to the climate, the animals have almost nowhere to go. With the drought of 2018, Anderson said, the number of koala joeys being brought in for care was overwhelming. They were starving, sunburnt, thirsty. A local vet would travel hundreds of kilometres a week to collect injured animals on a volunteer basis.

Anderson was fretting about the seven koalas in her care. Before they could be released they had to pass stringent tests for chlamydia and other diseases. Anderson needed to get them out and breeding, but there was nowhere to take them. 'If we have them too long we get into trouble,' she said, 'but we can't just throw them out to die.'

There weren't many possums and kangaroos when escaped convict George Clarke and surveyor Major Thomas Mitchell first got to the area. By the 1870s, the Aboriginal peoples had largely been run off or killed. The smaller fauna were being devastated: foxes and dogs killed native birds and mammals such as kangaroo rats, curlews and wallabies. 'Native bears' (koalas) and 'tiger cats' (quolls) were disappearing. As cultivated pastures spread, native grasslands were crushed or covered with scrub. Later, the tracks of tractors caught and spread pest predators and seeds, and took small lives.

Across the border in Queensland, a joint report by the RSPCA and WWF released in late 2017 found that, in the two years since loosening of regulations on landclearing in that state, an estimated 90 million native animals had been killed, largely by land-clearing activities. Most died painfully. Bulldozers weighing up to 100 tonnes typically charge over uneven ground, tipping into hollows and blind spots, and pushed trees crash, fall and splinter. Others simply starved. 'Nothing else in Queensland,' said Mark Townend of the RSPCA, 'causes as much suffering and death among animals as the escalating destruction of bushland habitat by bulldozers and other machinery.'

The report found that in the five years to 2014, more than 10,000 Queensland koalas were admitted to wildlife hospitals – out of 15,000 believed to exist in the state.

Australia has some of the world's most distinctive wildlife, and the worst mammal extinction rate in the world. We are home to one out of three mammal extinctions in the last 400 years, according to the Australian Wildlife Conservancy. That's thirty native mammal species in only 200-odd years

– three in the past decade alone, with a further seventeen likely in the next two. And those estimates do not include the devastating losses in the Black Summer bushfires of 2019–20. Another 30 per cent of the mammal species that have survived (not counting the innumerable bat species) are at risk. Insect populations, called 'the other 99%' of biodiversity, are crashing from habitat loss and chemical pesticide. The WWF's 'Living Planet Report 2018' shows that wildlife populations across the world have halved in only fifty years, and a million species are at risk of disappearance. What is described as the sixth extinction may indeed be the beginning of the last.

It is a swift, silent vanishing, and it can be deceptive. While cutting eucalyptus leaves for her koalas, Alaine Anderson has begun to notice animals she has never seen before, in thirty years of living in the district. They are not magically revived populations but survivors venturing from the back hills, prised forth by habitat disturbance, clearing and drought. The broadacre properties are coagulating: there are huge 'exclusion centres' hundreds of kilometres wide, Anderson says. There is the potential for those farmers 'to actually wipe out all the wildlife inside those properties, especially out here, where they might only be a ten-thousand-acre property: you've only got to turn the water off, and everything but the birds will die. And no one's supervising it.'

The specific will serve when it comes to the sequestration of property rights, of individual landholders and their personal profit, and of certain prestigious rural properties. But when it comes to particular endangered ecological communities such as greater gliders, brigalow or even the unique Great Barrier Reef, influential landowners and politicians with vast electorates take a sudden interest in landscape-scale offsetting or claims that threatened nature is plentiful in other places.

In the slow violence of local permissions, clearing in tiny, negligible pockets could, over time, destroy highly protected ecological communities. The red goshawks and koalas and skinks would quietly be isolated into smaller and smaller patches until, one day, there would simply be nowhere for them to be.

*

THE INCONVENIENT PRESENCE OF native vegetation on good farming land is managed thus: we move it somewhere more convenient. The solution is conceived of as a market-based mechanism, in which 'incentives' can boost 'cost-effective environmental goals'. Of all the models of offsetting available, the New South Wales government developed the Biodiversity Assessment Method (BAM), which, it explains, can 'assess impacts on biodiversity values' by using accredited assessors to balance 'risk of impacts on biodiversity from a proposal' with gains from 'improvements in biodiversity values from management actions undertaken at a stewardship site'.

The Environmental Defenders Office describes BAM as the weakest of all assessment models because it does not require like-for-like replacement. A destroyed area of scrub need not be replicated, the particular mix of plants replaced. Developers who need to offset can also make payments instead of replanting. Whole types of vegetation might be exempt from needing to be offset at all. And the level of significance of an ecological community is irrelevant: development can be made right on habitat for critically endangered species, so long as some offset or payment is made. If, that is, the clearing of the vegetation is reported at all, if it's not discounted under non-scientific grounds, if it's even assessed as coming under the rubric of the legislation.

When Hugh Possingham resigned from the Independent Biodiversity Legislation Review Panel in November 2016, he warned about the draft legislation's reliance on offsetting. 'Biodiversity offsetting, by definition,' he wrote, 'means no net decrease in the quality and quantity of native vegetation.' The new codes were too permissive, allowing for all sorts of exemptions, such as 'continuing use'. Under the proposed legislation, he warned, broadscale clearing in New South Wales could double, and much of that vegetation would not be replaced.

BAM relies almost entirely on vegetation mapping. Maps provided by the government show where low-conservation value areas are: especially, what might be summarily cleared or is not regulated. Peter Hannam at *The Sydney Morning Herald* reported in early 2016 that there were doubts over the reliability of the maps. Several local councils, instructed to use them for project planning, commissioned an independent review from a respected ecologist to test reality against the mapped. John Hunter found that the mapping was only about 17 per cent accurate in identifying some of the approximately 1500 individual plant communities in the state. The maps, combined from satellite, aerial and locally derived data, missed whole sets of endangered species, and mislocated others. They were, Hunter said, 'inherently unusable' for environmental assessment.

Adjustments were promised, though Hunter complained that he'd had no direct response from the OEH. As the new legislation geared up to take effect, conservation groups wrote to the chief executive at the OEH with a concern: even after the improvements, which involved relying less on satellite data, the maps were only about 60 per cent accurate. They wouldn't be used as regulation tools, the OEH promised. But they had already been used in the Hunter Valley on proposed coalmines.

The maps were still not all finalised when the laws came into effect in August 2017, and where they were absent, landholders were able to make their own assessments. By late 2017, several maps available for use in determining native grasslands were withdrawn. Mitchell Clapham of the NSW Farmers Association described the situation as a 'debacle'. An OEH map of his property had confused blackberries with eucalypts, he said. Other farmers mentioned water courses supposedly atop hills, or property boundaries wrongly ascribed, and a lack of response from the OEH to complaints.

New South Wales Minister for Primary Industries Niall Blair reassured the association that 'the government will not make any decision on the maps until consultation is complete and farmers are confident they will work'. In the interim, they would have to do without maps. The Local Land Services Land Management Code was designed as a work-around, allowing for yet more self-assessments.

In the case of grasslands – notoriously difficult to evaluate because they die back seasonally, and it is challenging to distinguish native from introduced (especially from aerial images) – it was easier to just give it all away. In November 2017, the OEH published an 'interim grasslands and other groundcover assessment method calculator' on its website, but trials at workshops had farmers again muttering of inaccuracies. It didn't seem to satisfy either landholders or environmentalists, and, judging from the intricacy of its instructions, only experts would be eager to test its advantages. Local Land Services 'worked with' the OEH to get native grasslands removed from the regulatory mapping system.

The confusion agreed with some. 'The farmers,' Phil Spark recalls, 'were actually saying, "We quite like it like this, and this is the way we want it to stay. We don't need maps!"' he chortles.

Into the chasm opened by the OEH mapping fiasco, NSW Farmers deftly inserted a wedge. In late 2018, members voted that the vegetation maps would have to be approved by the association. They should have veto over them. And no map could be used for regulatory purpose – used, for instance, by OEH compliance investigations on conservation values or remediation programs – unless the landholder had confirmed its accuracy. In late 2019 the OEH put up its newest Native Vegetation Regulatory Map for exhibition with an invitation for submissions from landholders 'and other interested parties', anticipating further updates. A map that shows an endangered ecological community would, if NSW Farmers had their way, have to be ratified by the owner who might want to remove it.

The association, on a roll, passed other motions. Invasive native species such as cypress pine should have a lower level of protection than non-invasive species. The prosecutor in a land-clearing case should be able to offer evidence of the clearing – even though such evidence is commonly raked, burnt and spread before it can be photographed. The OEH should grant a forgiving 'retrospective permission process' for 'non-permitted activities' under the last years of the old laws, rather than pursuing prosecutions. This last would be realised in 2019, when the state government declared an amnesty on new prosecutions for illegal clearing before 2016.

'We're in a dark spot,' Chris Nadolny admitted in 2018, 'where rates of clearing appear to be increasing but we don't even have figures to back that up.' As vice-president of the Armidale Tree Group, he had just written a summary and assessment of the law reforms as a whole and found they 'will certainly make it easier for landholders to clear land legally'. The system of offsets, he wrote, relies on honesty and compliance. Though it technically halves the gross areas lost to clearing, it 'will never compensate for the loss of habitat for wildlife'. In a strange personal experience of the revised laws, seventy-eight large and antique eucalypts in the grounds of the University of New England, where Nadolny works and where the OEH had an office, were suddenly marked for felling. Some of the trees probably pre-dated European settlement, and all were important habitat for fauna, many full of hollows and nests. A few were actually in the car park of the Natural Resources department. The reason cited for removal was safety; no further rationale was required, no alternatives had to be explored. Arborists were consulted, but no ecologists needed to be, despite the possums, gliders, parrots, bats and other animals that lived in the trees. Many had been cut down by the time Nadolny supported a student-led protest to save the rest. It can take over a hundred years for a young tree to form its hollows. Saplings were planted in their stead.

*

BY JULY 2018, THE Nature Conservation Council of NSW was loudly demanding that the OEH release recent figures on land clearing. The public data was four years out of date. After an eight-month wrangle with *The Guardian,* the government relented, and the information was as bad as conservationists had feared. From 900 hectares in 2013–14 to 7390 by 2015–16, the annual rate had risen, as the new laws were being anticipated, by an immense 800 per cent within three years. Regeneration and conservation programs were down – restoration that same year was less than half what it had averaged in the decade (though it still vastly exceeded the area cleared). Tree cover loss was huge: 106,100 hectares gone in one year, 40,000 hectares the next. This was mostly due to bushfires, infrastructure development – and rural projects. The rates would only continue to rise, and the government to bury the figures until they couldn't be contained.

It was all usefully seen in relation to activity just across the border. Queensland authorities' data showed nearly 400,000 hectares cleared in 2015–16, under new laws introduced by the Campbell Newman government. This had released about 45 million tonnes of greenhouse emissions, contributing to a nullification of all the tree-planting efforts by direct action projects and other mitigation schemes. Meanwhile, in the Northern Territory, landclearing permits had increased by ten times under a new Labor government, with interest in opening up more of the Kimberley to grazing.

Turnbull might seem like the last of a certain type of farmer, as he scraped away at the black soil. But he was a man very much of his moment. The dozers have been roaring across vast tracts of the nation in recent years. In New South Wales, with the re-election of the Berejiklian government in 2019, they were refuelled.

21

> The only good snake is a dead snake.
> **—Country saying quoted in Jock Marshall, *The Great Extermination*, 1966**

It was only six months after his father's death that Roger Turnbull's patience broke again. In September 2017, he took his mother to court, with Grant as secondary defendant. He and Annette were arguing their right to cross a corner of 'Yambin' to get to one of their own properties.

It was a nasty little dispute. It involved not just the family homestead but various other Turnbull properties, and gives an insight to the ways in which the family was adept at transferring property ownership. Proprietary in their property. They had excellent lawyers.

In the 1990s, Ian, Robeena and the four sons had together bought a station, 'Wallam', on the north side of the same east–west road as 'Yambin'. Five years later, under the partition arrangement when Roger stopped working for his father, it was made over to Roger and Annette alone. On the far side of 'Yambin', from 2008 on, was Roger's 'Royden'.

There was an access road across 'Yambin', which allowed Roger and Annette to avoid a very long detour along public roads from one of their properties to the other. Roger maintained that his father had pledged he could have access (reportedly saying irascibly that he didn't want Roger churning past the 'Yambin' homestead, casting up dust and making noise at all hours). But after Roger reached out to offer condolences to Alison McKenzie, the long-held tensions between Roger, Ian and Grant split them like a dead tree. The family foresaw that Glen Turner's family would sue for damages and make a claim on Ian and Robeena's properties, including 'Yambin' and 'North Yambin'. Roger was worried his right to the access road across 'Yambin' would be lost, and hastened to claim it officially.

He wasn't, he felt strongly, responsible for the crimes of his father, nor should he be penalised. In December 2014 he went to his mother, in what she would later testify was a state of agitation, and asked her to sign a document to prove his entitlement to the road. She signed it. He left. The next day Robeena rang her son and asked him to screw up the paper. He said he would, but he didn't.

In May 2015, Roger attempted to sue his parents for what he claimed was his lost inheritance. The old man was enraged. After that, Roger alleged, his mother got the lawyers onto her son, under her husband's instruction. Roger, Annette and their staff were not to use the access road. Roger was not even to enter the bounds of 'Yambin' or any other of Ian and Robeena's properties.

Roger and Annette continued to use the road. 'Yambin' was by now in Robeena's possession, after Turnbull had sold it to her for a dollar, and Grant, administering affairs on her behalf, let them use it. A tense family Christmas came and went. But in January the lawyers wrote again, warning, 'Any attempts by Roger Turnbull, Annette Turnbull or their employees, agents or contractors to enter, travel through or utilise any roads, paths or tracks on or through our clients' properties, specifically "Yambin", will be deemed as trespassing.' Letters flew between legal offices. Four months later, Ian Turnbull was in court for murder, and Roger was due to testify for the prosecution.

The boundary between 'Royden' and 'Yambin' is a strange one: the two properties don't touch. A creek runs between them. It and its banks are Crown land. So on one side was the land of the patriarch, and on the other the venture of the progeny, a line of nature imperviously trickling its little way through, separating father and son, but binding them together.

Marshalls Ponds Creek loops and careens its way in sine waves across the plains from the Golden Triangle to north of Moree. It crosses boundaries, upsets the geometry of block divisions, wobbles the composure of fencelines. It takes detours. Tiny trees stitch it tightly. Obtuse blocks of velvet green, cream yellow or the pale ones are cropped fields; one can tell the native vegetation from the colour, that familiar grey-olive. Most of the land is scraped clear like nap pared with a knife.

Marshalls Ponds Creek garners virtually no mentions on the internet. It appears not to be notable in any way, or to have any history that has been deemed worth transferring into new media. Google Maps barely deigns to identify it. Any attempt to follow it across scrolling screens of satellite maps is an exercise in frustration, as dark, unnamed undulating lines converge, branch and disappear from one zoomed-in view to the next, across the plains from the Golden Triangle to north of Moree. The hem of trees is supposedly protected, as part of the state waterways; satellite images show it wiggling restlessly, dark seam in a blanched fabric. It crosses boundaries, upsets the geometry of block divisions, wobbles the composure of fencelines. It takes detours.

For under the flat marquetry of the Moree plains and the jostle of perpendiculars and parallels are fugitive lines: the renegade curves and purposeless meanders of these waterways. The big rivers and the tributaries, the creeks and the flood paths. They surge diagonally over the maps; they loop and lope, dwindle and thicken according to moods invisible to cartography: gravity, habit, their own forms of profit. Around them cluster the last trees, at their densest here, where the roots may find moisture without incurring resentment. From above they form lines, too, irregular widenings and narrowings: so they spool across the land. This is a different kind of separation from the fences, the blocks with their property numbers, the roads, the gates and mapping polygons. There are no closed loops or rectangles in this wild espaliery, though the trees form lines, the water extends its silver threads. Every line has its gentle termination, with passage between them. Not so much a net as branches of a plant.

And the lines are permeable. Anything may pass through a thicket of trees: animals, seeds, breezes, sunshine and shade. Anything may pass over water: leaves and blossom, skimming insects, aerial animals, cloud shadow. Guilt.

*

THE OLDEST KNOWN EXAMPLE of primogeniture is the biblical story of Esau. For the Turnbulls, possessed of four sons, there was no question about a male inheriting; but like many an imperfect royal succession, the establishment of a classic dynasty would be complicated by its patriarch's ambitions.

Esau, eventually, was tricked from his inheritance by his younger brother, Jacob. It is Jacob who becomes spiritual leader of the family, heir to the lineage of Abraham. His mother, Rebecca, sides with him.

In September 2017, the Supreme Court of New South Wales heard that after the exchange of letters between lawyers in the summer, Grant Turnbull had had one of his staff drive a dozer, pulling a ripper attachment, right along the length of the access road. He then tore up another part of the road and planted crops on it.

According to his mother, Roger or someone acting for him had, in response, spitefully trespassed on 'Yambin' with a spray rig one winter night, driven along one boundary and poisoned a chickpea crop growing there.

The Turnbulls were literally gouging out each other's pathways, poisoning their mother's crops. The land was no longer simply friable soil into which one inserted seeds and saplings. It wasn't money anymore. It was a battleground, as it had been for nearly 200 years.

Grant took the stand. Under cross-examination, he said the Turnbulls, despite their keen interest in property, didn't keep written agreements between themselves, even as they worked on each other's land under various arrangements and understandings. He and Roger had worked together, along with their brothers Sam and Doug, for many years.

The family, the judge would later summarise, 'did not require a piece of paper to record what the agreements were'. Their father 'would tell his sons how things were going to be' and 'they would do it'.

In Grant's view, Roger 'did not give any support to Ian following his arrest'. Grant took a strong view about that, which he conveyed to Robeena. Roger told the court he and his brother 'have never been close'; Grant, in turn, agreed. Yet Grant, though positioned to do so, hadn't upheld Ian's command to block access on the road until nearly a year later, when a sharp letter, written at Grant's instruction, came from Cole & Butler spelling out the restriction. The path linking the brothers was literally being closed. For good measure Cory and his family were specifically exempted from the decree.

Roger lost the case. His testimony was, the judge decided, lamentably unreliable. He had knowingly misled the court in preparations for the trial by initially denying the incident spraying out the chickpeas; he had previously tried to get a loan by pretending, 'as bait', that he was about to sell his property and thus fund repayments. 'Sometimes you bend your figures to make it work,' he'd told the court. He'd admitted to these lapses under oath, which spoke of a desire to be honest but, at best, 'Roger's evidence may have been a subconscious construction. At worst,' said the judge bluntly, 'it was a deliberate fabrication'.

Roger and Annette wouldn't be compensated for the road dispute. Robeena was entitled to sue for damage to her chickpea crop, the judge ruled. The family left the court into a mild September day and headed to their various homes, all of them exhausted.

***

NSW FARMERS, UNDER AN abbreviated nomenclature and the leadership of Mitchell Clapham, was reasonably pleased with the laws it pushed for, passed by a sympathetic Liberal–National coalition government. Its website carries – as does the Local Land Services site – a case study featuring Nerinderjeet 'Nick' Lalli, a blueberry farmer from near Grafton. He cleared what he called 'mostly scrappy bush land' with a dozer. The land had been a peach farm, cleared by authorities for fear of fruit fly and then left to regrow scrub. 'The trees don't even grow straight,' Lalli said.

Blueberrries, however, enjoy the acidic soil, and he'd navigated the new legislation to clear a rectangular block in the middle of thick treed vegetation that stretched for many kilometres in every direction.

Under the law, Lalli was allowed to clear in exchange for set-aside areas of native vegetation: nearly 11 hectares of needlebark, stringybark and red bloodwood trees on another part of his property had to be protected 'in perpetuity'. Local Land Services, Lalli told NSW Farmers, spent hours auditing the biodiversity, and external auditors observed those staff at work. They chose the set-aside area for its connectivity to other timbered country on nearby properties. Of course, what it means is that there is now a cleared space where once there was none. It was a revelation to Lalli that clearing could be expanded under the new legislation. 'With the previous land management policy, I wouldn't have been able to clear my property at all,' he said, pleased. 'The new regulations have opened possibilities.'

His business, at high season, employs sixty people. Clearing the vegetation from one section of the property, he said, 'will unlock massive opportunities, not just for me but for the whole district'.

When the new laws came into effect in August 2017, the Nature Conservation Council of NSW and EDO were ready with a challenge: the state government's environment minister, Gabrielle Upton, had signed off on the legislation too late in the process, apparently without sufficient diligence. The implication was that the environment had been an afterthought. There was a spat in cabinet. In fact, according to *The Australian,* Minister for Primary Industries Niall Blair apparently shouted at Upton, in front of Premier Gladys Berejiklian and other ministers, 'Why didn't you bloody sign off on it in time?' The code was invalid, conceded the government in March 2018. The concession meant a second allegation, that the laws didn't address the legal principles of ecologically sustainable development, was never contested. The legislation was withdrawn, but only for a night. The very next day it was remade, without amendments, and carried on. Busy farmers like Lalli might barely have noticed.

***

ONLY THE DAY BEFORE Roger's claims over the 'Yambin' road were rejected, Robert Strange's case for damages was heard in the Supreme Court of New South Wales.

It was 28 September 2017, a year and three months since he had filed his documents alleging Turnbull had committed criminal negligence, assault and false imprisonment. He'd begun it when Turnbull was alive. Now the farmer was dead. But Strange would sue the estate.

The case lasted one day. His lawyer, Eugene Romaniuk SC, faced off against the Turnbulls' stalwart, Todd Alexis QC, who would be back again the next day as barrister for Robeena and Grant in the case against Roger. Alexis had been mastering the Turnbulls' affairs for years now, and his grasp of their claims and counterclaims was extraordinary. But in Robert Strange, he was facing a very credible witness. This man's life had been comprehensively ruined by the afternoon in Croppa Creek.

Strange had not worked since Turner's murder. The photographs he took of the burning stacks were the last task he did for the OEH. After the encounter with Turnbull, he kept mostly to his house, frightened and jumpy. He ensured the doors were always locked. Messages from friends went unanswered; he didn't have the energy for the conversations. Inside his house, he wept, alone. Telling that story again and again wore him out. There was no question of him returning as a compliance officer.

His family was concerned. When Strange had to leave the house, he needed one of his boys with him. He couldn't bear to do it alone. Eventually, his oldest son moved in with him permanently.

Six months after this court hearing, he would tell SBS's *Insight* program, on an episode devoted to the trauma of witnessing a violent crime, that for a long time after that day in Talga Lane he was braced for death: 'Expecting someone to come through the door with a gun. Expecting someone to shoot through the windows of the house. Expecting phone calls.' He shook his head before the camera. 'Paranoia and anxiety, absolutely rampant.' His ex-wife had taken him in for a while after he returned from Moree. It gave him some sense of normality, living there with her and their kids, as they'd done before. But he watched for a gun barrel through the window. His boys in the firing line.

He was, he'd written in his victim impact statement, constantly anxious, and full of self-doubt and anger. 'On a personal level I have become a recluse,' he admitted frankly. 'My anxiety levels are at a constant high. I have little if no energy to cope with the rigors of daily life that I have needed to get help in to do the basics of daily life like cleaning etc.' There were days when it was not bad just to make it from bed to the lounge room. A good day now was to do a little gardening, or play a game of golf. 'It's amazing,' he told Jenny Brockie on *Insight,* 'what something can do to your brain. You believe you're a reasonably sane and measured person. And then a switch goes off, and that's no longer the case.'

His health underwent a major change after the events of 29 July, he noted. 'I have suffered a heart attack which I believe is a direct result of the stresses that have been placed upon me from these events, have been diagnosed with Post Traumatic Stress Disorder and Major Depressive Disorder which has had a major impact upon my life,' he wrote in his statement.

Those with post-traumatic stress disorder experience both terror and numbness. They relive memories compulsively. They expect danger at any moment, and their bodies are constantly charging with stress hormones, rinsing them with cortisol and adrenaline. At the same time, they can suffer depression to the point of immobility. Even though they are acutely aware that any moment might be their last, should it come, that moment may well be spent lying listlessly on a couch, or crying in a toilet cubicle. They cannot stop awful images condensing in their minds. Strange would for a long time see

Turner lying on the cold ground, the smudge of soil on his brow, the fluid that gushed from his mouth when Strange tried to compress his heart. Strange would remember forever walking out into the road – the pale rust road, gone grey in the darkening landscape – the shadows around him, as headlights came down Talga Lane and he stepped out, hands up, eyes squeezed shut.

He would relive Turnbull turning the gun towards him three times; feel a bullet sing past his ear. He would always remember how dry his mouth was as he begged for Glen's life, and how the first thing he did before he went to assist the dying man was to drink some water himself. He will never forget how lonely it was, waiting there in the dark for someone to come and help him.

He had seen counsellors. He had seen psychologists, psychiatrists, doctors. He assumed modern medicine would solve the problem, but it could only help a bit. 'People call it, "you wake up with nightmares",' he scoffed to the television audience. 'Well, I wake up with reality.'

For his *Insight* appearance, he dressed in a neat shirt and shorts. Staying indoors had put weight on him. His large blue eyes were steady in a pale face under stiff, short hair. He reported the crime to the audience with the official language he had learned during fifteen years as a police officer: 'there was no more shallowness of breath', 'he had passed away'.

Preparing for court, he concluded his victim impact statement in firm, clear handwriting. 'I was at a place in my working life when I was extremely comfortable and proficient with the role that I was undertaking, but that has now all been taken from me and my future which once looked bright and planned is now bleak and dark.'

It would be years before he could return to any kind of paid work.

The Turnbulls, inevitably, fought Strange. In a statement written from jail before he died, Turnbull explained that he didn't know Strange, and hadn't known he was with Turner until he saw him on Talga Lane. 'During the ordeal,' he wrote, 'my focus was on Mr Turner. I had no intention of causing any harm, injury or death to Mr Strange. At the end, I recall telling him that he could go and that I would be waiting at home for the police. I regret any harm that I may have caused Mr Strange and I wish to apologise to him for this. As I say, it was not my intention to harm Mr Strange in any way, as I had not had any prior dealings or issues with him.'

Todd Alexis did not contest the count of criminal negligence. Turnbull had neglected to maintain Strange's sense of security and wellbeing when he pointed a gun at him and threatened to shoot him, when he'd ignored Strange's pleas to lower his weapon and when he'd left him in the dark without assistance. The judge immediately awarded Strange damages on that count.

But the charges of false imprisonment and assault were contested. The was no dispute over the facts, but about how much awareness Turnbull had had of his own actions. Could he have stopped himself, or was he substantially mentally impaired that evening on Talga Lane?

This was a chance to revisit the argument that had failed at the murder trial. A win here, if Turnbull were still alive, would certainly have helped an appeal on the murder conviction. It wasn't clear, Alexis argued again, that Turnbull had intended to harm Robert Strange. Turnbull didn't know him, hadn't shot him – had considered him superfluous to the scene, even, Alexis might have said, but tactfully did not.

The defence tendered David Greenberg's psychiatric evaluation statements from the murder trial. Greenberg had thought Turnbull had major depression at the time of the shooting, with abnormality of mind; his apparent lucidity was part of a 'dark sunglasses' perspective common to sufferers of major depression, a faux-rational conviction similar to the sudden cool levelheadedness of a potential suicide.

However, the judge pointed out that the defence of substantial impairment had been rejected at the trial, and the court had accepted Strange's evidence at the time. 'Move back or you'll get one in the heart,' Turnbull had said as he swivelled his gun towards him.

'Don't move. I've told you get back or I will fucking shoot you too,' he said the second time Strange attempted to get to the car.

And the third time, as Strange tried to shield his colleague and shots fired through the canopy and sank into the ute beside him, as Turnbull raised the gun and pointed it directly at Strange's head: 'I fucking told you, I will fucking shoot you. Now get back.'

The charge of assault does not require that physical violence be done to a person. It was, the judge observed, sufficient 'that [Turnbull] intentionally created in Mr Strange an apprehension of imminent harmful or offensive contact'. Alexis could argue that Turnbull hadn't intended to cause Strange harm, but he couldn't claim that Strange hadn't felt frightened that he would be hurt. The same logic applied to the false imprisonment: the physical intimidation and verbal threats were equivalent to a lock and key.

In the end, the judge couldn't grant Strange the satisfaction of summary judgement on all three allegations: Turnbull deserved to have the charges of assault and false imprisonment heard at a trial, but Strange's team decided to go no further. A settlement agreement was finally reached in October 2018. By 2020, the money still hadn't been paid. In October that year, Robeena Turnbull had to be ordered to arrange payment to Strange, and Alison McKenzie, for their separate dues. As the following year began, the matter was still not concluded.

22

> Let us make man in our image, in our likeness, and let them rule over all the earth.
> **—Genesis 1:26**

It goes without saying that farmers are not immune to the destruction of the land. They have a unique vantage from which to see it.

Farmers today see changes to rainfall. They see drought setting in again. They see dust storms and thunderheads once more rushing over the horizon. They see koalas stumbling out onto roads, the desiccated soil falling from their palms in clumps, the water running across glazed earth to flood elsewhere rather than soak. They see weather patterns changing, and many understand that this is because of climate change, and many know that carbon emissions from land clearing and degraded soil are significant. They see that where forty years ago they put half a litre of glyphosate on a hectare of soil, now they're up to two litres. They see their friends and family dying of cancer after a few decades' exposure to wet chemical spray. They see the empty stool at the pub where a friend who took their own life used to sit. They see the young people leaving the land.

The violation diffuses like vapour over the world. American scholar Rob Nixon has written of what he calls 'slow violence' – the ways in which damage from toxins, deforestation and climate change cascades gradually through echelons from the privileged world to the developing one. He examines 'disasters that are slow-moving and long in the making, disasters that are anonymous and that star nobody, disasters that are attritional and of indifferent interest to the sensation-driven technologies of our image-world', and how they are invisible to the very people who benefit from them, but borne by those who don't. He speaks of how continuity and consequence challenge our attention span, of how we have almost come to consider environmental damage as inevitable.

Few traditional family farmers – those raised on the land and of it – can face the agony of comprehension that a lifetime's work has been a lifetime's destruction. And few of the rest of us, in towns and cities far from farms, comprehend that our lifetime's consumption is the same.

*

IN 1955, THE VICTORIAN National Parks Association came under the direction of Dewar Wilson Goode, grazier and passionate conservationist. Born in 1907, in the time of the scarifying Federation Drought, his first years on the land in South Australia were revelatory. 'Droughts and soil erosion are devastating the arid pastoral properties of Australia,' he wrote urgently in 1935, in his first published work.

Non-Indigenous landholders, Goode realised, had taken a wrong turn. He developed an approach of 'sustained productivity basis' in arid regions: renovating unstocked or ruined properties, replanting trees and repairing water erosion. 'The original greenie', his son called him upon his death in 2002, by which time he had published or broadcast more than a thousand articles and lectures on conservation. From a grazier on devastated land, Goode became one of the founders of the Australian Conservation Foundation.

Since the settler James Atkinson published encouragements to heed native plants and resources, there has been a quiet fuse burning of farming more sympathetic to the peculiarities of Australian ecology. It has detonated in the past thirty or so years.

Every crisis of Australian agriculture has been noted in its time: the scrub incursions, the topsoil erosion, the salinity catastrophes, the extended droughts, the invasive pests, the soil degradation. At each cataclysm it was obvious to some that methods had to change or reverse. But how? The nation's top scientists set themselves to investigate. Their every solution seemed only to propel the trajectory further into hazard. And as technology led Australian agriculture into more and more specialised forms, a seditious questioning began to occur in whispers from the margins, speaking of what Charles Massy, farmer and author of *Call of the Reed Warbler* (2017), terms the organic mindset.

As Massy explains, what would become the 'organic' stream of agriculture pushed ahead after World War II, as 'sustainable agriculture', a riposte to the postwar industrialisation and conservative ambience. This fed in steady stages into counterculture movements, the New Age and the modern enthusiasm for things natural, traditional and 'eco-friendly'. By the 1980s, massive industrialised farming provoked a revulsion both instinctive and educated, and out of that reflex has come Massy's passion, the 'radical and transforming challenge' of regenerative agriculture. His book, published quietly, has become a sleeper hit among scientists, conservationists and a surprising number of farmers.

Regenerative agriculture imparts richness in the land, works in an attentive, humble, responsive mentality. It is an agriculture within nature, not against it. 'The key difference between industrial and regenerative agriculture,' says Massy, 'is that in the former humans generally believe they can control the chemical inputs while ignoring the biology. In the latter, the biology comes first.'

Leaves and grass blades are all solar panels, Massy emphasises. To get more energy in the system, it has to be seized from the sun by plants: the ambition is having more plants for longer. Ploughing stubble, overgrazing or bare fallow is the opposite of that.

Massy interviewed farmers and landholders across Australia who, like himself, had become disillusioned by accepted practices and curious about alternatives. The alternatives were found by renegade experimentation, collaboration, meticulous research, gut instinct, trial and error, forensic diligence and bloody-minded contrariness. One farmer may utterly change his or her approach while every neighbour, snorting scornfully, persists with chemical farming; in other places, networks of sympathetic experimenters will coordinate. Many report spectacular results that are visible in satellite images – healthy green in otherwise seared landscapes.

The main elements of regenerative farming are cover crops, crop diversification, reduced chemical and fertiliser use, rotational grazing and reduced or no tillage. One of the simplest adjustments is to return to the ancient relationship between animals and crops, a complement broken with the challenges of agriculture in the colony and the long obsession with grazing stock. Massy's book is full of examples of permutations, including the keyline system, which uses water flow across the contours of hillsides to retain moisture in soil. There is also 'pasture cropping', invented by two neighbours, Colin Seis and Darryl Cluff, four hours' drive south of Moree, who put various methods such as direct drilling (a system of seed placement) and cell grazing together. Seis summed up his approach: 'The thinking is that the only way you can grow a crop of wheat is to totally remove everything from the paddock to give that wheat every advantage you can. What we're talking about here is the complete opposite.'

He and Cluff call this 'farming without farming'.

The late Michael Jeffery, the country's first national soil advocate, wrote a report released in 2018 agreeing with a long line of scientists and farmers that soil regeneration is crucial. Our water, vegetation and soil are national strategic assets, and the world's six existential challenges – food, water and energy security, climate change abatement, biodiversity protection and human health – depend on soil security. Regenerative farming is 'a nobrainer', Jeffery told media. 'If we don't go to regenerative agriculture, we will continue to mine soils, particularly of carbon. This is the great loss and it is not being admitted. If you continue to mine carbon, you are shot.' But 'if we get agriculture right,' he said, 'we could pull down as much carbon as we are emitting.'

Vegetation clearing and land degradation contribute 20 per cent of annual global carbon emissions. The carbon that is stored in vegetation and soil, however, is three times greater than what's held in the atmosphere.

The healthier the soil, and the more microbes and worms and insects and fungi within it, the more carbon it can store. Some experts estimate that the world's cultivated soils have lost up to 70 per cent of their original carbon, through oxidisation from exposure and devastation to soil biota such as essential mycorrhizal fungi. But, stunningly, perhaps just 15 per cent more carbon in the planet's soil could pull down all the greenhouse gas emissions from fossil fuel since the beginning of the Industrial Revolution.

Regenerative farming promotes healthy soils and retaining vegetation to support them. It maintains functioning biodiversity that helps protect against other carbon-emitting degradation such as bushfires. It supports water retention and soil structure. It could, points out Massy, make 'a ready, effective and proven means of fixing enormous amounts of long-term carbon in the soil'.

In September 2019, Farmers for Climate Action, a nationwide advocacy group, launched a report by the Australian Farm Institute warning that agricultural production will fall and food insecurity increase in the absence of a proper policy on agriculture and climate change. The Liberal Party launched the report, but the National Party declined to send a single member to its launch.

*

THE USE OF THE term 'regenerative' in relation to farming, environmental historian George Main suggests, is powerful because it speaks of 'a painful history of suppression, fragmentation and disorder'. It can be confronting to open a discourse that admits of this, he concedes. But necessary. The health of soil systems and water courses are not the only things in need of regeneration and restoration in this country.

Alaine Anderson has read Massy's *Call of the Reed Warbler,* and it echoes her own instincts about the importance of getting Indigenous peoples back on country for management. 'Whenever we are fighting for the least of these animals, we are fighting for the least of our brothers and sisters who feel displaced. While ever we have these beautiful spaces, we need to celebrate them.' She names a local Elder. 'He is very sick. I know he wants his young people back as custodians, to get back in touch with nature and the culture that they had. And the animals, the koala totems or whatever: they will have a sense of purpose and meaning. Well, we all need that.'

She's not the only one to advocate turning back to agricultural systems practised here by First Nations peoples for millennia. Aboriginal people survived droughts and unpredictable climate, while maintaining a small population rather than expanding it. Bruce Pascoe, whose bestselling *Dark Emu* (2014) enthusiastically describes Indigenous agriculture, says that as drought returns many people are reading his work and asking questions about traditional methods. Native grasses, Pascoe says, are not as productive per acre as introduced cereals, but they grow themselves, sustain wildlife, stabilise soil and encourage water to soak in. And they could potentially draw down a fair amount of carbon. They are suited to

Australian soils, and they will withstand a drought.

Massy is from the Monaro, in southern New South Wales. The area is basaltic, volcanic, famous for its grasslands and its overclearing. When his property was devastated, first by his own incautious ploughing and then by drought, he began to ask questions: 'What is it that makes a landscape? And how, in the face of Australian summers that now, year by year, seem to be fiercer and more desiccating, do I continue to manage and regenerate this extraordinary world around me?' In fact, many of the experimenters and renegades he met had only been prompted to look for solutions after a disaster such as fire or drought had broken the complacency they had about institutional farming. A 'monoculture of the mind' dominates a farming mentality as compacted and sterilised of flexible feeling as a broadacre-crop field. 'The crucial point, however,' Massy writes urgently, 'is that *what* we farmers carry in our heads determines the health of a landscape.'

No coincidence, perhaps, that so many farm homesteads have much wall and small windows. It is agonising, Massy says from personal experience, to realise that a lifetime's work in good conscience, trying to build up a farm, following expert advice, traditions, common wisdom – a long dedication to building a future for one's children and grandchildren, years of sweaty slog put into shaping and insisting upon a recalcitrant bit of country – has all been wrong. You haven't built anything. Rather than ensure a secure future, you have pulled it down around you.

Ian Turnbull came, too late, to know this feeling.

But regenerative farming, sometimes called 'lazy farming', is taking hold. Funding is being secured for more research and ratification. Word is spreading. In February 2017, the *Moree Champion* ran a story of a Queensland family, the Trotts, who were using holistic grazing to negotiate the drought. 'After what we have seen this year and the position we are in now,' Jeff Trott said, 'I reckon we would be spending a lot of money on feed right now if we weren't doing what we are doing.'

Alaine Anderson tells of friends in Glen Innes who have put in permanent pasture with three different crops. 'Oh, the moisture in that paddock!' she crows. 'There's a full crop of native pasture because the roots are grown, the microbes are there. In five to ten years, if they so wish, they can put the land into full agriculture for another ten. It's giving the land a rest. And the trees!' She sighs. 'I went up there to release a koala. The trees in those paddocks, with no chemicals for twelve months, [had] three times the foliage of anything at home. Unbelievable! It was beautiful! She went up this gorgeous big tree and away she went.'

Some of the farmers Massy met had made the most astounding discovery: if they left their land alone, it got better. Sometimes it wasn't entirely subdued. There were seeds secret in the ground, biding, the ones not scraped away, the ones not split and crushed. People walked away from their land in despair and returned to find it grassed and lovely, the soil knitting once more, the green stitching it. They had stopped assaulting country. Damaged and changed, it seemed able to forgive them.

Of course, in some places it is less resilient. Others have found that when they abandon the land, species go extinct. Thoroughly ecologically modified, the land rewilds in monstrous form, overgrown and limited in diversity. Feral animals hunt unchecked. Weeds proliferate. We have pressed upon the earth, so in some places can things even function anymore, after our presence? We live in what is becoming known as the Anthropocene.

Walking off land isn't an absolute solution, but farming that is kind may help. 'I believe that love is *the* essential ingredient in human and human–Earth relationships,' Charles Massy concludes. 'An absence of love is seen in the ongoing colonial psyche in Australia and its ongoing lack of remorse for our Indigenous peoples' loss of sacred country.' Improving on the past 'means un-learning many things'.

***

THE SEEMINGLY ENDLESS SPILL of prosecution, trial, penalty and appeal, over three separate lots of clearing on two different properties, cascaded a little further on a warm spring day. Two weeks after the first part of Robert Strange's suit was settled, on 24 October 2017 Grant and Cory were convicted of the illegal land clearing of the second bout done on their respective properties in 2012 and given a fine: a total of $708,750.

Justice Preston, having heard the defence in April, now gave Grant the sternest penalty possible – minus a discount of 12.5 per cent for the belated guilty plea – after taking into account various technical considerations. The farmer would have to pay not only over a third of a million dollars, but also the OEH's costs for prosecution. It broke records for such penalties and made media headlines.

The penalty came on top of the remediation he had been ordered to do in 2016, estimated by Grant himself at $4.5 million, although it appeared still not to have been begun. Indeed, what the Turnbull family had done on

'Strathdoon' and 'Colorado' was, the judge said, 'irremediable'.

Grant had no prior convictions. A friend testified that he was known for his 'generosity, compassion and humility on many occasions'. But because he'd taken a year to plead guilty, the court had had to assemble for the case on nine separate occasions. He'd argued every point apart from his basic culpability; he even suggested that he should get a smaller fine in part because he had to pay for his defence team, including the inexhaustible Todd Alexis. The judge found that he showed no remorse, nor acknowledged the harm caused by his actions.

Cory appeared more sympathetically. A family friend who'd known Cory since childhood said he was 'an honest, respectful young man' now preoccupied with worry and anxiety. He understood his mistakes and wanted only to put the acts behind him and look forward to the future. But the judge reminded the room that, under cross-examination, Cory had said that 'at the end of the day it didn't matter' if groundcover on his property 'was native or non-native' because it was all going to go under crops. He did not express sadness that the land was unlikely to regenerate. He'd set out, he said, 'to achieve a goal of turning a grazing farm into a cropping farm'. To walk away now 'would mean the environment and myself would not benefit at all'. His admissions, the judge felt, were really 'statements of regret for being apprehended and prosecuted for committing the offence and for the sentence that might be imposed'.

'Strathdoon' cost Cory and his grandfather about $2 million when they bought it. By the time of the hearing in 2017, it was estimated to be worth two and a half times that. The court must ensure, said the judge, the penalty involved just punishment and denunciation: 'The community must be satisfied that the offender is given his just desserts.'

After a small discount for pleading guilty, the penalty for Cory was $393,750, plus the prosecutor's costs. The financial difficulties he pleaded were, the judge pointed out, because he was still paying off a fine for the previous illegal clearing.

Grant immediately launched an appeal against his own fine.

That same year, he appeared in an agricultural trade publication, extolling a new modified hybrid strain of corn. Its name was 'Pioneer'.

*

SO MANY MEMORIES, TESTIMONIES, interviews; so many laws, reviews, submissions; so many court cases, appeals; so many legal arguments, and press releases, and media reports; so much analysis, and debate, and discontent; so many shaken heads, so many disappointments. So much paperwork. So many trees felled to argue about the felling and keeping of trees.

Somewhere in the papier-mâché of this, caught in the gluey enclosure of regulation and terminology and argument, is the real world of animals with warm skin, of trees with rough bark, of the soil that crumbles between the palms. 'The wild,' wrote the activist scholar Vandana Shiva, 'is not the opposite of the cultivated. It is the opposite of the captivated.'

23

> The list of our disastrous failures, from forest obliteration and oceanic pollution to the raising of the extinction rate a thousandfold bears all the marks of a species which no longer believes itself to be part of the animal world at all.
> —**Richard Mabey, *Nature Cure,* 2006**

In December 2017, Roger Turnbull gave an extraordinary interview to *The Weekend Australian* in which he admitted his father had coldly premeditated Turner's murder. 'Glen Turner ... once he had his teeth into something, he wouldn't let go,' Roger told journalist Deborah Cornwall. 'And then you've got Dad, an old man who always gets his own way. And Dad just got more and more obsessed with Glen Turner. Neither of them was going to step back.' Perhaps this wasn't a revelation, but Roger went further. He said that his father had dug graves on the farm.

Chris Nadolny was horrified when he read this, especially the plural, 'graves'. He had accompanied Turner on most of the investigations. Turner had asked him to come on that late July trip, but he hadn't gone along because he was on leave. 'If it was going to require more than one grave, then who else had he in mind to kill?'

Nadolny had heard rumours of Turnbull's boasts to hide bodies before, even of a hole big enough for a four-wheel drive as well as a body. What chilled Nadolny's blood as he read Roger's words was the memory of a conversation he would not speak about publicly until 2019. Accounts in Turner's notebook and transcripts of the murder trial hadn't included it, but according to the ecologist, the day Ian Turnbull threatened Turner and Nadolny's lives in 2012, he had said more.

When Turner had said, 'I interpret that as a threat,' and Turnbull had riposted, 'I'm an old man. I can do anything I want,' Turner pressed him. Thinking of the law, Turner asked, 'Aren't you concerned about going to prison?'

And Turnbull smiled and said something like, 'If you were trespassing and I killed you with a single shot, it would only be treated as man slaughter.'

Nadolny admits his memory of the conversation was imprecise, even shortly after it occurred. The whole conversation took fifteen or so minutes. Neither he nor Turner recorded this comment in their notes; because, the ecologist explains, Turnbull said it in such a jovial, even-tempered tone, it was hard to take as seriously as the initial threat. There were other, more immediate elements to record. But Turnbull went on, he insists now: 'Especially as I'm such an old man. As an old man I'd be let out on bail.' He said dreamily, 'I could put up a million dollars, could stay in North Sydney. With the legal complications, the trial could be delayed for years. Til I was dead.' He had grinned at the two men. 'It could even be quite nice, retiring from farm work all these years. I deserve a bit of a holiday.'

Two years later, the morning news of a murder. He knew instantly what had happened.

A couple of days after Turner's death, Nadolny gave a statement to the police. He had, he says, 'a very foggy memory' of those further words, and so only confirmed the initial threat.

At the time, it had seemed strange to Turner and Nadolny that Turnbull would joke about stalling murder charges; probably, they thought, the farmer was awkwardly using humour to backtrack after his aggression. Or was he, Nadolny wondered, 'saying something so outlandish so that we'd think he was a nutter and be even more scared of him? I didn't know what to make of it,' he confesses, 'so my memory of that part of the conversation grew confused and faded.'

He has borne the memory, though, the weight of it, and wondered. His instinct today is that Turnbull, with his jokes about graves, manslaughter pleas and bail and holidays, was misleading his audience even as he experimented with scenarios and played a little mind game with his foes. How invigorating to talk of getting a gun and shooting a pest! The careless seeds of such talk, tossed lightly, landed in the deep earth of his brooding.

'This has affected me,' Nadolny admits. 'My wife says, "Chris, you've got to be positive." But it gets to you. Particularly seeing all this turning Glen into the villain.' He sighs. 'That hurts a lot. Half the people are thinking Glen was the villain for taking on my suggestions: my assessment of the seriousness of the clearing. That came from me, not Glen.'

Turnbull said genially that he would kill Glen Turner. Turner's life ended in murder; Turnbull's, as a convicted killer.

***

When twenty-eight children, women and Elders were killed at Myall Creek in 1838, there was no inquest: there was outrage. It was not on behalf of the beheaded victims, hacked to pieces in a creek and their bodies ineptly burned and left exposed. When the perpetrators of the atrocity – former convicts employed on his property by wealthy landowner Henry Dangar – were identified and brought to trial, the settler community was aghast.

Dangar, who had conveniently gone away during the crime, professed himself shocked, but defended his men, raised support and agitated for clemency. His fellow landholders rallied too, and when, after an initial acquittal, seven were re-tried and sentenced to execution, there was protest at this 'judicial murder'. Petitions were signed in support of their release. 'I would never,' a juror at the first trial told *The Australian,* 'see a white man hanged for killing a black.'

Their guilt was not at question. Rather, the murderers felt singled out when such killings had been committed by their neighbours with impunity. Men on the land had to do what they had to do, others agreed. When the law was unsympathetic, the law had no business there. The convictions were a scandal; these men were on trial for murder when they had only looked after their landholder's interests. The experience fatally weakened the authority of Governor Gipps, who had pursued the case; and those were the second, and last, executions for the murder of Aboriginal peoples in the colonial era.

Myall Creek is southeast of Warialda, 115 kilometres from Croppa Creek.

***

IN LATE MARCH 2018, many landholders and their advocates welcomed news, announced by federal Minister for the Environment and Energy Josh Frydenberg and Minister for Agriculture and Water Resources David Littleproud, of an interim review of the federal *Environment Protection and Biodiversity Act* as it concerned agricultural practice.

The review was convened under the authority of Dr Wendy Craik, who had been one of the four-member Independent Biodiversity Legislation Review Panel involved in the change in New South Wales' vegetation laws. It was planned 'to reduce red-tape [sic] and find practical ways to help farmers meet the requirements' of the Act. For three months in mid-2018, Dr Craik took submissions from stakeholders. The Environmental Defenders Office was one of them. There is no evidence, it said, that the Act put 'an undue regulatory burden' on landholders. The problem was not the Act, but the lack of resources to help farmers understand how it works. Nationals MP John 'Wacka' Williams had a say too. He'd been infuriated by a tale of a farmer, the brother of federal Liberal MP Angus Taylor, being prosecuted for spraying out native grasses that had been declared protected only a year earlier. Williams expected common sense would see the federal laws fall away in favour of the state ones so that 'farmers could be left out there to run their properties under state regulations to grow the food that feeds all Australians and tens of millions of others'. His wish would be supported.

The Craik report was completed by September 2018, though not published until June 2019. It recommended that farming interests, including options to lessen economic impacts, should be considered before a federal minister of the environment decided whether to list a threatened species under the Act; the public should also be consulted. The government should pay farmers and landholders to protect the environment through a billion-dollar fund, and landholders should be compensated if they suffered a 'financial burden' by hosting increases of threatened species.

A few months later, the full mandatory ten-yearly review of the whole *Environment Protection and Biodiversity Act* was announced by the new Minister for the Environment, Sussan Ley. The panel included a First Nations Wik-Ngathan representative, an environmental law and policy expert and a public administration expert alongside Dr Craik, but, as conservation groups pointed out, there was no ecologist or scientist of any kind. Its report was due in 2020.

*

THE WORLD IS NO longer in the same form as we knew it in as children, and the future is more profoundly uncertain than ever before. Though for thousands of years every generation has changed the world and seen it change around them, it has never occurred at this rate and scale. The trajectories of climate change numb the imagination as they soar off the charts. Ecosystem collapse is no longer a risk but a reality: we numbly contemplate the implications of lack of pollination, water insecurity and habitat loss, as well as greenhouse gas pollution. In the past twenty-five years alone, after 10,000 years of agriculture, humans are estimated to have destroyed a tenth of the Earth's remaining wilderness.

Some projections are apocalyptic. Others bet on adaptation. But one thing is certain: human life will not look as it does now. Solastalgia, that vaporous unease, is a gentle word for an experience that might sound like a scream.

The effect of solastalgia cannot be remedied by going home, as in homesickness, or by amassing mementoes, as with nostalgia; but it can be solaced, Glenn Albrecht suggests, 'by the simultaneous restoration and rehabilitation of mental, cultural and biophysical landscapes'.

Stranger things have happened. Tim Flannery describes how Europe is seeing a sudden increase in 'abandoned lands' as farming becomes more compact and mechanised, and fewer and fewer people are required or able to live on country, while across the globe, something towards 2 million square kilometres of cropland have already been emptied, most since the advent of industrial farming. Again, the 'old country' is instructive. There are 741 million people in Europe, but vast parts of it, like the regrowth in the depopulated region of Chernobyl in Ukraine, are transforming into untended, organic, astonishing wildernesses. In a sense, this is another kind of offsetting: the dense hazards of chemical industrial farming in some areas are what permits large natural reserves in others. And both the agricultural practice and the character of those reserves are potentially changing for the better. Regenerative farming is growing too. It is all, one might even say, improvement.

The continent is rewilding. Corners of fields are left uncultivated for haven, as they used to be. Programs of reintroduction are multiplying, and people are literally making wilderness, as in Oostvaardersplassen in the Netherlands, where land claimed from the sea has been devoted to recreating an Ice Age landscape complete with fauna and flora. Wolves are back. Bears are roaming. The population of carnivores, larger herbivores and scavengers are now, Flannery observes, healthier than they have been since the Middle Ages.

We cannot go back to what it was: Eden is lost. But human presence can, perhaps, chaperone healthy ecology once we accept that we are part of it.

More astoundingly, it seems that agriculture, now using half of the Earth's land surface, may one day require very little land at all. Already vegetables are being grown hydroponically – and vertically – with nothing more than water, distilled minerals and solar 'sundrop' heat. One day it is possible that crops, even something like wheat, will be cultivated not in the ground or even in hothouses but within the vessels of microbes. Minuscule grains, manufactured from genetic material and nutrients, will be manifested for our convenience; meat, cereals and vegetables will be grown in laboratories, no longer requiring their own agricultural supplies and devotion of water resources. With farming lands vacated for nature, we may yet live once more in a world of settlements separated by wildwoods and grass-plush plains.

Europe is pioneering once more. The continent that exported so much wrecking and revolution to the world is now a demonstration of how double occupancy is possible. Maybe there is just room enough for an intensity of humans and an intensity of natural environments. We could consider the natural world our habitat, not our garden or our factory.

It may be that we are at the apogee of malevolence to the Earth. Sympathetic, supportive forms of living are coming through, green buds. The question is, can nature hold on long enough? We are facing the sixth extinction. The trends and rates and trajectories are bad.

And, of course, we are animals at risk too. Our bodies, our food supplies, our habitats are as compromised as those of a quoll or a koala. We are each 'a flea in the pelt of a great living thing', in Wendell Berry's words.

'The Sympathetic Mind leaves the world whole,' writes Berry in an essay. 'It looks upon people and other creatures as whole beings. It does not parcel them out into functions and uses.'

Glenn Albrecht also coined other words: *eutierria* is a positive feeling of oneness with the Earth, obliterating distinctions between self and nature in 'a deep sense of peace and connectedness', and *soliphilia* is 'the love of and responsibility for a place, bioregion, planet and the unity of interrelated interests within it'. Our own libidinous greed, our bemusement; on the other hand, nature's imperviousness, its vulnerability, its forgiveness. Solastalgia is a painful wound, the sense of loving something and hurting for it. Its injury is the cost of finding a better way.

24

Moving into the future, forget not that it, like the present, is well served by the past. Let us resolve to preserve what is good, to discard what is not – to improve where practicable and not to damage or destroy. We can value our heritage, have confidence in ourselves and have faith in tomorrow.

—The Honourable Sir Kenneth McCaw, NSW attorney-general, raised in Bogamildi (near Croppa Creek), circa 1987

Gunnedah, south of Moree, still bears signs referring to it as Australia's koala capital. Now, after years of land clearing and the establishment of four Whitehaven mines, it is the coal capital.

'Our land management has changed forever,' Alaine Anderson laments. 'If we want to stay, well, we can't keep putting tens of thousands of dollars into chemicals every month. We're too small – we haven't got properties all over Australia where we can mitigate our risks. So I reckon the best way would be to rejuvenate the soil, go back to permanent pastures or rest it or something. We've all got to look at these different ideas because what we've been doing isn't *working*. The soil's *had* it.'

Footage in Gregory Miller's documentary *Cultivating Murder* shows Anderson with Deborah Tabart, CEO of the Australian Koala Foundation, comparing vegetation maps of the Croppa Creek area. In the 2008 maps of 'Strathdoon' and 'Colorado', koala habitat appears to cover about half the properties. Much less was visible in 2013, after the Turnbulls' clearing. The next map, from only a year later, shows virtually nothing left. The documentary shows a map of the broader region: those green patches of 2008 were among the largest in a sea of cleared, cropped country. Tabart puts it frankly: 'It's gone from quite a substantial piece of habitat to virtually nothing.'

Many Australians, Anderson says, imagine that state and national nature reserves comfortably accommodate sufficient koalas and other endangered species. 'They look at state forests and ask, why aren't the koalas there?' she says. 'Well, it is too dry, and as climate change increases they are going to need more water. They need 50 per cent water in every leaf, and the stress of the trees produces more tannins and more toxins.' We don't want them all on the coast in concentrated strips or reserves, she explains, because there the colonies have other problems, such as retroviruses. Those koalas afflicted with the retrovirus can't breed, or their young starve. 'Whereas at least with chlamydia we get a couple of babies sometimes and then mum will die,' she says frankly. And she points out that Local Land Services had in 2018 given permission for 55 acres of 'pristine virgin country, koala country, on the river here to be cleared'. On the one hand, the authorities give approvals for clearing, and at the same time they fund wildlife rescue programs. 'It beggars belief, in my book,' says Anderson.

Alison McKenzie had also been startled by the reduction in koala habitat when she was given the preview of the new laws in 2017. 'Under the new legislation,' she wrote in her open letter to state politicians, 'there is no protection provided for koala habitat and there is no protection provided for the thousands of mature hollow trees that provide vital habitat for at least seventy-two species.' The National Parks Association stated dramatically that koalas can lay claim to be 'the most poorly managed species in eastern Australia at present'. The loss of protection for up to 99 per cent of their habitat was, they said, 'hugely disappointing in light of their beloved status'.

By mid-2020, scientists were warning a parliamentary inquiry that the koala, under more pressure than ever following the horrendous bushfires of that year's Black Summer and the unending onslaught on its habitat, was facing extinction in New South Wales within thirty years. Everyone seemed amazed.

Just months later, the state Nationals threatened to quit government over faintly increased koala protections. Independent MP Justin Field spoke for many in his incredulity that 'the National

Party have decided to make this their hill to die on'. Yet though the state government had a $45 million Koala Strategy, habitat trees continued to fall, and grey-furred bodies to be crushed.

'I have no idea how many koalas were killed in those clearings,' Roger Turnbull told *The Weekend Australian*. 'But I do know about one incident in June 2012 where [my] father ordered more than 100 koalas to be shot on sight on the Colorado farm and thrown on a fire to burn because he knew the federal inspectors were planning to come and do a headcount that week. What kind of person does that?'

***

IF HUMANS ARE NOT willing or able to perceive equity between ourselves and other living things, the law will not privilege those living things over ourselves. What if the law ratified nature? What if it recognised that nature is not simply an object but the equivalent to a person: that it has rights?

Eco law is evolving. In Ecuador, natural flora and fauna have had rights since 2008, under the argument that this would expand Indigenous rights. New Zealand has granted legal personhood to the Te Uruwera forest, the Whanganli river and Mount Taranaki. The Ganges and Yamuna rivers in India, and the Atrato river in Colombia, have personhood too now. The Fitzroy and Margaret rivers in Australia may be next.

This 'raising' of natural elements to the status accorded humans is an idea first proposed by American lawyer and academic Christopher Stone in 1972 and since championed by the late environmental lawyer Polly Higgins: part land-rights movement, part human-rights push. It sways around the issue of whether nature is important in itself or only inasmuch as its health is significant to humans – the ambivalence within environmental movements between arrogance and abjection continues. But the Enlightenment confidence in nature as object is losing traction. A tree may be easily felled when a dozer gets to work. But the consequences are more powerful than any human concern: annihilating drought and climate change will be the response.

'Who will listen?' Anderson says bleakly. 'By the time they wake up, it'll be too late.'

***

IN THE MIDDLE of 2016, Ron Greentree reportedly sold 10,000 hectares of Milton Downs, just under a fifth of its total area, to an American corporation, Westchester, for $55 million. The price paid only six years earlier was $75 million for the lot.

In the end, Turnbull was small fry. He and his sons and grandsons are not a dynasty. He hadn't had enough protection. Perhaps he was even thrown to the pack. Perhaps he was bait.

***

THERE IS A PECULIAR quality to time on the land. It is slow as stone.

The western plains of New South Wales bloomed over millions of years, rising and falling beneath the oceans, gliding around the Southern Hemisphere, heaving up the Great Dividing Range on one side and scorching out the deserts on the other. As the mountains rose, writes Cameron Muir, 'low energy streams began carrying sediments from the highlands and deposited them inland over millions of years to form a vast alluvial plain'. Under the membranes of sediment, the plains 'are a palimpsest of abandoned riverways. Plains are old and secretive. You need to read them with a deeper sense of time.'

Like the light of stars, some of the life in the plains only comes to our eyes millions of years after it occurred. The white pebbles Turnbull saw exposed by erosion under the soil of 'Strathdoon' and 'Colorado' were rolled in rivers so long dried that they are written in stone. The nutrients that were stored in the soil had accreted for thousands and thousands of years, through floods and droughts in cycles as regular as breathing, as once the land itself rose and fell in the breath of the Earth. What comes up through the skin of the soil takes aeons. What wounds it may take an instant.

It was with shocking speed that Europeans began our work here. The land rang like a bell under the stroke;

with little axes and hooves, we undid the work of millennia. Now, a tiny 230 years later, we make decisions based on the infinitesimally small scale of political terms: three years, four. On farming budgets drawn up in five-year plans; on bank mortgage schedules over twenty or thirty years of repayments. A farming family's boarding-school fees may determine the destiny of a paddock by the time the child reaches high school. Two bad years in a row may sell a property, while a seasonal fashion or global market price fluctuation will tear out a vineyard thirty years in the growing for a crop that takes twelve weeks. A politician may need to weather a crisis that blows up in days; commitments are made now in thirty-second grabs on the news. Restoration may take thousands of years.

We have become used to the momentary. The age-old security of time has evaporated. We barely believe in it anymore; the future is as forgotten as the past. Australia, post-settlement, is unsure of how much of the past to clutch. It doesn't know how to imagine its future.

We seem so engrossed in our work that we forget how the tools came to be in our hands, how the earth that is in the shovel came to be made, that there must be a place to put that earth, that eventually everything must be laid down somewhere.

We like to consider our legacies, but not our mortality. One annihilates the other: genetics, bank accounts, property deeds, examples set, heirlooms, influences felt; we have so many ways to persist. It's comfortable to count the endowments we lay out for our children – the provisions, the advantages and the memories – but more difficult to countenance the damage, the dereliction. Who can bear to imagine they have squandered a fortune and cost their children a future?

Ian Turnbull mortgaged 'Yambin' to help guarantee loans for his son and his grandson and their families. He wanted to set them up, help Grant become secure and get young Cory established. That plan for succession, like the rest of Turnbull's hopes, ended in Talga Lane when he stopped his ute and put a gun to his shoulder.

But the Turnbull story isn't over. The generations go on, but they have spent much time in courts now, arguing to defend their wealth, arguing with each other over its division, explaining why it took blood to protect it. Their legacy is now one of dismay.

*

IN 1965, A LOCAL of Bingara, Len Payne, suggested a memorial to the twenty-eight men, women and children murdered at Myall Creek. He thought he'd make something, using the hinges and rails from the Myall Creek stockyards: a gate suspended from a pillar. The community was horrified, and called the idea 'mischievous and an insult'. Payne continued to privately lay a wreath every year until his death.

It wasn't until the late 1990s that the community was ready to recognise what had happened. Elders, local mob, non-Aboriginal locals and descendants of the culprits gathered in January 2000, and a huge granite boulder was placed at the site. *IN MEMORY,* it is inscribed, *OF THE WIRRA-YARAAY PEOPLE WHO WERE MURDERED ON THE SLOPES OF THIS RIDGE IN AN UNPROVOKED BUT PREMEDITATED ACT IN THE LATE AFTERNOON OF 10 JUNE 1838 [...] IN AN ACT OF RECONCILIATION, AND IN ACKNOWLEDGEMENT OF THE TRUTH OF OUR SHARED HISTORY. WE WILL REMEMBER THEM. NGIYANI WINAGAY GANUNGA.*

There are few sites left with traces of the Murri people who lived around Croppa Creek for millennia. The Barwon River Basin, which takes in the Moree plains, is described by one scholar as one of the major regions of archaeological disaster in New South Wales. Time and farming have erased almost all of it.

But in 2015, an anonymous donor sent an item to local Elder Noeline Briggs-Smith OAM. It was the damaged brass breastplate decorated with a kangaroo and an emu, which had been given in both mockery and a kind of honour, as these things were, to an Elder by a European figure of authority. The ones in Moree are usually from the late nineteenth century or later, even from Ian Turnbull's lifetime. Briggs-Smith believes the treasure was returned by a farmer who feared a land-rights claim based on its existence. That wouldn't happen, Briggs-Smith reassured, but she observed the plate had been damaged. It looked, she said, like it had been hit by a plough.

The lifestyle of the Murri people, the Moree Tourism website says, 'is to co-exist with, and maintain a balance with nature'. The first Kamilaroi Aboriginal people 'lived in harmony with the environment'. They hunted some species ferociously, perhaps even to extinction; they set whole landscapes on fire and reconstituted every element upon them. But what they did was maintain a functioning, equitable system that included humans – a threatened species themselves at times – in its calibrations. The Kamilaroi acted, to recall Charles Massy, 'with love', and since that time have watched their country transformed in only a few lifetimes more utterly than their ancestors did in millennia.

For his book *Heartland* (2005), George Main spoke to a Wiradjuri man from Main's own region around Cootamundra. The two men stood on country, gazing out. Look, the man said sorrowfully. Look at this ruined garden of ours.

***

ALAINE ANDERSON IS FACING three battles: to save the koalas in distress in her district, even if she cannot protect them long-term; to persuade her neighbours to more sympathetic forms of farming; and to prepare for passing on her own property. She is in her late sixties, her husband older. There is pressure to leave their land.

They bought 'Strangford' forty years ago, when the property had only about 10 per cent native vegetation left. This is still the case, despite their efforts. They've worked the land. Human-induced edge effect has killed off attempts to extend the green, due to spray drift and desiccation on the margins. When she began publicly criticising Turnbull for the clearing next door, her pumps mysteriously became blocked with dirt, wires were cut in the Spra Coupe, the letterbox was pulled out – twice. She still doesn't go out walking alone if she can help it. The sign out the front of their property looks ferocious: in red print, it says things like 'STOP', 'BEWARE', 'TRESPASSERS WILL BE PROSECUTED', and warns of CCTV. Other owners in the countryside have such signs, sometimes to daunt government compliance officers. Anderson has hers to warn off hostile neighbours.

While Turnbull was in jail, word had spread that the Andersons would retire soon and move on. In a phone call, a sullen Turnbull told his interlocutor he couldn't wait. The sooner, the better, he said. Someone would buy that property and clear it.

Anderson has no plans to let that happen. But it would be nice, she says wistfully, if they could retire. 'Wouldn't it be lovely if someone were guiding us,' she muses, 'to put this bit of land aside, and put it into writing as a covenant in perpetuity.' She has considered a covenant, but is cynical of its durability. 'You have to be able to say, this is so important that we will never clear this.' She and Lionel haven't been perfect, she admits: they've cleared and caused erosion in the past. 'Now we have to try and fix it. So I am not in a position to tell other farmers what to do, but I've seen a lot of changes for the worse. I just wish I was younger.' One day, choices will be made for them. Their children only say, *Get out, get out now.* What they hope is to move on from a life of farming and wildlife protection, and to 'leave a legacy of sustainable farming and robust environment'. That's, she says, 'all we've ever wanted'.

The Moree heatwave of 2017 – a nightmarish two months of incessant scorchers – broke records. Climate change is lengthening the extent of heatwaves, raising global temperatures and increasing the likelihood of drought and flood and extreme weather in general. It is creating less and less certainty, except of inevitable hardship.

'When it's been dry for a while and windy, the sky gets pink with dust,' said Moree's mayor, Katrina Humphries. The dry dust of the inland blew over Sydney in November 2018, followed by devastating rain and storms. They succeeded months of drought in the capital; out in the semi-arid interior, the dryness continued. 'Rain follows the plough,' people used to say. Not anymore. In the Moree region they plant water-intensive crops; they filch from rivers; they moisten the earth from bores. The sky is changing above Croppa Creek, but below, the tractors are still busy pushing trees.

Farmers are reporting serious issues with their ability to sustain crops. In 2018, the worst summer season since 1956, crops in the Golden Triangle failed. Many landholders didn't sow the following year. In 2019, after 231 years of agricultural effort, Australia was forced to import wheat.

Moree, said Humphries bravely, is adapted to hot weather. 'The climate's been changing for 20,000 years,' she told science magazine *Cosmos* after the heatwave. 'Mother Nature can be a bitch, she really can. We have to manage ourselves with what she does for us.'

Anderson and her friends discuss the prospect of the next few years. There are no windbreaks left since landholders began clearing right to the fencelines. There is no water in the dams. There have been dust storms, like in the 1930s. 'There will be more,' she sighs. Trees are now being taken out even from waterways. 'I can't believe it. They want the aerial spraying; they spray everything. The little birds' eggs aren't strong anymore, they won't hatch like they used to. Now they take out all the trees and they have open slather with their planes.

'They fill in the dams too,' she rushes on. 'That was the big push here: fill in the dams, fill in the dams. If we have a fire here this summer, god help us.'

That was in 2018. The apocalyptic bushfires that hit New South Wales at the end of the following year and burned throughout the summer didn't reach Croppa Creek: there was so little left to burn. But a photograph of a homeless koala licking rainwater from Croppa–Moree Road made headlines in British media, along with news that up to 3 billion of its wildlife cousins had been lost in the infernos.

The drought, Anderson and her friends had felt, was probably ultimately a good thing. It was a chance to rethink. We're all in it together, she reminds people. 'Can't we stand back now in the midst of this terrible drought,' she asks, 'and just say – right, enough is enough and let us not do this ever again?'

She's not entirely alone. North of Moree District, the Gwydir Shire Council has an energetic Landcare group, the Northern Slopes. In 2017, the group won a state award and became the state's representative at the federal awards. In February 2018, it invited Charles Massy and Colin Seis out to talk about regenerative farming. Their network of 'Future Farmers' now numbers about 600. They organise ecologists to talk to schoolchildren about spotting and guarding native wildlife. They have an Aussie Ark Threatened Species group to survey for fauna.

In North Star, Robeena Turnbull's brother Ran and his wife, Jenny, have put their property, 'Leyland', on the regenerative agriculture map. Mitchell, on inheriting the farm in 1954, noticed the returns from the soil were diminishing. So he took on no-till seeding, stopped fungicides and began composting. The property is now a stop on field tours through the Landcare group, and stars of the regenerative movement such as Massy and Dr Terry McCosker drop by. Relationships are being made where there were none, collaborations forming, competitions evaporating.

Phil Spark visits the shire regularly to give talks on koalas and other endangered species. For a while he also attended the Environmental Defenders Office workshops around the region, explaining the implications of the new legislation to farmers and conservation groups. He wheezes with humour. 'If you had a workshop specifically about how to manage native vegetation for biodiversity, they wouldn't turn up. But if you can capture them...' Most country people are good, Spark says. 'They're lovely people.' But there is the cone of silence around illegal clearing – it's like the concept of *omertà* in Sicily. 'It's just,' he says with a sigh, 'that one little problem they've got.'

He admits to ongoing unease over Turner's death. There are still questions about why Turner was left vulnerable. The Turnbull family welcomed the news of a coronial inquest, announced by the New South Wales coroner in 2017; they promised 'explosive' new evidence about Turner's harassment. But Sparks frowns when he explains the need for an inquest. 'We – we feel a little bit personally responsible because we were pressuring OEH staff to do more, all the time, you know,' he says. 'And poor Glen. He was the meat in the sandwich.'

Spark leans back, considering. He, Anderson and the liaisons in conservation organisations 'feel partly responsible that he was even there. Because there'd been some more clearing that we'd heard of down the road, and we were getting him to look at that.' He has hopes the inquest will illuminate a broken system, and clear Turner's name once and for all.

***

IN JULY 2019, FOLLOWING the re-election of the Berejiklian Liberal–National coalition government, the Office of Environment and Heritage was abolished. Its functions were absorbed into a newly created Department of Planning, Industry and Environment, its title perhaps indicative of the government's priorities.

The following month, the Berejiklian government announced an amnesty on new prosecutions of land-clearing transgressions committed in the lead-up to the new legislation implemented in 2017. Remediation orders would be a last resort from now on. The Nationals' Adam Marshall, the new agriculture minister, told 'concerned landowners' in Moree that landholders should not be prosecuted for acting against the law if the law had now changed. Farmers, continued the member for the Northern Tablelands electorate, which covers Croppa Creek, 'are our best environmental stewards and shoulder responsibility for the majority of land management in this state'. Marshall himself grew up on a farm near Gunnedah. He told his audience, 'I will not stand by and watch as activists and ideologues try to paint our farmers as criminals.'

Alison McKenzie, hearing this news from her property outside Tamworth, had to respond. 'I'm totally gutted by it,' she told the ABC. The premier sympathised. 'There's no doubt,' Gladys Berejiklian said helpfully, 'this is an emotional issue for many people.'

In late 2019, the government released more information. Some 27,000 hectares of woody vegetation had been cleared for agriculture in 2017–18 under the new laws. This scale of clearing triggered a mandatory review, initially kept secret, and the results were released on a Friday afternoon in March 2020, just as the COVID-19 pandemic engulfed Australia. Since the introduction of the new environmental laws, clearing rates had increased by thirteen times. In the region covered by Moree Plains Shire Council, encompassing the Golden Triangle and Croppa Creek, the area lost to cropping and pasture in just 2017–18 was about the size of greater Melbourne.

It's hard to set aside something already gone.

At the same time, Adam Marshall and other Nationals were attempting to wrest elements of environment protection from the New South Wales environment minister, Matt Kean, with a grab for final approval on activities including the clearing of native vegetation.

Then in January 2021, the report of the *Environment Protection and Biodiversity Act* review was made public. It categorically condemned the Act on its history of environmental protection. Two decades of failure since its inception had seen the nation's environment badly degrade, while the legislation was 'cumbersome' and unclear in its objectives. It was 'ineffective', not fit for purpose and needed significant revision if it were to counter the threats of the present and future. A full and immediate installation of rigorous national environment standards, and a new office of compliance and enforcement, were the centrepiece of the report's recommendations; a commissioner to evaluate and audit government policies, more consultation with First Nations peoples and their expertise, and a 'custodian' of information to the public were also part of the plan. The 'piecemeal' and compromised attitudes of the Act should cease. Responsible and effective administration of the nation's environment was envisaged, salvation of endangered species and mature management of natural resources.

Minister Ley responded, having sat on the report for three months before its release. 'This is a process that will take some time to complete,' she wrote, but she had committed to developing the national standards idea. The federal Liberal–National coalition government's other main intention, drafted even before the interim report, was to look into limiting the right of communities to bring legal challenges under the Act, and devolve environmental approval powers to the states and territories.

'Seems everything we do is a waste of time against a system that knows they can get away with it,' Phil Spark said, downcast after the 2019 state election outcome, which dashed hopes for a Labor repeal of the New South Wales land-clearing laws. 'Those of us that know the real picture are failures for allowing people and politicians to think that way. I don't know what it is going to take to bring about the change needed to seriously protect the environment.'

***

THERE WILL BE TREES in the future; there will be grain, though perhaps not as before. The continent is enormous, but then so is our appetite. We are renovating the very earth.

It is a question not often asked of conservationists: what do you ultimately want? Most environmental campaigns are fought defensively. When the future is mentioned, it is in caution: by such a date, some species will be likely be gone. Few, if any, tired conservationists dare imagine a future that involves planning beyond short-term campaigns. Few risk freeing the endangered species of hope.

First Nations peoples in Australia know this feeling well.

Most conservationists have in mind a country that is not diminished. The baseline of those who protest development is the moment when things still functioned with no loss of returns: the soil gave and received, the people used what the land could afford, change was sung into rhythm. We don't know if that is possible anymore. We don't know, either, if it would have any place for us in it.

Australians love the country in differing ways. For many, it is an inheritance made for them hundreds of years ago, formed by elders now only dust, put in words carried through years and landscapes. That legacy shapes continents. It scrapes forests from the soil. It sets a tool upon a trunk, sets trees on fire with the ferocity of its belief, scours animals from their hollows, tears meat from the bones of the land. It is a legacy so entire that those who carry it barely notice its weight in their hands.

It is the legacy of the Enlightenment – which came from the ambitions of property philosophy, from the Enclosures and the Clearances; which flexed from medieval agriculture and was ported across the oceans in little boats; which arrived in the hands of exiles who were ignorant, who tried to learn, who killed those who might have taught – to draw lines, to divide, to apply a compass and a ruler and an account book. The legacy of those who had nothing to lose; those who had everything to protect; the legacy of cities where people did not know the land, and country, where people did not like the rules. The legacy of the gun, of the waddy, of the plough and the dozer; of wheat that began thousands of years ago in the Fertile Crescent, and grass harvested here for hundreds of thousands of years; the legacy of hope and of despair. It all pressed on the earth of Australia like footprints, or the weight of a body.

The settlers live in us, whether we are their descendants or not. The landscapes we love now are as likely to be made by settlers as by nature. Our streets are asphalt, and our ability to forget the soil beneath is due to those settlers. We have changed the tracks of animals, rewritten their destinies, remapped a country erased by the shovel and the axe.

The richness of the soil has mostly gone. Much of what is left has been sucked dry. It took just six years for all the wealth of millennia to be eaten up in that soil around Port Jackson.

There is haunting in its grains, though. Blood. Bone. There are ghosts and guilt.

There is wealth, too. Many have been born here, and found haven and happiness. We have made gardens and grown flowers. We love our country. We love its fruits. How we adore to gobble them down.

***

IN MID-2018, GRANT PUT many of the family's Croppa Creek properties up for sale. 'Colorado' was among them. Huge 'Buckie' was too, on sale from Grant's company Qanagco; Robeena's 'North Yambin', 'Erralee' and 'Allandale'. They were leasing out 'Yambin' – the family homestead since the 1960s – and 'Elgin' and 'Lima', the properties bought by Robeena's father in 1932. Altogether, in a modest ad giving few details, the Turnbulls listed nearly 6000 hectares of their land.

Cory retained 'Strathdoon', by 2017 worth more than double what he had paid for it with the help of his grandfather. It is now a heavily cleared, thoroughly cropped monoculture, most of it bare to the soil but for the industrially farmed grains sown there.

None of the remediation ordered by the courts had, as far as observers knew, been made, and the real estate ads didn't mention the issue. A year after they went up, environment minister Matt Kean took the opportunity to make a statement that might have surprised his colleagues. 'Ian Turnbull was an evil man and people like him give good farmers a bad name,' he said. Anyone buying 'Colorado' needed to know 'the NSW government will make sure remediation orders are fully enforced'.

Aerial satellite photos of the property taken that year show cleared land, except a dribble of vegetation around the water gullies, to the margin. In early 2021, the properties were still unremediated and still unsold: the listing for 'Colorado' describes it as 'prime farming land' and 'predominantly timbered by Belah, Brigalow and Myall'. Remediation is still not mentioned.

Roger and Annette sold 'Royden' and 'Wallam' in late 2019. Combined, the sales to an American teachers' pension fund subsidiary made the couple more than $28 million, at $7500 a hectare.

Money from the sale of the other properties will be used to pay fines, and the settlements due to Robert Strange and Alison McKenzie. In the meantime, profits from crops on those properties may run into the millions.

*

THE PHOTOGRAPHS ON THE real estate listings for the Turnbull properties are studies in abstract. Many of them show cleared land: yellow-and-brown rectangles that fill nearly the entire frame. The earth is utterly flat, worn to the stubble. All the plough lines converge in the distance. Far, far away, almost at the top of the frame, is the horizon, under flat cumulus clouds and a pale blue sky, and the dark blotch of some tree. In some images the horizon is slightly tilted, so you feel woozy, tipped from the balance of the earth's surface.

There are shots of a shed full of expensive farm equipment. The corrugated iron walls of the workshed. A pale grey concrete floor.

There are images of the Turnbulls' wheat silos. Silver, smooth metal cylinders topped with grey metal cones, immensely high. They cast long shadows over the ground beneath them, pale orange, pressed by innumerable tyres. The gleaming metal, the magnificent height, the close ranking: they are like the magical towers of a fairytale castle, the battlements of a fortress.

And there is a photograph of a road. Not Talga Lane, but a yellow dirt track, a driveway probably. There is flat dark grass of some kind on each side, the edge of a metal fence and, beyond, a line of brigalow and there, just the sky, waiting.

*

ALISON MCKENZIE IS RAISING Alexandra and Jack alone. She grew into activism with the introduction of the new biodiversity laws, which she felt made a travesty of Glen's death. When the *Cultivating Murder* documentary was finished, with the help of crowdfunding, in 2017, she went to many of the screening events around New England and various cities, speaking to the audiences. Her friends were concerned at first, wondering if it would prolong the trauma, but McKenzie is committed to making change. She and Pearce adopted a favourite brand of Scotch: Glenlivet, which they like to call 'Glen Liveth'.

The year after Turner's death, a scholarship at the University of Newcastle was established in his name by the New South Wales government, offering a stipend to a student of natural or sustainable resource management. A few months later, a memorial bench was erected at a beach in Port Macquarie, where Turner had loved to run his dogs.

In September 2018, Robert Strange and Glen Turner received Australian Bravery Medals. Strange had already received a gold medal from the Royal Humane Society of NSW, and this second honour was for his selfless, courageous behaviour under danger. Turner was posthumously commended for valiant conduct in his attempts to escape with his life. 'Our family is proud and humbled to receive this honour for Glen,' Alison McKenzie wrote in a statement for the media. 'We try to focus on the man we knew and loved, rather than the final frightening half-hour of his life.' She accepted the medal from New South Wales governor David Hurley.

A sombre Strange said that 'what was done on that day' would never be forgotten. The medal, he explained, was for the families that had suffered.

The coronial inquest never happened. The coroner was satisfied the OEH had made changes, and little more was to be learned.

Every year, McKenzie and her children plant a tree for Turner, on the anniversary of his death, his birthday, Father's Day. In decades to come, there will be a little forest.

**

THE VIRGIN BRIGALOW IS gone. Clovers and lucerne grew in its traces, and cattle chewed that away. But the suckers and whipstick are there, defeating axe and dozer, chain and plough, napalm and fire, as they always have.

Salt has soaked through the soil, which has breathed away its carbon and its nitrogen. White crusts appear, and glazed earth washes away, flowing through rivers and out into the sea, leaving gullies and scoops. Invasive species finger their way across the fields and along the margins. Seeds blow into ground too stunned to receive them, and birds fly out looking to build nests in trees that are no longer there.

By 2009, the 7 million hectares of 1788 were half a million. Another three-quarters of a million were mixed brigalow growing back; most of it was just starting out after clearing.

There is still a little brigalow left. It is difficult to predict, says the country's expert in the species, Henry Nix, but it's possible it might one day regrow. 'Brigalow,' he writes, 'can wait.'

***

ROBERT STRANGE'S ELDEST SON, Joshua, was in the audience when Strange appeared on *Insight* in 2018. His father spoke frankly. 'Every day,' he said, 'there's something that reminds you.'

Jenny Brockie turned to speak to Josh. When the camera found him, the young man, wearing glasses and a youthful beard, was fighting tears. He composed himself and spoke. 'I lost my dad for twenty-four months after the event,' Josh said, in a voice constricted with feeling. His two younger brothers were in their early teens, going through their own stresses; he was doing HSC. He'd never been close with his mother, Josh said, and he relied a lot on his dad. 'To not have a father figure there – through no fault of Dad's own...' He swallowed and made himself keep going. The pitifully small outings, the child urging the father to attempt a walk in the fresh air, a visit to the shops. The hopes raised; the humiliation of the defeat. 'The hardest thing,' Josh said, glancing at his father, 'was not knowing what was going on, and not being told.'

Listening, Strange gazed back at him, or lowered his eyes to the floor, a look of the palest sorrow on his face. He said his reticence had been intended to protect the kids, as much as just not wanting to speak about the pain. He nodded, his eyes solemn. 'While you think you're protecting them, you're probably hurting them.'

***

IN JUNE 1938, WHEN Ian Turnbull was a little lad in the district, the anthropologist and linguist Norman Tindale spoke with and recorded two of the last fluent speakers of Kamilaroi language, a man called Harry Doolan and two other male Elders.

They told him a Dreaming story. They mumbled and hesitated at first, speaking the old words because they hadn't used their language for a long time. The only written record of their language was from a hundred years earlier – translations of pages from the Bible.

It took days for them to remember the right words, to shape them clearly in their mouths. They told the first part on one morning, the ending the next day. Slowly, the shape of the story was firmly formed again. The story was one that men would tell their children at a campfire at night.

It tells of Emu and Brolga: their envy and trickery of each other; the cost to them of their avarice. In most versions, parents are deceived into killing their own children. And in one, the Brolga must not only have her children killed for eating food she might eat herself, but she must eat them, too.

That story belongs here on the gold plains of the northwest of New South Wales. In Roman mythology, from the other side of the world, where white Australia's roots lie, stories tell of the god Saturn. That stern father rules the world of agriculture. But he is best known in a Goya painting: Saturn devouring his own children.

*

I WAS WALKING WITH my five-year-old son down the street one day as I was writing this book. We passed some spindly twigs carefully planted on the nature strip. They were new. 'What are those?' he asked.

I groaned. They were replacements for dozens of callistemons, the bushy red bottlebrushes popular in gardens and as street trees, found up and down the east and west coasts. But here no longer.

For years we had been walking down that inner-urban road to find the rough branches of the callistemons wrenched from the trunks and strewn across the footpath. Shredded joints remained pale on the trees. In the night, every few months, someone liked to rend these trees to pieces, yanking them until they cleaved, one after the other, down the line of the street. Sometimes whole trees were split in two, but somehow they survived; the wounds sealed, the trees endured and regrew. The consensus was that the damage was the work of drunks on their way home, but there was a relentlessness, a savagery required, that spoke of a deeper intent, a particular hatred for those trees. It went on for years. Someone wrenched those trees in the night, pulled with all their body weight, kept on pulling until something tore.

The council decided they'd had enough. They put notices on the surviving ones, proforma text saying they were 'diseased and/or growing badly', and one morning workers chopped them all down and pushed them into a shredder. In their place were planted spindly introduced species, those leafless twigs my son observed: Japanese elms, which would eventually grow to 13 metres but take years to cast shade; which would spread, casting leaves into the gutters and onto parked cars; which would nourish no native animals. Around the whippy little things someone had carefully packed a mulch of the shredded callistemons.

'Why don't Australians like native trees?' my son asked. I kissed him, and tried to explain.

CODA

In March 2012, Ian Turnbull was interviewed in his lawyers' offices in Moree, soon after contracts were signed on 'Strathdoon' and 'Colorado'. Glen Turner was there, but Gary Spencer, the special investigations officer for the OEH, did the running. Turnbull was candid, unperturbed by the questioning. He admitted he'd put on extra workers to finish a bout of clearing before the stop-work order came through and that, indeed, they'd finished the job.

'So what you're saying,' said Spencer, 'is you were trying to get as much done as you could before the stop-work order came.'

Turnbull shrugged. 'Yeah. There's an economical equation in there that we've always got a deadline to meet with banks and so forth, so we had to try and get somewhere. The area we've cleared plus the ground that's – that was already cleared – should get them through this year until we can do some negotiating with the EPA or the Gwydir Catchment Authority. Otherwise the place will have to be sold to someone else.'

'Can you tell me what your intention is with this property?' Spencer asked.

'To turn it into broadacre farming country,' explained Turnbull, 'because it's surrounded by broadacre farming properties. It's not as though it's an isolated property by itself, surrounded by undeveloped country.'

They asked if he had any last questions or comments. Imagine the old man standing, straightening his shoulders in his blue check shirt, speaking man to man, at ease in his lawyers' room, having seen off the interrogation, having explained his comfortable view of his actions. 'I'm hoping,' he said, 'you blokes have a bit of compassion so that we can clear it up and make it a farm for this younger generation. That's about it, yeah.'

ACKNOWLEDGEMENTS

Writing this book has been an exceptional education for me: very daunting but an enormous satisfaction. I am honoured to tell the story of Ian Turnbull and Glen Turner, the sorrows that came from their encounters and the lessons that may be learned. From the twilight scene on Talga Lane and my writing desk in suburban Melbourne I came to walk outwards in my research to the distant lands of Britain, the deep past of the First Nations legacy and the wide, gleaming wheatfields of New South Wales. It has been a revelation of place, identity and history to me. I finish it in a new home, in a new part of the continent, hearing the sea in the distance and looking out to a mountain dark with forest.

I've come, too, to a new understanding of my own creation: grown in a city that often resembles Europe, raised fond of lawns and English flowers and romantically habituated to the bare flanks of stripped country, I've learned to notice our native landscapes newly, and to comprehend my own 'shifting baseline' as I contemplate the future of the nation my son will grow up in, compared to the one I knew as a child; my lifetime alone covers nearly one-fifth of the period of white settlement in Australia. We face existential crisis with climate change, and everything is now to be reshaped. I was a city girl: now I see that I am as formed in nature as any brigalow.

The story of Ian Turnbull and Glen Turner is such a painful one that many involved struggled to speak of it. I am very grateful that Alison McKenzie, Fran Pearce, Rob Strange and Les Slater all generously agreed to share their experience and recollections with me. Phil Spark and Chris Nadolny were both endlessly patient with their expertise and recall of events, and Alaine Anderson took time in her busy day to talk. Others spoke cautiously on condition of anonymity, and I would like to thank JD, BO and JM, women of the northwest who spoke of life on the land and offered a female perspective on a very male narrative. From the OEH, former staff Simon Smith, John Lemon and John Benson, and Leah McKinnon at the Border Rivers–Gwydir Catchment Management Authority, lent their insight, while Andrew Picone at the Australian Conservation Authority also contributed information. Appreciation, too, to the four blokes at a Moree cafe who invited me to sit, bought me a coffee and told me of local life.

Inexperienced in research in legal archives, I was enormously and patiently helped by Anna Cooper at the Office of the Department of Public Prosecution; Sonya Zadel at the Office of the Chief Justice of the Supreme Court of New South Wales; and Linda at the Environment Line enquiry service at the OEH, who helped me untangle the OEH's evolution. Michael McNamara at the Gwydir Family Historical Society, and the staff and archives at the Moree Community Library, were very helpful as I delved into the town's past.

I would like to acknowledge the diligence, insight and work of Gregory Miller and Georgia Wallace-Crabbe for their documentary, *Cultivating Murder,* and Tanya Howard, who wrote the article that encouraged Morry Schwartz at Black Inc. to contemplate a full-length book.

Here, too, is my chance to show appreciation for the devoted and clever journalists on whose work I have hugely relied: Peter Hannam of *The Sydney Morning Herald;* Michael Slezak, Anne Davies, Adam Morton and Lisa Cox of *The Guardian;* Brianna Chillingworth of *Moree Champion;* Kerry Brewster, then of *Lateline;* and the various others who covered Ian Turnbull's murder trial and its aftermath. I also thank George Main and Cameron Muir, who wrote thoughtful and attentive histories of Australia's landscape; and Tom Griffiths, Libby Robin and their son, Billy Griffiths, who have all inspired me with their robust environmental histories, not to mention friendship, encouragement and example.

Julia Carlomagno and Chris Feik at Black Inc. were steady, exquisitely patient editors: Julia in particular never wobbled, even when I presented her with a manuscript twice as long as expected and a hundred times more complicated. Her attentiveness, canniness and expertise, even during national crisis, was a lesson in editorial virtue. I'm also thrilled to have Mary Callahan's beautiful cover design.

This book was written and edited on the country of various First Nations: the Boonwurrung people of the Kulin Nation in Narrm (Melbourne) and particularly the Yalukut Weelam (Port Phillip); the Gayemagal people of Kai'ymay (Manly); and the Wodi Wodi people of the Dharawal/Tharawal Nation in the Illawarra.

In my personal life I am always grateful for the presence of the following, and especially for their support as I toiled over this work: Vanessa Cross, Alice Williams, Matt Pritchard, Simon Tong, Ravenna and Shoshanah Keller, Cheryle Moore and Jeff Stein, Stacy Hoffman and Gino Mazzone, Daniel McGlone and many others for indelible friendship and just for taking an interest; Lee Kofman, James Norman, Chloe Hooper, Don Watson and Anna Krien, for friendship, writerly sympathy and advice; Jane Novak, for being my agent and friend and writing me the most encouraging email I've ever had; mentor and exemplar Erik Jensen; mentors and friends Anna and Morry Schwartz; Simeon and Tritian Glasson for hospitality as I visited court in Sydney; Julie and Mark Mills for the amazing house; Isabella Tree and Sir Charlie Burrell for hosting us at Knepp; the Fondation Segré and the Graduate Institute of International and Development Studies in Geneva for accommodating us; St Kilda & Balaclava Kindergarten for keeping my son safe and joyful as I worked; my cousin Tracey Callander, for the wise conversations about the world and help with my son as I wrote; everyone who asked kindly how the book was going, and listened as I told them. And as always, I'm full of gratitude for my gorgeous parents, Margot and Geoff, who helped with transcriptions and research and who provided love and coffee, and my patient and funny sister Jen, who bravely took the cat.

With all of the above guidance and help, it goes without saying that any errors contained in this book are my own.

I always write to music, and I encourage people to share with me the cinema soundtrack wonders of Max Richter, Nick Cave and Warren Ellis, Hildur Guðnadóttir, Ramin Djawadi, Clint Mansell; Justin Hurwitz's score for *First Man;* and the melodies of folk musicians Davy Graham, Duck Baker and Bert Jansch, Barry Dransfield and Fairport Convention, Shirley Collins, Pentangle, Anne Briggs, Judee Sill, Sibylle Baier, June Tabor, Linda Thompson, Bert Jansch and Martin Carthy. If anyone wants the sound of a countryside road in winter twilight, I recommend Richard Skelton's eerie soundscapes.

Last of all, I thank my incredible partner, Tim, who had the library I needed in his head or on the bookshelves, who made me lunch and listened to me, who has written his own exemplary histories and who is a beautiful, loving, exciting part of my own. And to our shining son, who will inherit all of our life, and live in the Australia that we have made – and the one yet to be loved.

BIBLIOGRAPHY

Articles

Albrecht, Glenn; Sartore, Gina-Maree; Connor, Linda et al., 'Solastalgia: The Distress Caused by Environmental Change', *Australasian Psychiatry,* vol.15, 2007, s95-98.

Austin, Peter & Tindale, Norman B., 'Emu and Brolga, A Kamilaroi Myth', *Aboriginal History,* vol.9, 1985, pp.9-21.

Barclay, Elaine & Bartel, Robyn, 'Defining Environmental Crime: The Perspective of Farmers', *Journal of Rural Studies,* vol.39, 2015, pp.188-98.

Barnes, Andrew & Hill, G.J.E., 'Estimating Kangaroo Damage to Winter Wheat Crops in the Bungunya District of Southern Queensland', *Wildlife Research,* vol.19, no.4, 1992, pp.417-27.

Bartel, Robyn & Barclay, Elaine, 'Motivational Postures and Compliance with Environmental Law in Australian Agriculture', *Journal of Rural Studies,* vol.27, no.2, 2011, pp.153–70.

Bartel, Robyn & Graham, Nicole, 'Property and Place Attachment: A Legal Geographical Analysis of Biodiversity Law Reform in New South Wales', *Geographical Research,* vol.54, no.3, 2016, pp.267–84.

Bellanta, Melissa, 'Clearing Ground for the New Arcadia: Utopia, Labour and Environment in 1890s Australia', *Journal of Australian Studies,* vol.26, no.72, 2002, pp.13–20.

Bettles, Colin, 'Williams Wants EPBC Act to Stop Treating Farmers Like Criminals', *The Land,* 5 April 2018.

Burton, Rosamund, 'Two of Us: Alison McKenzie and Fran Pearce', *Good Weekend,* 16 November 2016.

Butt, Nathalie & Menton, Mary, 'More Than 1,700 Activists Have Been Killed

This Century Defending the Environment', *The Conversation,* 6 August 2019.

Carrington, Damian, '$1m a Minute: The Farming Subsidies Destroying the World – Report', *The Guardian,* 16 September 2019.

Chan, Gabrielle, 'All About the Land: Drought Shakes Farming to Its Indigenous Roots', *The Guardian,* 6 October 2018.

——, 'Look After the Soil, Save the Earth: Farming in Australia's Unrelenting Climate', *The Guardian,* 22 October 2018.

Chillingworth, Breanna, 'Croppa Creek Killer Ian Robert Turnbull, Who Murdered Tamworth-Based Environment Officer Glen Turner, Dies in Sydney Hospital', *The Northern Daily Leader,* 28 March 2017.

——, 'Glen Turner and Robert Strange Recognised with Australian Bravery Awards After Fatal 2014 Croppa Creek

Clash', *Port Macquarie News,* 29 March 2018.

_____, 'Ian Robert Turnbull's Widow Robeena Ordered to Pay Damages for Murder of Glendon Turner Near Moree in 2014', *Northern Daily Leader,* 14 October 2020.

Clarry, Sarah & Noon, Samantha, 'Native Vegetation Laws – The Good, the Bad and the Farmers Making It Work', *The Farmer,* October 2018.

Cornwall, Deborah, 'Bloody-Minded Path to Croppa Creek Killing', *The Australian,* 16 December 2017.

Cox, Lisa, 'Five Countries Hold 70% of World's Last Wildernesses, Map Reveals', *The Guardian,* 1 November 2018.

_____, 'Land-clearing in NSW Rises Nearly 60% Since Laws Were Relaxed', *The Guardian,* 2 July 2020.

_____, 'Federal Minister Gives Green Light for Koala Habitat to be Bulldozed for Port Stephens Quarry', *The Guardian,* 27 October 2020.

_____, 'Australia Urged to Overhaul Environment Laws and Reverse "Decline of Our Iconic Places"', *The Guardian,* 28 January 2021.

_____, '"It's An Ecological Wasteland": Offsets for Sydney Toll Road Were Promised But Never Delivered', *The Guardian,* 10 February 2021.

Cranston, Matthew, 'Grain Farm Could Bring Up to $200m', *FarmOnline National,* 11 April 2014.

_____, 'Australia's Largest Wheat Grower Sells to US Westchester', *Australian Financial Review,* 5 September 2016.

Crawford, Sarah, 'Farmer Ian Turnbull "At Point of Despair" as He Shot Environment Officer', *The Daily Telegraph,* 17 May 2016.

Cubby, Ben, 'Koala Habitats in Danger as Bushland Areas Are Bulldozed', *The*

Sydney Morning Herald, 12 October 2012.

Davies, Anne, 'Clearing of Native Vegetation in NSW Jumps 800% in Three Years', *The Guardian,* 4 August 2018.

_____, 'Farmers Prosecuted for Land Clearing Allege Former NSW Minister Gave Them Green Light', *The Guardian,* 18 October 2019.

Dobney, Chris, 'Calls for "Incompetent" Environment Minister Upton to Be Sacked', *Echonetdaily,* 29 June 2018.

Druce, Alex, 'NSW Native Veg Details Revealed, Delays Expected', *The Land,* 10 May 2017.

_____, 'NSW Farmers Talk Tough on Land Conservation Costs, Grassland Fears', *The Land,* 18 July 2017.

Ellicott, John & Brown, Jamie, 'Hundreds of Prosecutions Still in Wings Under Old Veg Laws', *The Land,* 5 July 2019.

Feneley, Rick, 'The Farmers' Rights Tensions that Preceded Fatal Shooting of Environmental Officer Glen Turner', *The Sydney Morning Herald,* 1 August 2014.

Ferguson, Kathleen & Ingall, Jennifer, 'Native Vegetation Act Amnesty Angers Partner of Slain Environment Officer Glen Turner', *ABC News,* 2 August 2019.

Foley, Mike, 'Koala Wars: What Is Actually in the Law Threatening to Tear the Coalition Apart', *The Sydney Morning Herald,* 10 September 2020.

Gleeson-White, Jane, 'It's Only Natural: The Push to Give Rivers, Mountains and Forests Legal Rights', *The Guardian,* 1 April 2018.

Grear, Anna, 'It's Wrongheaded to Protect Nature with Human-Style Rights', *Aeon,* 19 March 2019.

Griffiths, Tom, 'How Many Trees Make a Forest? Cultural Debates about Vegetation Change in Australia',

Australian Journal of Botany, vol.50, no.4, 2002, pp.375–89.

Guilliatt, Richard, 'How A Row Over Land Clearing Left Compliance Officer Glen Turner Dead', *The Australian,* 13 September 2014.

Hall, Louise, 'Ian Turnbull, Accused of Murdering Environmental Officer Glen Turner, Refused Bail', *The Sydney Morning Herald,* 2 October 2014.

_____, 'Farmer Ian Turnbull Mentally Ill When He Shot Environmental Officer Glen Turner: Court', *The Sydney Morning Herald,* 13 May 2016.

Hannam, Peter, 'Losing the Plot: How Native Vegetation Mapping Went Feral', *The Sydney Morning Herald,* 15 January 2016.

_____, 'Murdered Environment Officer Glen Turner's Family Seeks Delay for Land-clearing Code', *The Sydney Morning Herald,* 3 August 2016.

———, 'Land Clearing in NSW Accelerates with Almost Two-Thirds of It Unexplained', *The Sydney Morning Herald,* 4 August 2016.

———, '"Too Complicated": New Land-clearing Laws Hard to Enforce, OEH Staff Widow Says', *The Sydney Morning Herald,* 17 November 2017.

———, 'NSW Koala Habitat Lost as Land Clearing Continues: "It Would Take the Army to Police These Blokes"', *The Sydney Morning Herald,* 6 August 2018.

———, 'Fears Family Behind "Evil" Land-clearing Act Will Avoid Court Order', *The Sydney Morning Herald,* 11 August 2019.

———, 'Dust-up Looms as NSW Nationals Seek to Cut Environmental Oversight', *The Sydney Morning Herald,* 29 July 2020.

Hinchcliffe, Joseph, 'Mystery Treasure Belonging to King Found at Moree', *The Border Mail,* 12 May 2015.

Hughes, Lesley, 'The Milk of Human Genius', *The Monthly,* March 2020.

Hunjan, Raveen, 'Proposed NSW Land-clearing, Biodiversity Laws Dealt Blow in Submissions', *ABC News,* 21 September 2016.

Kembrey, Melanie, 'Killer Farmer Ian Turnbull Taken to Court by Son Over Alleged Farm Promises', *The Sydney Morning Herald,* 30 July 2016.

Kinbacher, Lucy, 'When "Going Holistic" Helps You Through the Dry Times', *Moree Champion,* 21 February 2017.

King, Maddy, 'NSW Koalas Set to Become Extinct by 2050, Inquiry Reveals', *ABC News,* 30 June 2020.

Koubaridis, Andrew, 'Supreme Court Jury Finds Ian Turnbull Guilty of Murdering Glen Turner', News.com.au, 27 May 2016.

Lamacraft, Tim & Thomas, Kerrin, 'Croppa Creek Land Clearing Resumes After Environment Officer Fatal

Shooting, Footage Shows', *ABC News*, 7 August 2014.

Leonard, Sarah, 'Nature as an Ally: An Interview with Wendell Berry', *Dissent*, Spring 2012.

Levy, Megan & Hall, Louise, 'Elderly Man Charged with Murder of Environment and Heritage Worker Near Moree', *The Sydney Morning Herald*, 30 July 2014.

Lucas, Richard. M.; Clewley, Daniel; Accad, Arnon et al., 'Mapping Forest Growth and Degradation Stage in the Brigalow Belt Bioregion of Australia Through Integration of ALOS PALSAR and Landsat-Derived Foliage Projective Cover Data', *Remote Sensing of Environment,* vol.155, December 2014, pp.42–57.

Lucy, Michael, 'How Climate Change Is Driving Extreme Heatwaves', *Cosmos*, No.77, Summer 2018.

Manning, Adrian D., 'Scattered Trees are Keystone Structures – Implications for Conservation', *Biological*

Conservation, vol.132, no.3, October 2006, pp.311–21.

Martin, Paul & Hine, Donald W., 'Using Behavioural Science to Improve Australia's Environmental Regulation', *The Rangeland Journal,* vol.39, 2017, pp.551–61.

Martin, Sarah, 'Nationals MPs Snub Launch of Farming Group's Climate Change Report', *The Guardian,* 16 September 2016.

McQueen, Rob, 'Homesickness for a Foreign Country: Nostalgia and Colonisation', *International Journal of Law in Context,* vol.6, no.3, 25 August 2010, pp.257–75.

Monbiot, George, 'The Destruction of the Earth Is a Crime. It Should Be Prosecuted', *The Guardian,* 28 March 2019.

Morton, Adam, 'Letter by 240 Leading Scientists Calls on Scott Morrison to Stem Extinction Crisis', *The Guardian,* 28 October 2019.

_____, 'Review of Federal Environment Laws Will Cut "Green Tape" and Speed Up Approvals', *The Guardian,* 29 October 2019.

Morton, Adam & Davies, Anne, 'Australia Spends Billions Planting Trees – Then Wipes Out Carbon Gains by Bulldozing Them', *The Guardian,* 17 October 2019.

Nadolny, Chris, 'The New Biodiversity Laws: The Return of Broadscale Clearing or New Opportunities for Conservation-Minded Landholders?', in *Armidale Tree Group Newsletter,* vol.3, February 2018, pp.5–11.

Nason, James, 'Is There Any Money in Soil Carbon Projects? It Seems There Is Now', *Beef Central,* 9 December 2016.

No author, 'Agriculture' and 'The Kamilaroi', *Moree Tourism,* 2017, www.moreetourism.com.au

No author, 'Moree Shooting: The Reaction', *Moree Champion,* 30 July 2014.

No author, 'Moree Shooting: Farmer Ian Turnbull Jailed for 35 Years for Murdering Environmental Officer', *ABC News,* 23 June 2016.

No author, 'Farmers Thank Mike Baird,' *Western Magazine,* 19 January 2017.

No author, 'Ian Turnbull Obituary', *Moree Champion,* 11 April 2017.

No author, 'Saving Our Species Program', New South Wales Department of Planning, Industry and Environment, 20 January 2021, www.environment.nsw.gov.au/topics/animals-and-plants/threatened-species/saving-our-species-program

No author, 'Victim Impact Statements', *Victim Support Services,* https://victimsupportservices.org/help-for-victims/victim-impact-statements/

Olding, Rachel, 'Tragic End to Disputes Over Illegal Land Clearing', *The Sydney Morning Herald,* 30 July 2014.

———, 'Police to Allege Glen Turner Gunned Down While Inspecting an Unrelated Site in Croppa Creek', *The Sydney Morning Herald,* 5 August 2014.

Pike, Ben, 'Environmental Officer Glen Turner Gunned Down for Just Doing His Job: Wheat Farmer Ian Turnbull Charged with Murder', *The Daily Telegraph,* 30 July 2014.

———, 'Pushed Beyond Despair: Farmer Ian Turnbull's Family Says Feud Over Trees Consumed Hardworking Man of the Land', *The Daily Telegraph,* 31 July 2014.

Pike, Ben & Godfrey, Miles, 'Fresh Charges Laid Against Murder-accused Farmer Ian Turnbull', *The Daily Telegraph,* 5 August 2014.

Plumwood, Val, 'Shadow Places and the Politics of Dwelling', *Australian Humanities Review,* vol.44, 2008, pp.139–50.

Pontin, Ben, 'Environmental Law-Making Public Opinion in Victorian Britain: The

Cross-currents of Bentham's and Coleridge's Ideas, *Oxford Journal of Legal Studies,* vol.34, no.4, Winter 2014, pp.759–90.

Popova, Maria, 'Pioneering Conservationist Mardy Murie on Nature, Human Nature, and the Wealth of the Wilderness', *Brain Pickings,* no date.

Richardson, Miles; Cormack, Adam; McRobert, Lucy et al., '30 Days Wild: Development and Evaluation of a Large-Scale Nature Engagement Campaign to Improve Well-Being', *PLoS ONE,* vol.2, no.2, 18 February 2016.

Rule, Susan; Brook, Barry; Haberle, Simon et al., 'The Aftermath of Megafaunal Extinction: Ecosystem Transformation in Pleistocene Australia', *Science,* vol.335, no.6075, pp.1483–86.

Schlesinger, Larry, 'Nuveen Adds Moree Farms to $3.5b Global Agriculture Fund', *Australian Financial Review,* 10 November 2019.

Schwartz, Judith D., 'Soil as Carbon Storehouse: New Weapon in Climate Fight?', *Yale Environment 360,* 4 March 2014.

Slezak, Michael, 'NSW Farmers Member Quits Executive in Dispute Over Land Clearing', *The Guardian,* 2 February 2016.

_____, 'Conservation Groups Storm Out of Consultations Over Land-clearing Law', *The Guardian,* 19 February 2016.

_____, 'Koalas "Under Siege" from Policy Changes Set to Destroy Habitat, Report Finds', *The Guardian,* 7 November 2016.

_____, 'Call for Inquiry After Nationals MP Urged Land-clearing Investigation Be Dropped', *The Guardian,* 15 November 2016.

_____, 'Can Queensland Labor End Broadscale Land Clearing, As Promised?', *The Guardian,* 12 March 2018.

———, 'Death by a Thousand Cuts: The Familiar Patterns Behind Australia's Land-clearing Crisis', *The Guardian,* 14 March 2018.

Symons, Mark, 'Tree-Clearing Causing Queensland's Greatest Animal Welfare Crisis', WWF Australia, 6 September 2017.

Tyson, Ross, 'Moree Shooting: Croppa Creek Unites for Glen Turner's Family', *Moree Champion,* 30 July 2014.

Vanclay, Frank, 'Social Principles for Agricultural Extension to Assist in the Promotion of Natural Resource Management', *Australian Journal of Experimental Agriculture,* vol.44, no.3, pp.213–22.

Vaughan, Adam, 'Humans Have Destroyed a Tenth of Earth's Wilderness in 25 Years – Study', *The Guardian,* 9 September 2016.

Vergotis, Paul, 'Power to the People: What the Draft Biodiversity Conservation Bill 2016 Means for

Developers and Landowners', *McCabe Curwood,* 17 May 2016.

Ward, Michelle; Simmonds, Jeremy & Reside, April et al., 'Lots of Loss with Little Scrutiny: The Attrition of Habitat Critical for Threatened Species in Australia', *Conservation Science and Practice,* 8 September 2019, https://conbio.onlinelibrary.wiley.com/doi/full/10.1111/csp2.117

Watts, Jonathan, 'Latest Land Defender Murder Cements Mexico's Deadly Reputation', *The Guardian,* 27 October 2018.

Wetherell, Rodney, 'The "Original Greenie": Dewar Wilson Goode AM, Grazier, Conservationist and Writer, 1.2.1907–28.6.2002', *Habitat Australia,* vol.30, no.6, 2002, p.24.

Wharton, Jane, 'Thirsty Koala Risks Life to Lick Rainwater Off Road in Fire-Ravaged Australia', *Metro,* 18 January 2020.

Books

Atkinson, James, *An Account of the State of Agriculture and Grazing in New South Wales,* Sydney University Press, Sydney, 1975 (facsimile edition 1826).

Barr, Neil & Cary, John, *Greening a Brown Land: The Australian Search for Sustainable Land Use,* Macmillan Education Australia, Melbourne, 1992.

Berry, Wendell in Kingsnorth, Paul (ed.), *The World-Ending Fire: The Essential Wendell Berry,* Penguin Books, Middlesex, 2017.

Blomfield, Charles Edwin, *Reminiscences of Early New England: Memoirs of a Pioneer,* Southern Publishers, Bega, 1978.

Bolton, Geoffrey, *Spoils and Spoilers: A History of Australians Shaping Their Environment* (second ed.), Allen & Unwin, Sydney, 1992.

Bonyhady, Tim, *The Colonial Earth,* Melbourne University Press, Melbourne, 2000.

Boyce, Dean, *Clarke of the Kindur: Convict, Bushranger, Explorer,* Melbourne University Press, Melbourne, 1970.

Curthoys, Ann, 'Mythologies' in Richard Nile (ed.), *The Australian Legend and Its Discontents,* University of Queensland Press, St Lucia, 2000.

Flannery, Tim, *The Future Eaters: An Ecological History of The Australasian Lands and People,* Reed Books, Melbourne, 1994.

_____, *Europe: A Natural History,* Text Publishing, Melbourne, 2018.

Frawley, Kevin, 'Evolving Visions: Environmental Management and Nature Conservation in Australia', in Pawson, Eric & Dovers, Stephen (eds), *Australian Environmental History: Essays and Cases,* Oxford University Press, Melbourne, 1994, pp.55–78.

Gascoigne, John with Curthoys, Patricia, *The Enlightenment and the Origins of European Australia,* Cambridge University Press, Port Melbourne, 2002.

Gibson, Ross, *Seven Versions of an Australian Badland,* University of Queensland Press, St Lucia, 2002.

Griffiths, Jay, *Wild: An Elemental Journey,* Hamish Hamilton, London, 2007.

Haines, Robin F., *Emigration and the Labouring Poor: Australian Recruitment in Britain and Ireland, 1831–60,* Macmillan Press, Houndsmills and London, 1997.

Korff, Jens, 'Myall Creek Massacre (1838)', *Creative Spirits,* 2017, available at www.creativespirits.info/aboriginalculture/history/myall-creek-massacre-1838#axzz4q04fpEl5

Lines, William J., *Taming the Great South Land: A History of the Conquest of Nature in Australia,* Allen & Unwin, Sydney, 1991.

Locke, John, *Second Treatise on Civil Government,* Awnsham Churchill, London, 1869.

Macfarlane, Robert, *Mountains of the Mind: A History of a Fascination,* Granta Books, London, 2003.

Madden, Pat; Swinburn, Doug; Fuller, Shirley et al., *And So the Story Goes: The Croppa Creek District, 1848–87,* National Library of Australia, Canberra, 1987.

Main, George, *Heartland: The Regeneration of Rural Place,* University of New South Wales Press, Sydney, 2005.

Maitland, Sara, *Gossip from the Forest: The Tangled Roots of Our Forests and Fairytales,* Granta, London, 2012.

Massy, Charles, *Call of the Reed Warbler: A New Agriculture, A New Earth,* University of Queensland Press, St Lucia, 2017.

Mitchell, Major Thomas L., *Three Expeditions Into the Interior of Eastern Australia: With Descriptions of the Recently Explored Region of Australia Felix, and of the Present Colony of New South Wales, Vol.1* (second ed.), 2004 (originally published 1838).

_____, *Journal of an Expedition Into the Interior of Tropical Australia In Search of a Route from Sydney to the Gulf of Carpentaria,* 1848, available at http://gutenberg.net.au/ebooks/e00034.html

Muir, Cameron, *The Broken Promise of Agricultural Progress: An Environmental History,* Routledge, Melbourne, 2014.

Nix, Henry, 'The Brigalow', in Pawson, Eric & Dovers, Stephen (eds), *Australian Environmental History: Essays and Cases,* Oxford University Press, Melbourne, 1994, pp.198–233.

Nixon, Rob, *Slow Violence and the Environmentalism of the Poor,* Harvard University Press, Massachusetts and London, 2011.

Paine, Thomas, *Agrarian Justice,* 1795, available at www.cooperative-individualism.org/painethomas_agrarian-justice-01.htm

Pascoe, Bruce, *Dark Emu: Aboriginal Australia and the Birth of Agriculture,* Magabala Books, 2014.

Plumwood, Val, *Feminism and the Mastery of Nature,* Routledge, London, 1993.

Proudfoot, Lindsay & Hall, Dianne, *Imperial Spaces: Placing the Irish and Scots in Colonial Australia,* Manchester University Press, Manchester, 2013.

Ratcliffe, Francis, *Flying Fox and Drifting Sand: The Adventures of a Biologist in Australia,* Chatto & Windus, London, 1938.

Robin, Libby, *Defending the Little Desert: The Rise of Ecological Consciousness in Australia,* Melbourne University Publishing, Melbourne, 1994.

_____, *How a Continent Created a Nation,* University of New South Wales Press, Sydney, 2007.

Rolls, Eric, 'More a New Planet Than a New Continent', in Pawson, Eric & Dovers, Stephen (eds), *Australian Environmental History: Essays and Cases,* Oxford University Press, Melbourne, 1994, pp.22–36.

_____, *A Million Wild Acres: 200 Years of Man and an Australian Forest,* Hale & Iremonger, Sydney, 2011.

Rousseau, Jean-Jacques (trans. Cole, G.D.H.), *The Social Contract,* Digireads, 2018 (originally published 1762).

Solnit, Rebecca, *A Book of Migrations: Some Passages in Ireland,* Verso, London and New York, 1997.

Stubbins, Ted & Smith, Paulette, *The Myall Creek Massacre: Its History, Its Memorial and the Opening Ceremony,* The Myall Creek Memorial Committee, Bingara, 2001.

Tan, Shaun, *Tales From Outer Suburbia,* Allen & Unwin, Sydney, 2008.

Thomas, Keith, *Man and the Natural World: Changing Attitudes in England 1500–1800,* Penguin Books, Middlesex, (1983).

Warialda and District Historical Society, *Legacy of the Years: Notes from the Warialda Historical Society,* Warialda, 1973.

Webb, R.J. (ed.), *The Rising Sun: A History of Moree and District 1862–1962,* The Council of the Municipality of Moree, Moree, 1962.

Young, Ann, *Environmental Change in Australia since 1788,* Oxford University Press, Melbourne, 1996.

Judgements

Chief Executive of the Office of Environment and Heritage, Department of Premier and Cabinet v Turnbull [2014] NSWLEC 150, Land and

Environment Court, New South Wales, September 2014.

Chief Executive of the Office of Environment and Heritage v Turnbull [2014] NSWLEC 153, Land and Environment Court, New South Wales, September 2014.

Chief Executive of the Office of Environment and Heritage v Turnbull (No.2) [2014] NSWLEC 155, Land and Environment Court, New South Wales, September 2014.

Chief Executive of the Office and Environment and Heritage v Cory Ian Turnbull [2017] NSWLEC 140, Land and Environment Court, New South Wales, October 2017.

Chief Executive of the Office of Environment and Heritage v Grant Wesley Turnbull NSWLEC 141, Land and Environment Court, New South Wales, October 2017.

Chief Executive of the Office of Environment and Heritage v Grant

Wesley Turnbull (No.3) [2019] NSWLEC 165, Land and Environment Court, New South Wales, November 2019.

Chief Executive of the Office of Environment and Heritage, Department of Premier and Cabinet v Turnbull [2014] NSWLEC 150, Land and Environment Court, New South Wales, September 2014.

Chief Executive of the Office of Environment and Heritage v Turnbull (No.4) [2016] NSWLEC 66, Land and Environment Court, New South Wales, June 2016.

R v Turnbull (No.1) [2016] NSWSC 189, Supreme Court of New South Wales, March 2016.

R v Turnbull (No.23) [2016] NSWSC 802, Supreme Court of New South Wales, May 2016.

R v Turnbull (No.25) [2016] NSWSC 831, Supreme Court of New South Wales, June 2016.

R v Turnbull (No.26) [2016] NSWSC 847, Supreme Court of New South Wales, June 2016.

Strange v Turnbull [2017] NSWSC1363, Supreme Court of New South Wales, Sydney, 2017, paragraph 12.

Strange v Turnbull; McKenzie v Turnbull [2021] NSWSC 27, Supreme Court New South Wales, Sydney, January 2021.

Turnbull v Chief Executive of the Office of Environment and Heritage [2015] NSWCCA 278, Court of Criminal Appeal, Supreme Court of New South Wales, October 2015.

Turnbull v Director-General, Office of Environment and Heritage (No.2) [2014] NSWLEC 112, Land and Environment Court, New South Wales, July 2014.

Turnbull v Turnbull [2017] NSWSC 1316, 'Statement in the Matter of Ian Turnbull', Supreme Court of New South Wales, September 2017.

Witness statements

Bailey, Terrence, 'Statement in the Matter of Ian Turnbull', 2016.

Joseph, Sylvester, 'Notice of Intention to Adduce Tendency Evidence', 2016.

Snook, Arthur, 'Statement of Arthur James Snook in the Matter of Ian Turnbull', 2014.

Strange, Robert, 'Witness Testimony', Supreme Court of New South Wales, 2014.

Transcripts

Holden, Kate, 'Excerpts from OEH Correspondence Relating to Management of Turnbull Investigation', Supreme Court, New South Wales State Archives, March 2018.

_____, 'Notes from Typed Edition of Glen Turner's Compliance Notebook Concerning Turnbull Illegal Clearing Investigations', Supreme Court, New

South Wales State Archives, March 2018.

———, 'Notes from Victim Impact Statements', Supreme Court, New South Wales State Archives, March 2018.

———, 'Notes on Autopsy Report on Glendon Eric Turner by Dr Rexson Tse at Northern Hub, Newcastle Department of Forensic Medicine, August 2014', March 2018.

———, 'Notes on Court Debate on Holding Turnbull Trial in Moree', Supreme Court, New South Wales State Archives, March 2018.

———, 'Notes on Defence Case for Provocation and Notice to Adduce Tendency', Supreme Court, New South Wales State Archives, March 2018.

———, 'Notes on Ian Turnbull Witness Statement', Supreme Court, New South Wales State Archives, March 2018.

_____, 'Notes on Ian Turnbull's Psychiatric Testimonies', Supreme Court, New South Wales State Archives, March 2018.

_____, 'Notes on OEH Prosecution of Ian Turnbull for Landclearing: Transcript of Interview with Gary Spencer of OEH, Roger Butler and Ian Turnbull, and Glen Turner, Interview 22 March 2012', March 2018.

_____, 'Notes on the Crown Case Statement for Glen Turner's Murder', Supreme Court, New South Wales State Archives, March 2018.

_____, 'Notes on Transcript of Robert Strange Police Walk-Through', 30 July 2014.

_____, 'Notes on Witness Statements in Trial of Ian Turnbull', Supreme Court, New South Wales State Archives, March 2018.

Turnbull, Ian, 'Audio Recordings from Cessnock Correctional Centre, Long Bay Correctional Complex and Long Bay

Hospital', Office of the Director of Public Prosecutions NSW, June 2020.

Interviews and correspondence

Anderson, Alaine, interview with author, 3 September 2018.

McKenzie, Alison, open letter to the Premier and Minister for the Environment, August 2017.

McKenzie, Alison, correspondence to author, 11 August 2020.

Rendell, Trish, 'Re: Clearing Vegetation for High-Value Agriculture at [Redacted]', letter to [redacted], 10 December 2015.

Mitchell, Ranald, correspondence to author, 18 November 2019.

Nadolny, Chris, interview with author, 18 February 2018.

———, interview with author, 19 August 2019.

———, correspondence to author, 15 October 2020.

———, correspondence to author, 24 October 2019.

———, correspondence to author, 31 October 2019.

Slater, Leslie, correspondence with Peter Dunphy, executive director of SafeWork NSW, July 2016.

———, correspondence to New South Wales State Coroners Court, Glebe, 20 October 2018.

———, reproduced correspondence, various dates, sent to author July 2020.

———, correspondence to author, 17 December 2020.

Smith, Simon, interview with author, 24 October 2010.

Spark, Phil, 'Submission Requesting a Coronial Investigation Into the Circumstances That Led To Glen Turner's Murder at Croppa Creek on 29th July 2014', file 2014/224477, May 2017, sent to author December 2017.

———, interview with author, 27 November 2017.

———, correspondence to author, 31 March 2019.

———, correspondence to author, 8 May 2020.

Strange, Robert, interview with author, 24 July 2020.

Turner, Glen, 'Correspondence to Managers Regarding Turnbull Threat', Office of Environment and Heritage files, 2012.

Reports

Auditor-General, 'Referrals, Assessments and Approvals of Controlled Actions under the Environment Protection and Biodiversity Conservation Act 1999: Department of Agriculture, Water and the Environment', Auditor-General Report No.47 2019–20, Performance Audit, Australian National Audit Office, Canberra, 2020.

Blanch, Stuart; Sweeney, Oisín; Pugh, Dailan, 'The NSW Koala Strategy: Ineffective, Inadequate and Expensive. An Assessment of the NSW Koala Strategy Against Recommendations Made in the Independent Review Into Decline of Koalas in NSW', WWF Australia, Sydney, pp.1–17.

Bombell, Alec & Montoya, Daniel, 'Native Vegetation Clearing in NSW: A Regulatory History', Briefing Paper No.05/2014, NSW Parliament, Sydney, 2014.

Byron, Neil; Craik, Wendy; Keniry, John et al., 'A Review of Biodiversity Legislation in NSW: Final Report', Independent Biodiversity Legislation Review Panel, 18 December 2014.

Ecologically Sustainable Development Steering Committee, 'National Strategy for Ecologically Sustainable Development', Department of Agriculture, Water and the Environment, Australian Government, Canberra, December 1992.

Environment, Energy and Science, 'Biodiversity Assessment Method', Department of Planning, Industry & Environment, New South Wales, 2020.

General Purpose Standing Committee No.5, 'Examination of Proposed Expenditure for the Portfolio Areas Environment, Heritage', Budget Estimates, Australian Government, Canberra, 11 October 2012.

Lee, Derek, 'Inquest Into the Death of Ian Turnbull', State Coroner's Court of New South Wales, Sydney, file number 2017/95138, October 2018.

Natural Resources Commission, 'Land Management and Biodiversity Conservation Reforms: Final Advice on a Response to the Policy Review Point', NSW Government, Sydney, July 2019.

No author, 'Compliance Policy', State of New South Wales and Office of Heritage and the Environment, Sydney, 2018, p.4.

No author, 'NSW Biodiversity Reforms 2016: Issue 2 – Offsets and Ecologically Sustainable Development', Environmental Defenders Office, Sydney, 2017.

No author, 'NSW Woody Vegetation Change 2017–18 Spreadsheet', Department of Planning, Industry and Environment, Australian Government, Canberra, 2019.

No author, 'Paradise Lost – The Weakening and Widening of NSW Biodiversity Offsetting Schemes, 2005–2016', Nature Conservation Council of NSW, Sydney, 2016.

Office of Environment and Heritage, 'Biodiversity Legislation Review: Submissions Report', New South Wales

Office of Environment and Heritage, December 2014.

OzArk Environmental & Heritage Management, 'Newell Highway Heavy Duty Pavements, North Moree: Aboriginal and Historic Archaeological Survey Report', Roads and Maritime Services, May 2018.

Pain, Nicola & Wright, Sarah, 'The Rise of Environmental Law in New South Wales and Federally: Perspectives from the Past and Issues for the Future', National Environmental Law Association Annual Conference, Broken Hill, 2003.

Samuel, Graeme, 'Independent Review of the EPBC Act: Interim Report', Department of Agriculture, Water and the Environment, Australian Government, Canberra, June 2020.

Smith, Peter; Wilson, Brian; Nadolny, Chris et al., 'The Ecological Role of the Native Vegetation of New South Wales: A Background Paper of the Native Vegetation Advisory Council of New South Wales', Native Vegetation

Advisory Council of New South Wales, Sydney, January 2000.

Taylor, Martin F.J. & Dickman, Christopher R., 'NSW Native Vegetation Act Saves Australian Wildlife', WWF Australia, Sydney, April 2014.

Taylor, Martin F.J.; Booth, Carol; Paterson, Mandy, 'Tree-clearing: The Hidden Crisis of Animal Welfare in Queensland', WWF Australia, Sydney, 2017.

Television, film and video

Brewster, Kerry, 'NSW Government Accused of Failure to Act on Alleged Illegal Land Clearing', *Lateline,* ABC-TV, 14 November 2016.

Miller, Gregory (dir.), *Cultivating Murder,* Film Projects and Sensible Films, Australia, 2007.

Pennells, Steve, 'Cultivating a Murder', *Sunday Night,* Channel 7, 2 October 2016.

Pauly, Daniel, 'The Ocean's Shifting Baseline', TED Talk, *YouTube,* April 2010.

Piatek, Alix, 'Witness Part 1', *Insight,* SBS, season 2, episode 8, April 2018.

NOTES

Prologue

'If it wasn't help, he didn't want to see what was going to happen': Robert Strange's actions and thoughts, including the realisation of Turner's death, paraphrased from Holden, 'Notes on Transcript of Robert Strange Police Walk-Through', and Strange, 2014.

Chapter 1

'Turnbull himself is known for his quiet generosity': Slater, July 2020.

'...the Environmental Protection Agency had written a letter...': Bailey.

'Flinders, Kangaroo, and perennials ... edible herbs once grew between the clumps': Rolls, 2011, p.111.

"The plains are like flat, black ocean...": ibid., p.42.

'Moree is wealthy...': Back in 1965, the Freedom Ride, led by Charles Perkins, came to Moree to protest the segregation of the baths. Black children had been forbidden to bathe alongside whites. Fifty years later, there is a lavish Dhiiyaan Aboriginal Centre, and an Aboriginal art gallery and café in the centre of town. Ten years ago, the first corroboree since 1938 was held, gathering clans from Tamworth to Taree to dance, smoke the grounds and speak languages once forbidden. Tools were made, stories told, spears thrown. It was broadcast on local radio and live-tweeted. At the same time, there is tension in Moree. Ice and young black people are blamed for vandalism and violence. Their elders lament. Though of course it is impossible to tell a person's heritage from sight, the prosperous landholders gathering in Moree district pubs appear overwhelmingly white.

'The Moree Plains Shire produces an average of a million tonnes of wheat': 'Agriculture', Moree Tourism.

"At different times of the year...": ibid.

"disposed of in one determined engagement": Rolls, 2011, p.94.

'It was the year of a grasshopper plague...': Madden, p.157.

"The way was now open...": Madden, p.43.

"My happy childhood...": Robeena Turnbull in ibid., p.161.

'By the 1940s Croppa had houses and a railway line': ibid., p.114.

"The phone was connected in 1952", "Often a storm had been across the road": Robeena Turnbull in ibid., p.164, p.160. Despite the growth of the community, parts of Moree remained undeveloped through this period. Deirdre Magill, a co-author of the Croppa Creek history, remembers arriving in the area in the 1960s as a newlywed, to camp in the scrub with her husband as they cleared their property with the help of two friends.

It was a scene appreciably little different from a century earlier, something from a Frederick McCubbin painting.

'Ran ... began to love his small patch...': Mitchell.

'Now in 1987': Robeena Turnbull in Madden, p.161.

"land of an equal richness...", "Nobody could think himself injured": Locke, Chapter V, paragraph 33.

"[T]he earth, in its natural, uncultivated state...": Paine, paragraph 11.

"...is always subordinate to the right which the community has over all": Rousseau, Book I, Chapter IX.

'...the ineluctable mark of a British citizen was land ownership': The dilemmas of humans in the landscape are of course older than Enlightenment arguments. Not expecting to find a sophisticated culture in Australia, most Europeans made few records of First

Nations concepts of property. But the Cadigal people of the Eora Nation in Sydney, though judiciously practising communal arrangements of resources, had their own system of ownership rights. 'Strange as it may appear,' David Collins of the First Fleet wrote, 'they also have their real estates.' Eora man Woollarawarre Bennelong told Collins that Me-Mel (Goat Island) in Sydney Harbour was 'his own property', inherited from his father, and that such hereditary arrangements were common. Proof of entitlement was through knowledge of song. Access was controlled and exclusive; hunting and fishing rights were assumed. And these rights were passed from generation to generation. Was it so very different from the Europeans?

'Suffrage was only granted to British men...': Universal male suffrage wasn't given in Britain itself until 1918, sixty years after a form of it was bestowed on British male subjects in most of the Australian territories.

Chapter 2

'First named scientifically in 1864...': Nix, p.203.

'...almost everything about the plant is designed to impede fire...': Flannery, pp.227–28.

'They house biodiversity ... they work on the land as surely as farm labourers': Smith, Wilson & Nadolny.

'...conversion of grazing to cropping land was where the money was now': Years later, it was noted in court that 'a primary practice that the Turnbull family had engaged in was to identify a cheaper property that was not being cultivated effectively and then acquire the property at the best price possible'. They 'would try to identify underdeveloped farming properties that had either been poorly developed or had a mixture of grazing and farming, then acquire such properties and try to increase the level of cultivation'. See *Turnbull v Turnbull,* 2017, paragraph 57.

'...it swallowed whole herds': Croppa Creek man Stan Bischoff remembered the 'Mungle Scrub' east of Croppa Creek at the start of the twentieth century: 40,000 acres thick with prickly pear as high as a man's head. It was home to dingoes, wild turkeys and reptiles. A term arose: scrub cattle, tracked by Aboriginal experts, legends for their dauntlessness: Billy Uglymug, Black Albert Williams, Old Gunta, Ginger Lang, Jack Tommy Tommy. See Madden, pp.81–82.

"a massive suckering response": Nix, p.204.

'At the surface the roots are braided and set...': ibid.

'Turnbull, in exchange for mortgaging his own place...': *Turnbull v Chief Executive.*

'...a developer could buy a block now and double its worth in a couple of years': Country in that district could be bought for $800–900 per acre, and sell after conversion for $3000. See Smith, 2019.

'...the crop's failure baffled the colonists': Barr, Chapter 2.

'Australian soils are formed in the crucible of a very dry, hot environment...': Massy, pp.16–17.

'...cut Panicum (panicgrass) with stone knives, tossed it to be winnowed by the wind and ground it for flour': Mitchell, 1848, entry dated 19 Feb 1846.

'They stored seeds in granaries and baked bread ... for many thousands of years': Muir, p.91.

'...to confirm James Cook's scanty impressions from decades earlier...': Where were the demarcated fields, the fences, the captive stock and domesticated companions, the tidy rows of crop? Cook's scant investigation served as a pretext for Britain to argue within international law that – in the words of the Swiss lawyer Emer de

Vattel, the pre-eminent legal sage of the eighteenth century and author of *The Law of Nations* (1758) – 'unsettled habitation in these immense regions cannot be accounted a true and legal possession' (see McQueen, p.259 and Muir, p.92). In addition, Aboriginal peoples were patently not Christian, so the prohibition in British law against seizing the lands of Christians didn't apply. There need be no legal impediment to seizure and possession of what seemed a radiant instance of that rare and remarkable phenomenon, *terra nullius*.

'The force of this willed perception was so phenomenal that it has persisted to the present day': The virtues of Indigenous management are well attested. But some palaeontologists, ecological and Indigenous historians also argue that the impact of Aboriginal settlement brought drastic and apocalyptic change to the land. The strong implication of surviving palaeontological evidence is that humans, arriving on a 'virgin' land, ate the large herbivorous mammals.

Uneaten, overabundant vegetation burned easily, and eventually, under the influence of human-directed 'fire-stick farming', the character, behaviour and thickness of vegetation changed radically across Australia (see Flannery, pp.224–27). To ignore this likelihood collaborates in a disingenuous concept of Aboriginal peoples as 'creatures of nature': unconscious, instinctual, primaeval, faunal. This was exactly the sentiment European colonists expressed when they weighed their sophistication and entitlements against those of the people they were about to dispossess.

'...the soil had a mulch of thousands of years...': Rolls, 1994, p.22.

"[N]o person, to my knowledge": Atkinson, p.21. Subsequent quotations in this paragraph, p.17 and p.8.

"...the land in a few years gets exhausted...": ibid., p.32.

'...farmers welcomed artificial, controllable technology, applied mechanically': Massy, p.45. The stump-jump plough, invented in South Australia, was a game-changer; so was H.V. McKay's 1884 stripper harvester, perfected over the next century and introduced to the north by the early twentieth century. That miraculous compendium machine reaped, winnowed and filled bags with clean grain as it moved. It was named, McKay said, for an image of God as sunshine, penetrating even through the cloudy skies of despair (see Main, p.158).

'Tined seed drills...': Rolls, 2011, p.215.

'...defoliants like Agent Orange were liberally poured from aircraft': Lines, p.204. One who made his fortune in that employ was a man called Joh Bjelke-Petersen.

'The town has little tidy brick houses, plush green winter paddocks...': But in the hills beyond there are still farmers who get their sons working the land from sixteen. Education levels are low, and in many places there is little television reception or internet connectivity. Telegraph Point was hard-hit by bushfires in November 2019.

"I didn't perceive him as gung-ho": Chris Nadolny's memories of Glen Turner in Nadolny, 18 February 2018.

'...Roger reacted with fury': Smith.

"While the EPA fully expects that you will comply...": *Chief Executive v Cory Ian Turnbull.*

"illegal clearing is not degradation, it is restoration": Muir, p.83.

'Some farmers waited it out': Nadolny, 'The New Biodiversity Laws', p.6.

'They all used the same agent, and Turnbull's lawyer...': Holden, 'Notes on Ian Turnbull Witness Statement'.

'The brothers were allowed to stay on...': ibid.

'He didn't realise the application couldn't be granted...': Nadolny, 24 October 2019.

'After the ground was settled...': Holden, 'Notes on OEH Prosecution'.

'She had stood up in the Croppa Creek hall...': Spark, 2017.

'Satellite images of vegetation cover...': Explanation of the EPA process for tracking vegetation clearance and Simon Smith's comments in Smith.

'There were ... usually two or three compliance officers...': Hannam & Smith.

'"Cory," he said, when his call was answered': call between Glen Turner and Cory Turnbull as recorded by Glen Turner in Holden, 'Notes from Typed Edition of Glen Turner's Compliance Notebook', s.32.

'The old man watched...': Description of the clearing and Scott brothers' presence in Nadolny, 24 October 2019.

'Nadolny voiced it...': Holden, 'Notes from Typed Edition of Glen Turner's Compliance Notebook', s.32, entry dated 14 February 2012.

'Smith ... was about to leave his position': Smith.

'Back at Tamworth...': Conversation between Glen Turner and Simon Smith in Smith.

'As much as ethics or practicalities...': Martin.

"He was quite a progressive farmer...": Smith's view of Turnbull and his motivations for clearing in Smith.

"I felt very confronted by him": Quoted in Joseph.

'They met on the verandah in the hot March air': Holden, 'Notes from Typed Edition of Glen Turner's Compliance Notebook', s.82, entry dated 21 February 2012.

"Glen was just doing his job": Nadolny's view of Glen Turner, and the quad-bike incident, in Nadolny, 24 October 2019.

"Simon, Simon": Quotations from Turnbull and Smith's guilt in Smith.

'...the precious grasses and groundcover had been ploughed': Holden, 'Notes from Typed Edition of Glen Turner's Compliance Notebook', ss.84–86, entry dated 13 March 2012.

"He's guaranteed the loan, so it's hard to disagree with him": Testimony given by Cory Turnbull in Holden, 'Notes from Typed Edition of Glen Turner's Compliance Notebook', s.97, entry dated 27 March 2012.

'Turner allegedly said to Turnbull...': Testimony given by Ian Turnbull in ibid.

'Simon Smith admits...': Smith's admission and the OEH response in Smith, and Nadolny, 19 August 2019.

'the state minister for the environment would be closely questioned...': Spark,

'Submission Requesting a Coronial Investigation'.

"I was very disappointed": Smith.

'The Turnbulls boasted to neighbours...': Spark, 'Submission Requesting a Coronial Investigation'.

Chapter 3

'He spoke of a great river and fertile lands': Clarke gave a vivid report to *The Sydney Monitor* in 1832, available at https://trove.nla.gov.au/newspaper/article/32076934

'Life in Australia had begun excitingly...': Clarke's life and Mitchell's condemnation in Boyce & Rolls, 2011.

'...two years later Mitchell took Clarke's lead north': Rolls, 2011, p.85.

'...though not a single plough...': The first plough didn't arrive until 1796, and there were hardly enough horses or oxen to drag it.

'The Exodus and Eden myths...': Curthoys. Indeed, a century later, in the 1890s, there was a project for a New Arcadia in the wastelands of Queensland, Victoria and South Australia; it is regarded as having failed, leaving abandoned villages and crushed hopes (see Bellanta). But Edward Wakefield's dream, realised in South Australia and the Swan River settlement in Western Australia, drew comparisons in Britain with Goshen, the biblical land of plenty, and Hesperia, the Isles of the Blessed (see Young, p.3).

"if you new what i now nough...": Quoted in Haines, p.258.

'Fencing and enclosing land': Atkinson, p.91. The history of ecological change since settlement is full of 'what if?' moments. What if the colonists had been better informed about the place that awaited them; if Joseph Banks had not had gout and vanity that impeded him fully publishing his researches and findings? What if the British administrators hadn't also been trying to establish a penal colony and so had short-term, practical issues on their minds? What if it had been Indonesia or China who colonised the continent, or the Dutch or French, with their diverse approaches to agriculture and portfolios of skill? What if settlers had been better able to negotiate initial encounters with the Eora and Dharug people, and welcomed their wisdom and expertise?

'...had versatile agrarian skills': Haines, p.22.

'...the countryside soon rustled': Rolls, 1994, p.30. Following a French example, the London Acclimatisation Society was founded in 1860. A year later, Edward Wilson, the future owner of *The Argus* newspaper, returned from a visit to London to found local branches with a project to introduce starlings, peafowl, common pheasant, white swans and linnets. His efforts were followed enthusiastically by the Society.

'...more than 1300 plants have been introduced...': Bolton, p.85.

"The Thirties made the squatters and the Forties broke them": Blomfield, p.20.

'Sheep began to be killed...': Rolls, 2011, p.141.

'Restraint ... seemed unnecessary': Bolton, p.40.

'By 1860, the country had twenty million sheep...': ibid., p.81.

'It was a fair idea and an awful reality': effects of the Land Acts, including property names, in Webb, p.36–37.

'The Land Acts, supposed to distribute land democratically...': Lines, p.95.

'The third time Ian Turnbull and Glen Turner met': Encounter and dialogue in Holden, 'Notes from Typed Edition of Glen Turner's Compliance Notebook', ss.125–57, entry dated 28 June 2012, and Nadolny, 31 October 2019.

'As evicted Aboriginal tribes had discovered...': Galarrawy Yunupingu has pointed out the irony that Aboriginal people have for two centuries now been described as 'nomads', while the Europeans, who were constantly careening around the globe, were called 'settlers' (see Curthoys, p.31).

'He had licences for two shotguns and two rifles': From author's notes on witness statements to murder.

"Of course I will abide by your direction...": Quotations in this and next paragraph from Turner's email dated 7 August 2012 in Holden, 'Excerpts from OEH Correspondence'.

'most people want to do the right thing': 'Compliance Policy', p.4.

"You should not plan to go to Strathdoon...": Manager's comments to Turner and decision on team support in email dated 7 August in Holden, 'Excerpts from OEH Correspondence'.

"…Gary's experience and training…": Turner in a letter dated 15 August 2012 in ibid.

'…other staff had also received threats…': 'Submission Requesting a Coronial Investigation'.

"Australians inherited the strong British dislike…": Bolton, p.18.

'On the ground was a huge chain…': Nadolny, 24 October 2019.

'illegal clearing of Belah…': Holden, 'Notes from Typed Edition of Glen Turner's Compliance Notebook', s.158, entry dated 9 July 2012.

Chapter 4

"My work takes me all around the northwest": Spark's description of his job, involvement with Turnbull and suspicions that Turnbull was being protected in Spark, 2017.

"I think a lot of the attitude there relates...": Nadolny, 18 February 2018.

"Farmers do what they consider to be the 'right thing'": Vanclay, p.214.

"I started out assisting with the Landcare movement": Nadolny, 18 February 2018.

"Farmers ... do not believe they are 'raping the earth'": Vanclay, p.216.

"As an ecologist...": Nadolny, 18 February 2018.

"...sustainability means something along the lines of...": Vanclay, p.215.

"Glen was a reasonably experienced officer...": Smith.

'They entered through the "Strathdoon" gate': Description of clearing, presence of koalas and Turner's expression in Nadolny, 19 August 2019 and 24 October 2019.

"He was really aggro when he was speaking to me...": Joseph.

"You're just a selfish bitch": Smith.

'Simmons was on the phone to her landlord...': Joseph.

'...he'd keep at the Turnbulls...': Quoted in Holden, 'Notes on Ian Turnbull Witness Statement'.

'The legislation would ... not just be amended but wholly trashed': By late 2019, two farmers had testified, while being sentenced in the Land and Environment Court, about this alleged advice. They reported that Humphries had indicated to them there would be no prosecutions, as the law was soon due to change. Both farmers were convicted and fined. Humphries faced calls for investigation of his remarks by the Independent Commission Against Corruption (see Davies).

"I think I can get the Turnbulls to stop clearing": Nadolny, 24 October 2019.

"Governance is a behaviour management system": Martin & Hine, p.556.

"They may become ... game-players": Bartel & Barclay, pp.160–61. They identify what they call the exploitative type, the grouping into which Turnbull would most likely fit. These individuals are a tiny minority, the rusted-on, the intransigent. They don't participate in nature conservation programs. They don't consider the environment when they vote. They aren't interested in Landcare and tend to be the most sceptical of climate change. They don't like government intervention – not even of the supportive kind, say in weed control – and they aren't likely to make sacrifices or plan for a sustainable future. Ian Turnbull had been a conservation farmer, with a pragmatic, more than esoteric attitude to country. Now, faced with an opportunity for wealth, the OEH and the obstacle of environmental regulation, it seems he clenched into this pose.

'A person with a resistant, intransigent posture to authority': Bartel & Barclay, pp.160–61. Nearly half of game-players didn't have involvement with local environment groups; they explained it was pragmatic concern for profit and loss, and the risk of weeds and pests getting out of control, that constrained their enthusiasm. They didn't like social change in their districts and weren't much interested in further education. They farmed rice, beef and wool, had lived the longest on their properties and were mainly from New South Wales. Ian Turnbull fit this profile well: he was in his late seventies when he oversaw illegal clearing on his family's blocks, after a lifetime spent farming in the Moree district, mostly in mixed agriculture and sheep grazing. Untypically, he had been a conservation champion at one time; but when the authorities said 'no' to him, the long devotion to pragmatism showed through.

'Criminal subcultures ... are shaped by the same foundations': Bartel & Barclay.

'The federal government was quick to investigate the clearing...': Spark, 'Submission Requesting a Coronial Investigation', p.11.

'Weak relationships with the environment go with strained social relationships': Muir, p.31.

"[I]t is no coincidence...": ibid., p.31.

Chapter 5

'...federal and state environment departments rarely shared knowledge...': Spark, 'Submission Requesting a Coronial Investigation'.

'...Phil Spark rang Glen Turner': Conversation in Holden, 'Notes from Typed Edition of Glen Turner's Compliance Notebook', s.187–89.

'...Gary Spencer had called Grant Turnbull': Conversation in *Chief Executive v Grant Wesley Turnbull*, 2017, pp.44–45.

'They too saw the pushed trees': *Chief Executive v Turnbull,* NSWLEC150, 2014, s.142 and Spark, 'Submission Requesting a Coronial Investigation'.

"The lighting of those fires...": Quoted in *Chief Executive v Grant Wesley Turnbull,* 2017, p.47.

"We have heard all the political spin...": Spark, 'Submission Requesting a Coronial Investigation'.

"Once adequate information is gathered...": ibid.

'Almost all settlers to northwest New South Wales...': Robin, 2007.

'To many, Australian nature was eccentric...': Frawley, p.65.

"...trees retained their leaves...": Young, p.9.

"The country is horrible": Daniel Brock quoted in Griffiths, Jay, p.216. Major Mitchell had tried hard, on his surveys, to learn and bestow local Aboriginal names, but many of the replies, allegedly, actually meant "I don't understand what you're asking", and so, as Jay Griffiths observes, 'he dutifully transcribed the terms of incomprehension; a truer representation of the colonial mind than any "correct" place names could be' (see Griffiths, p.217).

"...looking actively *dead*...": descriptions of the bush and Charles Darwin quoted in Bonyhady, p.118.

'Traditional cultures were not much interested in an ideology of progress': Gascoigne, p.12.

'...there was growing defensiveness among settlers...': That ambivalence, resolving into aggression, can be sensed in a letter by a settler's teenage son who spoke Kamilaroi fluently and describes an alarming encounter. 'I am sorry to inform you that the blacks have driven off all our horses. They are now ten times more troublesome than they have been,' said Andrew Doyle Jnr on the Barwon River after finding forty cattle killed. 'I fear that unless some prompt steps are adopted by the Government for our protection, the blacks will carry out their threats of either killing or driving off all the whites from the Barwon and McIntyre River' (see Madden, pp.11–12).

"Shoot them all...": Quoted in Rolls, 2011, p.57. Some whites were periodically killed; many blacks, in reprisals. A magistrate had to go along on punitive expeditions so it would be lawful killing; he could later attest it was necessary.

"I often think about 'Murdering Gully'...": William Henry Weick quoted in Society, p.14. Massacres have been attested near the region at Ardgowan Island on the Gwydir River, and Gravesend Mountain, both near Warialda, and at Slaughterhouse Creek, just a few kilometres away, near Pallamallawa. The total dead at these three relatively unknown events is estimated at five hundred. Other atrocities, to the north, are reported at Cramptons Corner and the Macintyre

River in the 1840s. Then there were the twenty-eight killed at Myall Creek, just 115 kilometres from Croppa Creek.

'...a proxy for the traditional masculine challenges...': Muir, p.70; see also Robin, 2007.

"[t]he self-chosen white victim...": Curthoys, p.37.

"No matter how much self-conviction...": Gibson, p.92. Subsequent quotation p.94.

"If I go to jail, I won't be there long": Quoted in Cornwall, 2017.

Chapter 6

"I haven't got an underpinning of science studies...": Anderson.

'...place attachment fosters a healthy investment in those sites': Bartel & Graham.

'Landholders arguing a special privilege...': ibid.

"subdued, tilled and sowed any part of it...": Locke. For example, a property owner might claim 'takings' if government regulation inhibits the owner from doing what he or she might normally expect to do, such as use the water resources on the owned land, or profit from agricultural products planted there. Much depends on the expectations of the owner on acquisition and on what is considered an accepted use – damming a river that flows through a property is not an expected privilege, but using the water in a private dam probably is.

'Anything that reduces that ownership is an affront': In 2009, a sad saga commenced in southern New South Wales when grazier Peter Spencer claimed he was refused permission to clear native vegetation on his property and wasn't compensated. His 52-day hunger strike up a pole drew national attention. He was the star attraction at a 2000-strong rally in Canberra, attended by Alan Jones and Tony Abbott, against the Rudd government's alleged suppression of property rights, despite the situation being a state matter and Spencer's family suggesting his issues had deeper origins. His grievance, however disordered, was evidently shared by others.

'...a pushing and shoving over boundaries...': Bartel & Graham.

'Property Rights Australia is an illustrative Australian lobby group...': See www.propertyrightsaustralia.org.au

'In times of natural disaster...': In 2019, for example, Gwydir Shire Council hosted family gatherings with drought assistance services for farmers in Warialda, North Star and Croppa Creek, all within the wealthy Golden Triangle.

"I'm an old man...": *R v Turnbull (No.26)*, 2016.

"just shook his head": Holden, 'Notes on Ian Turnbull Witness Statement'.

'Financial penalties, rather than jail time...': Some new terms are entering legal spaces. 'Environmental crime' or 'offences', still evolving concepts, transgress regulations or laws. 'Environmental harm' comprises acts that damage the environment but aren't actually against the law; 'environmental problems', paler still, are what a community perceives as concerns. Penalties have risen – though the total penalties awarded are lower than ever, as prosecutions have failed to eventuate (see Barclay & Bartel, pp.188–89).

'...one of the most commonly recognised environmental crimes is trespass': Examples and quotations in ibid.

'Nearly 60 per cent of landholders in their survey...': Figures and examples in ibid, p.194. Quotation from Farmer, also p.194.

Chapter 7

"It becomes boring...": Tan, p.66. Subsequent quotation p.69.

'Phil Spark was in touch with the Environmental Defenders Office...' Spark, 'Submission Requesting a Coronial Investigation', p.12.

"That was always our cry": Spark, 2017.

'In the New South Wales parliament...': General Purpose Standing Committee No.5, p.29.

'The Environmental Defenders Office helpfully wrote...': Correspondence from Kirsty Ruddock at EDO to Phil Spark on 10 October 2012 in Spark, 'Submission Requesting a Coronial Investigation'.

'Jeff Angel of the Total Environment Centre...', 'The OEH ... said that a prosecution was imminent': Cubby.

'The OEH launched the prosecution...':
Chief Executive v Turnbull, NSWLEC150, 2014, section 13.

'...trees were being torched...':
Description of fire and response in correspondence from Phil Spark to Fairfax Media on 7 December 2012 in Spark, 'Submission Requesting a Coronial Investigation'.

'They were allegedly seen to burn stacks on days of total fire ban':
Correspondence from Alaine Anderson to Mark Coulton on 25 January 2013 in ibid.

'Anderson was putting water out...':
Description of dozer incident and koalas fleeing in ibid.

"All the best for the coming year":
Correspondence from Mark Coulton to Alaine Anderson on 25 January 2013 in Spark, 'Submission Requesting a Coronial Investigation'.

"a very poorly designed piece of legislation": Smith.

'Turnbull was entering a guilty plea...': *Chief Executive v Turnbull,* NSWLEC150, 2014, s.164.

"Crop extends ... to the fence running North–South...": 'Notes from Typed Edition of Glen Turner's Compliance Notebook', s.200, entry dated 21 June 2013.

'Nadolny read a novel in the park...': Description of events in September 2013 in Nadolny, 2020.

'The two officers had permission to enter...': Cornwall.

"I felt pretty exposed...": Events of December 2013 visit to 'Colorado' in Nadolny, 18 February 2018.

'The work was back on...': Witnesses' accounts provided to Turner in *Chief Executive v Grant Wesley Turnbull,* 2019.

'Luc Farago testified...': Farago's testimony in *Chief Executive v Cory Ian Turnbull.*

"I was on the stand for a day and a half": Nadolny, 18 February 2018.

"Your Honour...": Todd Alexis quotations in *Chief Executive v Cory Ian Turnbull*.

"We never intended to clear it all": Ian Turnbull and prosecutor quoted in Holden, 'Ian Turnbull Witness Statement'.

'Turner had his colleague Robert Strange...': *Chief Executive v Grant Wesley Turnbull,* 2017.

'In April 2014, there was big news in the district': Greenacre's property listing and asking price for Milton Downs in Cranston, 2016.

"This is succession planning": Cranston, 2014.

'...Turnbull told Roger he'd dug two graves for Turner': Cornwall.

Chapter 8

"There are three characteristics peculiar to the farmers...": Joseph Jenkins quoted in Barr & Cary, p.34.

"It came up so quickly": Rolls, 1994, p.30.

'...white, dead stalks': Bonyhady, p.179.

'So when the soil was wet again...': ibid., p.285.

"The stump...": Lines, p.41.

'Nor would they set aside fodder for bad times...': Bonyhady, p.285.

'He'd moved farm equipment onto the property...': *Turnbull v Turnbull,* 2017.

'There had been remediation orders...': Penalties and Roger's response to the OEH officers in June 2014 in Guilliatt.

"Roger wasn't formally indicted...": Nadolny, 18 February 2018.

"My grandfather is eighty…": Quoted in Guilliatt.

"There's every farm in the 30 kilometres…": Quoted in Holden, 'Ian Turnbull Witness Statement'.

'Justice Preston … ruled…': Justice Preston's quotations and details of ruling in *Turnbull v Director-General*, 2014.

'Pastoralism seemed finished': Cameron Muir describes the 'horror of the interior': 'Whenever the coast-hugging settlers turned their gaze towards the great interior plains, they glimpsed broken country, bloodshed and extinction. They saw skulls pierced with blunt lead bullets, ribcages cracked open with heavy spears, red country littered with ringbarked timber and the desiccated carcasses of millions of sheep; they saw clay-pans, silted creeks and sagging slab huts; they saw the material remains of initial hopes and land-lust bleached by an unrelenting sun. For governments, the frontier quickly became a liability; for pioneering colonisers, it was a path to ruin.' See Muir, pp.3–4.

'By 1891, there were about 13.5 million sheep...': ibid., p.30.

'Victoria and South Australia ... had already surged their agricultural efforts': ibid., p.43.

'Wheat would feed and build the country': Muir charts spectacularly what happened next: enthusiasms of various government and leadership programs, new departments of agriculture, prizes awarded to farmers for yield and quality and even the 'cleanliness' of their operations. Against a background anxiety about 'degeneration' in the bush, a kind of atavistic regression into horror and unshaven lawlessness, 'agriculture promised to bring civilisation even to the frontier'. See Muir, p.4.

"Where golden grain is golden gain": 'Australian Agriculture and Rural Life', State Library of New South Wales, 2021, www.sl.nsw.gov.au/stories/austr

alian-agricultural-and-rural-life/settlersguides-and-emigrant-publications

'...unlike the rice cultivated by the non-whites to the north': As Australia, cutting loose from the empire, contemplated its new vulnerability in the Pacific, there was an anxiety that rice-eating people might see our unused, 'wasted' lands in the interior and invade, just as the British had moved upon the apparent absence of Indigenous cultivation. See Muir, p.4.

"Wheat created the white race": Quoted in ibid., p.96.

"He had this belief...": Quoted in Holden, 'Notes on Ian Turnbull's Psychiatric Testimonies'.

'He was overheard saying he was willing to do something...': McKenzie, 2017.

'...his name was on an affidavit...': *R v Turnbull (No.26)*, 2016.

"The fact that Cory Turnbull was indicted...": Nadolny, 18 February 2018.

"This will finish us…", "He was at a point of despair…": Quoted in Crawford.

'Turnbull instructed his lawyer to file a complaint…': Sylvester Joseph's letter and the OEH response in Cornwall.

'…Ian and Robeena hosted their old friends…': Holden, 'Ian Turnbull Witness Statement'. "If by shooting Glen…": Nadolny, 18 February 2018.

"If anything happens to me…": Cornwall.

'The incantation … was taken up': Barr & Cary, p.175.

'With this knowledge…': Rolls, 2011, p.220.

'Diesel-engine tractors with rubber tyres…': Rolls, 1994, p.32.

'Rolls gives a dreamlike description…': Rolls, 2011, p.220.

'Then, the Depression crashed the wheat price': Barr & Cary.

'The phrase "balance of nature" was in people's mouths': Muir, p.157.

'Good seasons boosted confidence...': Robin, 2007, p.161.

"I just wanted to get that [clearing]...": Quoted in Holden, 'Ian Turnbull Witness Statement'.

"The second and third generation on the land before I retire": Quoted in ibid.

Chapter 9

'Ian's mother Beryl had been so stricken...': Quoted in Holden, 'Notes on Ian Turnbull's Psychiatric Testimonies'.

"I had the feeling that I had to get things done": Quoted in ibid.

'Some called the parching of 2014...': Bureau of Meteorology rainfall records at nearby Crooble Station showed 431 millimetres for 2014, compared to a median of 571 millimetres. It was low, but not the worst ever. The year 2018 showed only 348 millimetres.

"Turner in my mind. Turner": Quoted in Holden, 'Notes on Ian Turnbull's Psychiatric Testimonies'.

"They have to be resilient and stoical": Quoted in ibid.

"I'm virtually finished": Quoted in ibid.

'They rouse with martial talk of a "clash"...': Main, p.151.

'Turnbull's father...': Robin, 2007.

"...agriculture ... as an engineer might conceive it to be": Quoted in Main, 2005, p.123.

"They don't hop out of the airconditioned cab": Anderson.

"If the community wants farmers...": Quoted in Bartel & Graham, p.273.

'...constant vigilance and maintenance of order': Some ecologists point out that even highly managed agricultural landscapes include biodiversity, in the sense that soil formation, nutrient cycling and pollination of crops continues, albeit mostly through human agency. And biodiversity persists even despite exclusion controls: paddock trees host birds, insects, small mammals, reptiles; woodland birds nest and explore the landscape; deep roots draw nutrients back to the surface. It is uncomfortable, for some environmentalists and deep ecologists as well as colonial-heritage landholders, to remember that nature is not divisible, and human action is ineluctably part of, not apart from, nature.

"If you've got a neighbor...": Quoted in Leonard.

'Another yet might ... send in a gang of workers': Feneley.

"They're in the tips of the trees", "Pretty paltry out here": Anderson.

"Waste ... ravage, damage, injury": Griffiths, Jay, p.218.

'The scrub-covered land...': Bellanta, p.16.

'The plants of the scrub are imagined...': Muir, p.66.

'It became a metonym...': Muir, p.66.

"I wish I wasn't going to Moree": Quoted in Holden, 'Notes from Victim Impact Statements'.

"Arthur, we're on the road at 'Strathdoon' and 'Colorado'": Conversation between Glen Turner and Arthur Snook in Snook.

"one immense crime scene": Ross Gibson writes that settlers, in the aftermath of dispossession and murder, living on land figuratively and literally scattered with unburied bones, '[w]ith no professional mourners to help them live on this funeral-ground', tried to 'regard the place as new and unstained, as if there were nothing residual to see, touch, feel and believe. But they were overwhelmed by the fact that death had been recently and prodigiously abroad. Fear and denial have ghosted Queensland ever since.' See Gibson, p.83.

"No man who disappears...": Muir, p.67.

'When Ian Turnbull spoke of digging graves...': Nadolny, 19 August 2019.

'Only one of the three properties...': Nadolny, 19 August 2019 and Snook.

'He had been with the OEH for a while...': Strange, 2014.

"Okay. Talk to you in the morning": Call between Glen Turner and Arthur Snook in Snook.

Chapter 10

Events and quotations in this chapter are taken from the various witness statements contained in the Supreme Court archives. I used the statements of: Andrew Uebergang, Scott Kennett, Nicola Kennett, Robbie Maas, Ivan Maas, Adam Baxter, Felicity Whibley, Arthur Snook,

Detective Timothy McCarthy and Terrence Bailey. The material relating to Robert Strange is taken from Holden, 2014 and Strange, 2014.

Chapter 11

'Turnbull was already walking towards his ute...': Holden, 'Notes on Ian Turnbull Witness Statement'.

'...Turner asked his colleague to pull over': Strange, 2014 and Holden, 2014.

"Sir, put the gun down...": This scene is based on Robert Strange's witness testimony, given in a police walk-through and in the stand at the Supreme Court. This paragraph in particular is paraphrased closely from his own words. Some additional details are taken from Ian Turnbull's testimony under cross-examination in his murder trial in Holden, 'Ian Turnbull Witness Statement'.

'And about a kilometre along...': Uebergang's testimony in Holden, 'Notes on Witness Statements'.

'He had gone to the police a few weeks earlier...': Alleged in Nadolny, 19 August 2019.

'Meanwhile, in Tamworth...': Holden, 'Notes from Victim Impact Statements'.

'Nadolny knew immediately who it was...': Nadolny, 24 October 2019.

'Media outside the court clustered...': Pike, 30 July 2014.

'At the morgue, Glen Turner's body was autopsied...': Holden, 'Notes on Autopsy Report'. There was evidence of cannabinoids in his bloodstream. In his request for a coronial inquest, Leslie Slater states: 'Mr Turner had illicit substances in his blood stream and one or more administered close to his time of death, The Toxicology Report showed "Delta-9-tetrahydrocannabinal" at 0.013mg/l and "Delta-THC Acid at 0.030" Canabis/Marijuana. I have proof that Mr Turner was a habitual drug user.' But Matthew J. Atha's study suggests that passive smoking of marijuana can give blood results up to 20ng/ml up to four days later ('It was concluded that presence of cannabinoids in urine or blood is not unequivocal proof of active cannabis smoking') and notes that other studies have 'recommended a threshold of 65ng/ml to differentiate between active and passive smoking of cannabis' (see Altha, Matthew J., 'Blood and Urine Drug Testing for Cannabinoids', Independent Drug Monitoring Unit, Wigan, United Kingdom, both quotations p.4). Note the measurement is 'ng/ml', not 'mg/ml', as Slater has it.

"focused and determined...": Holden, 2014.

"Glen told me on at least one occasion...": ibid.

"Ten days of wondering where he was...": Quoted in Holden, 'Notes from Victim Impact Statements'.

'McKenzie suppressed her tears...': Burton.

"the combination of a harmful act...": Barclay & Bartel.

'There was a large yellow dozer...':

'The journalist took photos': Lamacraft.

Chapter 12

"They are all thinking of you...": All comments of support in Holden, 'Notes on Court Debate on Holding Turnbull Trial in Moree'.

"Travelling to court in Sydney...': Chris Nadolny, 24 October 2019. He wrote: "It was Sydney; I don't know who attended. I think the main ruling was earlier, before Glen was murdered."

"We just want some good to come of it": Quoted in Tyson.

"He has done different work...": Quoted in ibid.

"Glen was clearly a beautiful man...": Pike & Godfrey.

"This is a terrible tragedy": Quoted in Tyson.

"That millisecond has affected so many people": Quoted in 'Moree Shooting: The Reaction'.

"Ian is a well-known and respected member of the community": Quoted in Pike, 30 July 2014.

"Violence was always going to happen": Quoted in Levy & Hall, 2014.

"pushed beyond despair...": Pike, 31 July 2014.

"the kind of behaviour that leads people to murder": Quoted in Olding, 30 July 2014.

'Members of the Turnbull family': see Pike, 31 July 2014.

"'No one, but no one...': Quoted in Feneley.

"It's a tragic event...': Quoted in Pike, 31 July 2014.

"enforced by Big-Brother-style satellites": ibid.

"You have this crazy situation...": Olding, 5 August 2014.

'...Governors Hunter and Collins...': Bonyhady, pp.3–6.

'The tenant argued...': ibid., p.161.

"an almost pet-like status": Trees were given personas and names, either of their own or of their protectors. They were sung at, decorated, pressed with coins for luck, assigned emotions. People sensed a proprietorial custodianship. 'They cherished their associations, their antiquity, their link with the past,' writes Keith Thomas. Eighteenth-century writers such as William Marsden mourned that the felling of an aged tree 'appears a violation of nature, in the exercise of a too arbitrary right'. See Thomas, p.213.

"To future ages, may'st thou stand...": Quoted in ibid.

"Everyone who has the least pretension...": Quoted in ibid., p.221.

'The foliage of Britain...': See Maitland.

"aspects of a much wider reversal...": Thomas, p.243.

"it was a commonplace...": Bonyhady, p.10

"In a rising colony": Quoted in ibid., p.44.

'...individuals began to challenge the government...': ibid., p.9.

'There was even a claim tried...': ibid.

"We all put to our OEH chief executive...": Nadolny, 18 February 2018.

'Simon Smith ... spoke up too': Smith.

'Six weeks after that ... the OEH was back in court': *Chief Executive v Turnbull,* NSWLEC153, 2014 and *Chief Executive v Turnbull,* NSWLEC155, 2014.

"to restrain any further unlawful clearing": Bailey, p.6.

'supported ... by the NSW Farmers Association...': Spark, 2017.

'On Baird's retirement...': No author, 'Farmers Thank Mike Baird.'

'The term "heritage" came to be used': Bonyhady.

"A nationalist movement...": Solnit, p.32.

"They were ultimately producing...": ibid, p.34.

'Jay Griffiths reminded herself...': Griffiths, Jay, p.3.

"For much of European history...": Solnit, p.103.

Chapter 13

'Chris Nadolny and fellow ecologist Terry Mazzer...': Bailey, p.44.

'Nadolny was reassured by their presence...': Nadolny, August 2019.

"I find that the level of the environmental harm...": *Chief Executive v Turnbull,* NSWLEC150, 2014, section 136.

"A wilderness...": Quoted in Popova.

"[w]e attribute qualities to a landscape...": Macfarlane, p.18.

"[a] fine case can be made...": Solnit

"We were born wild...", "To me, humanity is not a stain...": Griffiths, Jay, p.73, p.4.

'...strong critical comments about the OEH...': *R v Turnbull (No.25)*, 2016.

"just a nasty piece of work": Turnbull.

"I didn't mean to kill him": Quoted in Hall, 2014.

'In 2014, at least 116 people...': Butt & Menton.

"Julián is irreplaceable": Quoted in Watts.

'For twenty-six years...': Kembrey.

"You've made a bad choice in wife": Quoted in Cornwall.

"Your second best friend Turner...": ibid.

Chapter 14

"west of the highway...": Anderson.

"shifting baseline syndrome": See Pauly.

"...a state of extreme depletion...": Muir, p.154.

'Almost half of the 3.7 million hectares...': Muir, p.31.

"With the disappearance of the forest...": Quoted in Young, p.5.

'Royal National Park...': The park was designed more as a recreation area for Sydneysiders than a refuge for wildlife. It had picnic facilities and broad paths for strolling. Nevertheless, it did feature indigenous plants. Meanwhile, the wonderful government botanist of Melbourne, Baron Ferdinand von Mueller, promoted the use of native plants, pioneering the export of eucalypts across the world to revegetate arid regions. Argentina, South Africa and parks in Rome and Naples still sport his efforts (see Young, pp.7–9). Mueller did much to revise attitudes to indigenous species, though those good works were undercut when he chose to introduce blackberries to the country.

'Rural citizens ... could be more preoccupied...': Bonyhady.

'...an alert, thoughtful researcher called Robert Peacock...': Muir, p.79. Meanwhile, at the commission, settlers denied water was a problem, and continued to overstock, complaining there wasn't enough grass. Thousands of water bores were sunk through the state, searching to extend the arable land into the interior (see Muir, pp.30–32).

"too familiar landmarks...": ibid., pp.77–78.

'...those hardy souls led by Myles Dunphy...': Frawley, p.70.

"every reason to be intensely proud...": Ratcliffe, p.332.

'...he proposed nature as a balm to the spirit...': Robin, 1994. Crosbie Morrison wanted people to safeguard nature, and become more scientifically qualified to study it and more engaged to defend it. After World War II he agitated for a 'New Deal', not of Eisenhower's kind but for 'the wild things', particularly to redress the 'patriotic sacrifice' of land at Wilson's Promontory in Victoria during its wartime occupation by the military.

'...wedge-tailed eagles, galahs, cockatoos and kangaroos...': Robin, 2007, p.163.

'Their value as natural assets...': Young, p.188.

'The scientific approach cooled emotional pleas...', "science of crisis": Robin, 2007, p.165.

'...biological diversity was at dreadful risk from development': ibid., p.167.

'Thus by late in the twentieth century...': Main, p.152.

"shadow places": Plumwood, 2008.

'Robin identifies a difference...': Robin, 1994, p.3.

'Nature was not yet political': ibid., p.109.

'And would-be conservationists liked...': Muir, p.157. Balance, it was promised, could be restored.

"these people, whose numbers are swelled...': Quoted in Lines, p.232.

'...the benefits of human contact with natural places...': Richardson, et al.

'It would be hard to find an impartial jury in Moree...': The Moree courthouse in Frome Street is a heritage building of Federation Free architecture, ironically protected by the Office of Environment and Heritage, the same office that employed Glen Turner.

"What you've done has done more for the cause...": Quoted in Holden, 'Notes on Court Debate on Holding Turnbull Trial in Moree'.

"Beliefs regarding the policing...", "for reason of local prejudice...': *R v Turnbull (No.1)*, 2016.

"Eight weeks...": Miller.

"consumed with Glen's death...": Quoted in Holden, 'Notes from Victim Impact Statements'.

Chapter 15

"That was a difficult moment...": Quoted in Miller.

"a reasonable person in his or her position...": 'Manslaughter', Criminal Trial Courts Bench Book – Offences, Judicial Commission of New South Wales, www.judcom.nsw.gov.au/publications/benchbks/criminal/manslaughter.html

'...they would go to buy waterproof mascara...': Miller.

"I needed to talk about it one day...": Quoted in Piatek.

"I wanted him to know that Glen...": Quoted in Pennells.

"Their livelihood was on the line...": Todd Alexis quoted in Hall, 2016.

"totally obsessed": Robyn Cush and Dorothy Sampson quoted in ibid.

"We didn't feel like...": Quoted in Koubaridis.

'Turner had a "tendency" to harass...': *R v Turnbull (No.25)*, 2016.

'The incident with Anna Simmons...': Evidence of Anna Simmonds, Ivan Mass, John Kennedy, Judith Grills and Lynn Hudson in Holden, 'Notes on Defence Case for Provocation'.

'...support the case for provocation': Roger Turnbull was summonsed to testify at the murder trial. But in the end the Crown case was so overwhelming he wasn't needed. The defence wanted to use Turner's notebook to prove he had had a series of vendettas, first against Roger, but since Roger hadn't appeared as a witness, the judge didn't admit the notebook (notebook MF151). See *R v Turnbull (No.23)*, 2016.

'He said Turner had a fixation...', 'After hearing the evidence...': Comments from Todd Alexis and Justice Johnson in ibid.

'...Turnbull was in the witness stand': Turnbull's testimony in Holden, 'Notes on Ian Turnbull Witness Statement'.

Chapter 16

"Well, I do...": Quoted in Holden, 'Notes on Ian Turnbull's Psychiatric Testimonies'.

'Grant Turnbull stepped into the witness stand...': Grant's testimony quoted in Crawford.

"I mean, literally constantly...": Nielssen's testimony in Holden, 'Notes on Ian Turnbull's Psychiatric Testimonies'.

'Dr David Greenberg took the stand...': Greenberg's testimony in ibid.

"He appeared to be functioning pretty well": Hall's testimony in ibid.

"The politicians need to listen": 'Moree Shooting: Farmer Ian Turnbull Jailed for 35 Years for Murdering Environmental Officer'.

'...a jury, they learned with surprise...', "I just want it to be justice for Glen": Alison's description of events and quotations in Miller.

'Nadolny sat alone, and felt it': Nadolny, 24 October 2019.

'The two women pressed their faces...': Miller.

Chapter 17

'The statements ... helped to illustrate': *R v Turnbull (No.26)*, 2016.

'Alison McKenzie's statement was carefully composed': Summary of and quotations from victim impact statement in Holden, 'Notes from Victim Impact Statements'.

"Don't directly express your anger...": Victim Support Services.

"I drink too much...": Summary of and quotations from victim impact statement in Holden, 'Notes from Victim Impact Statements'.

'Wealthy landowners were concerned...': Pontin, p.761.

'...a respect for "natural law"...': Coyle & Morrow.

'Locke had proposed ... Coleridge spoke of...': Pontin, p.771.

"The two antagonist powers...": ibid., p.778.

"preserve the stores...": ibid., p.779. Coleridge was no hoarse voice in the wilderness: he influenced Benjamin Disraeli, later prime minister of England. Disraeli delivered a speech in Manchester in 1872 in which he proposed the axiom of *Sanitas sanitatum, omnia sanitas:* 'The first consideration of a Minister should be the health of the people [defined as] pure air, pure water, the inspection of unhealthy habitations [of] the adulteration of food' (see Pontin, p.784). He and his Tories won the election two years later, and soon passed landmark legislation to prevent river pollution. The bill positioned itself in contrast to the Manchester School and Adam Smith's faith in the market, with its appetite for development and profit in the human world at the expense of natural resources. According to Pontin, the famous *Sea Birds*

Preservation Act 1869, enacted under Disraeli's authority, was an expression of Coleridge's sentiment that natural beauty was a moral quality equal to economic presence, as it defended migrating birds from having their feathers pillaged to adorn women's hats.

'When Australia was federated...': Pain & Wright.

'When the Hawke government...': Wilderness was assessed by the Australian Heritage Commission when in 1987 it first surveyed the continent according to two criteria: remoteness and naturalness. Today, this system is known as the National Wilderness Inventory, and one of its main principles of assessment is that 'wilderness indicators ... are not indicative of the value of remote and natural lands. Remote and natural areas will be considered "wilderness" (or similar) where the intrinsic existence of these attributes is recognised in society.' Wilderness sites, to qualify for this title, are ranked on a stern catalogue of criteria few places in coastalzone Australia might fully meet. 'They will be protected,' warns the inventory, 'when the value of these attributes is considered greater than those of competing alternative uses.'

'...town planning and environmental law weren't merged...': Pain & Wright, p.2.

'It is composed both of judges and trained commissioners...': ibid., p.7.

"bring proceedings in the Land and Environment Court...": *Native Vegetation Act 2003,* New South Wales, Section 41 (2).

'...open standing cases are not infrequently...': Pain & Wright, p.10.

"how far do the public have to go...": Spark, 2020.

'...the Act has been used to stop two developments...': Office, 2020. *The Guardian* established that environment minister Josh Frydenberg blocked the turbines against the advice of both his department and the wishes of the inhabitants of Lord Howe Island, ensuring they continue to rely on diesel generators. See 'Josh Frydenberg Overruled Department to Block Lord Howe Island Wind Turbines', 18 September 2019. Meanwhile, nearly 80 per cent of approvals were actually non-compliant or contained errors.

'Those cleared lands included...': Ward.

"I just want justice for Glen": Miller.

'Justice Johnson spoke...': Justice Johnson quoted in *R v Turnbull (No.26)*, 2016.

'Justice Johnson had been satisfied...': Miller.

Chapter 18

"the 'green' and the 'black' began to negotiate shared ground": Robin, 1994, p.108.

'The environment was now a moral cause': Griffiths, Tom, p.376.

"the green movement...": ibid., p.383.

'...it works on a separating principle...': Manning.

'Offsetting, popular with conservative administrations...': In early 2021, *The Guardian* revealed that an offset arrangement for a public reserve, made twenty years ago by the New South Wales government in exchange for approval to clear bushland for housing and highway developments, still had not seen the land gazetted, protected or remediated. Instead, ecologist Steve Douglas described the site as 'an ecological wasteland' of rusted vehicles, feral animals and weeds. See Cox, 10 February 2021.

'One could grandly shift ecologies from here to there...': In October 2020, federal environment minister Sussan Ley approved for the clearing of 52 hectares of koala habitat as part of a quarry expansion project at Port

Stephens. Critics, including New South Wales Liberal environment minister Matt Kean, were vocal on the decision, as habitat loss is the greatest threat to the vulnerable species. Ley explained that 74 hectares of habitat would be established by the quarry company as an offset, a 'net gain'. Campaigners questioned where the koalas might live while saplings grew to maturity (see Cox, 27 October 2020).

"You can destroy what you've got": Spark, 2017.

'...it now forms the structural rationale...': Office, 2020.

'In a 2016 report...': 'Paradise Lost'.

"It's like it has some kind of credibility": Spark, 2017.

"must be understood in the context of events": Quotations from Justice Craig and outcome of the case in *Chief Executive v Turnbull (No 4)*, 2016.

"I've never been to any meeting": Quoted in Miller.

'How are we going...': ibid.

"using, conserving and enhancing...": Ecologically Sustainable Development Steering Committee.

"four main planks...": Environmental Defenders Office, 2017.

'Rural communities felt disenfranchised...': Nadolny, August 2019.

"It was ... a bloodbath": Spark, 2017.

"There is no doubt...": Pain & Wright, p.23. One of the more interesting entryways into conservation policy is through intergenerational rights. It can include something called the 'right to an open future', usually discussed in terms of the human rights of children. Under the United Nations Convention of the Rights of the Child, children, as vulnerable humans with limited agency, possess the right to have their 'best interests' as the first consideration of any actions concerning them. A child's existence will be diminished if it grows up in a world infringed by environmental degradation.

'WWF Australia released a report...': Taylor et al., 2014.

"What I have done...": Holden, 'Notes on Court Debate on Holding Turnbull Trial in Moree'.

'A terrorist act': Nadolny, 19 August 2019.

"maintained or improved environmental outcomes": Bombell & Montoya.

"It's all part of the disconnect": Spark, 2017.

'...the OEH published two reports': Information on both OEH reports in Bombell & Montoya.

"We reviewed all the legislation": Spark, 2017.

"Educational, suasive and incentive measures": Details of the report in Byron et al. Bartel & Graham also make the point about the report's 43 recommendations on p.269, and Bombell & Montoya note the underlying assumptions of the plan on p. vi.

'There would be significant funding...': Nadolny, 'The New Biodiversity Laws', p.8.

"What greater slap in the face...": Spark, 2017.

Chapter 19

"an arrogant, disgusting pig": Quoted in Cornwall.

'...the abrupt dropping of the investigation...': Brewster.

'There were rumours...': Spark, 2020.

"It is too explosive and not warranted": Brewster.

"They're driven by this little core minority": Spark, 2017.

"We don't want to go back to the stage...": Quoted in Brewster.

"...the comments of Mr Humphries...": Quoted in Davies, 2019.

"to postpone": Quoted in Brewster.

'There was a clear implication...': Slezak, 15 November 2016.

"The current native vegetation law...": Quoted in Hannam, 6 August 2016.

'Two farmers would later testify...': Davies, 2019.

"the devil was in the detail": Nadolny, 18 February 2018, p.8. The promise that agricultural development would be treated the same as non-agricultural didn't eventuate: conversion to cropping, one of the most lucrative forms of land exploitation, was not to be treated as 'new development'. The laws set a target of only about 10 per cent retention of native vegetation on private land.

'...the conservation groups ... had had enough': Slezak, 19 February 2016.

'The NSW Farmers Association declared...': Joshua Gilbert, an Indigenous farmer and member of NSW Farmers during the 2016 push to change the native vegetation laws, ended up quitting the association, alleging that threats were made to him over his resistance to their policy and their support for self-assessment. Gilbert had previously tried to move the association towards a greater acceptance of climate science. He told *The Guardian* that 'the policies, if implemented, would allow more land to be cleared, which was not sustainable'. 'We can't just think about the short term and what we can put in our pockets now,' he said. 'We need to think about farming in the future and how we will feed an additional 2.3 billion people in the next 34 years sustainably, so that we can keep doing it into the future as well.' As with the general farming community, not all members of the association were so devoted to loosening regulation (see Slezak, 2 February 2016).

'The state environment department reported just over 1000 submissions': Breakdown of submissions in 'Biodiversity Legislation Review', December 2014 and Hunjan.

"The take away message...": Vergotis.

"We believe many farmers...": Quoted in Druce, 18 July 2017.

'...underestimating clearing by six-fold': Hannam, 4 August 2016.

'The Gwydir Wetlands...': Hannam, 6 August 2016.

"threaten the most significant remnants...": Chris Nadolny, Mark Speakman, Penny Sharpe and Mehreen Faruqi quoted in Hannam, 17 November 2016. Clearing permissions could be granted even on Crown lease land.

"If we all did a little bit...": Anderson.

"...very little is known about Mr Turnbull's personal life": Lee.

"He's always been a mudguard": Quoted in Cornwall.

"We will never have closure...': Quoted in Chillingworth, 2017.

"It didn't sit well with me": *R v Turnbull (No.26)*, 2016.

'Ian Robert Turnbull, Late of "Yambin", Moree': *Moree Champion*, 11 April 2017.

Chapter 20

"Dear Premier and Minister for the Environment...": McKenzie, 2017.

"Glen Turner was a highly valued and experienced environment officer": Quoted in Hannam, 17 August 2017.

"You can't help thinking...": Spark, 2017.

"From what we have heard...': McKenzie, 2017.

'The office was pained...': In 2011, the science division, representing the mapping staff, secured $4.5 million over four years without the knowledge of other OEH divisions. A report was commissioned from an outside source but cancelled before it could be delivered. The author, Nicole Campbell, was instructed to hand over all electronic files but apparently circulated a handful of hard copies to senior OEH executives. When the Greens submitted a freedom of information request the next year, the OEH was unable to find a copy (see Hannam, 15 January 2016).

"It's very, very big...": Spark, 2017.

'Turnbull had no prior record...': Olding, 5 August 2014.

"a great injustice", "Ian Turnbull would not hurt a fly...", "This is all on record": Slater, July 2020.

'A person, unknown to Robert Strange...': Chris Nadolny, asked whether he could imagine Turner having trespassed that evening, says, 'It doesn't sound right to me. I've been with Glen on a number of occasions. He wouldn't have crossed the fence. He'd have known he'd get into trouble for doing that, so he'd have been on the right side of the barbed-wire fence' (see Nadolny, 19 August 2019). Robert Strange always denied they trespassed, and his photographs were taken from the established points on the public reserve to the side of Talga Road.

"...if this employee...": Slater, 2016.

"a rogue employee...": Slater, 2018.

"From their point of view...': Slater, July 2020.

"It is hoped...": Spark, 'Submission Requesting a Coronial Investigation'.

'[S]ome accountability is required...": Slater, 2016.

"If government continues to restrict...": Quoted in Druce, 18 July 2017. There is a legal term, *solatium,* which describes payment in compensation for an injury to the feelings, rather than a physical or financial harm. That is how the term, from the Latin *solace,* is understood in Scots and American law. In Australia its concern is, tellingly, very financial and physical – usually applied to payment in return for compulsory government acquisition of property. It is not generally used in land management restrictions, but the implication that the government has appropriated something and someone should have to pay remains in the reactions and rhetoric of landholder lobby groups.

'Part of the package...': 'Saving Our Species Program.' The provisions come in three tiers. A biodiversity stewardship agreement encourages the permanent sequestering of private land, known as 'covenanting'. Conservation agreements are a less binding form in which an owner might pledge to conserve land with special features such as native habitat or Aboriginal heritage sites after they sell or die. They can also be used to convert perpetual Crown leases into freehold, and entitle the owners to government assistance with maintenance, and land rate and tax breaks. Wildlife refuge agreements support more general conservation work on farming properties. All tiers are administered by the NSW Biodiversity Conservation Trust.

'Meanwhile, only *critically* endangered species...': Nadolny, 'The New Biodiversity Laws'.

'Paddock trees shelter...': Main.

'Ecologists propose protecting them...': Manning, p.317.

'Phil Spark has seen several extinctions...': Phil Spark quoted in Spark, 2017.

'Now they too were open for clearing...' In October 2020, the New South Wales cabinet agreed to change regulations, allowing property owners to clear up to 25 metres from a fenceline without environmental approval, not for development but under the *Rural Fires Act 1997 No.65,* with the rationale of protection against bushfire risk. Such allowances had not been included in any of the recommendations of the New South Wales bushfire inquiry.

"Solastalgia": Quotations from Glenn Albrecht in Albrecht et al. It is a corollary of another instinct: spirituality, Godhead, paganism, animism; E.O. Wilson's biophilia, or 'love of place'; geographer Yi-Fu Tuan's topophilia, or love of country. These are complicated, portmanteau words, from other times and the other side of the world, but perhaps they are appropriate here in Australia, to name the effect of awkward importation of ourselves.

'...a 1992 CSIRO report...': Barnes & Hill, 1992.

"a young generation who don't give a stuff...": Anderson.

'"Native bears" (koalas) and "tiger cats" (quolls)': Blomfield.

'...a joint report by the RSPCA and the WWF...': Taylor et al., 2017.

"Nothing else in Queensland...": Symons.

'...one out of three mammal extinctions...': Figure quoted in Morton, 28 October 2019.

'What is described as the Sixth Extinction...': Taylor et al., 2017. The United Nations released a report in May 2019 by its Intergovernmental Science-Policy Platform on Biodiversity and Ecosystem Services. It described stunning trajectories of diminishment and extinction, and indicated the possibility of massive insect population loss, jeopardising food systems, as well as an 82 per cent fall in the biomass of wild mammals.

"to actually wipe out all the wildlife...": Quoted in Anderson.

"assess impacts on biodiversity values": 'Biodiversity Assessment Method'.

'The Environmental Defenders Office describes BAM...': 'NSW Biodiversity Reforms 2016: Issue 2 – Offsets and Ecologically Sustainable Development'.

"Biodiversity offsetting, by definition...": Quoted in Slezak, 15 November 2016.

"inherently unusable": Discussion of vegetation map flaws, promised improvements and John Hunter quoted in Hannam, 15 January 2016.

"the government will not make any decision...": Quoted in Druce, 18 July 2017.

"The farmers ... were actually saying...": Spark, 2017.

'The association, on a roll, passed other motions': Clarry & Noon.

"We're in a dark spot...": Nadolny, 18 February 2018.

"will certainly make it easier for landholders...": Nadolny, 'The New Biodiversity Laws', p.9. The article also recounts the experience at the University of New England.

'...the government gave it out to *The Guardian*': Davies, 2018.

'...in relation to activity just across the border': Slezak, 12 March 2018.

Chapter 21

'Ian, Robeena and the four sons...': Details of 'Yambin' road access; feud between Ian, Roger, Grant and Robeena; Grant's testimony and the judge's summation in *Turnbull v Turnbull,* 2017.

"Any attempts by Roger Turnbull, Annette Turnbull or their employees...": Quoted in *Turnbull v Turnbull,* 2017, paragraph 21.

'Its website ... carries a case study...': Clarry & Noon.

'The very next day it was remade, and it carried on': Three months later, in June 2018, the Nature Conservation Council of NSW and the Environmental Defenders Office tried again, hazarding that the code's lack of reference to the ecologically sustainable development principles made it unlawful. This time, the allegation was that Upton had not, in the brief hours before the code was reinstated in March, had time to 'properly, genuinely, and realistically' contemplate the implications of her assent, and the ecologically sustainable development principles still weren't discernible. 'The role of the Environment Minister outlined in the law is not one of rubber stamping, nor one of symbolism,' said David Morris, the chief executive officer of the Environmental Defenders Office. 'It is the crucial check and balance to ensure the integrity of our state's unique biodiversity in a changing climate.' See Dobney, 2018.

'After the encounter with Turnbull, he kept mostly to his house...': The impacts of Glen Turner's murder on Robert Strange in Holden, 'Notes from Victim Impact Statements'.

"Expecting someone to come through the door with a gun...": Quoted in Piatek.

'On a personal level I have become a recluse': Quoted in Holden, 'Notes from Victim Impact Statements'.

"It's amazing ... what something can do to your brain": Quoted in Piatek.

'During the ordeal ... my focus was on Mr Turner': *Strange v Turnbull*, paragraph 12.

'A settlement agreement was finally reached in October 2018': Strange, 2020.

Chapter 22

"slow violence": Quoted in Nixon.

'grazier and passionate conservationist': This description appears in Robin, 1994, p.38.

"Droughts and soil erosion...", "The original greenie": Dewar Wilson Goode and his son quoted in Wetherell, p.24.

'As Massy explains...': The growth of an organic mindset in Massy, p.50. Ironically, as he points out, it was those old Commonwealth ties to Britain, even in the 1950s, that gave experimental farmers here access to British research and publishing. A group of 'organic' farmers formed in Sydney in 1944, after receiving *The Living Soil* by Lady Eve Balfour and hearing her speak. Soil was a subject for enthusiasm over in the next ten or so years, with several works on its properties and significance.

"The key difference between industrial and regenerative agriculture...": Massy, p.161. George Main takes issue with the term 'sustainable agriculture', seeing it as a furphy for the sustainability of industrial farming, not the broader, more holistic term disingenuously implied. Massy, too, exposes some double-talk in the claims made for direct-drilling. In 'diabolically clever reframing', the United Nations Food and Agriculture Organization and others like Australia's CSIRO rebranded direct drilling (also known as 'zero tilling') as the cosy 'conservation agriculture', although there are hazards for this too. Both 'conservation agriculture', or cropping, and 'sustainable agriculture' aim for healthful soil, but come at solutions with different compromises: benefits to soil structure are usually at the price of intense chemical additives and the destruction of life within it (see Main). Turnbull practised 'minimum-' or 'zero-till' techniques, also using traditions of burning stubble, minimal ploughing and fallow, but herbicides too, which have implications for human health, soil health and plant health.

'Leaves and grass blades are all solar panels...': Massy, p.67.

'Massy's book is full of examples of permutations...': The keyline system, p.128, and pasture cropping, pp.194–97, in Massy. Quotation from Colin Seis on p.201. Interestingly, it was a Zimbabwean farmer, Allan Savory, who popularised the idea of what he called 'holistic planned grazing' or 'cell grazing'. The concept was brought to Australia by a disciple in 1989, and Massy considers it 'one of the greatest forward leaps in agriculture since domestication 10,000 years ago'. Savory was inspired by the wild herds of migratory animals in Africa and the after-effects of their presence on land: not devastation, but regeneration. Rather than let stock roam over wide areas, eating each out and then requiring bought grain, graziers put massed stock in small fenced areas, allowing dung to fall and grass to be picked, then moved them on in coordinated rotations while each area was allowed to rest and absorb the stimulation of forage and manure. It is a demanding, but not arduous, system in which natural functions are allowed to do their work (see Massy).

"If we don't go to regenerative agriculture...": Quoted in Chan, 22 October 2018.

'...perhaps just 15 per cent more carbon...': Schwartz.

"a ready, effective and proven means...": Massy, p.442.

'The Liberal Party launched the report...': Martin, 2019.

"a painful history of suppression, fragmentation and disorder": Main, p.225.

"Whenever we are fighting for the least of these animals...": Anderson.

'Native grasses ... grow themselves': Bruce Pascoe is quoted in Chan, 6 October 2018. STIPA Native Grasses Association Inc., named for the generic term for corkscrew or speargrass, is an association formed to promote native grass as pasture and an instrument of conservation. They document what exists and run courses and restoration projects – for example, in the box woodlands of New South Wales – in conjunction with farmers and community groups. They published Darryl Cluff's *Farming Without Farming,* and they have government funding for a trial in carbon sequestration using planned grazing and pasture cropping.

"What is it that makes a landscape?": Massy, p.351.

"monoculture of the mind": Vandana Shiva.

"The crucial point...": Massy, p.411.

"After what we have seen this year...": Quoted in Kinbacher.

"Oh, the moisture in that paddock!": Anderson.

"I believe that love is *the* essential ingredient...": Massy, p.499. Knepp, a radical regenerative project in Sussex, England, has also dared leave nature to reestablish its own equilibrium, albeit with initial management. The owners of the estate, Isabella Tree and Charles Burrell, allowed vegetation to freely reestablish, then introduced large herbivores to graze and manure. Species are reappearing that haven't been seen in hundreds of years; ecological texts are being rewritten. Tree explains in her bestseller *Wilding* (2018) that the seedbed for re-emergent vegetation has been hosted in the hedgerows that border old fields. Fenceline vegetation in Australia might work the same way. But those frail lines of refuge are being cleared. Tree and Burrell find it essential to keep a certain percentage 'open' by strategic reintroduction of herbivores, and have had qualms about the vulnerability of reemergent species; surrounded by mainstream practices, fire risk, invasive pests and diffuse climate change, their work is an experiment, still inconclusive.

'The farmer would have to pay...': The judge made an interesting diversion into the subject of Grant's finances in light of Grant's claim that he'd be financially ruined by a big fine.

'Colorado' was owned by his trust, but Grant had owned the property on the title, though the judge couldn't work out who owned it now. Grant had sold 'Buckie' in 2015, with a capital gain, according to his tax return (the clerks of the court had done their work), of more than a million dollars – but Qanagco now seemed to own 'Buckie'. Qanagco appeared to pay some of the environmental regulation costs on 'Colorado', and it had paid four million dollars in dividends to Grant himself over two years. 'These financial statements,' said Justice Preston, 'are unsatisfactory in in many respects' (see *Chief Executive v Grant Wesley Turnbull,* 2017, pp.62–63).

'...what the Turnbull family had done on "Strathdoon" and "Colorado"...' Judge's statements, details of charges and arguments, and witness testimony for Grant and Cory in ibid. An old friend of Cory's, who went to boarding school with him in Toowoomba, told the court that Cory had always had a passion for farming – and wildlife. He 'is one of the most responsible, driven and next-generation farmers that agriculture in Australia will need and will be proud to have. He is leading the way in minimal-till farming, reduced chemical usage and environmentally friendly practices.'

"at the end of the day...": ibid., p.60.

"statements of regret...": ibid., p.71.

"The community must be satisfied...": ibid., p.72.

"The wild ... is not the opposite of the cultivated": Quoted in Griffiths, Jay, p.37.

Chapter 23

"And then you've got Dad...": Quoted in Cornwall.

"If it was going to require more than one grave...": Nadolny, 18 February 2018. Roger had allegedly told a senior OEH official to warn Nadolny to stay away from Grant after Turner's death.

Following newly cautious protocol, Nadolny and his legal team at the agency had requested an armed marshal at one of his expert testimonies in the Land and Environment Court. 'Which turned out to be overkill,' he remembers in his slight voice, 'because Grant Turnbull never showed up anyway.' Previously Grant, indeed, had come up to him at an airport after a court appearance and apologised for the legal team's aggression. 'Grant has never expressed anger towards me,' Nadolny says. But his father certainly had.

'...the memory of a conversation...': Nadolny's recall of Turnbull's comments to him and Turner in Nadolny, 31 October 2019.

"a very foggy memory": ibid. Nadolny expected that his statement to police would be followed by an interview. A year or so later he realised it wouldn't, so he sent in a second, more detailed statement. During the trial, the prosecution felt that such a scandalous, late piece of evidence might only compromise what seemed a clear-cut case. In the witness box, Nadolny wasn't asked about the whole conversation.

"This has affected me": Nadolny, 19 August 2019.

"I would never ... see a white man hanged for killing a black": Korff.

'...many landholders and their advocates welcomed news...': Clarry, 2018. Some might have wondered why landholder lobbies felt so oppressed. In late 2015 and early 2016, the federal environment department under then minister Greg Hunt wrote to fifty-one prominent landholders in Queensland who had state approval to clear land near the Great Barrier Reef, asking them to show how the proposed clearing wasn't unlawful under the act. The existence of the letter got around. The farming lobby exploded. Nationals figures began shouting. Within two months, an apology was issued to the landowners. The environment department, assistant secretary Shane

Gaddes wrote, 'deeply' regretted any distress caused. Enquiries had now shown that at least eighteen of the landowners didn't need government approval. Department staff would meet other owners and talk it through. Labor and the Greens, the letter concluded pointedly, were blocking the creation of a streamlined process for handling clearing approvals to 'remove the bureaucratic double handling that occurs when the Queensland government issues permits but ignores national environment law' (see Rendell, 2015 and Slezak, 14 March 2018). But as *The Guardian* journalist Michael Slezak explained, in three years just three voluntary referrals to the federal government had been made, during a period in which land-clearing was dramatically increasing. 'The story each time,' he wrote, 'is of some sort of action taken to reign in clearing, either by government bureaucrats or even by the minister for the environment, and then outrage from a farming lobby group, backed up in parliament', usually by Nationals MPs. Josh Frydenberg, Slezak wrote, 'has repeatedly talked up the federal government's powers to control land clearing, but action has not yet matched the tough words' (see Slezak, 14 March 2018).

'...the authority of Dr Wendy Craik...': Department of Environment and Energy website. Craik is highly experienced: she's chaired the Climate Change Authority and the National Rural Advisory Council, been a board member of Dairy Australia and was a former executive director of the National Farmers' Federation. She has a doctorate in zoology and a diploma in management; she was made a Member of the Order of Australia in 2007 for, among other achievements, her service to the natural resources sector. She was assisted by then Assistant Minister for the Environment, Melissa Price, who had previously worked in the farming and mining sectors.

'...Dr Craik took submissions from stakeholders': EDO and John Williams quoted in Bettles. The Angus Taylor #Grassgate saga continued for months, including reports of a meeting with

Frydenberg's office, prompting the office to ask if protections for critically endangered grasslands might be quietly scrapped. Taylor himself had an interest in the company that was investigated for the illegal spraying, but insisted any meeting had had no connection with his own situation.

'The government should pay farmers and landholders...': Craik's report can be found at www.environment.gov.au/epbc/publications/review-interactions-epbc-act-agriculture-final-report. Meanwhile, a 2019 report established that globally, only 1 per cent of the at least $700 billion (£560 billion) of public subsidies for farmers was used to prosecute environmental aims. Much of the rest contributed to what the authors, using OECD data, guessed was about $12 trillion a year of *costs* to environment, human health and development (see Carrington).

'In the past twenty-five years alone...': Vaughan; Cox, 1 November 2018. Most of the remaining wild places are within just five countries: Brazil, the United

States, Russia, Canada and Australia. Each of those five has governments that have stated their devotion to increasing productivity and development, though US president Joe Biden has committed to answering what he called in his inauguration speech 'a cry for survival' from the planet, 'a cry that can't be any more desperate or any more clear'. It remains to be seen if his focus will be solely on climate change and transition to renewable energy economics, or address other concerns related to sustainability.

"by the simultaneous restoration and rehabilitation...": Albrecht. Soliphilia, Albrecht says, is 'the love of and responsibility for a place, bioregion, planet and the unity of interrelated interests within it'. See Albrecht's post dated Thursday, 19 February 2009 on his blog *Healthearth.*

'...Europe is seeing a sudden increase...': Flannery, 2018.

'...human presence can, perhaps, chaperone healthy ecology': It is worth remembering that, after the cataclysms of the Blitz in London, the firehoses watered seeds stored in the Botanical Gallery, where they had been dormant since collection 150 years earlier. Others were activated in bomb sites. Heated by the blaze of incendiaries and watered by desperate firemen amid carnage and demolition, flowers not seen since Napoleon, not smelt since the Tudor era, bobbed their heads in the sunshine of hundreds of years later. Even tumult and violence can germinate revival.

'...meat, cereals and vegetables may be grown in laboratories': Taking inspiration from a NASA concept, in 2019 a Finnish company announced its successful production of Solein, a flour-like substance containing carbohydrates, fats and high levels of protein, manufactured from only carbon dioxide, water and electricity. Its production is carbon-neutral, retail costs low and ingredients prolific (see Hughes).

"The Sympathetic Mind leaves the world whole": Berry, p.186.

Chapter 24

"Our land management has changed forever": Anderson.

"It's gone from quite a substantial piece of habitat...": Miller.

'...why aren't the koalas there?': Anderson.

'Under the new legislation...': McKenzie, 2017.

"the most poorly managed species in eastern Australia at present": Quoted in Slezak, 7 November 2016.

"the National Party have decided to make this their hill to die on": Quoted in Foley.

'...the koala ... was facing extinction...': King.

'Yet though the state government had a $45 million Koala Strategy...': The strategy pledged $20 million to buy 5000 hectares of koala habitat, while permitting the clearing of seven million hectares of it across the state (see Blanch, Sweeney & Pugh).

"I have no idea how many koalas were killed...": Cornwall.

'Eco law is evolving': Gleeson-White. Drafts of the Rome Statute, listing international crimes against humanity, included ecocide as a crime until it was dropped under pressure from the United Kingdom, France and the Netherlands. But ten countries do recognise the offence, and activists are lobbying to have it reintroduced to Article 8. It would bring perpetrators of ecocide to the Hague.

'...first proposed by ... Christopher Stone': Monbiot.

'the ambivalence ... between arrogance and abjection continues': Grear.

"Who will listen?": Anderson.

"low energy streams began carrying sediments...": Muir, p. xviii.

'...a local of Bingara ... suggested a memorial...': Stubbins & Smith.

'...one of the major regions of archaeological disaster...': OzArk.

'Briggs-Smith believes the treasure was returned by a farmer...': Hinchcliffe.

'The Moree Tourism website says...': 'The Kamilaroi', Moree Tourism.

'Look, the man said sorrowfully': Main.

"Wouldn't it be lovely if someone were guiding us": Anderson.

"leave a legacy of sustainable farming and robust environment": Quoted in Miller.

"When it's been dry for a while...", "The climate's been changing for 20,000 years": Lucy, pp.26–27.

"There will be more": Anderson.

'But a photograph of a homeless koala...': Wharton.

"Can't we stand back now...": Anderson.

'Ran and his wife, Jenny, have put their property...': Jenny Mitchell is also an OAM for her work with country women's groups in the South Pacific. One prominent visitor to their property, Dr Terry McCosker, estimates that at the carbon pricing models of 2016, sequestering two tonnes of carbon per hectare per year would make the soil itself worth more than cattle raised on it (see Nason, 2016).

"If you had a workshop...": Spark, 2017.

'The Turnbull family welcomed the news...': Cornwall.

"concerned landowners": Ellicott & Brown. Marshall has pushed for 'regional codes', allowing some areas more licence than others. There is already a pilot scheme at Walgett, west of Moree. 'Because of the scale of the farming enterprises out there,' said David Witherdin, chief executive of Local Land Services, which grants permissions, the codes 'don't really work as well as they could'. That may be because there is so little native vegetation left: in the northwest, 'unexplained' clearing jumped about five-fold in a year (see Cox, 2 July 2020).

"I'm totally gutted by it", "There's no doubt ... this is an emotional issue...": Ferguson & Ingall.

'Some 27,000 hectares of woody vegetation...': Commission DPIE, 2019 and Nadolny, 24 October 2019.

'In the region covered by Moree Plains Shire Council...': Morton & Davies, 2019.

"The current environmental trajectory is unsustainable": Samuel.

'...with a grab for final approval...': Hannam, 29 July 2020.

"This is a process that will take some time to complete...": Quoted in Cox, 28 January 2021. The report is available at https://epbcactreview.environment.gov.au/resources/final-report

"Seems everything we do is a waste of time...": Spark, 2019.

'By 2017, the property was estimated by Cory himself to be worth about $5 million': *Chief Executive v Cory Ian Turnbull.*

'None of the remediation...': Anderson.

"Ian Turnbull was an evil man...": Hannam, 11 August 2019.

"prime farming land": See listing: www.domain.com.au/-colarado-croppa-creek-nsw-2411-2014808843

'Money from the sale of the other properties will be used to pay ... Robert Strange and Alison McKenzie...':

Strange v Turnbull. By June 2020, the estate of Ian Turnbull had failed to make the settlement payments to Strange and McKenzie. In October 2020, the New South Wales Supreme Court ordered the estate's executor, Robeena Turnbull, to pay the settlements, plus hundreds of thousands in interest, and legal costs (see Chillingworth, 14 October 2020). As this book went to print, the money still had not been paid.

'Roger and Annette sold...': Schlesinger.

'She and Pearce adopted a favourite brand of Scotch': McKenzie, 2020.

"Our family is proud and humbled...", "What was done on that day...": Alison McKenzie and Robert Strange quoted in Chillingworth, 2018.

'The coronial inquest never happened': McKenzie, 2020.

'...the seven million hectares of 1788 were half a million': Lucas et al., 2014.

"Brigalow ... can wait": Nix.

"Every day ... there's something that reminds you": Robert and Joshua Strange in Piatek.

'...the anthropologist and linguist Norman Tindale...': For a discussion of Tindale's methodology and legacy, see Monaghan, Paul, 'Laying Down the Country: Norman B. Tindale and the Linguistic Construction of the North-West of South Australia', PhD, 2003, University of Adelaide, available at https://digital.library.adelaide.edu.au/dspace/bitstream/2440/21991/2/02whole.pdf

'It tells of Emu and Brolga': Austin & Tindale; see also 'Burraalga bulaarr Dhinawan/The Brolga and the Emu', *Guwaabal: Yuwaalaraay and Gmilaraay Stories,* available at http://yuwaalaraay.org/stories/burraalgaV2.html.

BACK COVER MATERIAL

'Beautifully written, meticulously researched, carefully plotted and seamlessly stitched.'
CHARLES MASSY

'An agonising and powerful parable.'
TOM GRIFFITHS

'Ecological, humane and grounding.'
ANNA KRIENTHS

*

An epic true story of greed, power and a desire for legacy from an acclaimed Australian storyteller.

July 2014, a lonely road at twilight outside Croppa Creek, New South Wales: 80-year-old farmer Ian Turnbull takes out a .22 and shoots environmental officer Glen Turner in the back.

On one side, a farmer hoping to secure his family's wealth on the richest agricultural soil in the country. On the other, his obsession: the government man trying to apply environmental laws.

The brutal killing of Glen Turner splits open the story of our place on this land. Is our time on this soil a tale of tragedy or triumph – are we reaping what we've sown? Do we owe protection to the land, or does it owe us a living? And what happens when, in pursuit of an inheritance for his family, a man creates terrible consequences?

Kate Holden brings her discerning eye to a gripping tale of law, land and entitlement. It is the story of Australia.

Kate Holden is the author of two highly praised memoirs, *In My Skin* and *The Romantic*, and a regular contributor to *The Saturday Paper*, *The Monthly* and *The Age*.

www.ingramcontent.com/pod-product-compliance
Lightning Source LLC
Chambersburg PA
CBHW010555020526
44111CB00054BA/2929